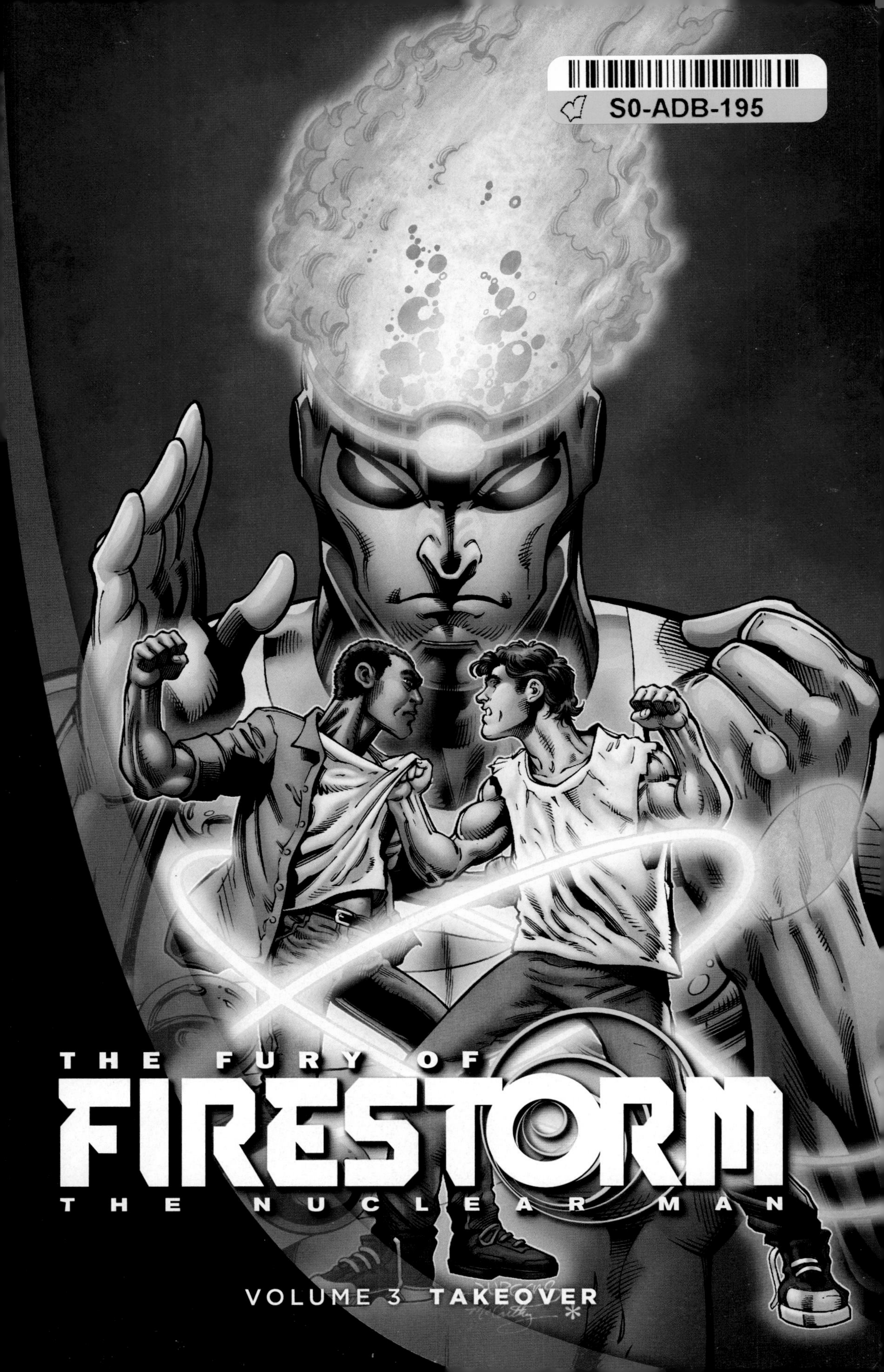
THE FURY OF
FIRESTORM
THE NUCLEAR MAN
VOLUME 3 TAKEOVER

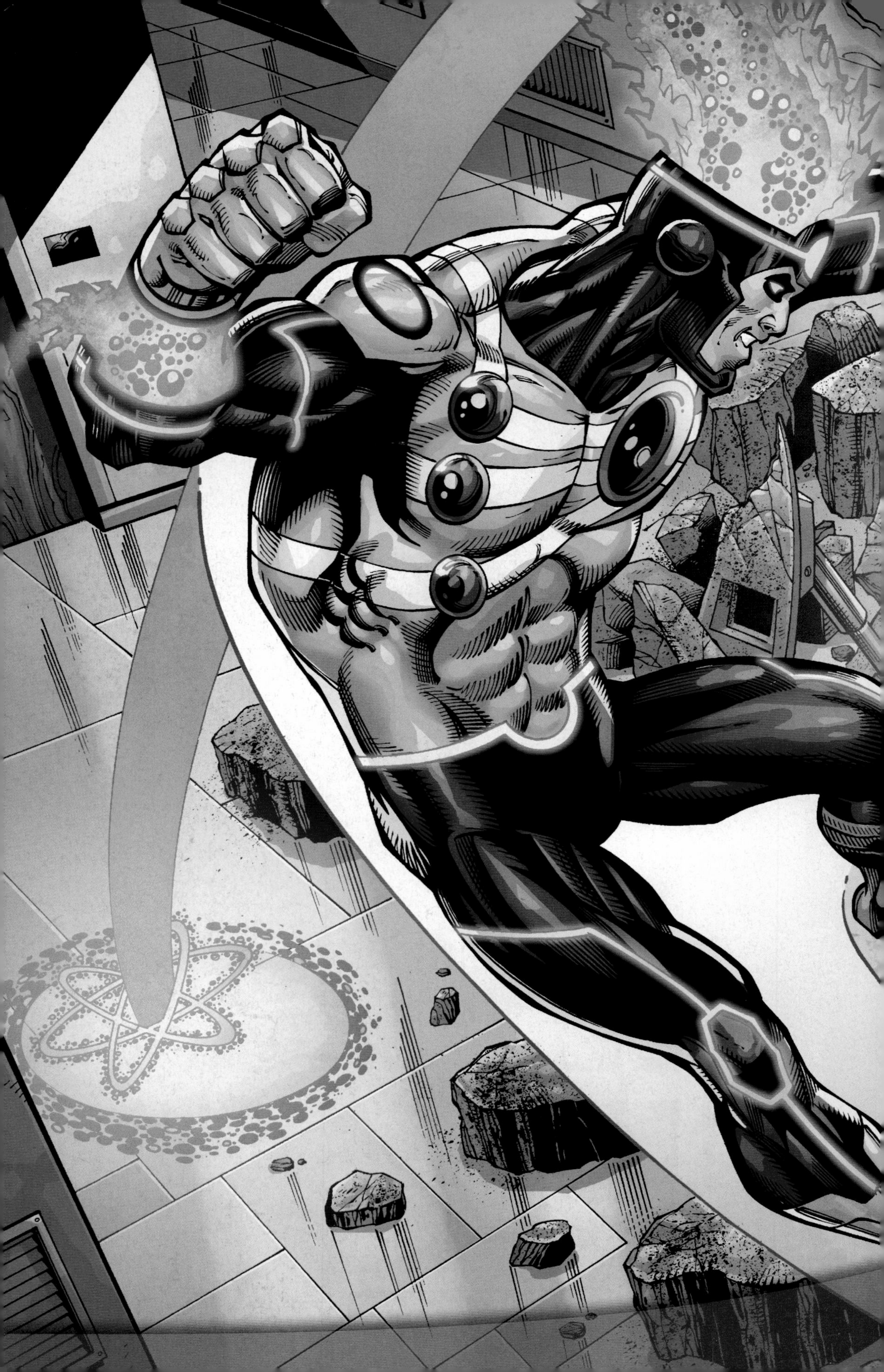

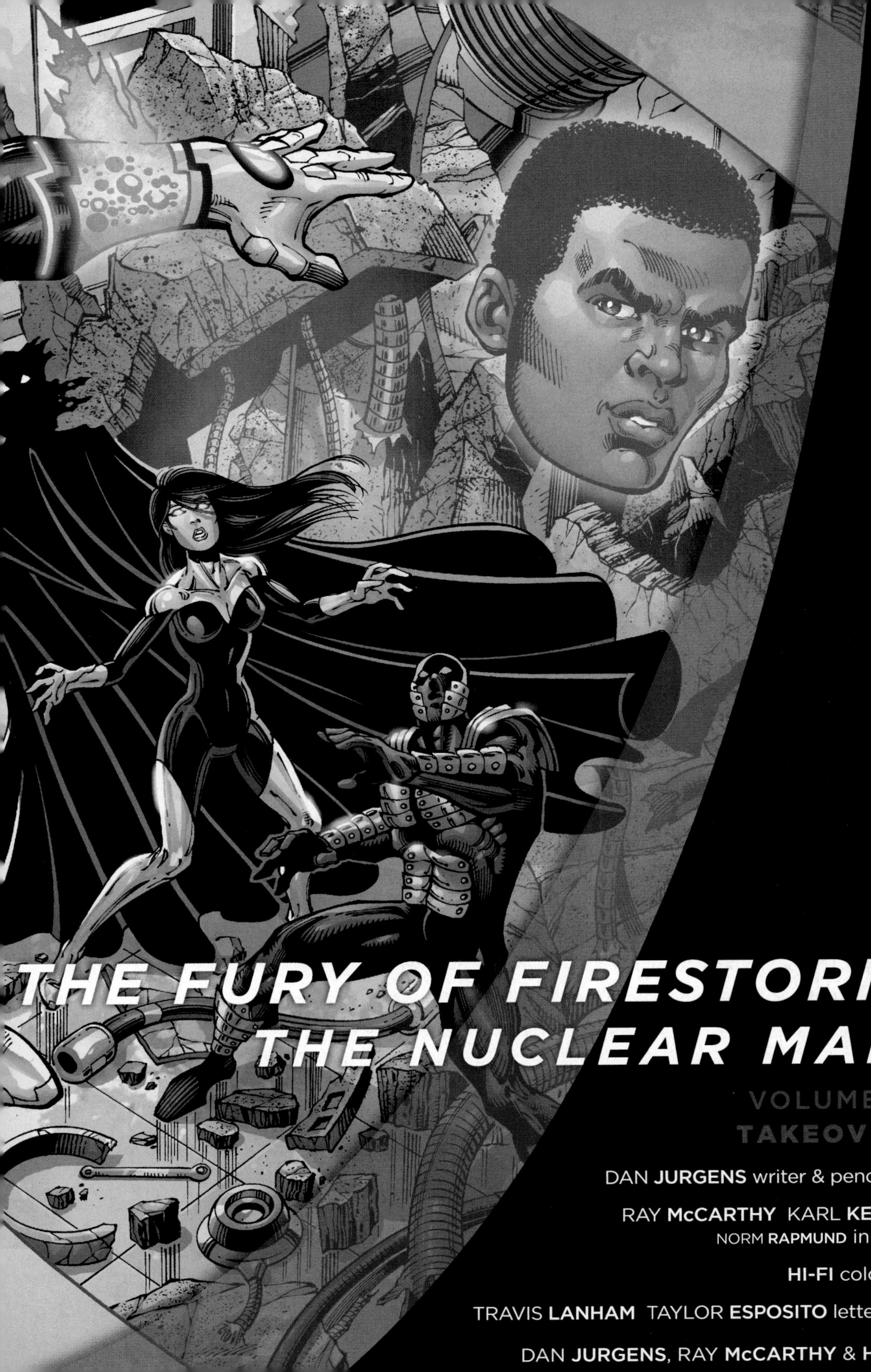

THE FURY OF FIRESTORM THE NUCLEAR MAN

VOLUME 3 TAKEOVER

DAN JURGENS writer & penciller

RAY McCARTHY KARL KESEL NORM RAPMUND inkers

HI-FI colorist

TRAVIS LANHAM TAYLOR ESPOSITO letterers

DAN JURGENS, RAY McCARTHY & HI-FI

MIKE COTTON RACHEL GLUCKSTERN Editors – Original Series
ANTHONY MARQUES RICKEY PURDIN Assistant Editors – Original Series RACHEL PINNELAS Editor
ROBBIN BROSTERMAN Design Director – Books ROBBIE BIEDERMAN Publication Design

BOB HARRAS Senior VP – Editor-in-Chief, DC Comics

DIANE NELSON President DAN DIDIO and JIM LEE Co-Publishers
GEOFF JOHNS Chief Creative Officer
JOHN ROOD Executive VP – Sales, Marketing and Business Development
AMY GENKINS Senior VP – Business and Legal Affairs NAIRI GARDINER Senior VP – Finance
JEFF BOISON VP – Publishing Planning MARK CHIARELLO VP – Art Direction and Design
JOHN CUNNINGHAM VP – Marketing TERRI CUNNINGHAM VP – Editorial Administration
ALISON GILL Senior VP – Manufacturing and Operations HANK KANALZ Senior VP – Vertigo & Integrated Publishing
JAY KOGAN VP – Business and Legal Affairs, Publishing JACK MAHAN VP – Business Affairs, Talent
NICK NAPOLITANO VP – Manufacturing Administration SUE POHJA VP – Book Sales
COURTNEY SIMMONS Senior VP – Publicity BOB WAYNE Senior VP – Sales

THE FURY OF FIRESTORM: THE NUCLEAR MAN: VOLUME 3: TAKEOVER

DC Comics, 1700 Broadway, New York, NY 10019
A Warner Bros. Entertainment Company.
Printed by RR Donnelley, Salem, VA, USA. 11/15/13. First Printing.

ISBN: 978-1-4012-4292-3

SUSTAINABLE
FORESTRY
INITIATIVE

Certified Chain of Custody
At Least 20% Certified Forest Content
www.sfiprogram.org
SFI-01042
APPLIES TO TEXT STOCK ONLY

Library of Congress Cataloging-in-Publication Data

Jurgens, Dan, author.
The Fury of Firestorm, The Nuclear Men. Volume 3, Takeover / Dan Jurgens, Ray McCarthy.
pages cm. — (The New 52!)
ISBN 978-1-4012-4292-3 (pbk.)
1. Graphic novels. I. McCarthy, Ray, illustrator. II. Title. III. Title: Takeover.
PN6728.F4797J87 2013
741.5'973 — dc23

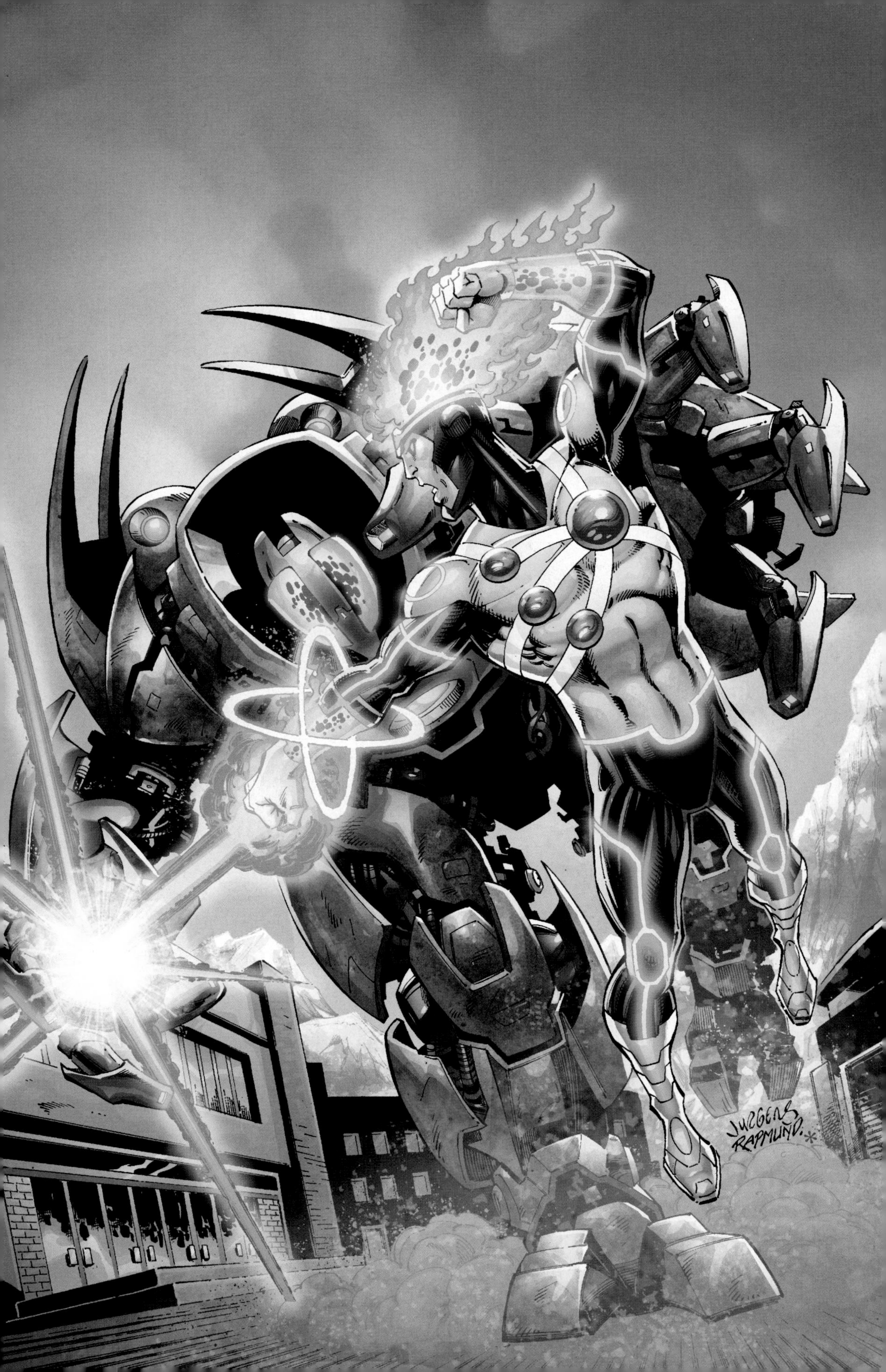
JURGENS
RAPMUND.

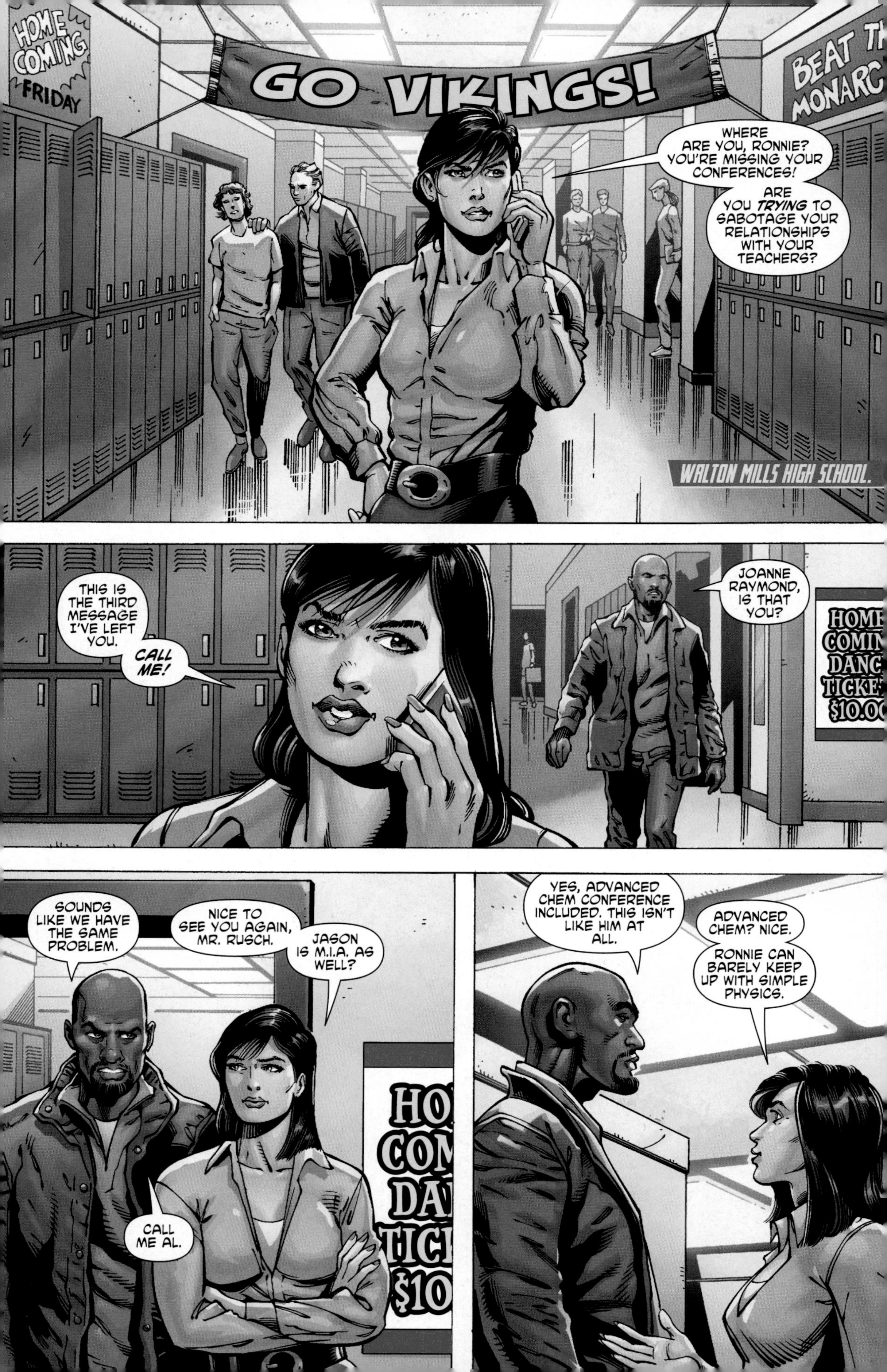
HOME COMING FRIDAY
GO VIKINGS!
BEAT TH MONARC
WHERE ARE YOU, RONNIE? YOU'RE MISSING YOUR CONFERENCES!
ARE YOU TRYING TO SABOTAGE YOUR RELATIONSHIPS WITH YOUR TEACHERS?
WALTON MILLS HIGH SCHOOL.
THIS IS THE THIRD MESSAGE I'VE LEFT YOU.
CALL ME!
JOANNE RAYMOND, IS THAT YOU?
HOME COMIN DANC TICKET $10.0
SOUNDS LIKE WE HAVE THE SAME PROBLEM.
NICE TO SEE YOU AGAIN, MR. RUSCH.
JASON IS M.I.A. AS WELL?
CALL ME AL.
YES, ADVANCED CHEM CONFERENCE INCLUDED. THIS ISN'T LIKE HIM AT ALL.
ADVANCED CHEM? NICE.
RONNIE CAN BARELY KEEP UP WITH SIMPLE PHYSICS.

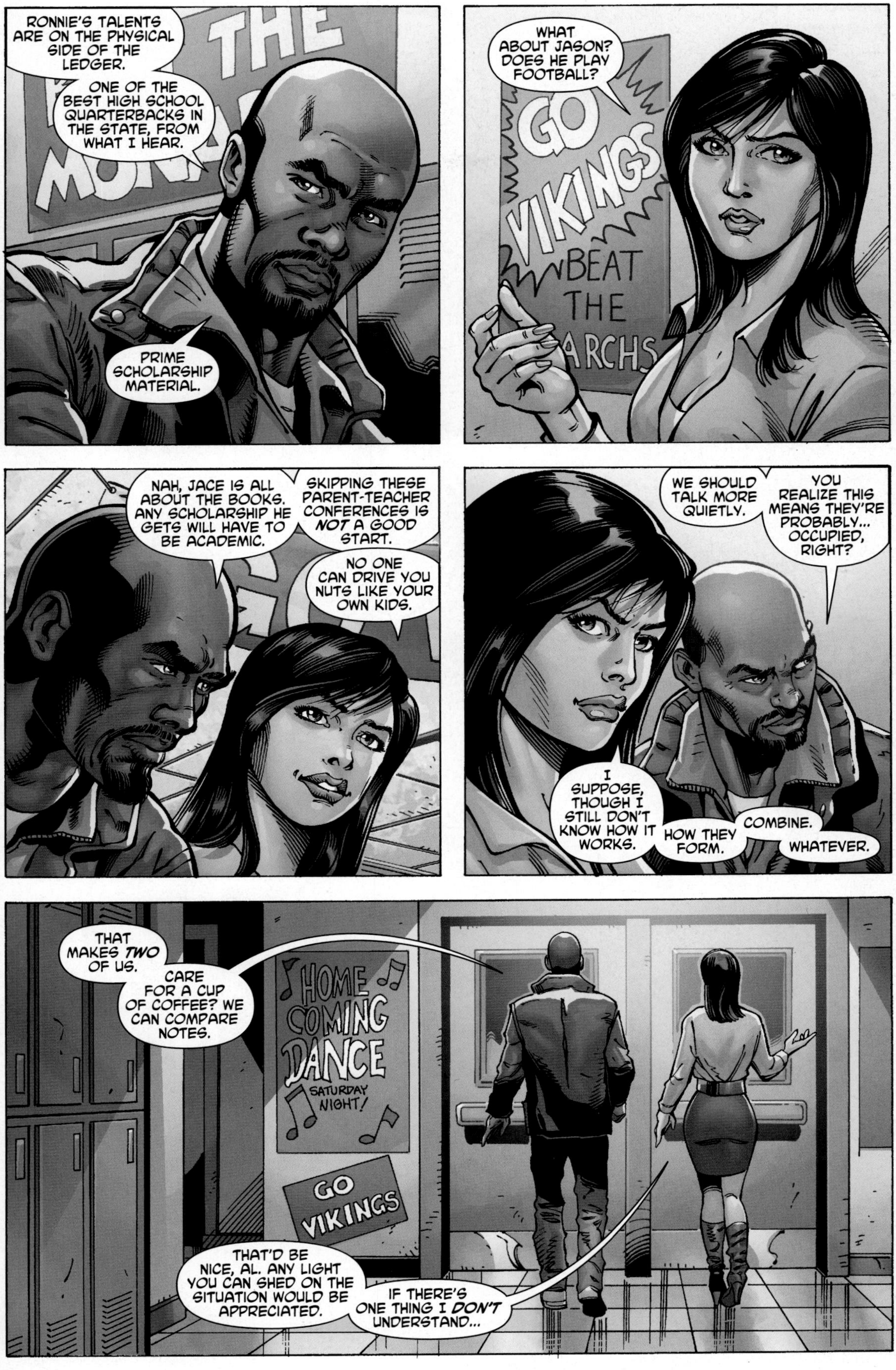
RONNIE'S TALENTS ARE ON THE PHYSICAL SIDE OF THE LEDGER.
ONE OF THE BEST HIGH SCHOOL QUARTERBACKS IN THE STATE, FROM WHAT I HEAR.
PRIME SCHOLARSHIP MATERIAL.
WHAT ABOUT JASON? DOES HE PLAY FOOTBALL?
GO VIKINGS BEAT THE ARCHS
NAH, JACE IS ALL ABOUT THE BOOKS. ANY SCHOLARSHIP HE GETS WILL HAVE TO BE ACADEMIC.
SKIPPING THESE PARENT-TEACHER CONFERENCES IS *NOT* A GOOD START.
NO ONE CAN DRIVE YOU NUTS LIKE YOUR OWN KIDS.
WE SHOULD TALK MORE QUIETLY.
YOU REALIZE THIS MEANS THEY'RE PROBABLY... OCCUPIED, RIGHT?
I SUPPOSE, THOUGH I STILL DON'T KNOW HOW IT WORKS.
HOW THEY FORM.
COMBINE.
WHATEVER.
THAT MAKES *TWO* OF US.
CARE FOR A CUP OF COFFEE? WE CAN COMPARE NOTES.
HOME COMING DANCE SATURDAY NIGHT!
GO VIKINGS
THAT'D BE NICE, AL. ANY LIGHT YOU CAN SHED ON THE SITUATION WOULD BE APPRECIATED.
IF THERE'S ONE THING I *DON'T* UNDERSTAND...

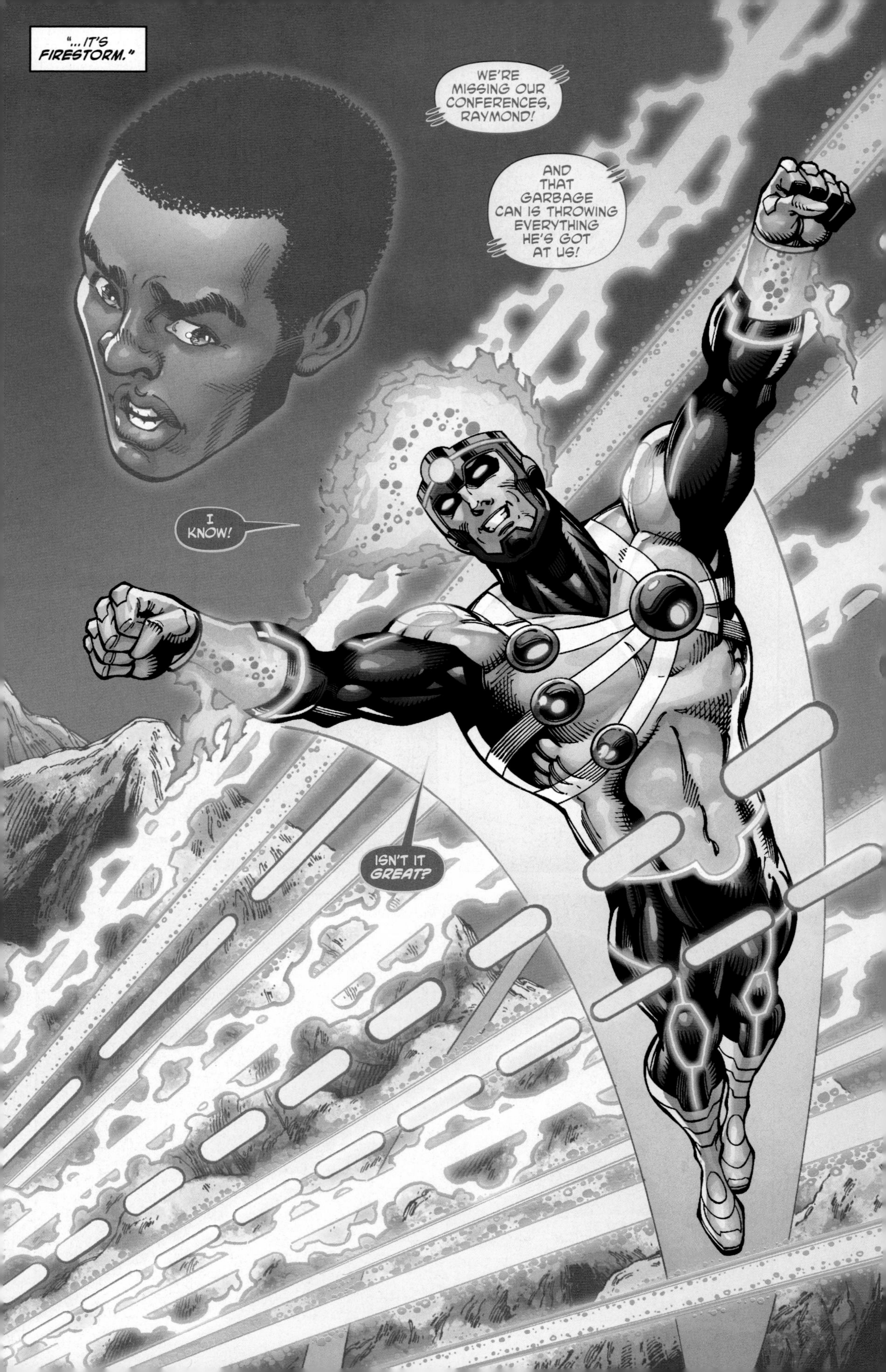
"...IT'S FIRESTORM."
WE'RE MISSING OUR CONFERENCES, RAYMOND!
AND THAT GARBAGE CAN IS THROWING EVERYTHING HE'S GOT AT US!
I KNOW!
ISN'T IT GREAT?

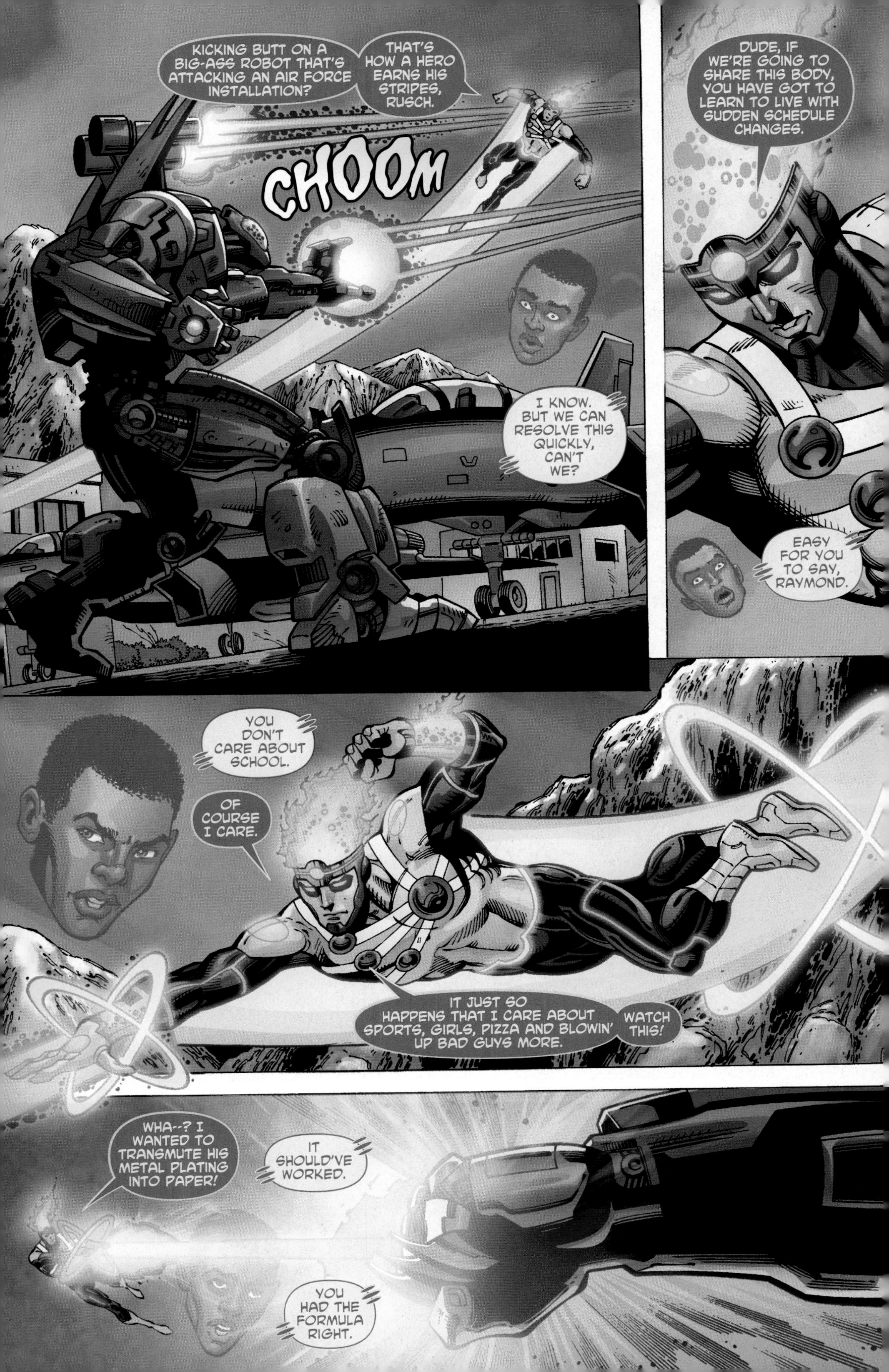
KICKING BUTT ON A BIG-ASS ROBOT THAT'S ATTACKING AN AIR FORCE INSTALLATION?
THAT'S HOW A HERO EARNS HIS STRIPES, RUSCH.
CHOOM
I KNOW. BUT WE CAN RESOLVE THIS QUICKLY, CAN'T WE?
DUDE, IF WE'RE GOING TO SHARE THIS BODY, YOU HAVE GOT TO LEARN TO LIVE WITH SUDDEN SCHEDULE CHANGES.
EASY FOR YOU TO SAY, RAYMOND.
YOU DON'T CARE ABOUT SCHOOL.
OF COURSE I CARE.
IT JUST SO HAPPENS THAT I CARE ABOUT SPORTS, GIRLS, PIZZA AND BLOWIN' UP BAD GUYS MORE.
WATCH THIS!
WHA--? I WANTED TO TRANSMUTE HIS METAL PLATING INTO PAPER!
IT SHOULD'VE WORKED.
YOU HAD THE FORMULA RIGHT.

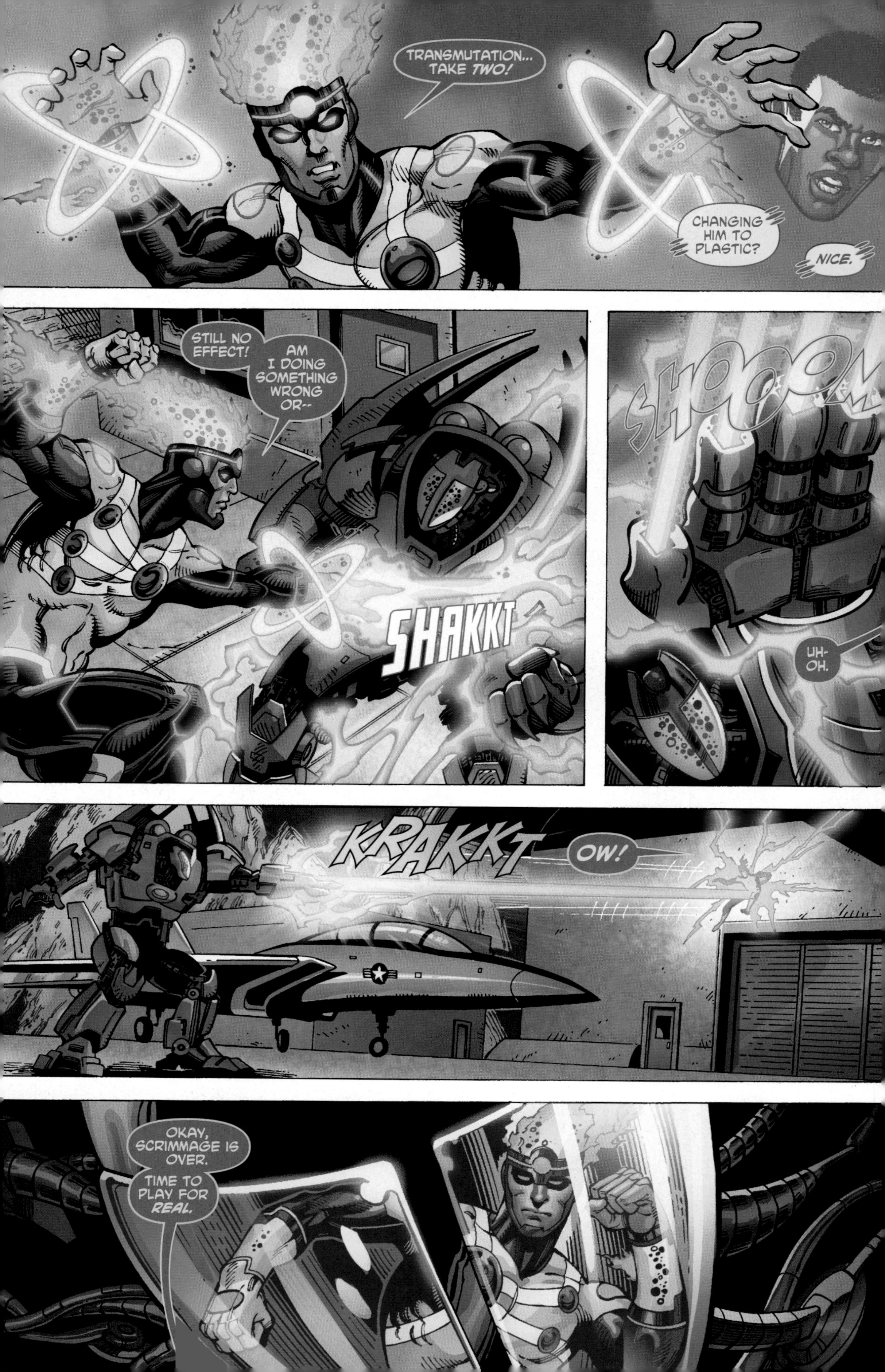

TRANSMUTATION... TAKE TWO!
CHANGING HIM TO PLASTIC?
NICE.
STILL NO EFFECT!
AM I DOING SOMETHING WRONG OR--
SHAKKT
SHOOOM
UH-OH.
KRAKKT
OW!
OKAY, SCRIMMAGE IS OVER.
TIME TO PLAY FOR REAL.

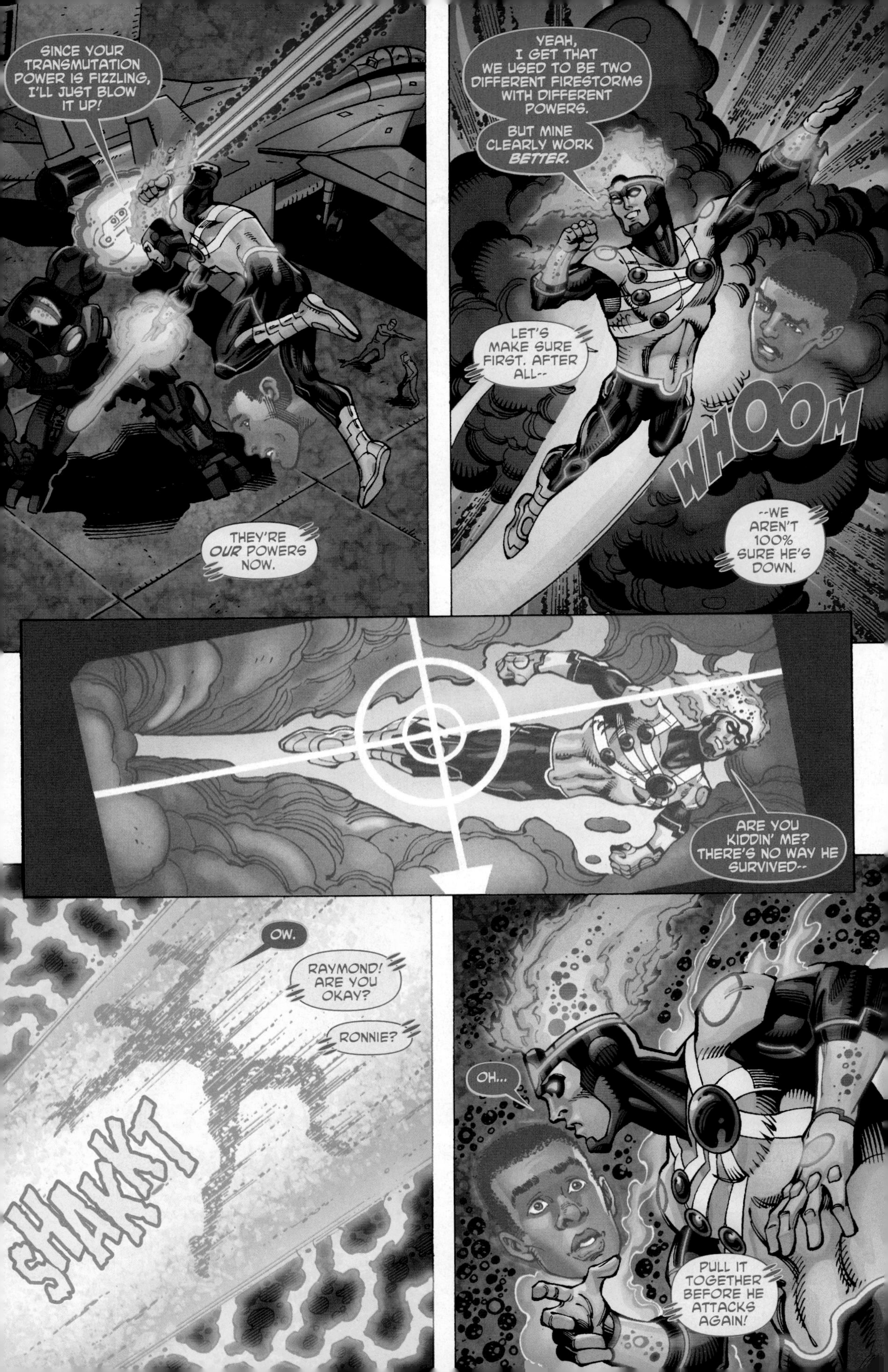

SINCE YOUR TRANSMUTATION POWER IS FIZZLING, I'LL JUST BLOW IT UP!
THEY'RE *OUR* POWERS NOW.
YEAH, I GET THAT WE USED TO BE TWO DIFFERENT FIRESTORMS WITH DIFFERENT POWERS.
BUT MINE CLEARLY WORK *BETTER.*
LET'S MAKE SURE FIRST. AFTER ALL--
WHOOM
--WE AREN'T 100% SURE HE'S DOWN.
ARE YOU KIDDIN' ME? THERE'S NO WAY HE SURVIVED--
OW.
RAYMOND! ARE YOU OKAY?
RONNIE?
SHAKKT
OH...
PULL IT TOGETHER BEFORE HE ATTACKS AGAIN!

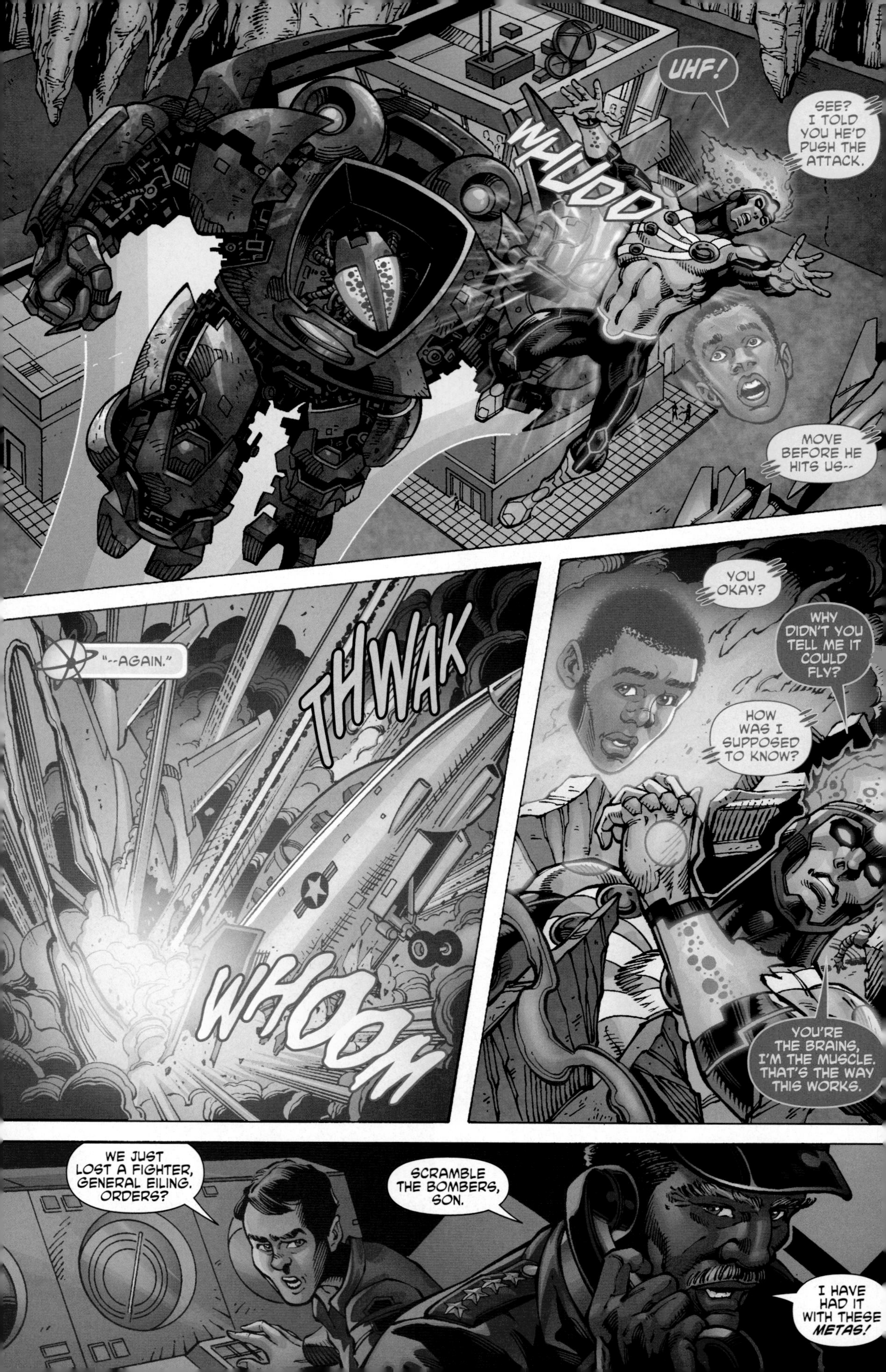

UHF!
WHUDD
SEE? I TOLD YOU HE'D PUSH THE ATTACK.
MOVE BEFORE HE HITS US--
"--AGAIN."
THWAK
WHOOM
YOU OKAY?
WHY DIDN'T YOU TELL ME IT COULD FLY?
HOW WAS I SUPPOSED TO KNOW?
YOU'RE THE BRAINS, I'M THE MUSCLE. THAT'S THE WAY THIS WORKS.
WE JUST LOST A FIGHTER, GENERAL EILING. ORDERS?
SCRAMBLE THE BOMBERS, SON.
I HAVE HAD IT WITH THESE *METAS!*

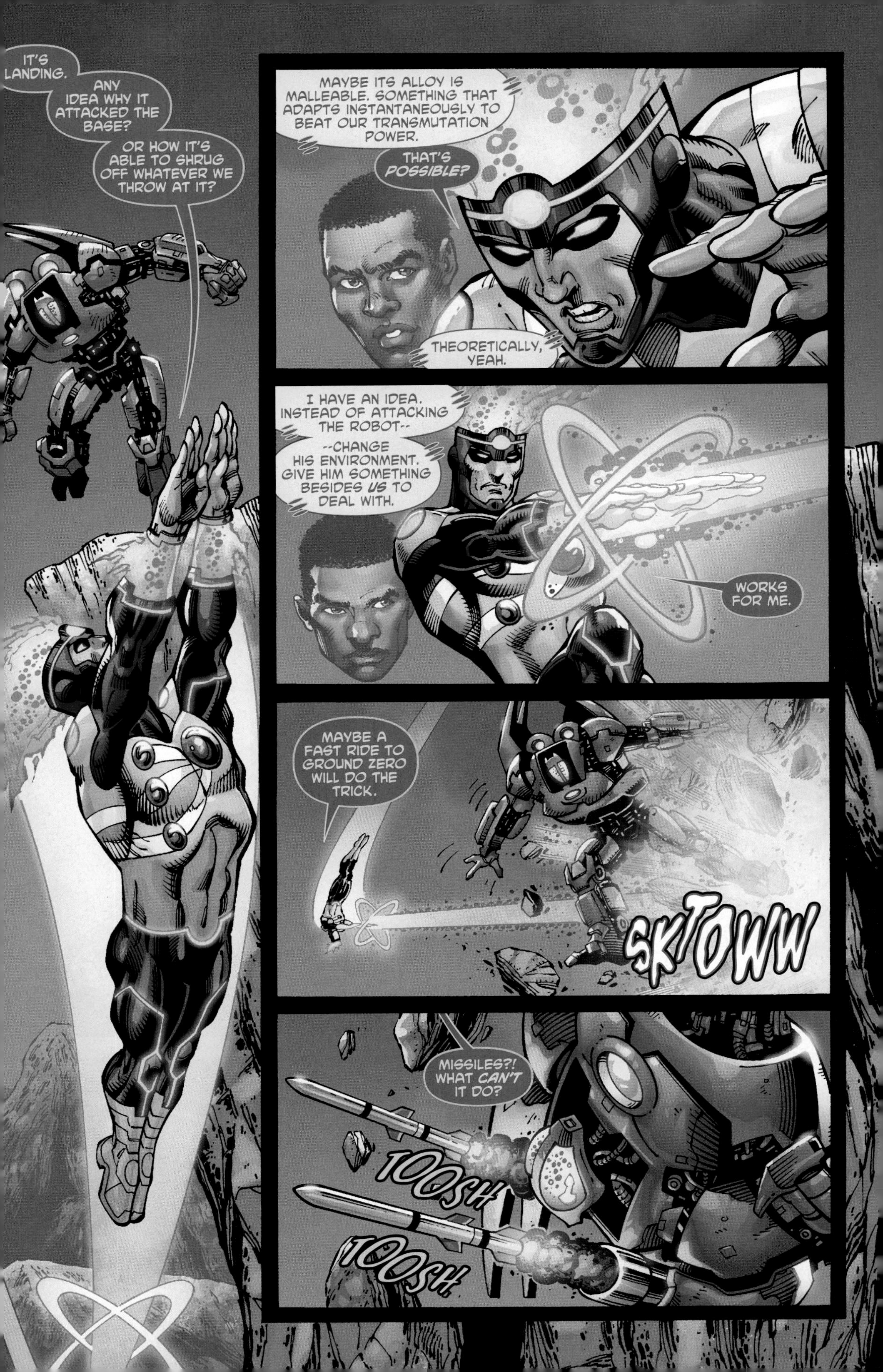
IT'S LANDING.
ANY IDEA WHY IT ATTACKED THE BASE?
OR HOW IT'S ABLE TO SHRUG OFF WHATEVER WE THROW AT IT?
MAYBE ITS ALLOY IS MALLEABLE. SOMETHING THAT ADAPTS INSTANTANEOUSLY TO BEAT OUR TRANSMUTATION POWER.
THAT'S POSSIBLE?
THEORETICALLY, YEAH.
I HAVE AN IDEA. INSTEAD OF ATTACKING THE ROBOT--
--CHANGE HIS ENVIRONMENT. GIVE HIM SOMETHING BESIDES US TO DEAL WITH.
WORKS FOR ME.
MAYBE A FAST RIDE TO GROUND ZERO WILL DO THE TRICK.
SKTOWW
MISSILES?! WHAT CAN'T IT DO?
TOOSH
TOOSH

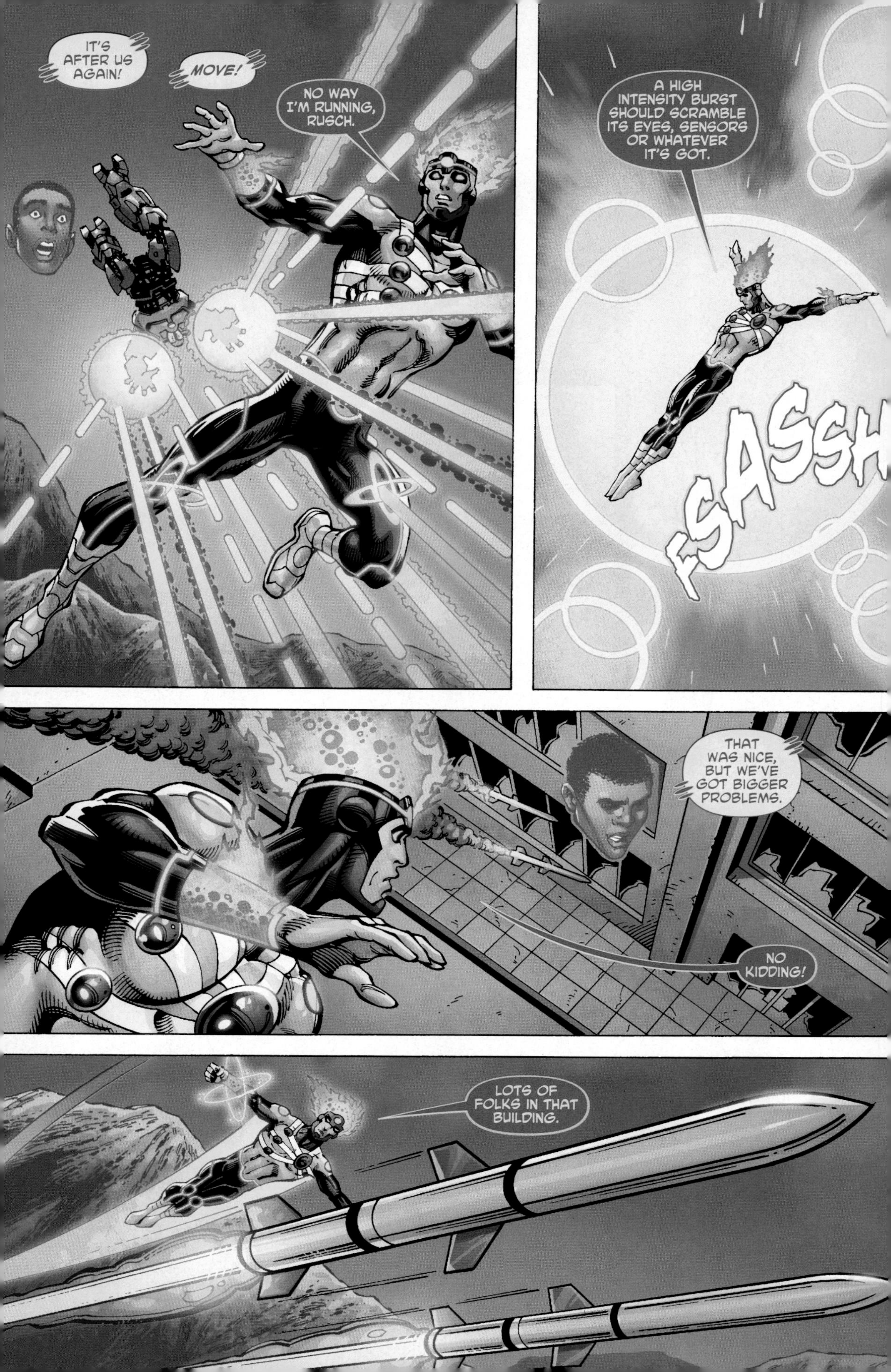

IT'S AFTER US AGAIN!
MOVE!
NO WAY I'M RUNNING, RUSCH.
A HIGH INTENSITY BURST SHOULD SCRAMBLE ITS EYES, SENSORS OR WHATEVER IT'S GOT.
FSASSH
THAT WAS NICE, BUT WE'VE GOT BIGGER PROBLEMS.
NO KIDDING!
LOTS OF FOLKS IN THAT BUILDING.

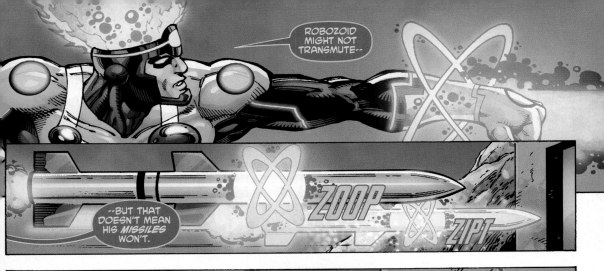

ROBOZOID MIGHT NOT TRANSMUTE--

--BUT THAT DOESN'T MEAN HIS *MISSILES* WON'T.

ZOOP

ZIPT

KRIKT

TINK

TUNK

KRINK

AWESUMMMM! SCORE ONE FOR THE GOOD GUYS!

NO HIGH FIVES UNTIL WE TAKE CARE OF THE MONSTER.

GOOD POINT. LET'S--

HE'S GONE?

CAN IT BE... THAT EASY? WHY WOULD HE VANISH?

--THE JUSTICE LEAGUE WILL COME KNOCKING!

THEY DON'T EVEN KNOW WE EXIST.

ONE LOOK AT THAT ROBOT AND THEY'D BE IMPRESSED. I WONDER WHERE HE CAME FROM?

WHO CARES, DUDE? WE *WON!*

EVEN SUPERMAN WOULD GIVE US A PAT ON THE BACK FOR THIS! IF WE KEEP IT UP--

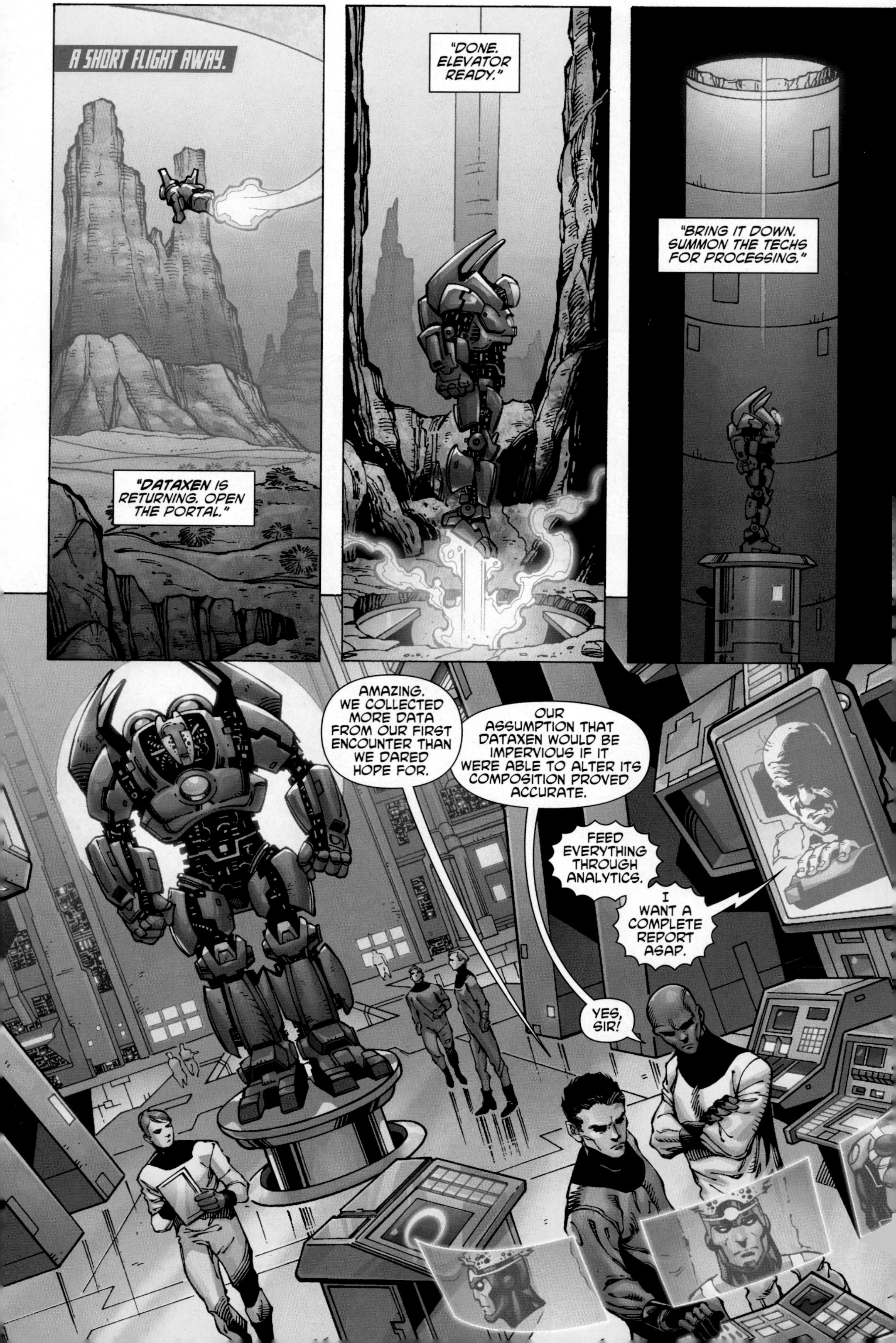
A SHORT FLIGHT AWAY.
"DATAXEN IS RETURNING. OPEN THE PORTAL."
"DONE. ELEVATOR READY."
"BRING IT DOWN. SUMMON THE TECHS FOR PROCESSING."
AMAZING. WE COLLECTED MORE DATA FROM OUR FIRST ENCOUNTER THAN WE DARED HOPE FOR.
OUR ASSUMPTION THAT DATAXEN WOULD BE IMPERVIOUS IF IT WERE ABLE TO ALTER ITS COMPOSITION PROVED ACCURATE.
FEED EVERYTHING THROUGH ANALYTICS.
I WANT A COMPLETE REPORT ASAP.
YES, SIR!

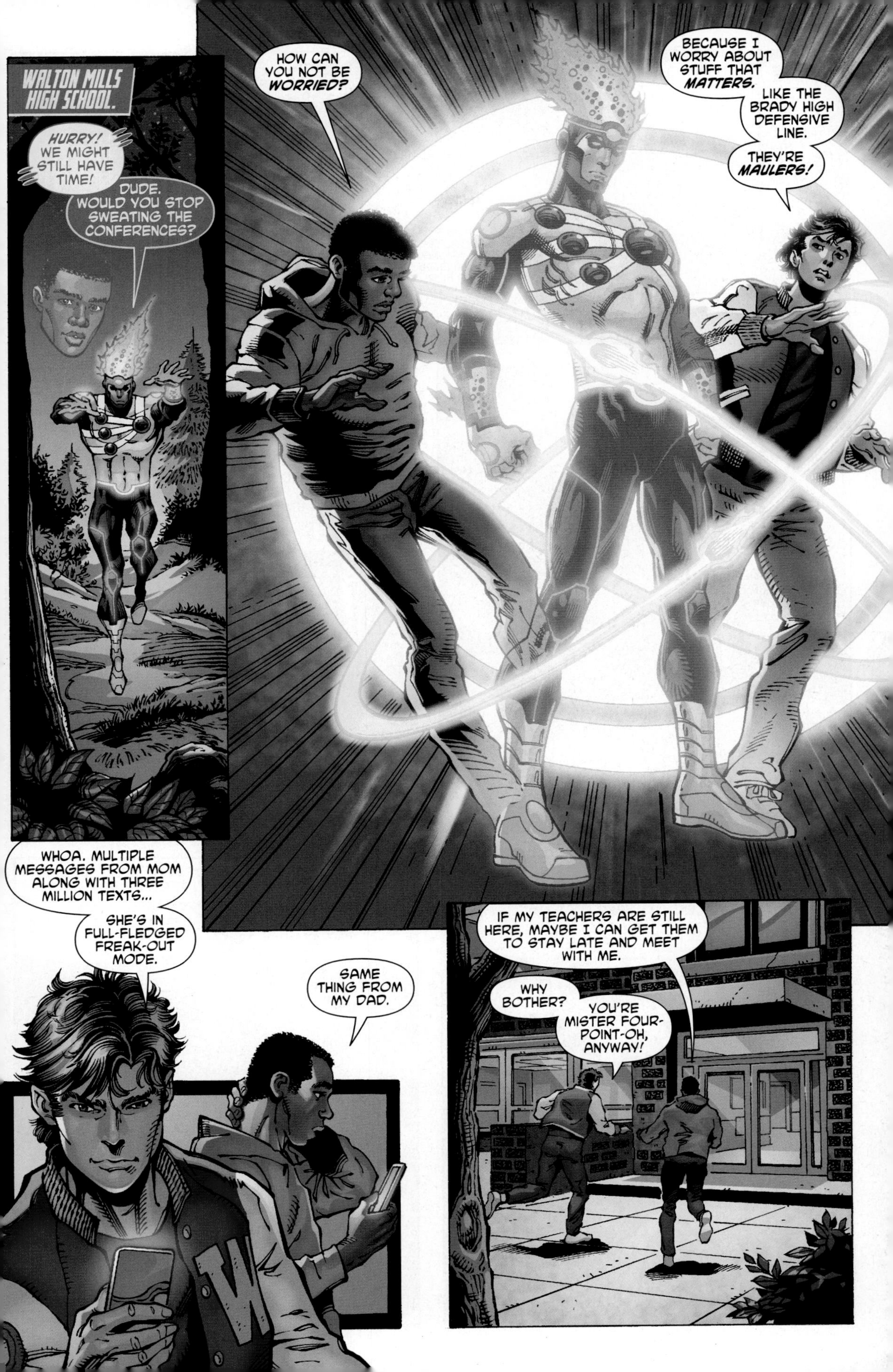
WALTON MILLS HIGH SCHOOL.
HURRY! WE MIGHT STILL HAVE TIME!
DUDE. WOULD YOU STOP SWEATING THE CONFERENCES?
HOW CAN YOU NOT BE WORRIED?
BECAUSE I WORRY ABOUT STUFF THAT MATTERS.
LIKE THE BRADY HIGH DEFENSIVE LINE.
THEY'RE MAULERS!
WHOA. MULTIPLE MESSAGES FROM MOM ALONG WITH THREE MILLION TEXTS...
SHE'S IN FULL-FLEDGED FREAK-OUT MODE.
SAME THING FROM MY DAD.
IF MY TEACHERS ARE STILL HERE, MAYBE I CAN GET THEM TO STAY LATE AND MEET WITH ME.
WHY BOTHER?
YOU'RE MISTER FOUR-POINT-OH, ANYWAY!

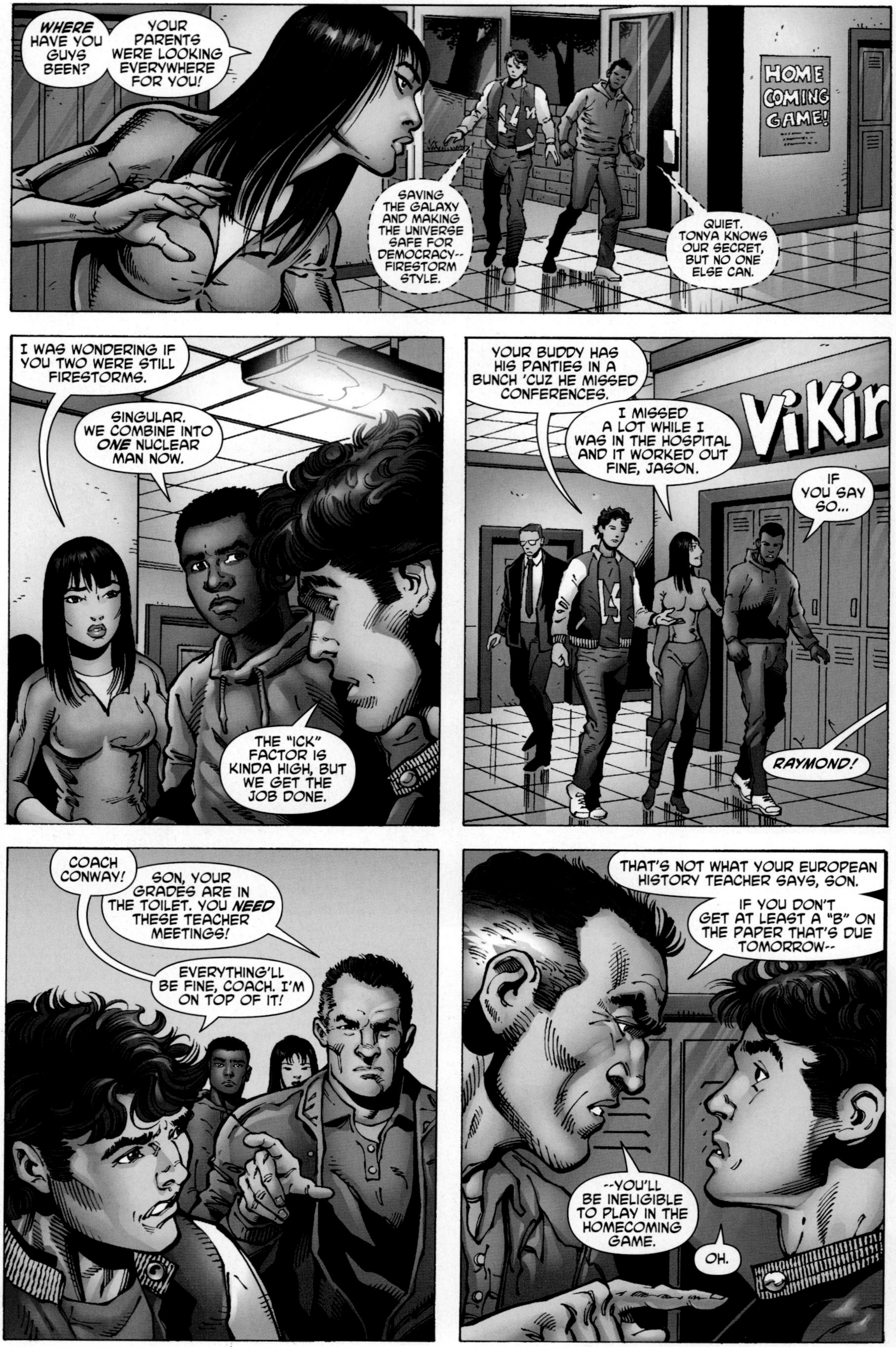
WHERE HAVE YOU GUYS BEEN?
YOUR PARENTS WERE LOOKING EVERYWHERE FOR YOU!
HOME COMING GAME!
SAVING THE GALAXY AND MAKING THE UNIVERSE SAFE FOR DEMOCRACY-- FIRESTORM STYLE.
QUIET. TONYA KNOWS OUR SECRET, BUT NO ONE ELSE CAN.
I WAS WONDERING IF YOU TWO WERE STILL FIRESTORMS.
SINGULAR. WE COMBINE INTO ONE NUCLEAR MAN NOW.
THE "ICK" FACTOR IS KINDA HIGH, BUT WE GET THE JOB DONE.
YOUR BUDDY HAS HIS PANTIES IN A BUNCH 'CUZ HE MISSED CONFERENCES.
I MISSED A LOT WHILE I WAS IN THE HOSPITAL AND IT WORKED OUT FINE, JASON.
IF YOU SAY SO...
RAYMOND!
COACH CONWAY!
SON, YOUR GRADES ARE IN THE TOILET. YOU NEED THESE TEACHER MEETINGS!
EVERYTHING'LL BE FINE, COACH. I'M ON TOP OF IT!
THAT'S NOT WHAT YOUR EUROPEAN HISTORY TEACHER SAYS, SON.
IF YOU DON'T GET AT LEAST A "B" ON THE PAPER THAT'S DUE TOMORROW--
--YOU'LL BE INELIGIBLE TO PLAY IN THE HOMECOMING GAME.
OH.

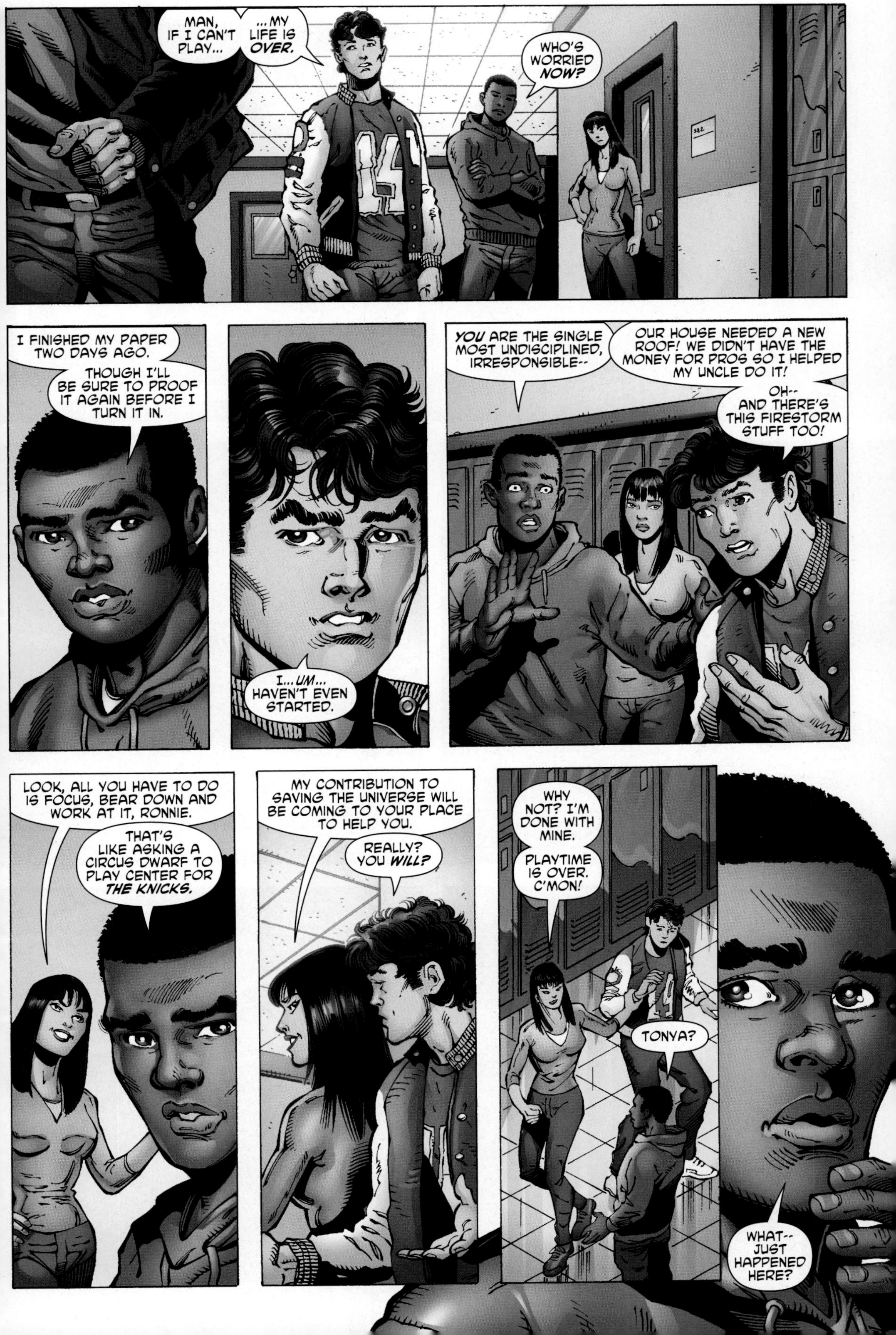

MAN, IF I CAN'T PLAY...
...MY LIFE IS OVER.
WHO'S WORRIED NOW?
I FINISHED MY PAPER TWO DAYS AGO.
THOUGH I'LL BE SURE TO PROOF IT AGAIN BEFORE I TURN IT IN.
I...UM... HAVEN'T EVEN STARTED.
YOU ARE THE SINGLE MOST UNDISCIPLINED, IRRESPONSIBLE--
OUR HOUSE NEEDED A NEW ROOF! WE DIDN'T HAVE THE MONEY FOR PROS SO I HELPED MY UNCLE DO IT!
OH-- AND THERE'S THIS FIRESTORM STUFF TOO!
LOOK, ALL YOU HAVE TO DO IS FOCUS, BEAR DOWN AND WORK AT IT, RONNIE.
THAT'S LIKE ASKING A CIRCUS DWARF TO PLAY CENTER FOR THE KNICKS.
MY CONTRIBUTION TO SAVING THE UNIVERSE WILL BE COMING TO YOUR PLACE TO HELP YOU.
REALLY? YOU WILL?
WHY NOT? I'M DONE WITH MINE.
PLAYTIME IS OVER. C'MON!
TONYA?
WHAT-- JUST HAPPENED HERE?

WHY CAN'T I GET THIS RIGHT?

S.T.A.R. LABS

THIS SHOULD BE *EASY*.

BUT ALL THESE LITTLE *BIRDS* DO IS MAKE ME *ANGRY!*

MAYBE IF I BLOW THE BACK PART UP FIRST...

YES!

I'M HOME FR--

THUK

--EE?

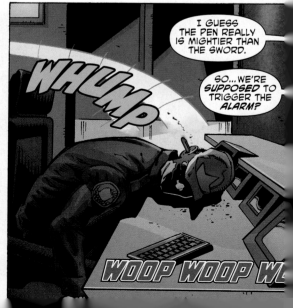

I GUESS THE PEN REALLY IS MIGHTIER THAN THE SWORD.

SO...WE'RE *SUPPOSED* TO TRIGGER THE *ALARM?*

WHUMP

WOOP WOOP W

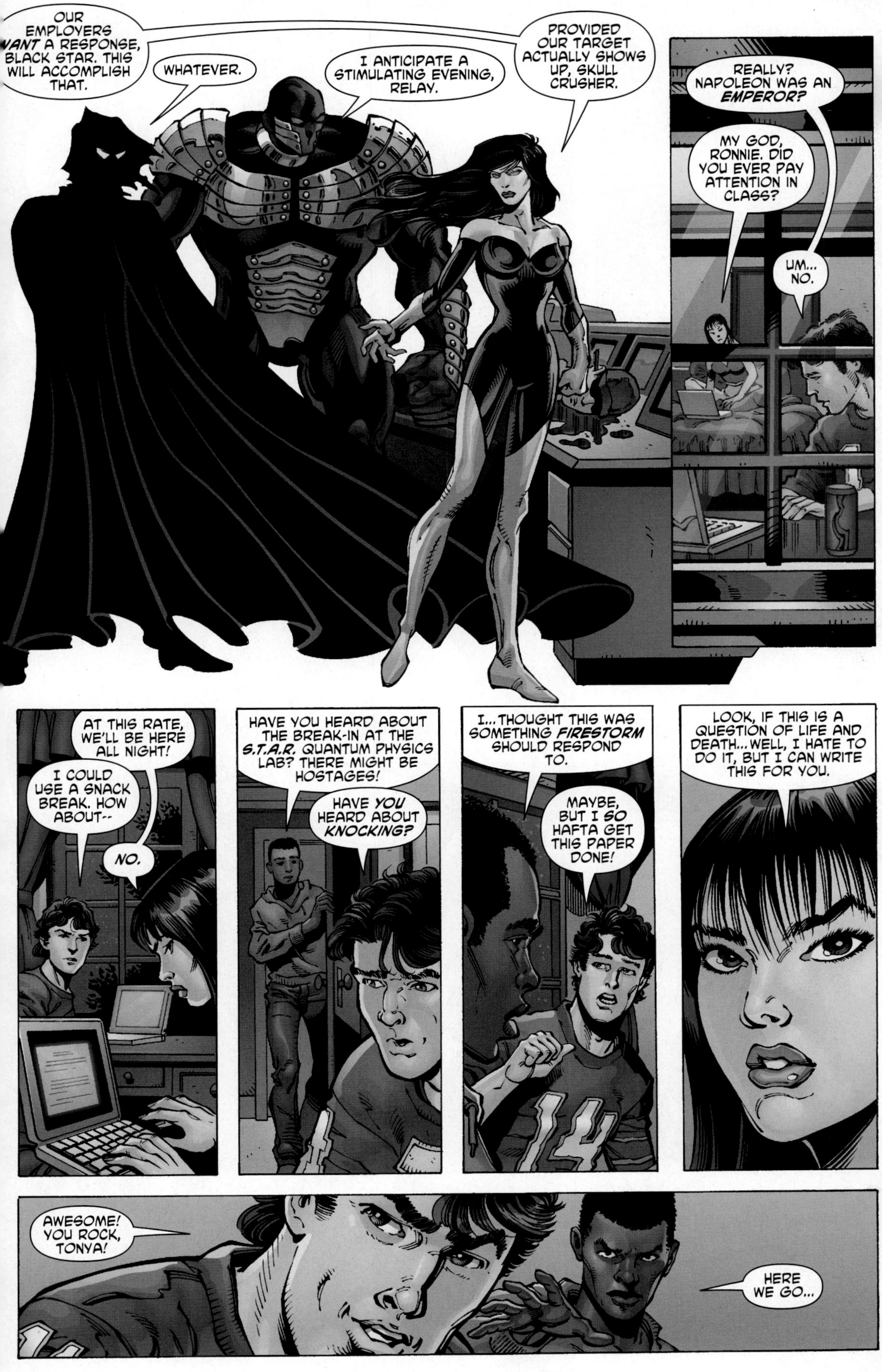

OUR EMPLOYERS WANT A RESPONSE, BLACK STAR. THIS WILL ACCOMPLISH THAT.
WHATEVER.
I ANTICIPATE A STIMULATING EVENING, RELAY.
PROVIDED OUR TARGET ACTUALLY SHOWS UP, SKULL CRUSHER.
REALLY? NAPOLEON WAS AN *EMPEROR?*
MY GOD, RONNIE. DID YOU EVER PAY ATTENTION IN CLASS?
UM... NO.
AT THIS RATE, WE'LL BE HERE ALL NIGHT!
I COULD USE A SNACK BREAK. HOW ABOUT--
NO.
HAVE YOU HEARD ABOUT THE BREAK-IN AT THE *S.T.A.R.* QUANTUM PHYSICS LAB? THERE MIGHT BE HOSTAGES!
HAVE *YOU* HEARD ABOUT *KNOCKING?*
I...THOUGHT THIS WAS SOMETHING *FIRESTORM* SHOULD RESPOND TO.
MAYBE, BUT I *SO* HAFTA GET THIS PAPER DONE!
LOOK, IF THIS IS A QUESTION OF LIFE AND DEATH...WELL, I HATE TO DO IT, BUT I CAN WRITE THIS FOR YOU.
AWESOME! YOU ROCK, TONYA!
HERE WE GO...

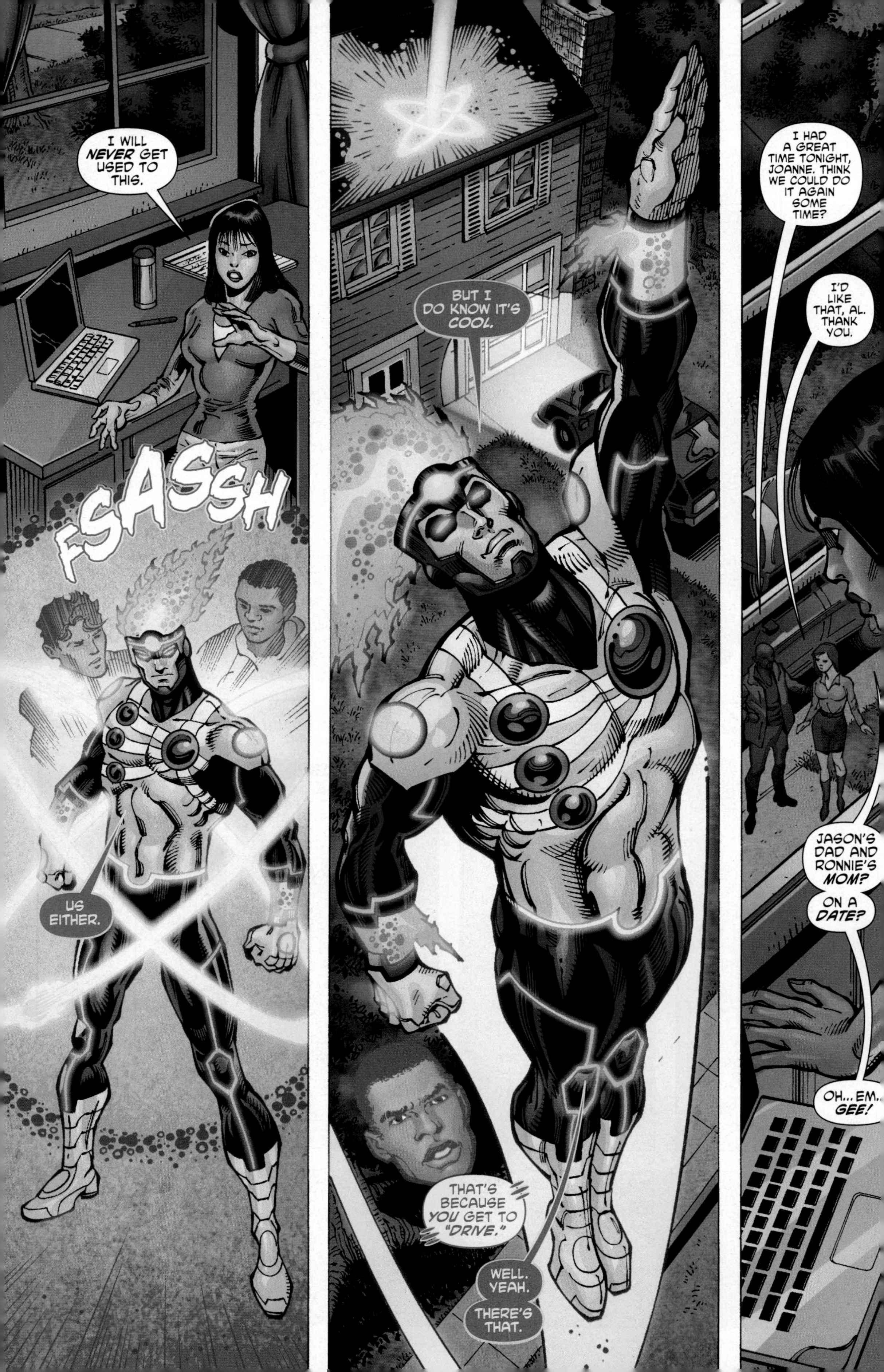
I WILL NEVER GET USED TO THIS.
FSASSH
US EITHER.
BUT I DO KNOW IT'S COOL.
THAT'S BECAUSE YOU GET TO "DRIVE."
WELL. YEAH.
THERE'S THAT.
I HAD A GREAT TIME TONIGHT, JOANNE. THINK WE COULD DO IT AGAIN SOME TIME?
I'D LIKE THAT, AL. THANK YOU.
JASON'S DAD AND RONNIE'S MOM?
ON A DATE?
OH... EM. GEE!

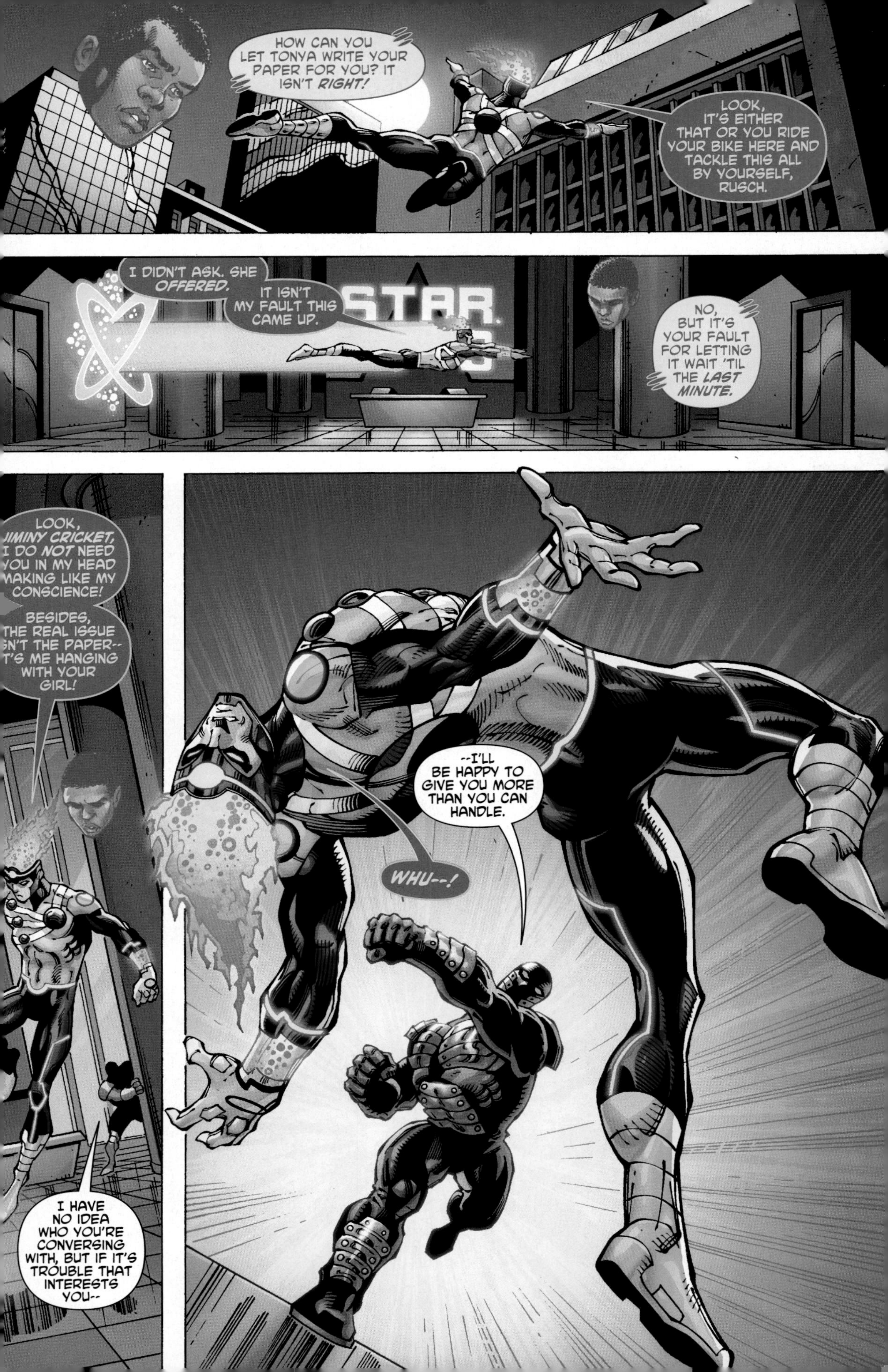
HOW CAN YOU LET TONYA WRITE YOUR PAPER FOR YOU? IT ISN'T RIGHT!
LOOK, IT'S EITHER THAT OR YOU RIDE YOUR BIKE HERE AND TACKLE THIS ALL BY YOURSELF, RUSCH.
I DIDN'T ASK. SHE OFFERED.
IT ISN'T MY FAULT THIS CAME UP.
S.T.A.R.
NO, BUT IT'S YOUR FAULT FOR LETTING IT WAIT 'TIL THE LAST MINUTE.
LOOK, JIMINY CRICKET, I DO NOT NEED YOU IN MY HEAD MAKING LIKE MY CONSCIENCE!
BESIDES, THE REAL ISSUE ISN'T THE PAPER-- IT'S ME HANGING WITH YOUR GIRL!
I HAVE NO IDEA WHO YOU'RE CONVERSING WITH, BUT IF IT'S TROUBLE THAT INTERESTS YOU--
--I'LL BE HAPPY TO GIVE YOU MORE THAN YOU CAN HANDLE.
WHU--!

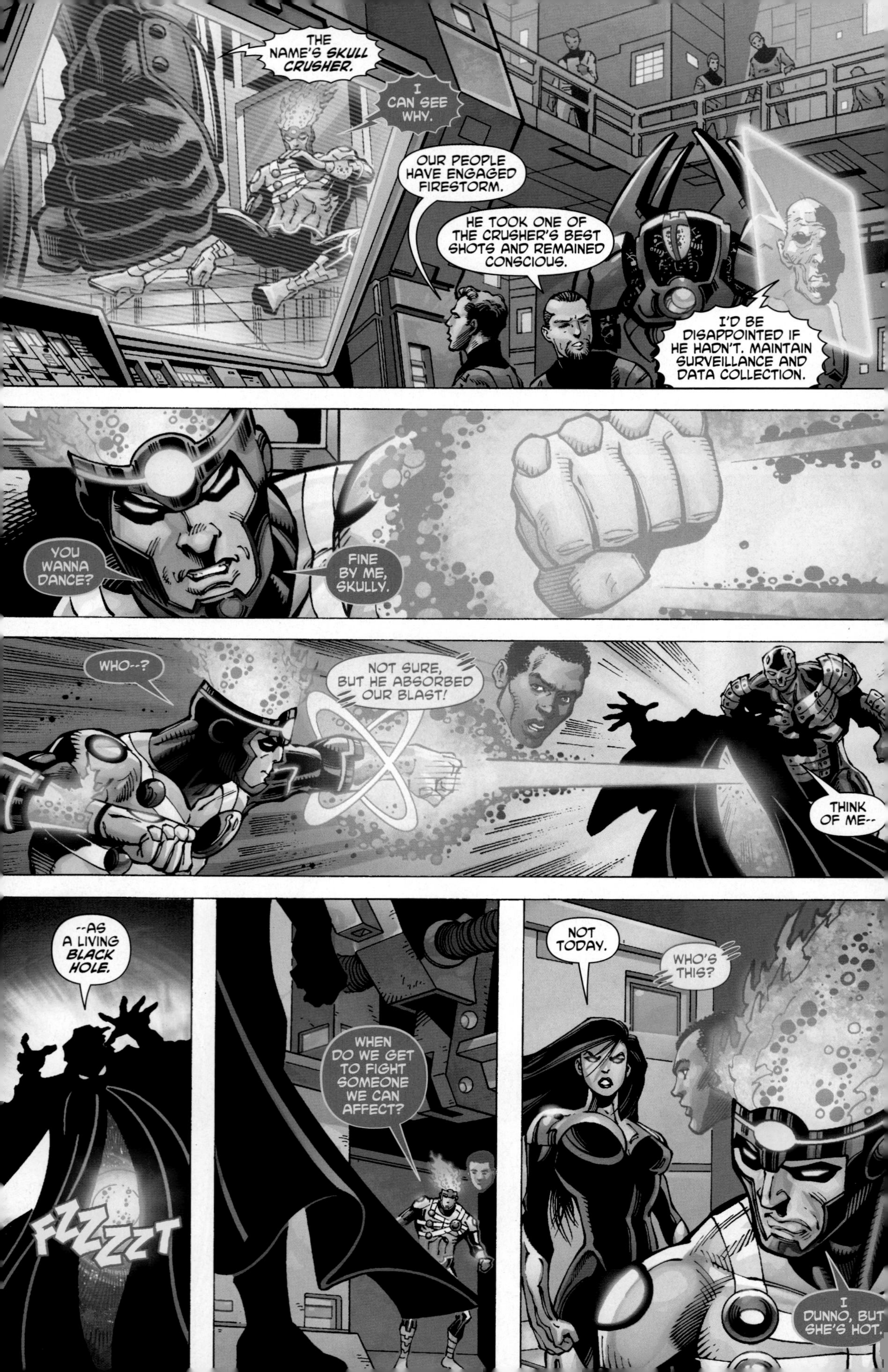
THE NAME'S SKULL CRUSHER.
I CAN SEE WHY.
OUR PEOPLE HAVE ENGAGED FIRESTORM.
HE TOOK ONE OF THE CRUSHER'S BEST SHOTS AND REMAINED CONSCIOUS.
I'D BE DISAPPOINTED IF HE HADN'T. MAINTAIN SURVEILLANCE AND DATA COLLECTION.
YOU WANNA DANCE?
FINE BY ME, SKULLY.
WHO--?
NOT SURE, BUT HE ABSORBED OUR BLAST!
THINK OF ME--
--AS A LIVING BLACK HOLE.
FZZZZZT
WHEN DO WE GET TO FIGHT SOMEONE WE CAN AFFECT?
NOT TODAY.
WHO'S THIS?
I DUNNO, BUT SHE'S HOT.

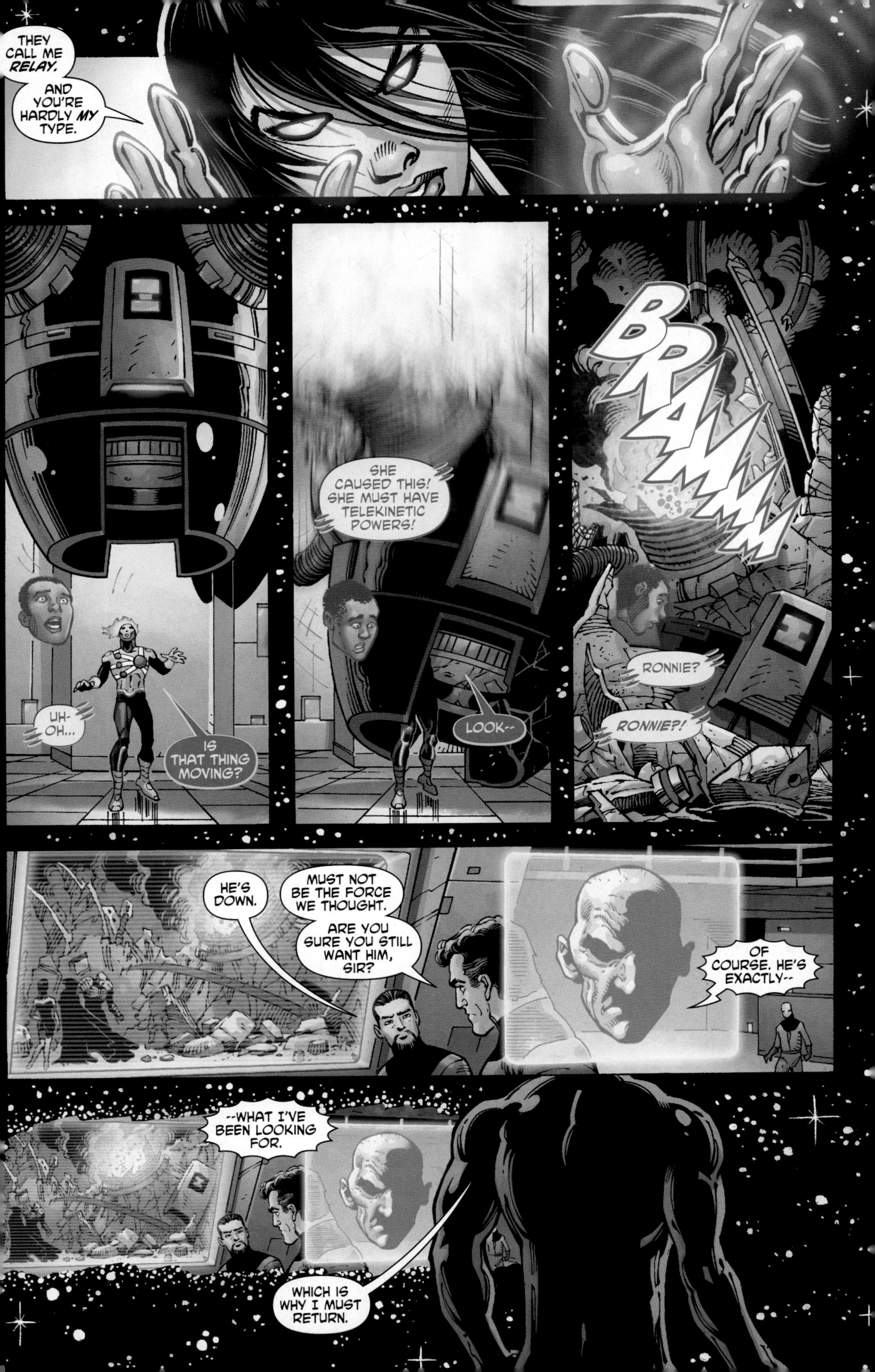
THEY CALL ME RELAY.
AND YOU'RE HARDLY MY TYPE.
UH-OH...
IS THAT THING MOVING?
SHE CAUSED THIS! SHE MUST HAVE TELEKINETIC POWERS!
LOOK--
BRAMMMM
RONNIE?
RONNIE?!
HE'S DOWN.
MUST NOT BE THE FORCE WE THOUGHT.
ARE YOU SURE YOU STILL WANT HIM, SIR?
OF COURSE. HE'S EXACTLY--
--WHAT I'VE BEEN LOOKING FOR.
WHICH IS WHY I MUST RETURN.

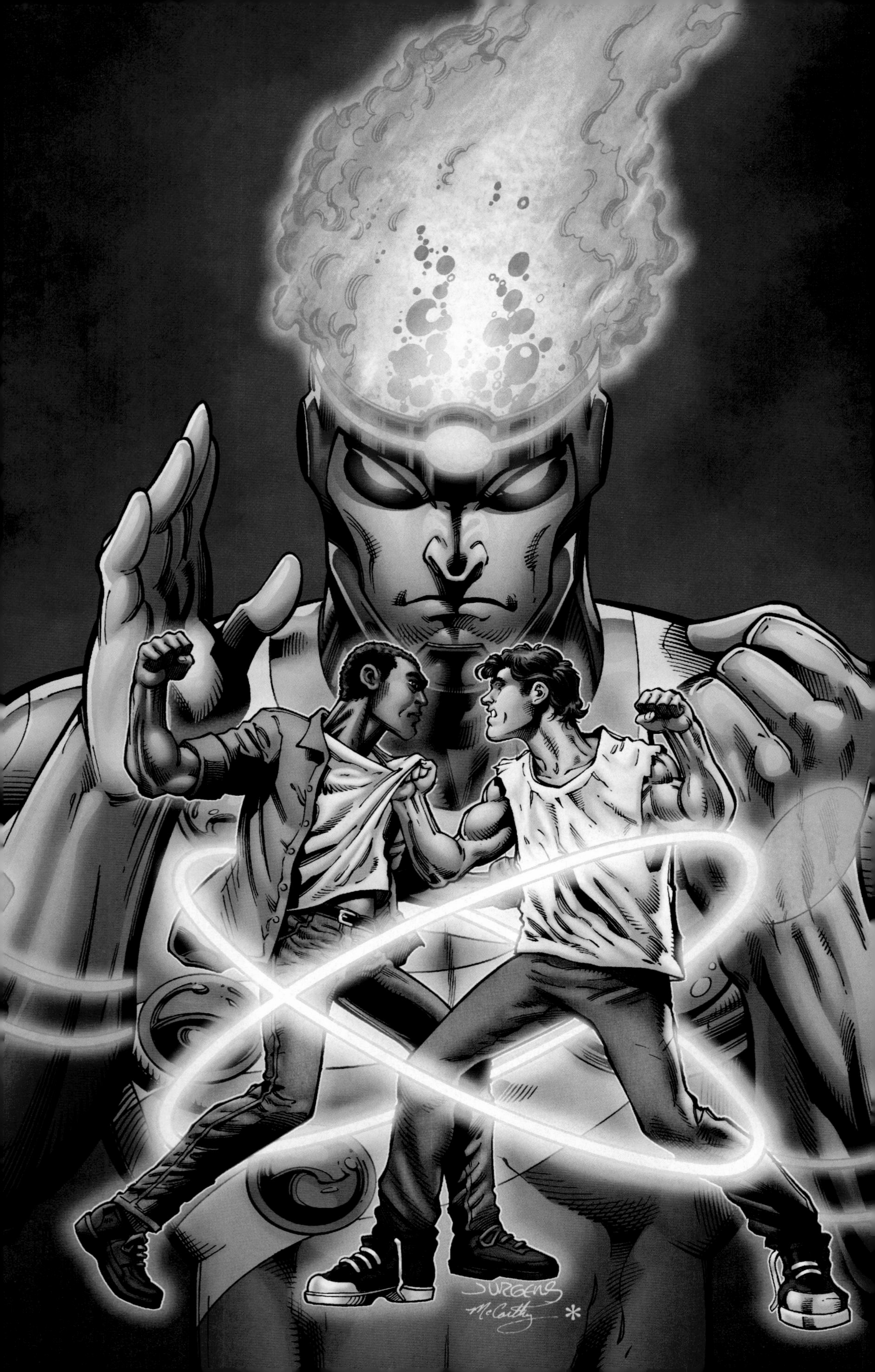
JURGENS
McCarthy

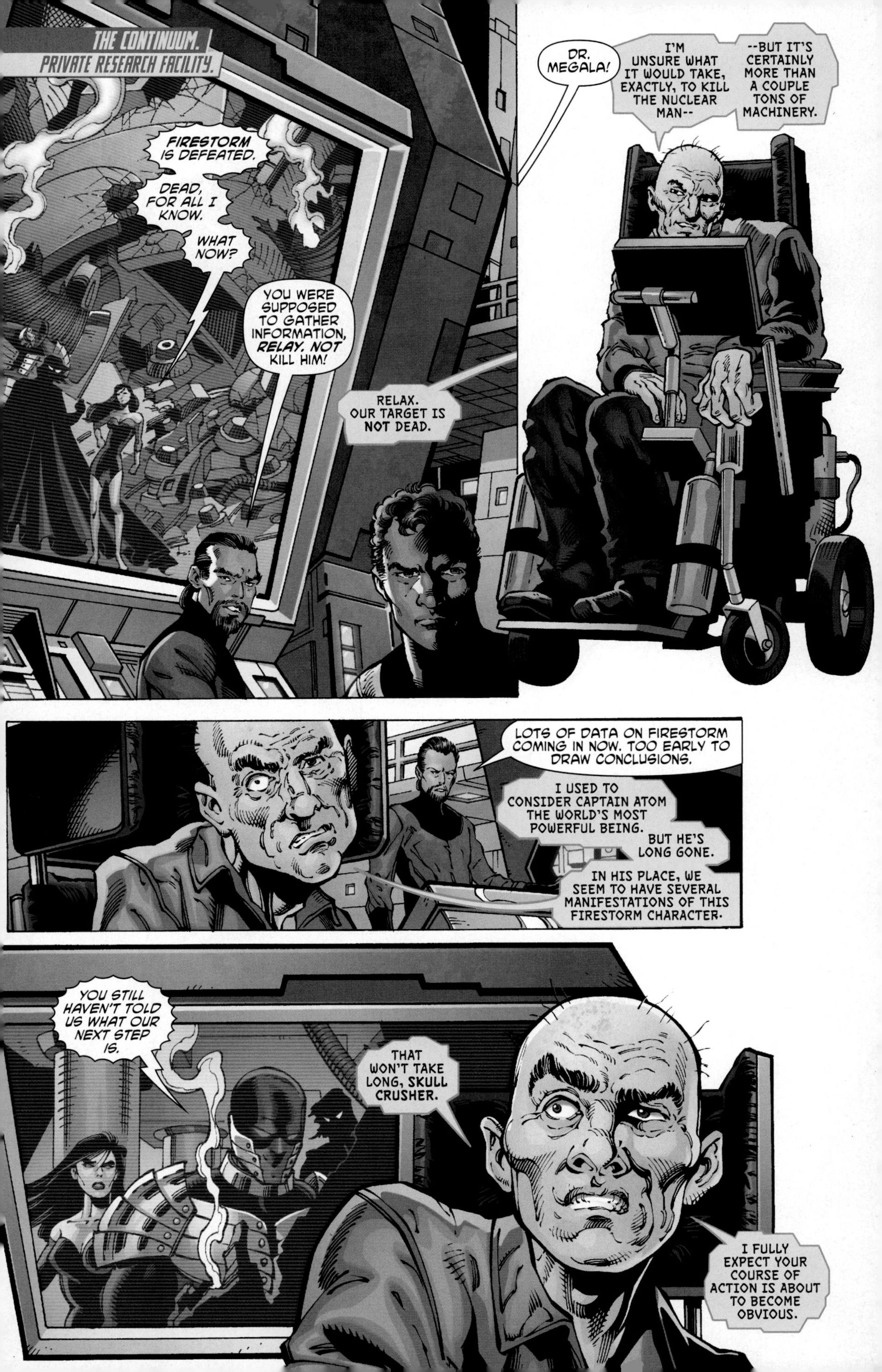
THE CONTINUUM. PRIVATE RESEARCH FACILITY.
FIRESTORM IS DEFEATED.
DEAD, FOR ALL I KNOW.
WHAT NOW?
YOU WERE SUPPOSED TO GATHER INFORMATION, RELAY. NOT KILL HIM!
RELAX. OUR TARGET IS NOT DEAD.
DR. MEGALA!
I'M UNSURE WHAT IT WOULD TAKE, EXACTLY, TO KILL THE NUCLEAR MAN--
--BUT IT'S CERTAINLY MORE THAN A COUPLE TONS OF MACHINERY.
LOTS OF DATA ON FIRESTORM COMING IN NOW. TOO EARLY TO DRAW CONCLUSIONS.
I USED TO CONSIDER CAPTAIN ATOM THE WORLD'S MOST POWERFUL BEING.
BUT HE'S LONG GONE.
IN HIS PLACE, WE SEEM TO HAVE SEVERAL MANIFESTATIONS OF THIS FIRESTORM CHARACTER.
YOU STILL HAVEN'T TOLD US WHAT OUR NEXT STEP IS.
THAT WON'T TAKE LONG, SKULL CRUSHER.
I FULLY EXPECT YOUR COURSE OF ACTION IS ABOUT TO BECOME OBVIOUS.

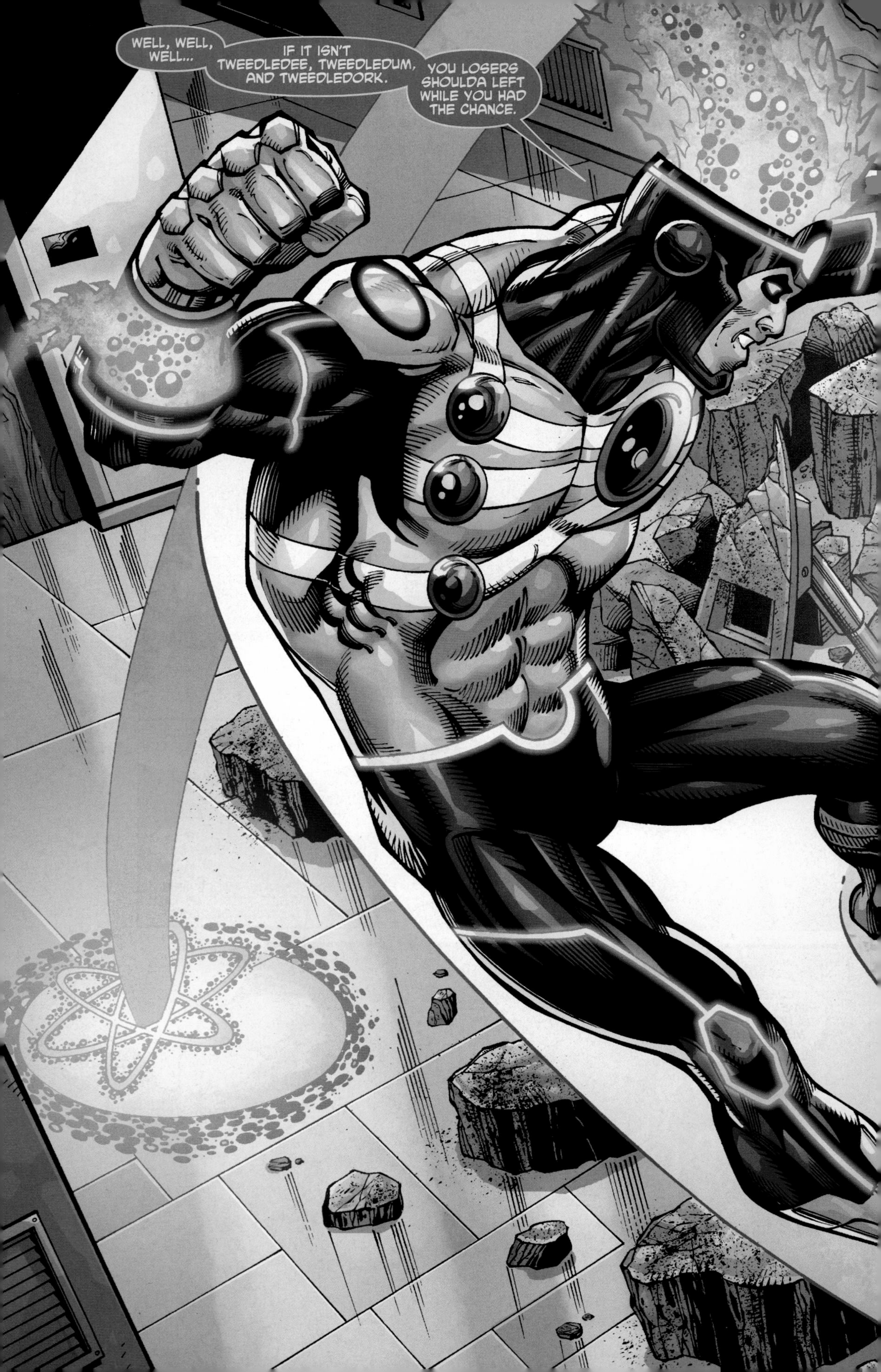
WELL, WELL, WELL...
IF IT ISN'T TWEEDLEDEE, TWEEDLEDUM, AND TWEEDLEDORK.
YOU LOSERS SHOULDA LEFT WHILE YOU HAD THE CHANCE.

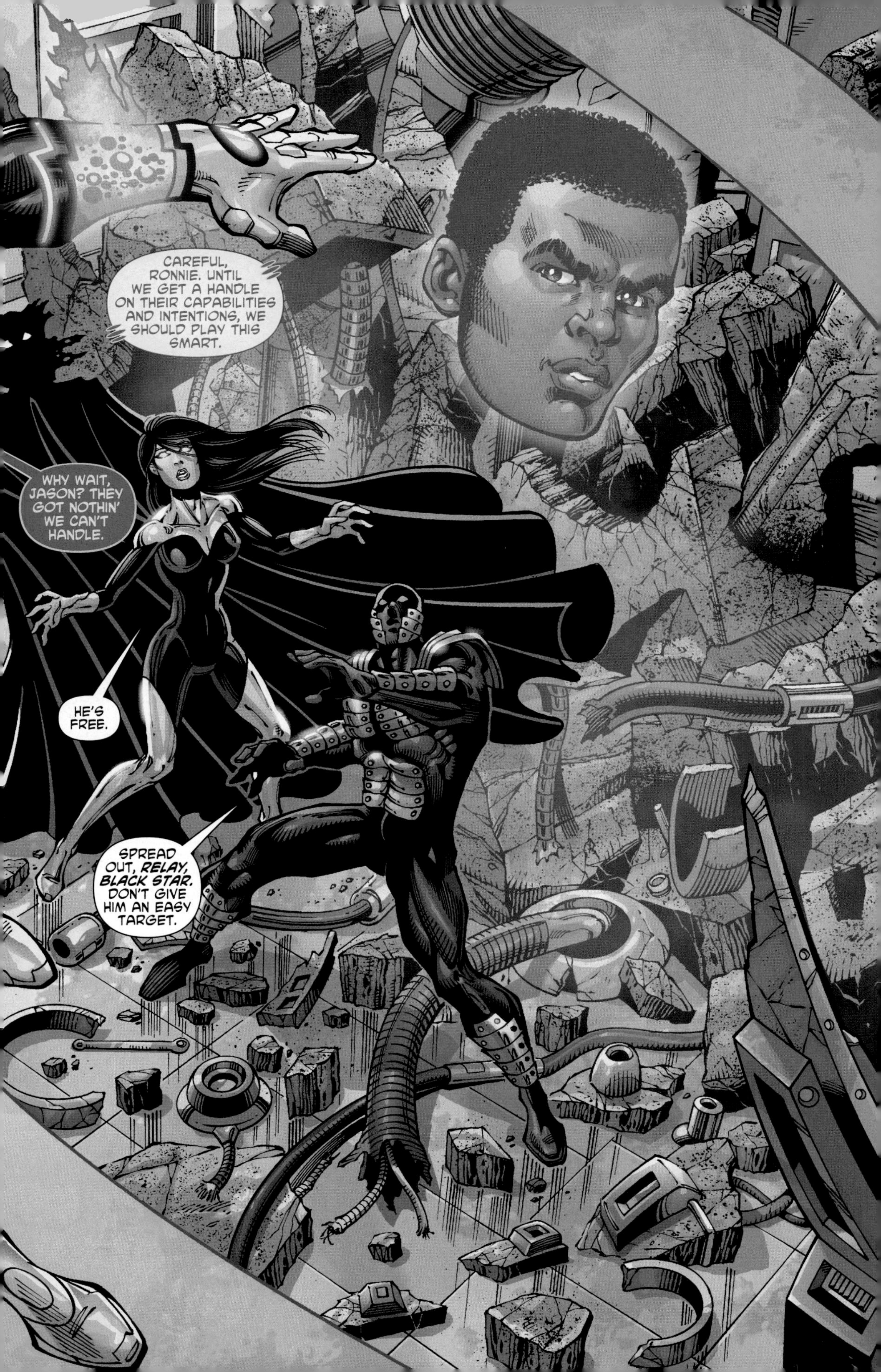
CAREFUL, RONNIE. UNTIL WE GET A HANDLE ON THEIR CAPABILITIES AND INTENTIONS, WE SHOULD PLAY THIS SMART.
WHY WAIT, JASON? THEY GOT NOTHIN' WE CAN'T HANDLE.
HE'S FREE.
SPREAD OUT, RELAY, BLACK STAR. DON'T GIVE HIM AN EASY TARGET.

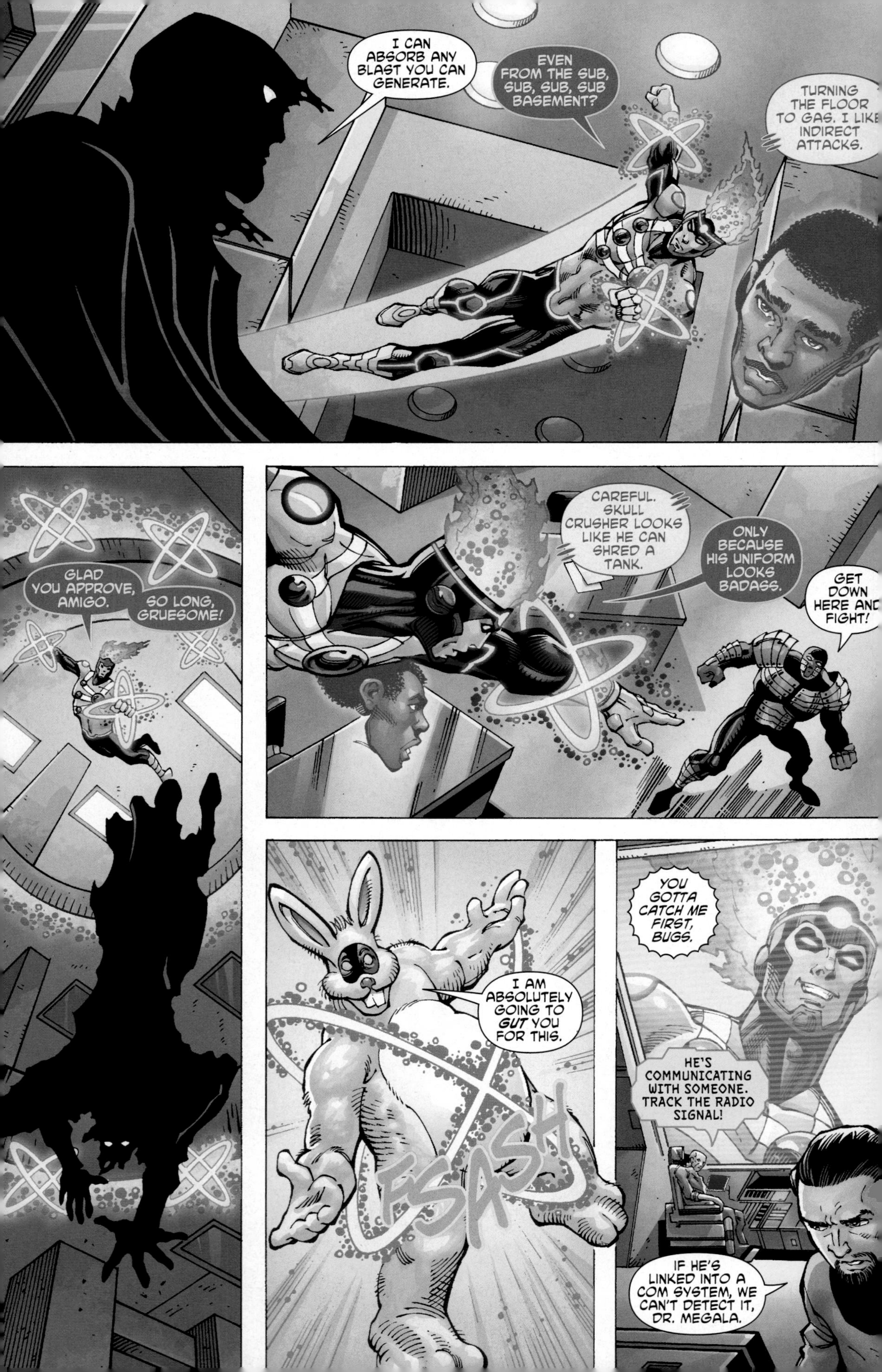
I CAN ABSORB ANY BLAST YOU CAN GENERATE.
EVEN FROM THE SUB, SUB, SUB, SUB BASEMENT?
TURNING THE FLOOR TO GAS. I LIKE INDIRECT ATTACKS.
GLAD YOU APPROVE, AMIGO.
SO LONG, GRUESOME!
CAREFUL. SKULL CRUSHER LOOKS LIKE HE CAN SHRED A TANK.
ONLY BECAUSE HIS UNIFORM LOOKS BADASS.
GET DOWN HERE AND FIGHT!
I AM ABSOLUTELY GOING TO *GUT* YOU FOR THIS.
FSASH
YOU GOTTA CATCH ME FIRST, BUGS.
HE'S COMMUNICATING WITH SOMEONE. TRACK THE RADIO SIGNAL!
IF HE'S LINKED INTO A COM SYSTEM, WE CAN'T DETECT IT, DR. MEGALA.

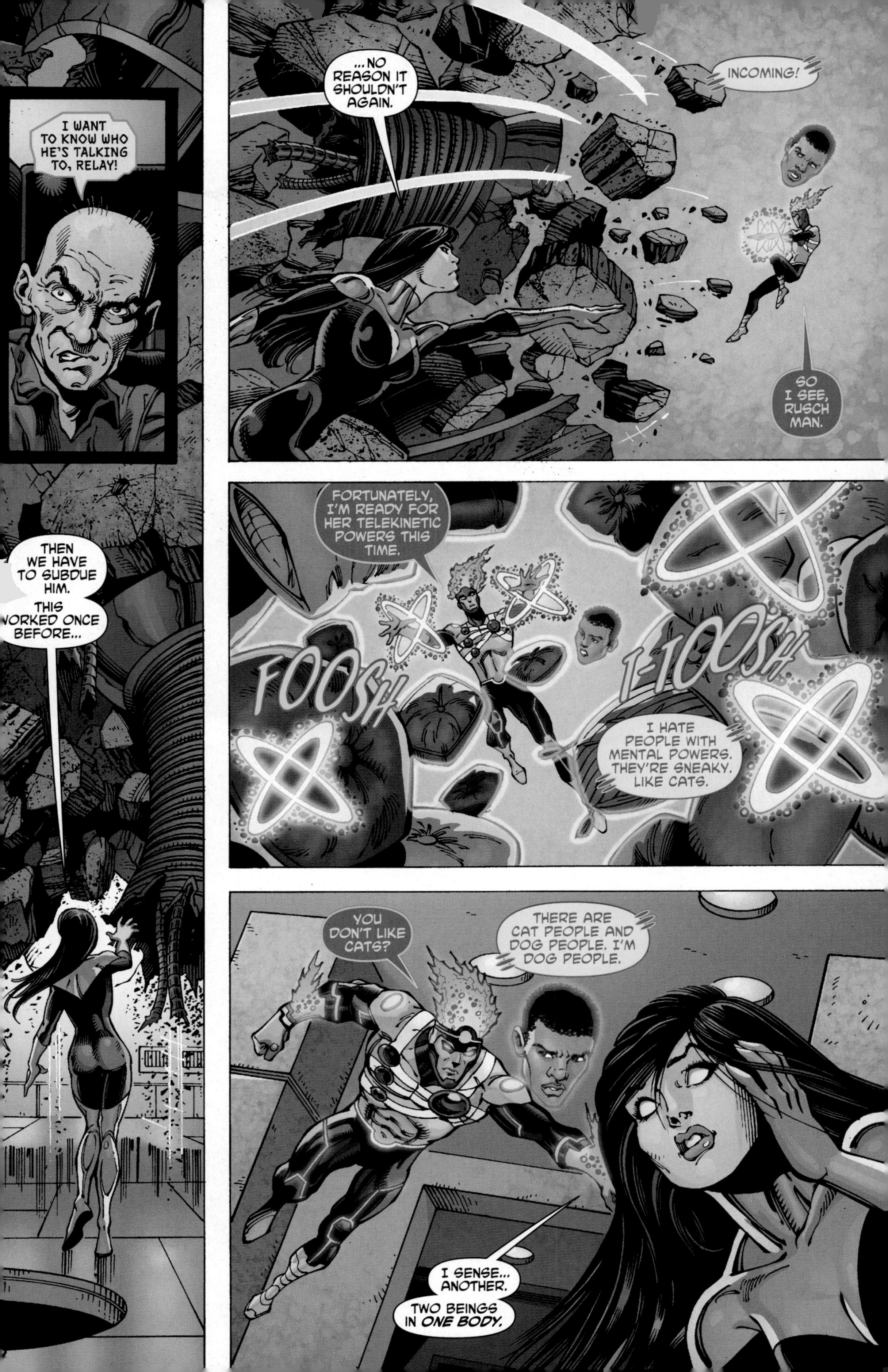

I WANT TO KNOW WHO HE'S TALKING TO, RELAY!
...NO REASON IT SHOULDN'T AGAIN.
INCOMING!
SO I SEE, RUSCH MAN.
THEN WE HAVE TO SUBDUE HIM.
THIS WORKED ONCE BEFORE...
FORTUNATELY, I'M READY FOR HER TELEKINETIC POWERS THIS TIME.
FOOSH
F-FOOSH
I HATE PEOPLE WITH MENTAL POWERS. THEY'RE SNEAKY. LIKE CATS.
YOU DON'T LIKE CATS?
THERE ARE CAT PEOPLE AND DOG PEOPLE. I'M DOG PEOPLE.
I SENSE... ANOTHER.
TWO BEINGS IN ONE BODY.

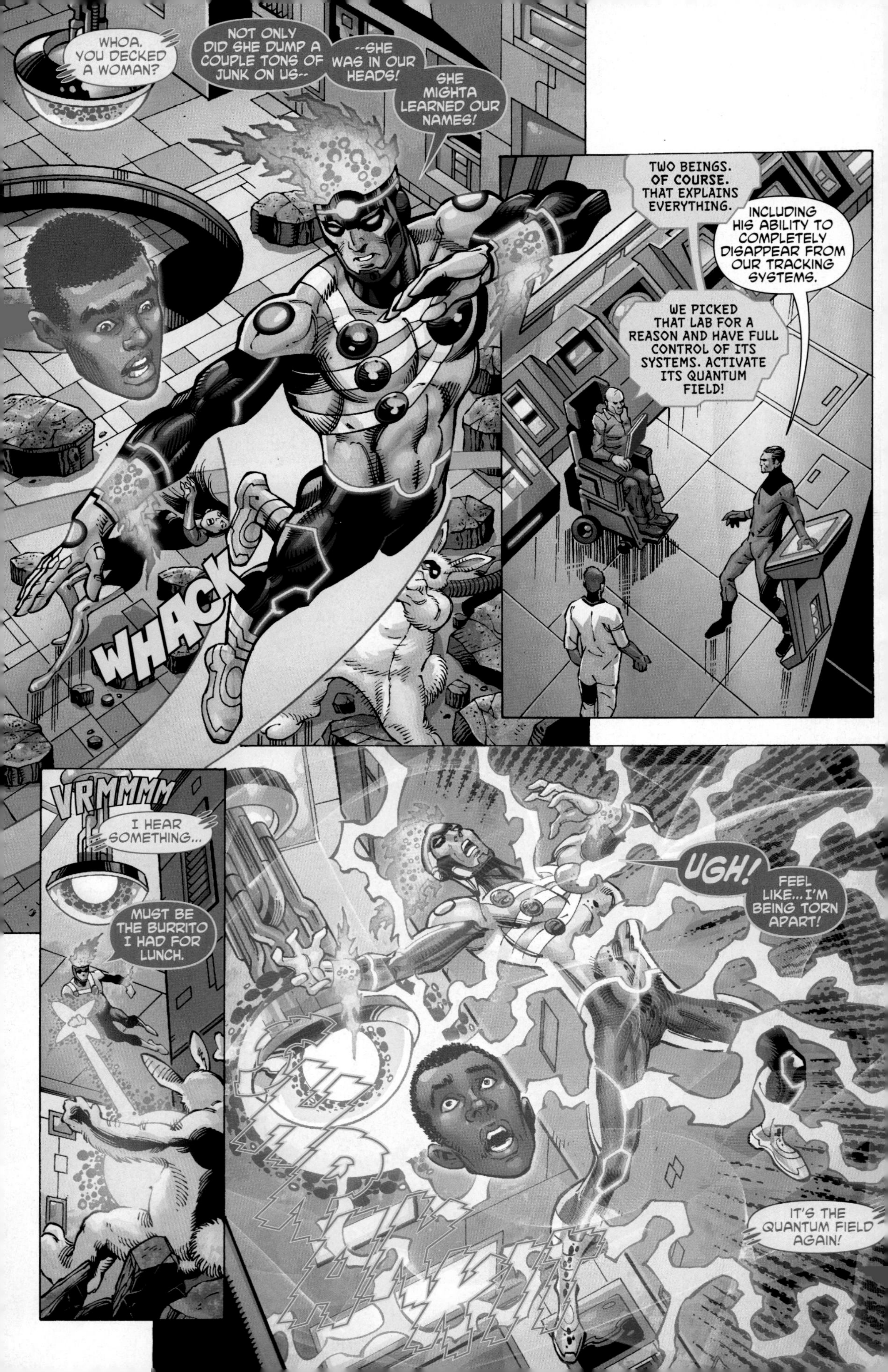
WHOA. YOU DECKED A WOMAN?
NOT ONLY DID SHE DUMP A COUPLE TONS OF JUNK ON US--
--SHE WAS IN OUR HEADS!
SHE MIGHTA LEARNED OUR NAMES!
WHACK
TWO BEINGS. OF COURSE. THAT EXPLAINS EVERYTHING.
INCLUDING HIS ABILITY TO COMPLETELY DISAPPEAR FROM OUR TRACKING SYSTEMS.
WE PICKED THAT LAB FOR A REASON AND HAVE FULL CONTROL OF ITS SYSTEMS. ACTIVATE ITS QUANTUM FIELD!
VRMMMM
I HEAR SOMETHING...
MUST BE THE BURRITO I HAD FOR LUNCH.
UGH!
FEEL LIKE...I'M BEING TORN APART!
IT'S THE QUANTUM FIELD AGAIN!

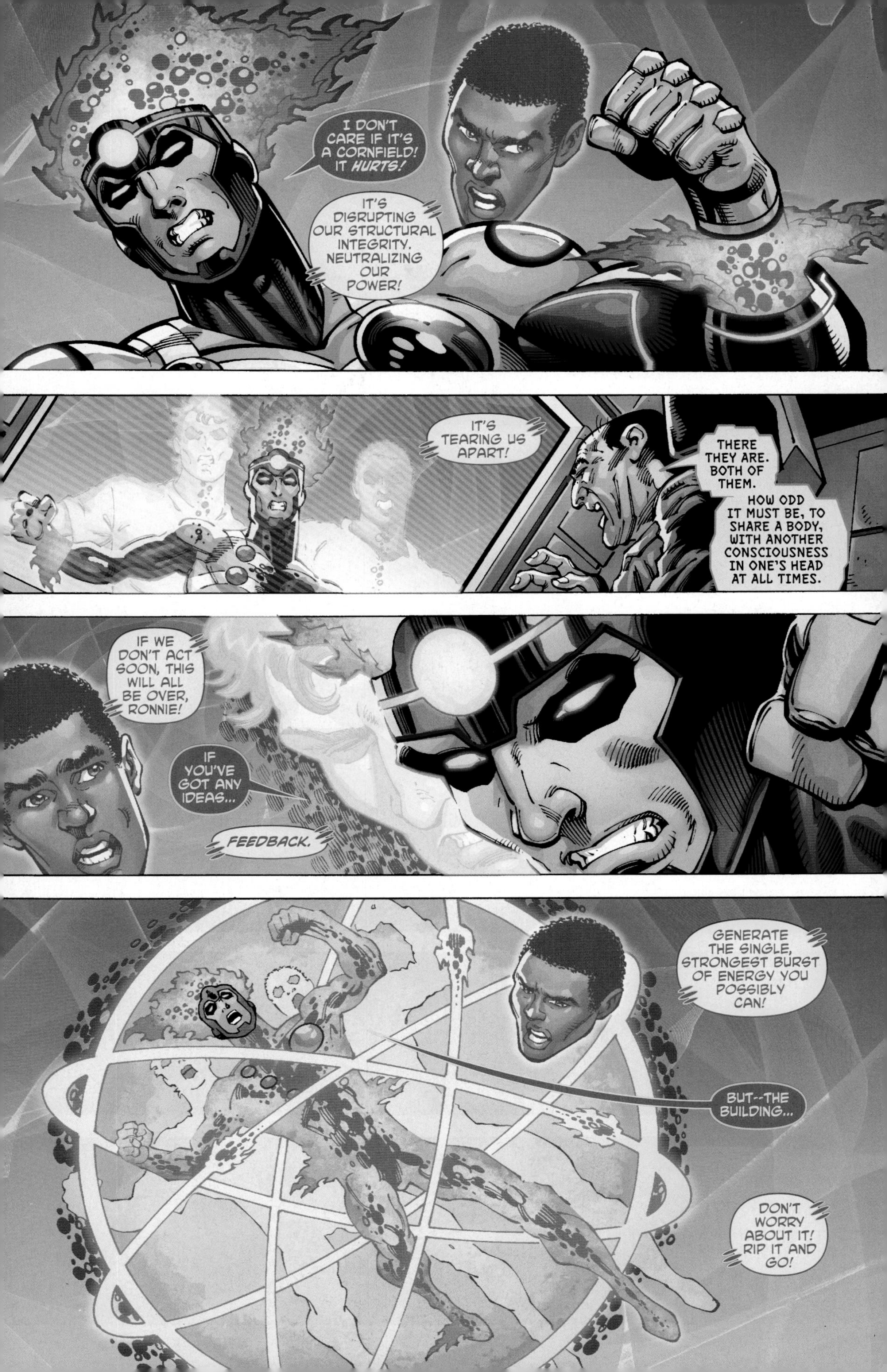
I DON'T CARE IF IT'S A CORNFIELD! IT HURTS!
IT'S DISRUPTING OUR STRUCTURAL INTEGRITY. NEUTRALIZING OUR POWER!
IT'S TEARING US APART!
THERE THEY ARE. BOTH OF THEM.
HOW ODD IT MUST BE, TO SHARE A BODY, WITH ANOTHER CONSCIOUSNESS IN ONE'S HEAD AT ALL TIMES.
IF WE DON'T ACT SOON, THIS WILL ALL BE OVER, RONNIE!
IF YOU'VE GOT ANY IDEAS...
FEEDBACK.
GENERATE THE SINGLE, STRONGEST BURST OF ENERGY YOU POSSIBLY CAN!
BUT--THE BUILDING...
DON'T WORRY ABOUT IT! RIP IT AND GO!

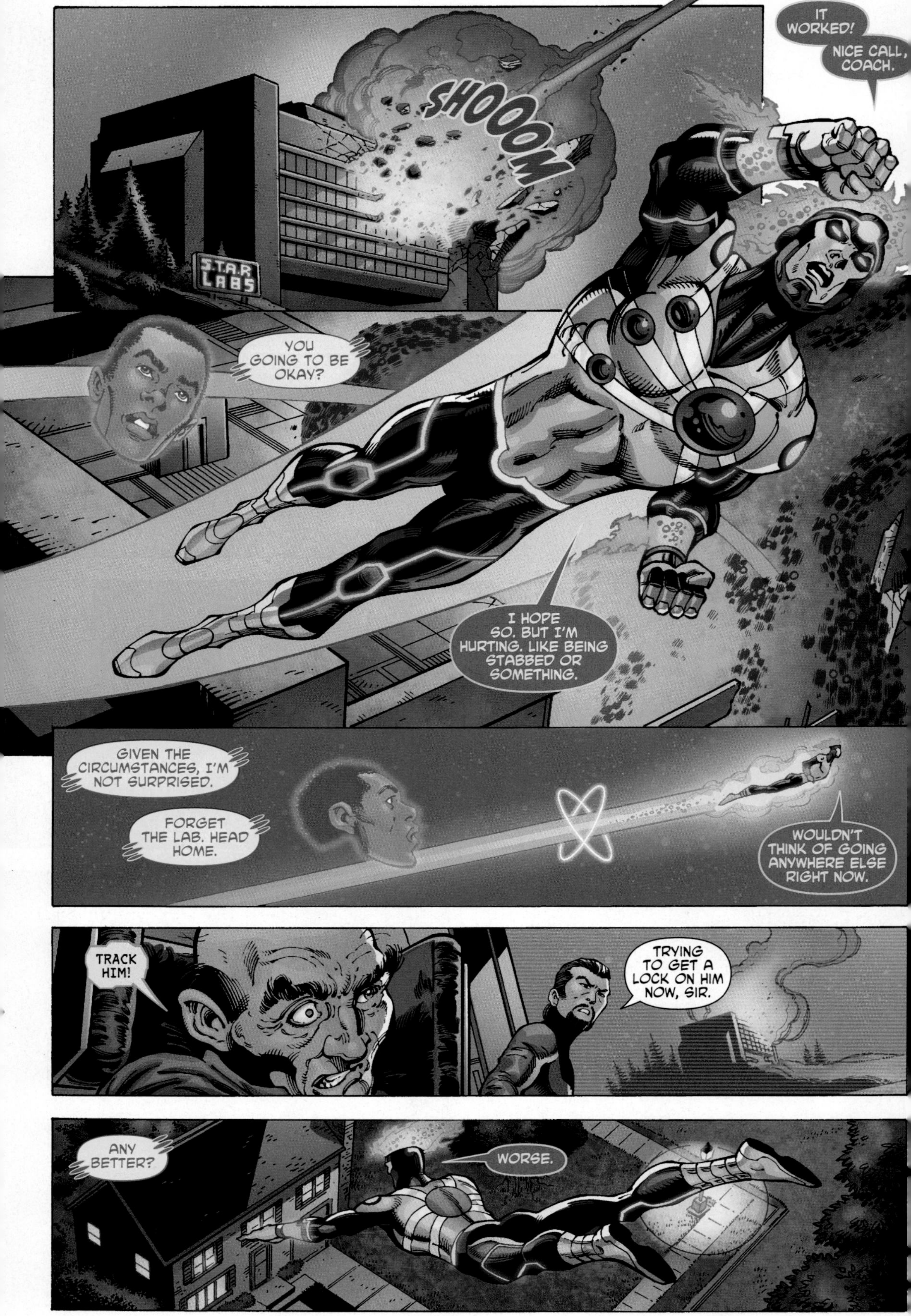

SHOOOM
IT WORKED!
NICE CALL, COACH.
YOU GOING TO BE OKAY?
I HOPE SO. BUT I'M HURTING. LIKE BEING STABBED OR SOMETHING.
GIVEN THE CIRCUMSTANCES, I'M NOT SURPRISED.
FORGET THE LAB. HEAD HOME.
WOULDN'T THINK OF GOING ANYWHERE ELSE RIGHT NOW.
TRACK HIM!
TRYING TO GET A LOCK ON HIM NOW, SIR.
ANY BETTER?
WORSE.

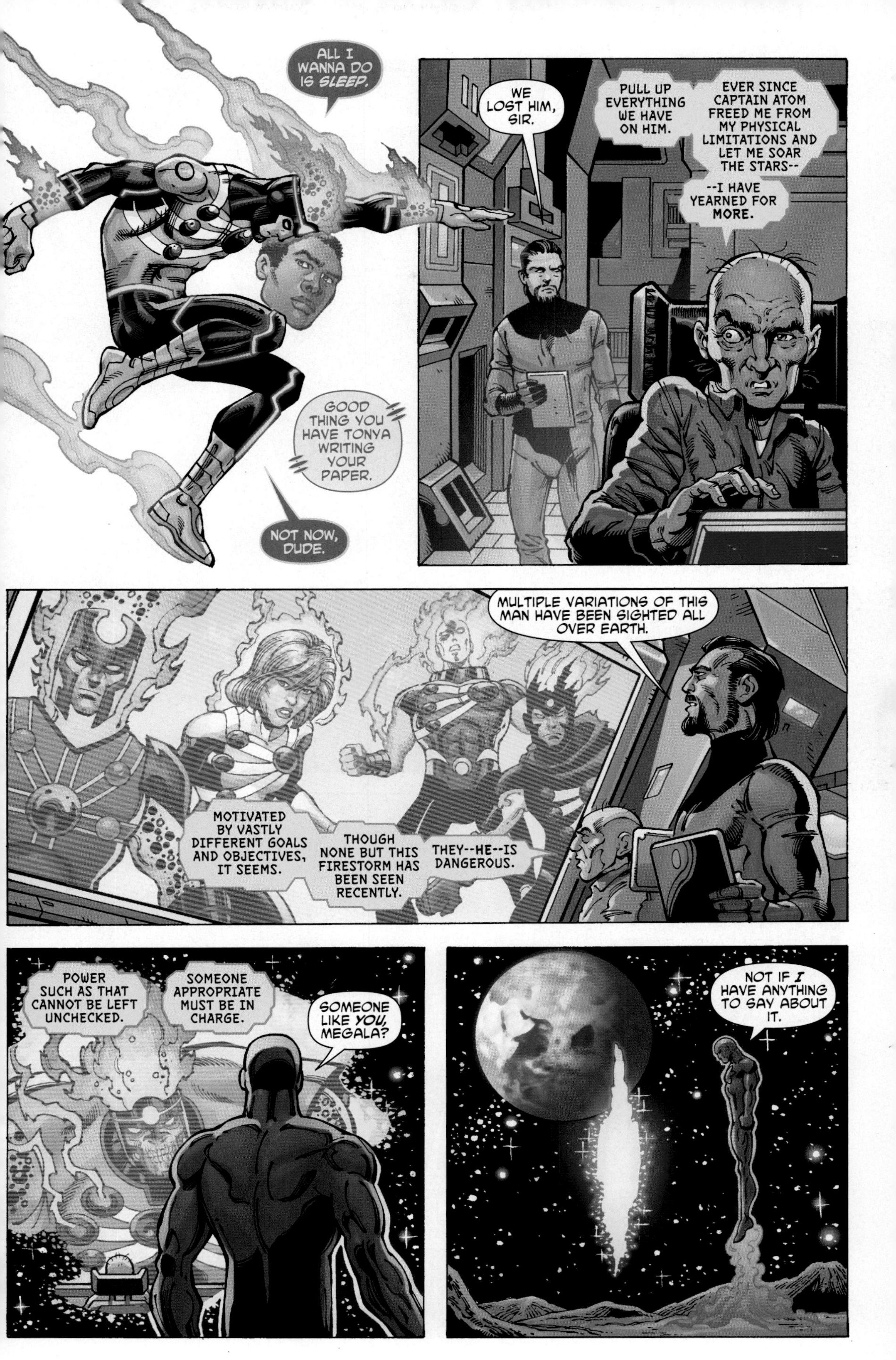
ALL I WANNA DO IS SLEEP.
GOOD THING YOU HAVE TONYA WRITING YOUR PAPER.
NOT NOW, DUDE.
WE LOST HIM, SIR.
PULL UP EVERYTHING WE HAVE ON HIM.
EVER SINCE CAPTAIN ATOM FREED ME FROM MY PHYSICAL LIMITATIONS AND LET ME SOAR THE STARS--
--I HAVE YEARNED FOR MORE.
MULTIPLE VARIATIONS OF THIS MAN HAVE BEEN SIGHTED ALL OVER EARTH.
MOTIVATED BY VASTLY DIFFERENT GOALS AND OBJECTIVES, IT SEEMS.
THOUGH NONE BUT THIS FIRESTORM HAS BEEN SEEN RECENTLY.
THEY--HE--IS DANGEROUS.
POWER SUCH AS THAT CANNOT BE LEFT UNCHECKED.
SOMEONE APPROPRIATE MUST BE IN CHARGE.
SOMEONE LIKE YOU, MEGALA?
NOT IF I HAVE ANYTHING TO SAY ABOUT IT.

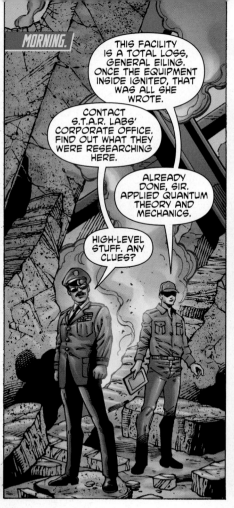

THIS FACILITY IS A TOTAL LOSS, GENERAL EILING. ONCE THE EQUIPMENT INSIDE IGNITED, THAT WAS ALL SHE WROTE.

CONTACT S.T.A.R. LABS' CORPORATE OFFICE. FIND OUT WHAT THEY WERE RESEARCHING HERE.

ALREADY DONE, SIR. APPLIED QUANTUM THEORY AND MECHANICS.

HIGH-LEVEL STUFF. ANY CLUES?

WE PULLED THIS PHOTO OFF A SECURITY CAM...

...CAM...

A FIRESTORM.

WE HAVE COMPANY, GENERAL.

LOOK!

HE'S LEAVING.

BUT IF THAT'S WHO I THINK IT IS, THIS IS GOING TO GET A WHOLE LOT MESSIER.

RONALD ROY RAYMOND!

WHOA. IT'S SERIOUS WHEN THE MIDDLE NAME GETS USED.

FOR THE LAST TIME--

--GET UP!

YOUR UNCLE WOULDN'T STAND FOR YOU CUTTING SCHOOL, BUSTER.

WHICH STARTS IN TWENTY MINUTES!

MOVE IT!

YES, SIR! RIGHT AWAY, SIR! AS YOU COMMAND, SI--

ENOUGH.

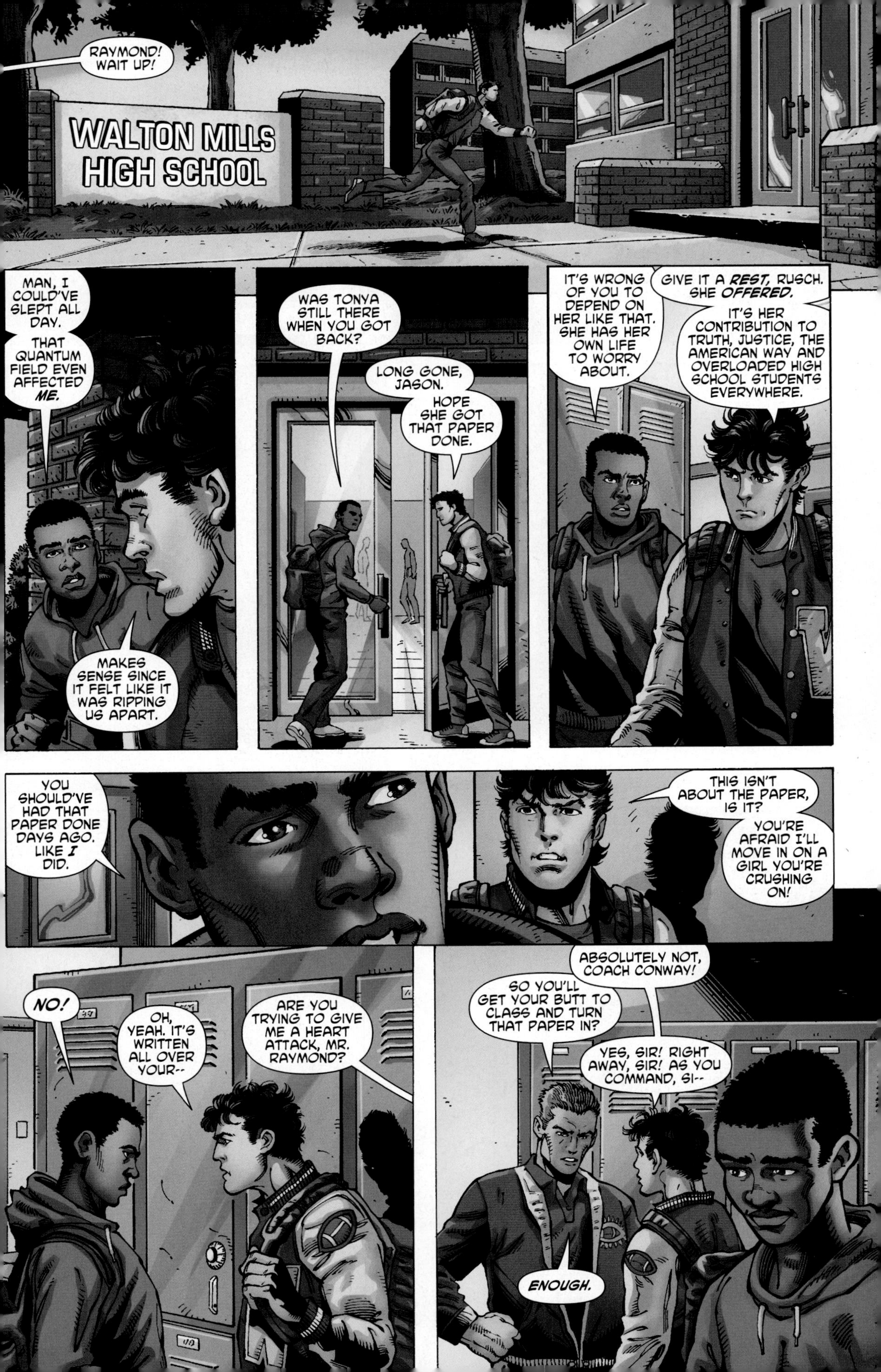
RAYMOND! WAIT UP!
WALTON MILLS HIGH SCHOOL
MAN, I COULD'VE SLEPT ALL DAY.
THAT QUANTUM FIELD EVEN AFFECTED ME.
MAKES SENSE SINCE IT FELT LIKE IT WAS RIPPING US APART.
WAS TONYA STILL THERE WHEN YOU GOT BACK?
LONG GONE, JASON.
HOPE SHE GOT THAT PAPER DONE.
IT'S WRONG OF YOU TO DEPEND ON HER LIKE THAT. SHE HAS HER OWN LIFE TO WORRY ABOUT.
GIVE IT A REST, RUSCH. SHE OFFERED.
IT'S HER CONTRIBUTION TO TRUTH, JUSTICE, THE AMERICAN WAY AND OVERLOADED HIGH SCHOOL STUDENTS EVERYWHERE.
YOU SHOULD'VE HAD THAT PAPER DONE DAYS AGO. LIKE I DID.
THIS ISN'T ABOUT THE PAPER, IS IT?
YOU'RE AFRAID I'LL MOVE IN ON A GIRL YOU'RE CRUSHING ON!
NO!
OH, YEAH. IT'S WRITTEN ALL OVER YOUR--
ARE YOU TRYING TO GIVE ME A HEART ATTACK, MR. RAYMOND?
ABSOLUTELY NOT, COACH CONWAY!
SO YOU'LL GET YOUR BUTT TO CLASS AND TURN THAT PAPER IN?
YES, SIR! RIGHT AWAY, SIR! AS YOU COMMAND, SI--
ENOUGH.

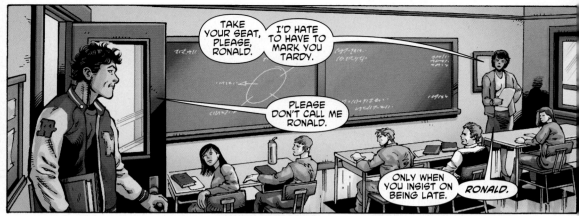

TAKE YOUR SEAT, PLEASE, RONALD.

I'D HATE TO HAVE TO MARK YOU TARDY.

PLEASE DON'T CALL ME RONALD.

ONLY WHEN YOU INSIST ON BEING LATE. *RONALD.*

YOU HAVE YOUR PAPER DONE, I ASSUME?

OF COURSE, MRS. SCHMIDT.

LEMME SIT DOWN AND I'LL GET IT FOR YOU.

HERE.

GOT IT.

NAPOLEON BY RONNIE RAYMOND

HERE YOU GO.

YOU LOOK MORE UNKEMPT THAN USUAL THIS MORNING. LATE NIGHT?

WORKING ON THE PAPER. THAT NAPOLEON IS A TOUGH DUDE TO GET A HANDLE ON.

YOU'LL NEED AT LEAST A C-PLUS, YOU KNOW.

MORTAL LOCK, MRS. SCHMIDT. BEST THING I EVER WROTE, GUARANTEED.

AND BE SURE TO TELL COACH I GOT IT IN ON TIME, OKAY? THE HOMECOMING GAME IS FRIDAY, AND I GOTTA *PLAY.*

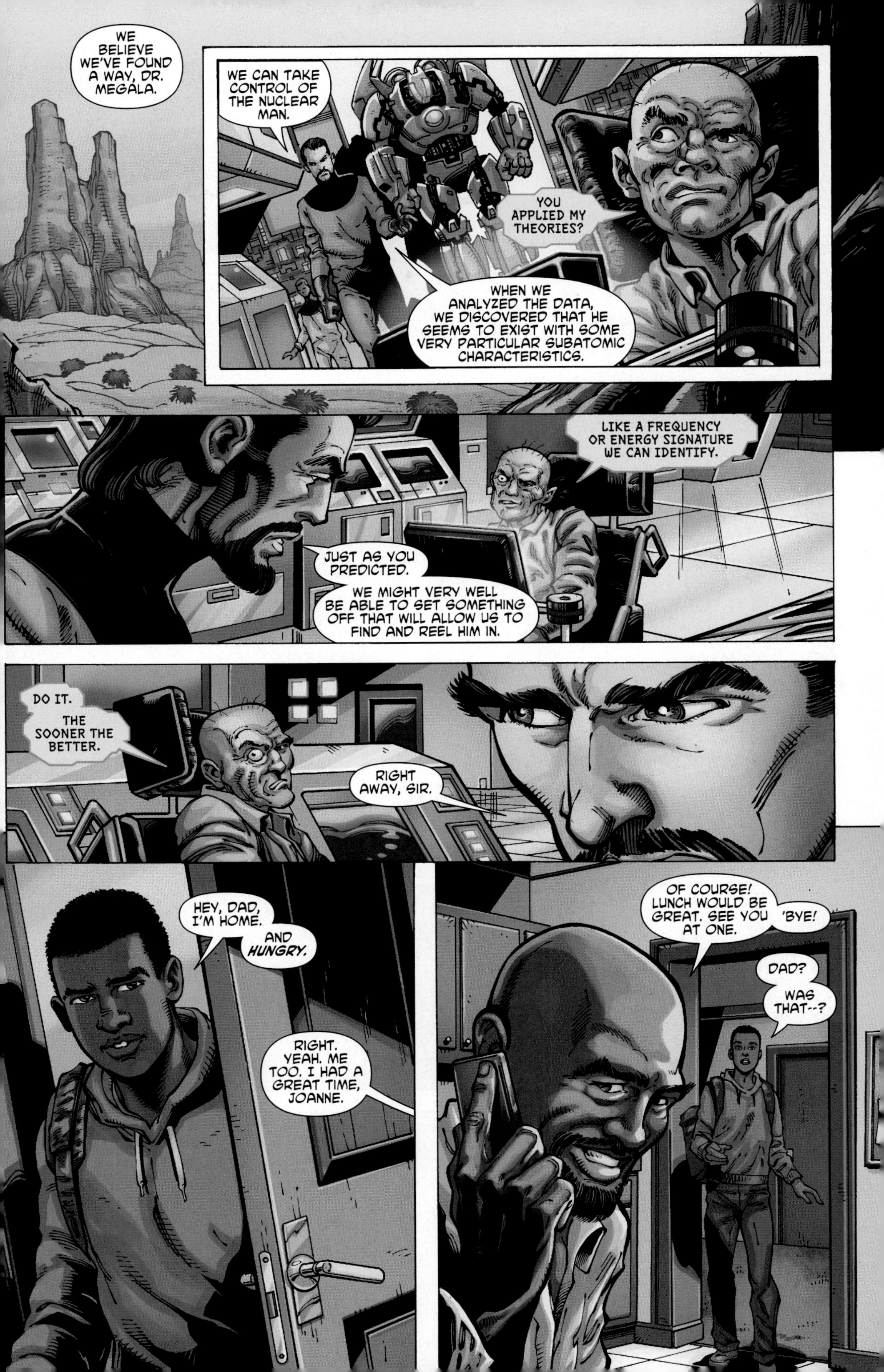
WE BELIEVE WE'VE FOUND A WAY, DR. MEGALA.
WE CAN TAKE CONTROL OF THE NUCLEAR MAN.
YOU APPLIED MY THEORIES?
WHEN WE ANALYZED THE DATA, WE DISCOVERED THAT HE SEEMS TO EXIST WITH SOME VERY PARTICULAR SUBATOMIC CHARACTERISTICS.
LIKE A FREQUENCY OR ENERGY SIGNATURE WE CAN IDENTIFY.
JUST AS YOU PREDICTED.
WE MIGHT VERY WELL BE ABLE TO SET SOMETHING OFF THAT WILL ALLOW US TO FIND AND REEL HIM IN.
DO IT.
THE SOONER THE BETTER.
RIGHT AWAY, SIR.
HEY, DAD, I'M HOME.
AND *HUNGRY.*
RIGHT. YEAH. ME TOO. I HAD A GREAT TIME, JOANNE.
OF COURSE! LUNCH WOULD BE GREAT. SEE YOU AT ONE.
'BYE!
DAD?
WAS THAT--?

RONNIE RAYMOND'S MOM. JOANNE. WE'RE GETTING TOGETHER FOR LUNCH.

BUT... SHE... WHAT DOES THIS MEAN?

I'M NOT REALLY SURE MYSELF. BUT WE'RE FRIENDS, JASON.

WHOA. THAT JUST ISN'T-- ISN'T--

UGH!

JASON?!

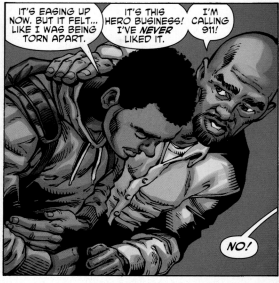

IT'S EASING UP NOW. BUT IT FELT... LIKE I WAS BEING TORN APART.

IT'S THIS HERO BUSINESS! I'VE NEVER LIKED IT.

I'M CALLING 911!

NO!

IT HAPPENED TO ME, TOO--JUST LIKE WITH FIRESTORM LAST NIGHT.

SOME KIND OF LASTING EFFECT?

OR SOMEONE TRYING TO GET TO US?

EITHER WAY, THIS CRAZINESS HAS TO STOP.

THE ONLY WAY FOR THAT TO HAPPEN--

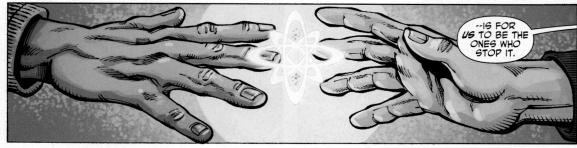

--IS FOR US TO BE THE ONES WHO STOP IT.

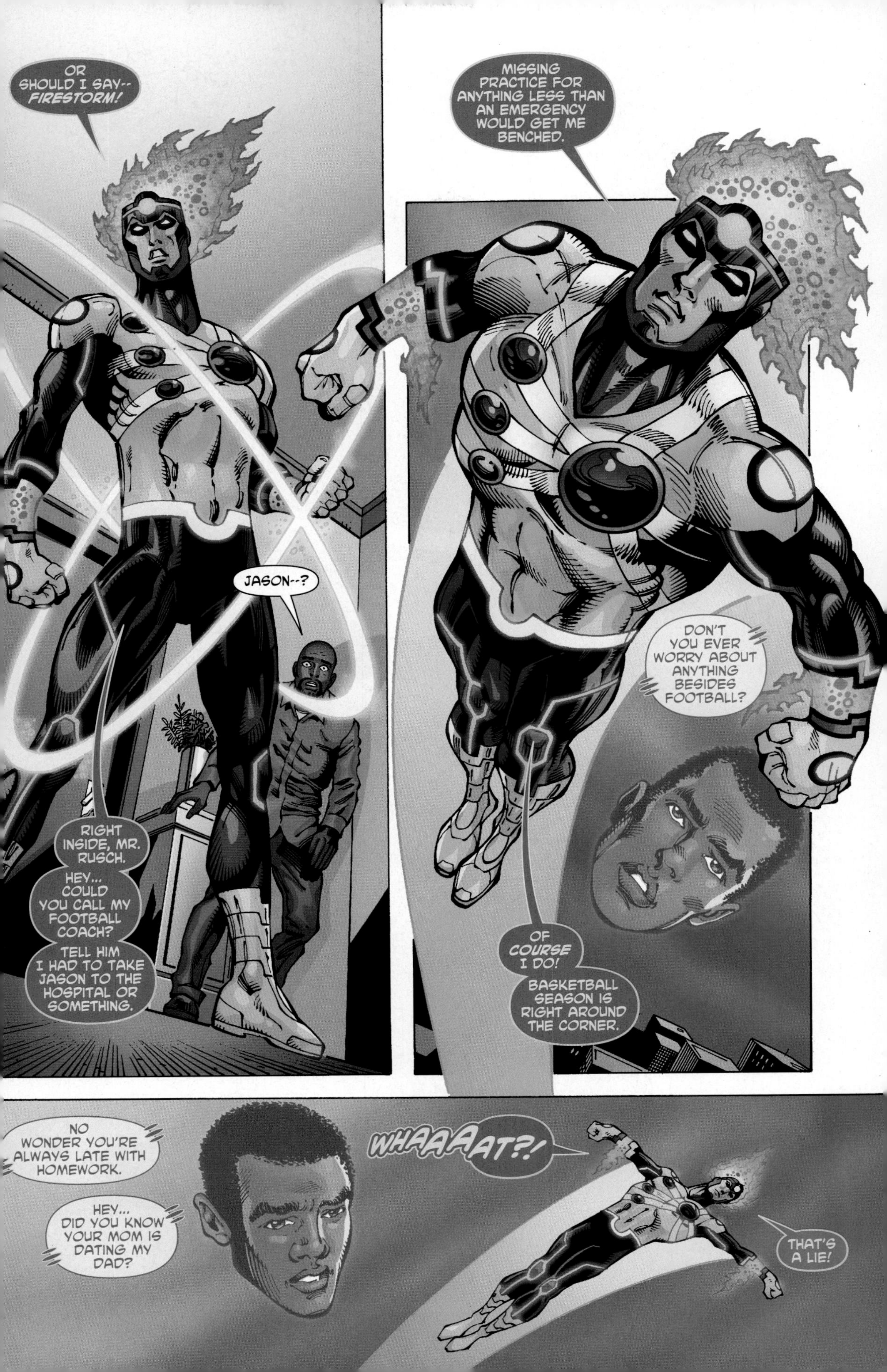
OR SHOULD I SAY-- FIRESTORM!
JASON--?
RIGHT INSIDE, MR. RUSCH.
HEY... COULD YOU CALL MY FOOTBALL COACH?
TELL HIM I HAD TO TAKE JASON TO THE HOSPITAL OR SOMETHING.
MISSING PRACTICE FOR ANYTHING LESS THAN AN EMERGENCY WOULD GET ME BENCHED.
DON'T YOU EVER WORRY ABOUT ANYTHING BESIDES FOOTBALL?
OF COURSE I DO!
BASKETBALL SEASON IS RIGHT AROUND THE CORNER.
NO WONDER YOU'RE ALWAYS LATE WITH HOMEWORK.
HEY... DID YOU KNOW YOUR MOM IS DATING MY DAD?
WHAAAAAT?!
THAT'S A LIE!

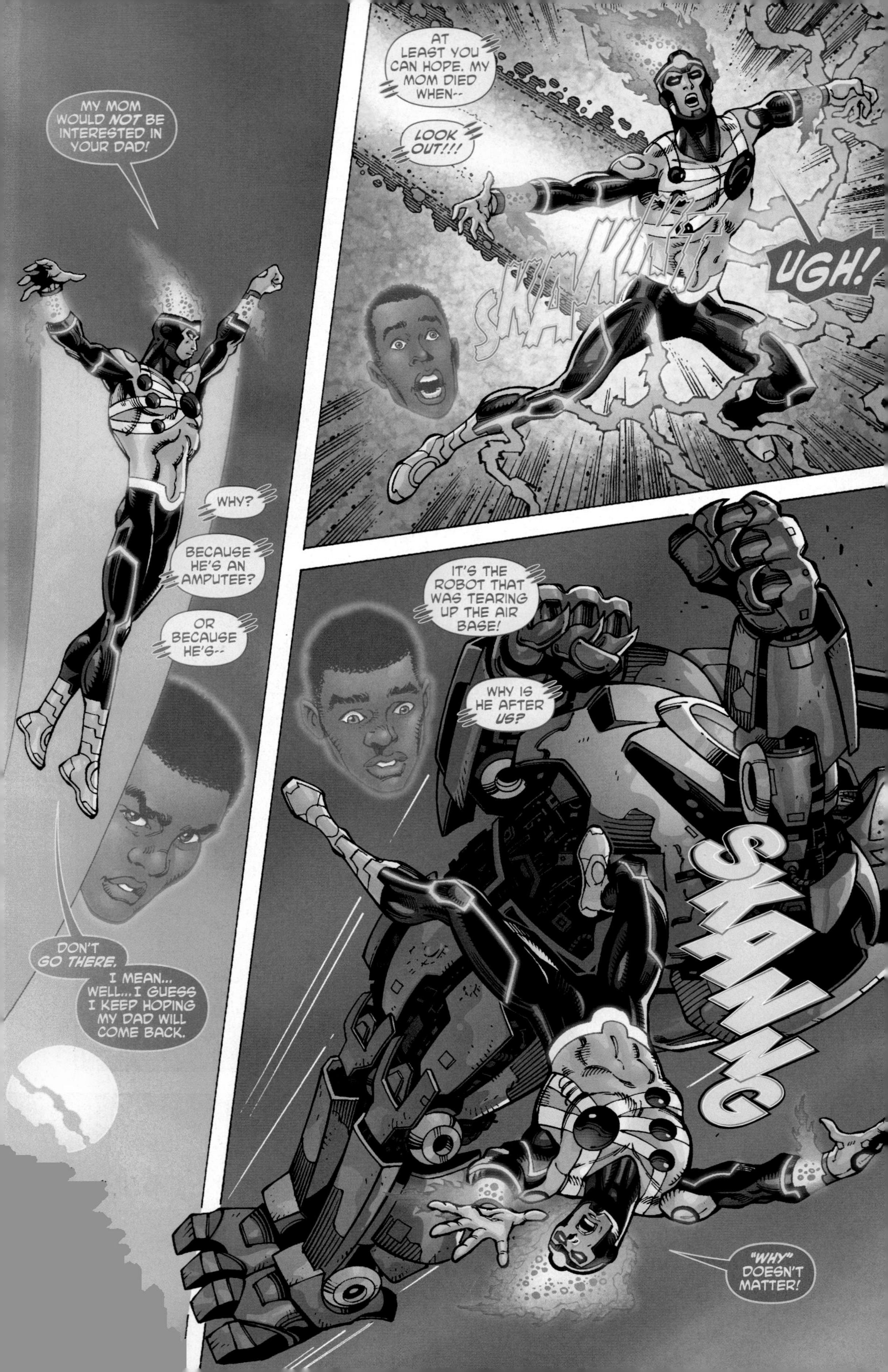
MY MOM WOULD *NOT* BE INTERESTED IN YOUR DAD!
AT LEAST YOU CAN HOPE. MY MOM DIED WHEN--
LOOK OUT!!!
SHANKT
UGH!
WHY?
BECAUSE HE'S AN AMPUTEE?
OR BECAUSE HE'S--
DON'T *GO THERE.*
I MEAN... WELL... I GUESS I KEEP HOPING MY DAD WILL COME BACK.
IT'S THE ROBOT THAT WAS TEARING UP THE AIR BASE!
WHY IS HE AFTER *US?*
SKANNG
"WHY" DOESN'T MATTER!

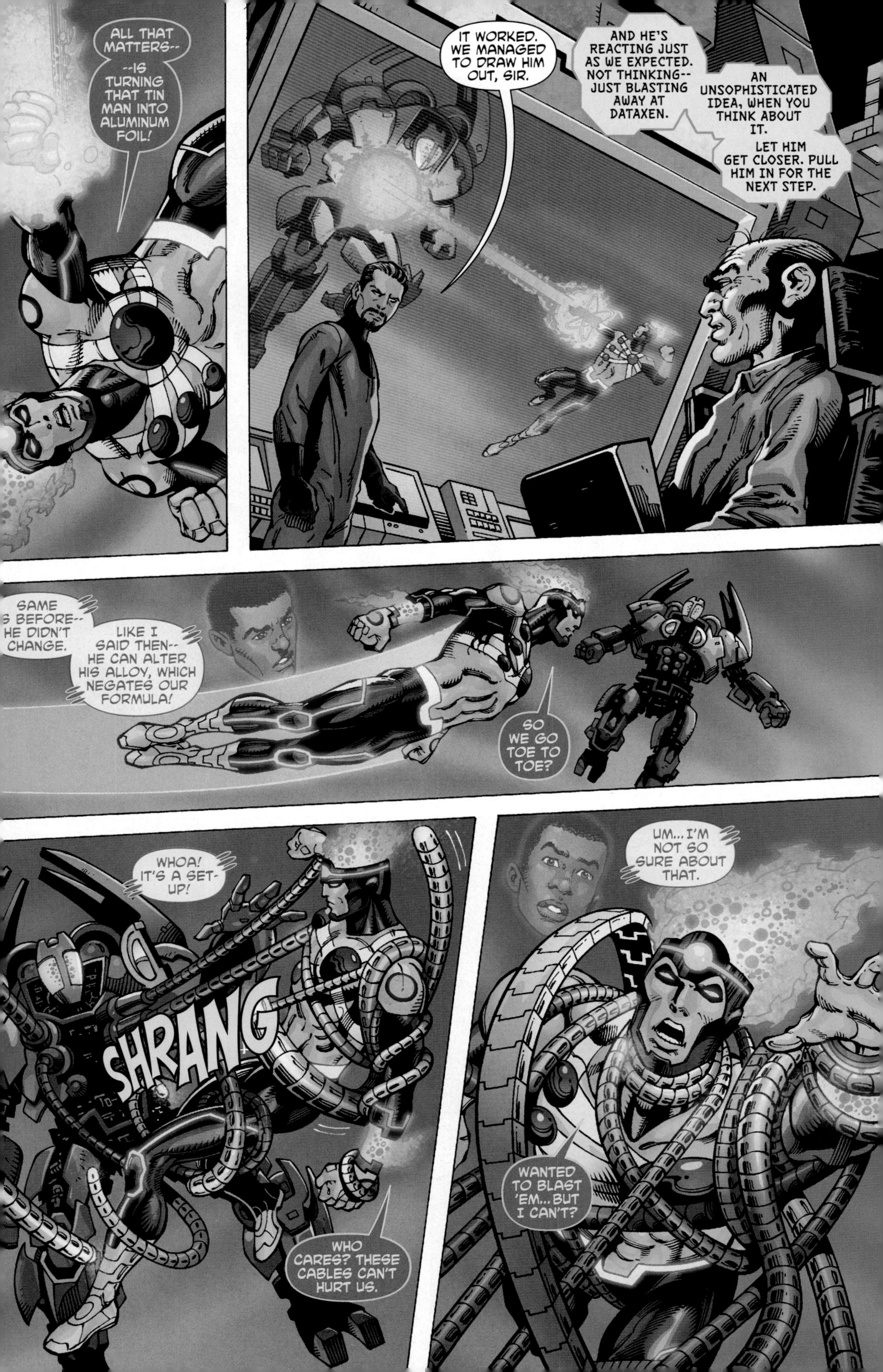
ALL THAT MATTERS--
--IS TURNING THAT TIN MAN INTO ALUMINUM FOIL!
IT WORKED. WE MANAGED TO DRAW HIM OUT, SIR.
AND HE'S REACTING JUST AS WE EXPECTED. NOT THINKING-- JUST BLASTING AWAY AT DATAXEN.
AN UNSOPHISTICATED IDEA, WHEN YOU THINK ABOUT IT.
LET HIM GET CLOSER. PULL HIM IN FOR THE NEXT STEP.
SAME S BEFORE-- HE DIDN'T CHANGE.
LIKE I SAID THEN-- HE CAN ALTER HIS ALLOY, WHICH NEGATES OUR FORMULA!
SO WE GO TOE TO TOE?
WHOA! IT'S A SET-UP!
SHRANG
WHO CARES? THESE CABLES CAN'T HURT US.
UM... I'M NOT SO SURE ABOUT THAT.
WANTED TO BLAST 'EM... BUT I CAN'T?

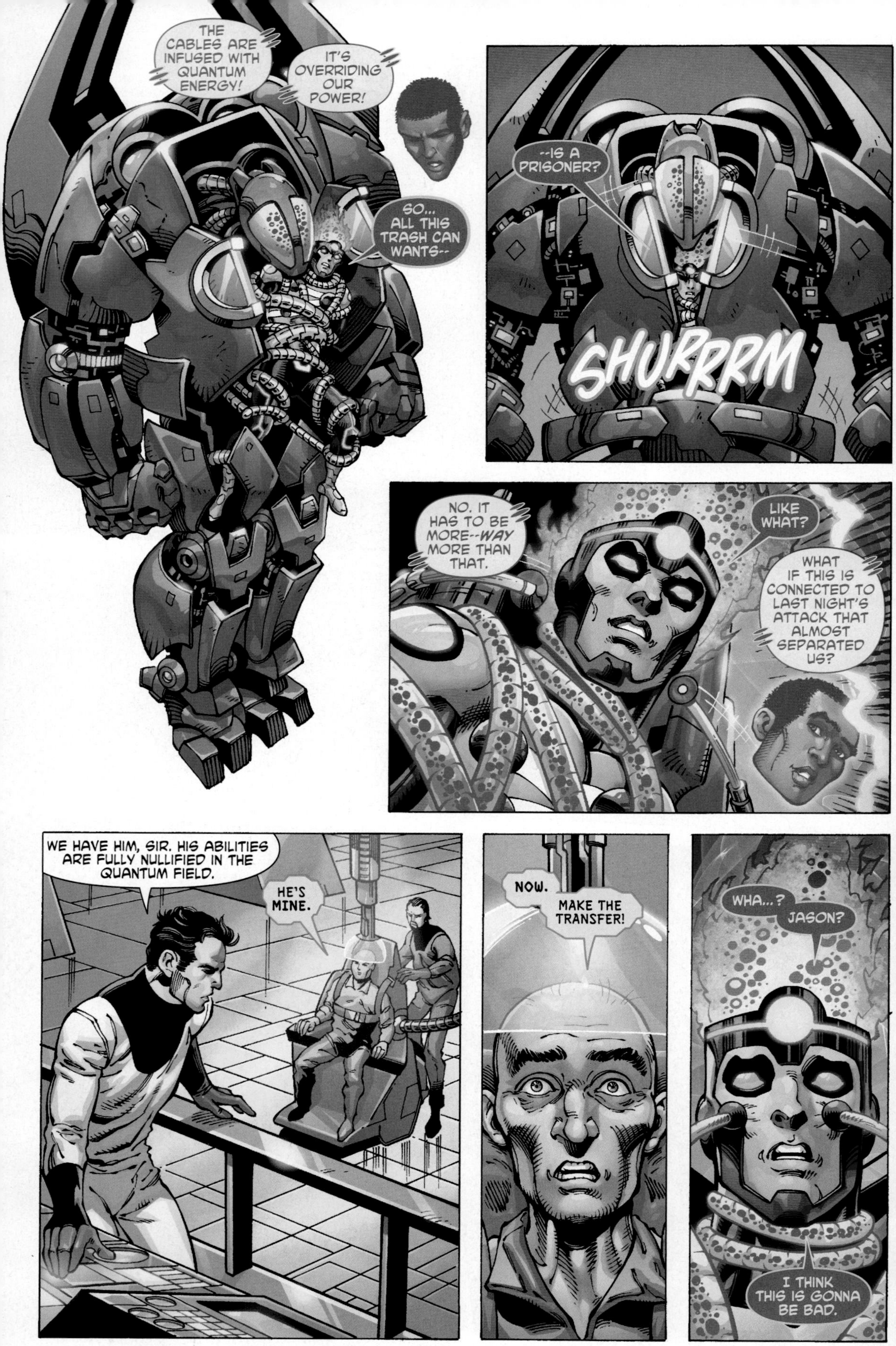
THE CABLES ARE INFUSED WITH QUANTUM ENERGY!
IT'S OVERRIDING OUR POWER!
SO... ALL THIS TRASH CAN WANTS--
--IS A PRISONER?
SHURRRM
NO. IT HAS TO BE MORE--*WAY* MORE THAN THAT.
LIKE WHAT?
WHAT IF THIS IS CONNECTED TO LAST NIGHT'S ATTACK THAT ALMOST SEPARATED US?
WE HAVE HIM, SIR. HIS ABILITIES ARE FULLY NULLIFIED IN THE QUANTUM FIELD.
HE'S MINE.
NOW.
MAKE THE TRANSFER!
WHA...? JASON?
I THINK THIS IS GONNA BE BAD.

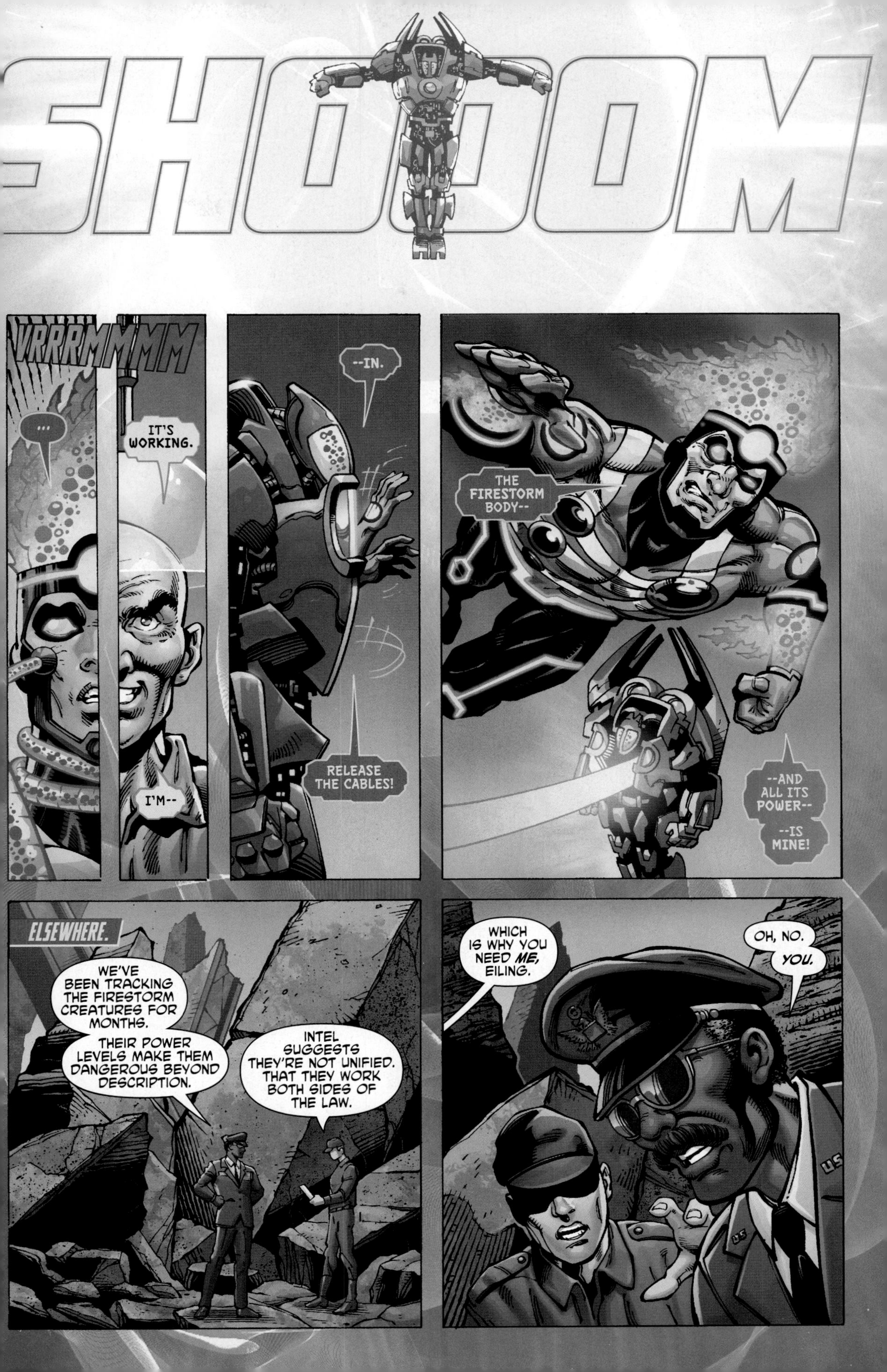
SHOOOM
VRRRMMMMM
...
IT'S WORKING.
I'M--
--IN.
RELEASE THE CABLES!
THE FIRESTORM BODY--
--AND ALL ITS POWER--
--IS MINE!
ELSEWHERE.
WE'VE BEEN TRACKING THE FIRESTORM CREATURES FOR MONTHS.
THEIR POWER LEVELS MAKE THEM DANGEROUS BEYOND DESCRIPTION.
INTEL SUGGESTS THEY'RE NOT UNIFIED. THAT THEY WORK BOTH SIDES OF THE LAW.
WHICH IS WHY YOU NEED ME, EILING.
OH, NO. YOU.

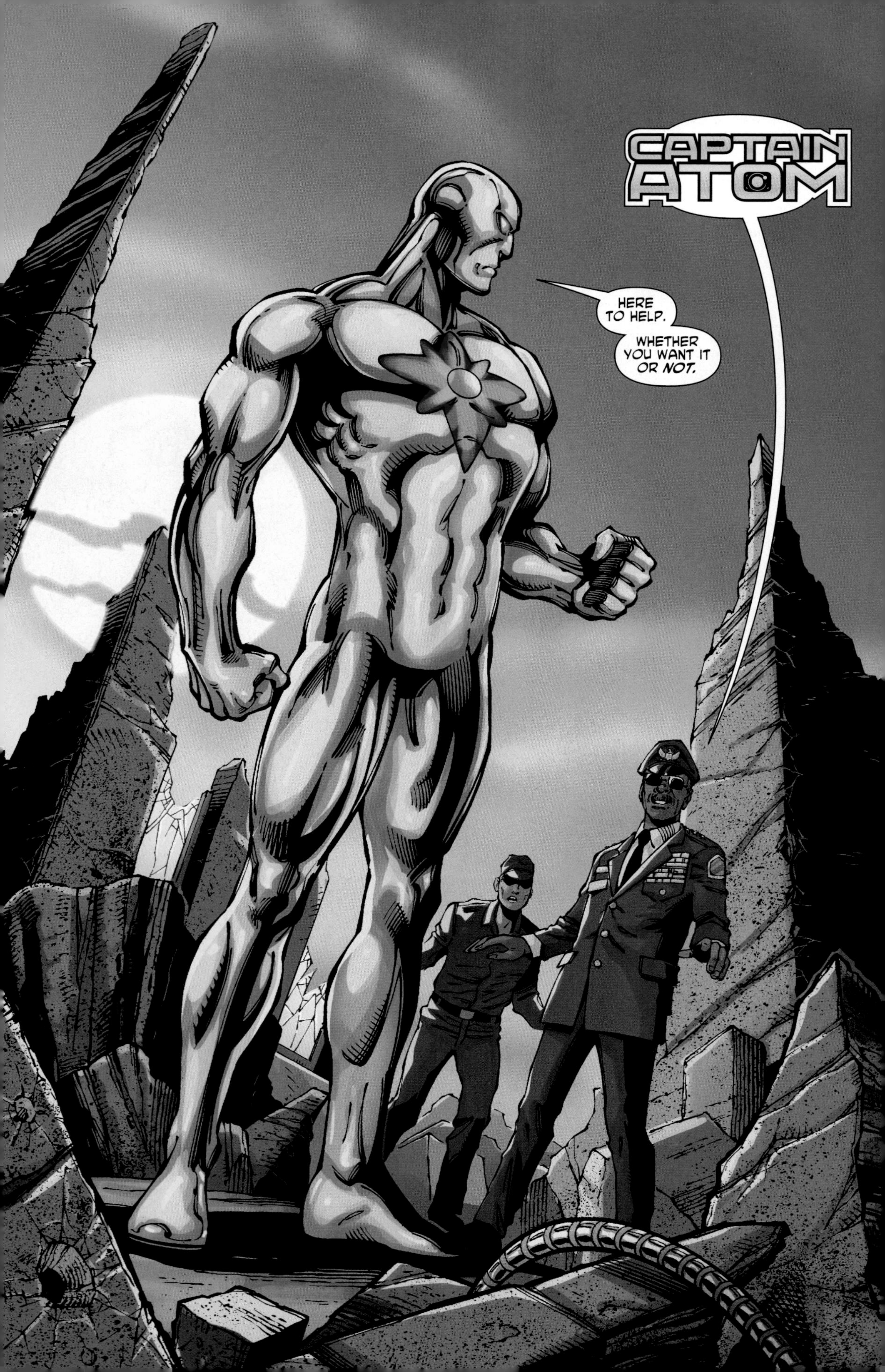
CAPTAIN ATOM
HERE TO HELP.
WHETHER YOU WANT IT OR *NOT*.

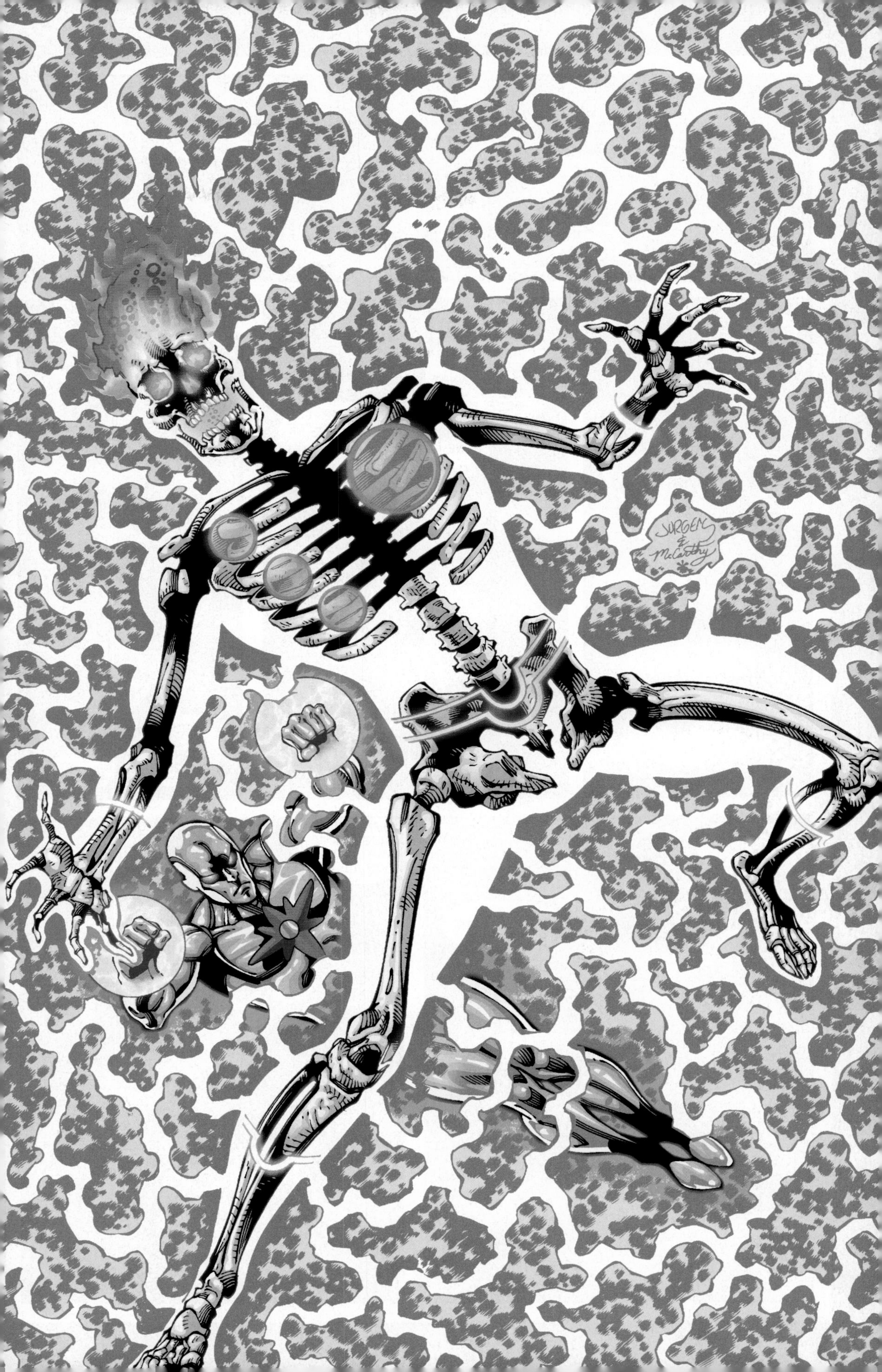
JURGENS & McCarthy

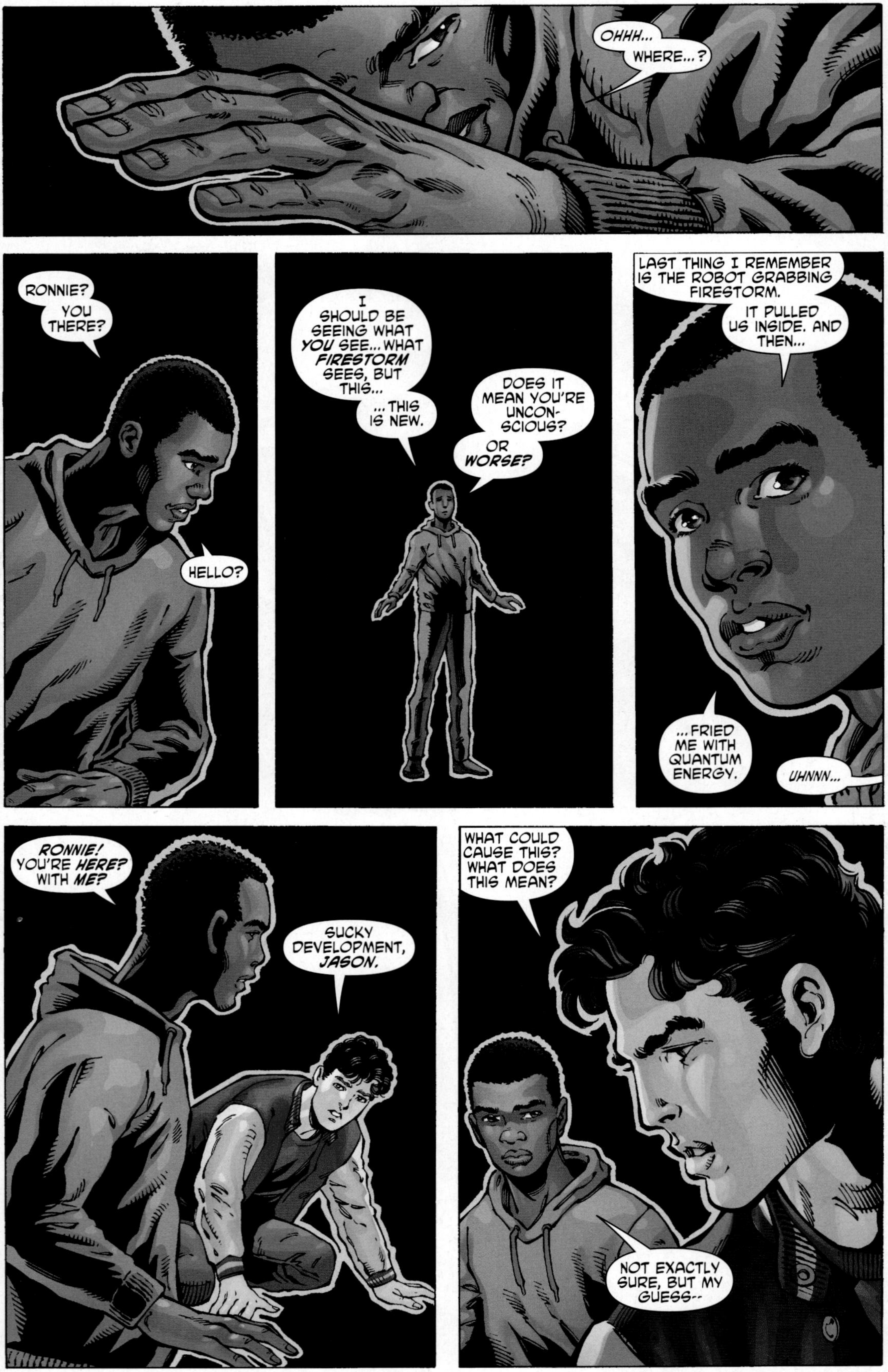
OHHH...
WHERE...?
RONNIE? YOU THERE?
HELLO?
I SHOULD BE SEEING WHAT *YOU* SEE...WHAT *FIRESTORM* SEES, BUT THIS...
...THIS IS NEW.
DOES IT MEAN YOU'RE UNCONSCIOUS?
OR *WORSE?*
LAST THING I REMEMBER IS THE ROBOT GRABBING FIRESTORM.
IT PULLED US INSIDE. AND THEN...
...FRIED ME WITH QUANTUM ENERGY.
UHNNN...
RONNIE! YOU'RE *HERE?* WITH *ME?*
SUCKY DEVELOPMENT, *JASON.*
WHAT COULD CAUSE THIS? WHAT DOES THIS MEAN?
NOT EXACTLY SURE, BUT MY GUESS--

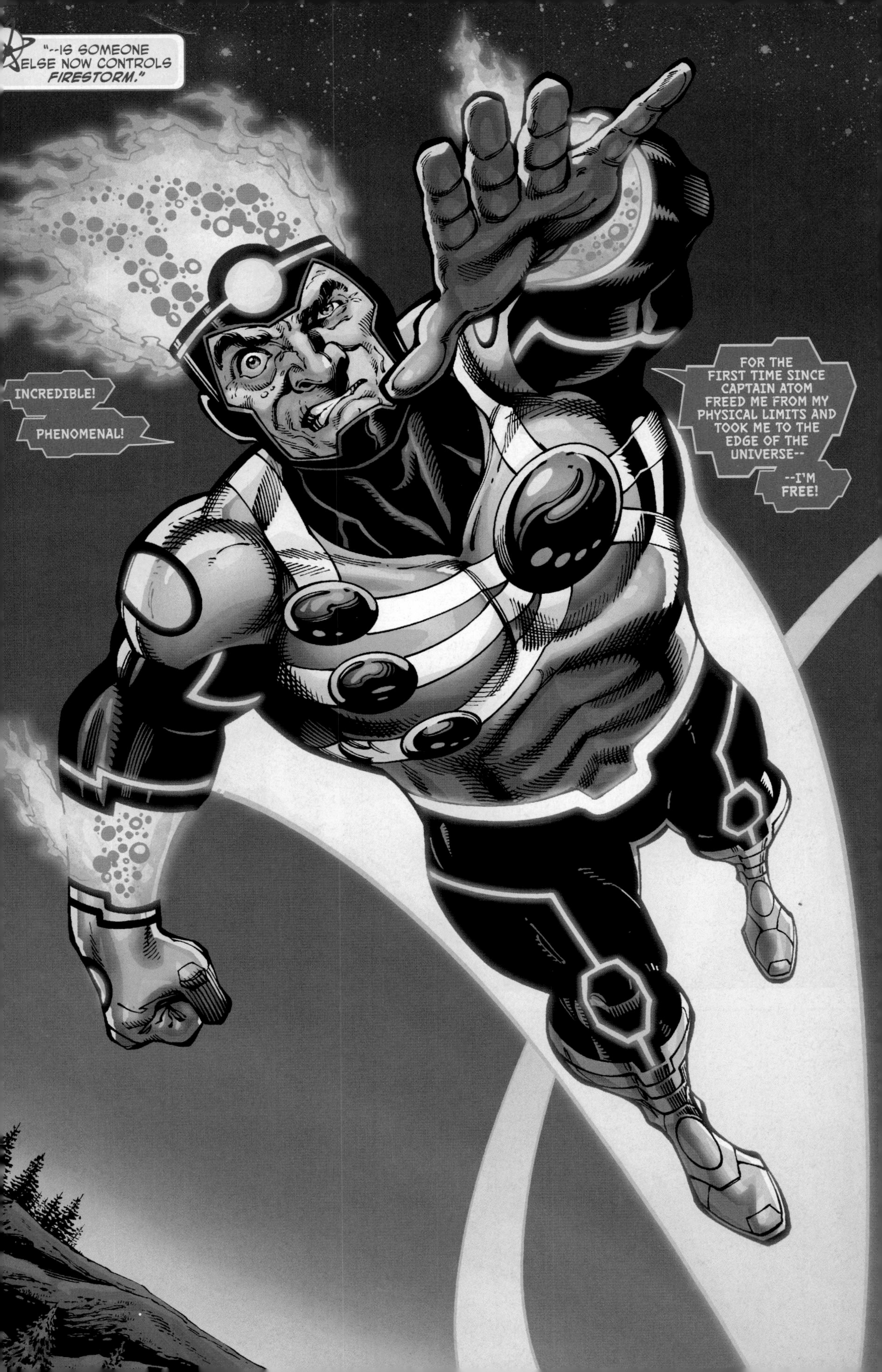
"--IS SOMEONE ELSE NOW CONTROLS FIRESTORM."
INCREDIBLE!
PHENOMENAL!
FOR THE FIRST TIME SINCE CAPTAIN ATOM FREED ME FROM MY PHYSICAL LIMITS AND TOOK ME TO THE EDGE OF THE UNIVERSE--
--I'M FREE!

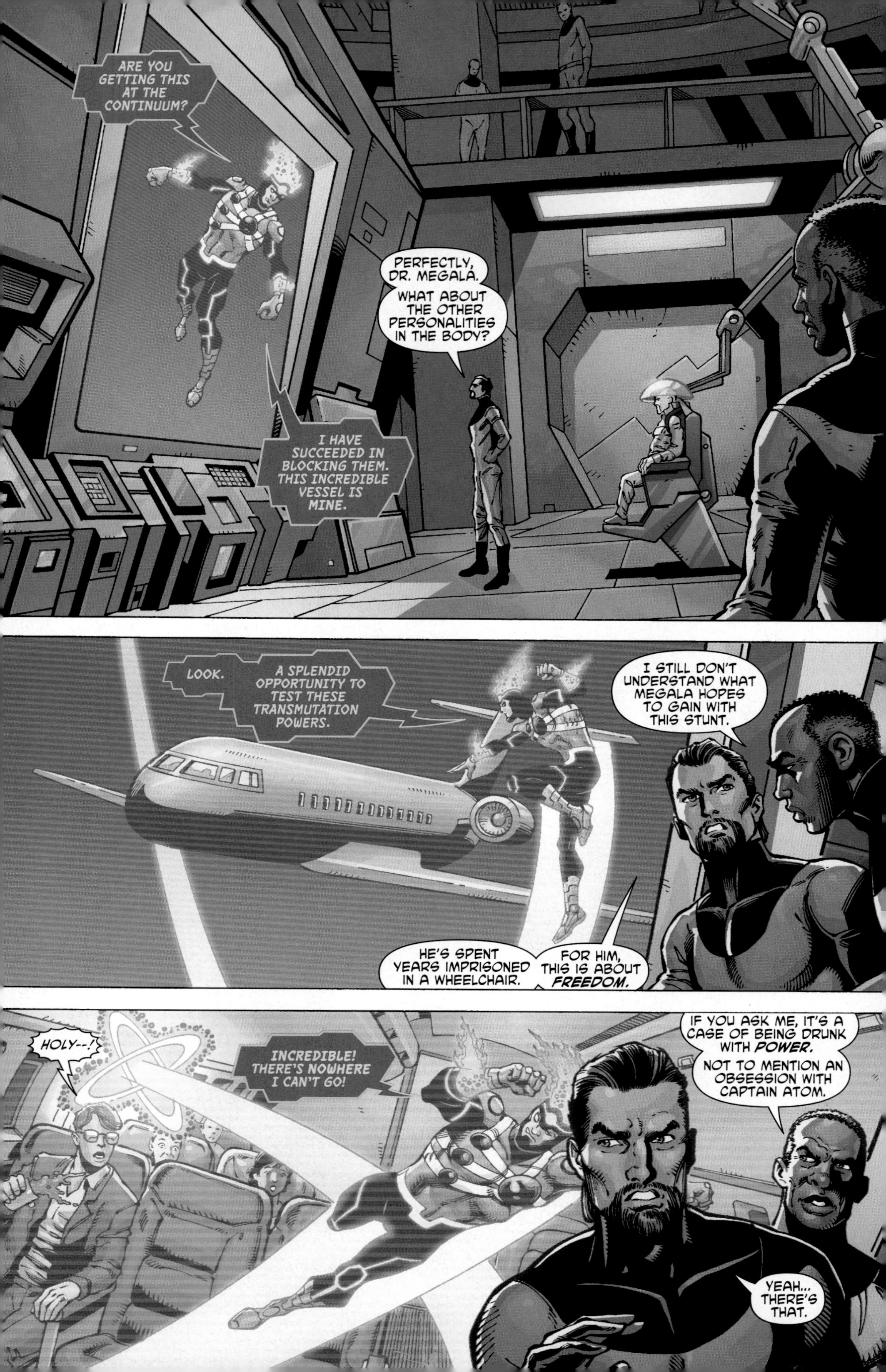
ARE YOU GETTING THIS AT THE CONTINUUM?
PERFECTLY, DR. MEGALA.
WHAT ABOUT THE OTHER PERSONALITIES IN THE BODY?
I HAVE SUCCEEDED IN BLOCKING THEM. THIS INCREDIBLE VESSEL IS MINE.
LOOK.
A SPLENDID OPPORTUNITY TO TEST THESE TRANSMUTATION POWERS.
I STILL DON'T UNDERSTAND WHAT MEGALA HOPES TO GAIN WITH THIS STUNT.
HE'S SPENT YEARS IMPRISONED IN A WHEELCHAIR.
FOR HIM, THIS IS ABOUT FREEDOM.
HOLY--!
INCREDIBLE! THERE'S NOWHERE I CAN'T GO!
IF YOU ASK ME, IT'S A CASE OF BEING DRUNK WITH POWER.
NOT TO MENTION AN OBSESSION WITH CAPTAIN ATOM.
YEAH... THERE'S THAT.

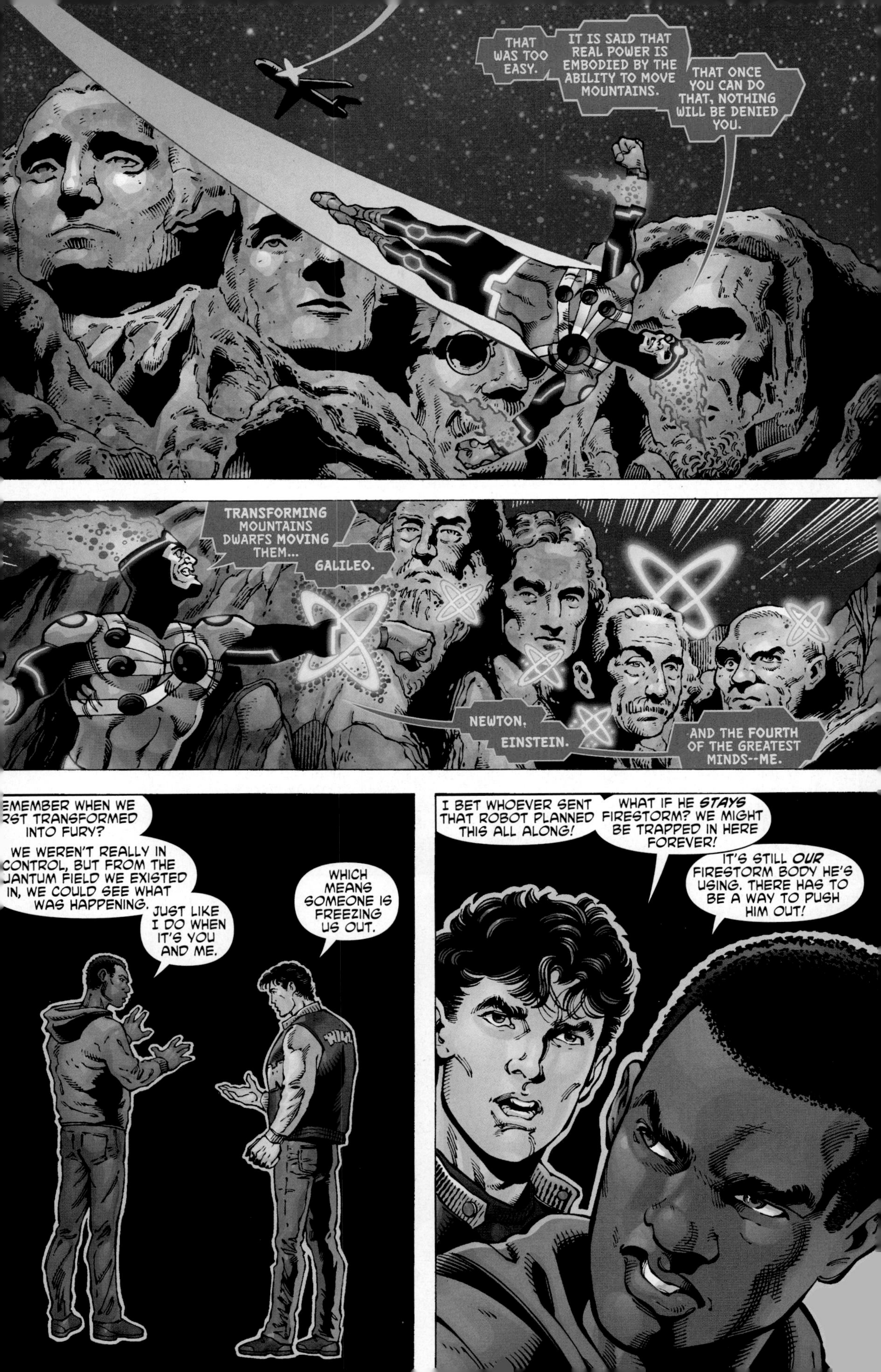
THAT WAS TOO EASY.
IT IS SAID THAT REAL POWER IS EMBODIED BY THE ABILITY TO MOVE MOUNTAINS.
THAT ONCE YOU CAN DO THAT, NOTHING WILL BE DENIED YOU.
TRANSFORMING MOUNTAINS DWARFS MOVING THEM...
GALILEO.
NEWTON.
EINSTEIN.
AND THE FOURTH OF THE GREATEST MINDS--ME.
EMEMBER WHEN WE RST TRANSFORMED INTO FURY?
WE WEREN'T REALLY IN CONTROL, BUT FROM THE UANTUM FIELD WE EXISTED IN, WE COULD SEE WHAT WAS HAPPENING.
JUST LIKE I DO WHEN IT'S YOU AND ME.
WHICH MEANS SOMEONE IS FREEZING US OUT.
I BET WHOEVER SENT THAT ROBOT PLANNED THIS ALL ALONG!
WHAT IF HE STAYS FIRESTORM? WE MIGHT BE TRAPPED IN HERE FOREVER!
IT'S STILL OUR FIRESTORM BODY HE'S USING. THERE HAS TO BE A WAY TO PUSH HIM OUT!

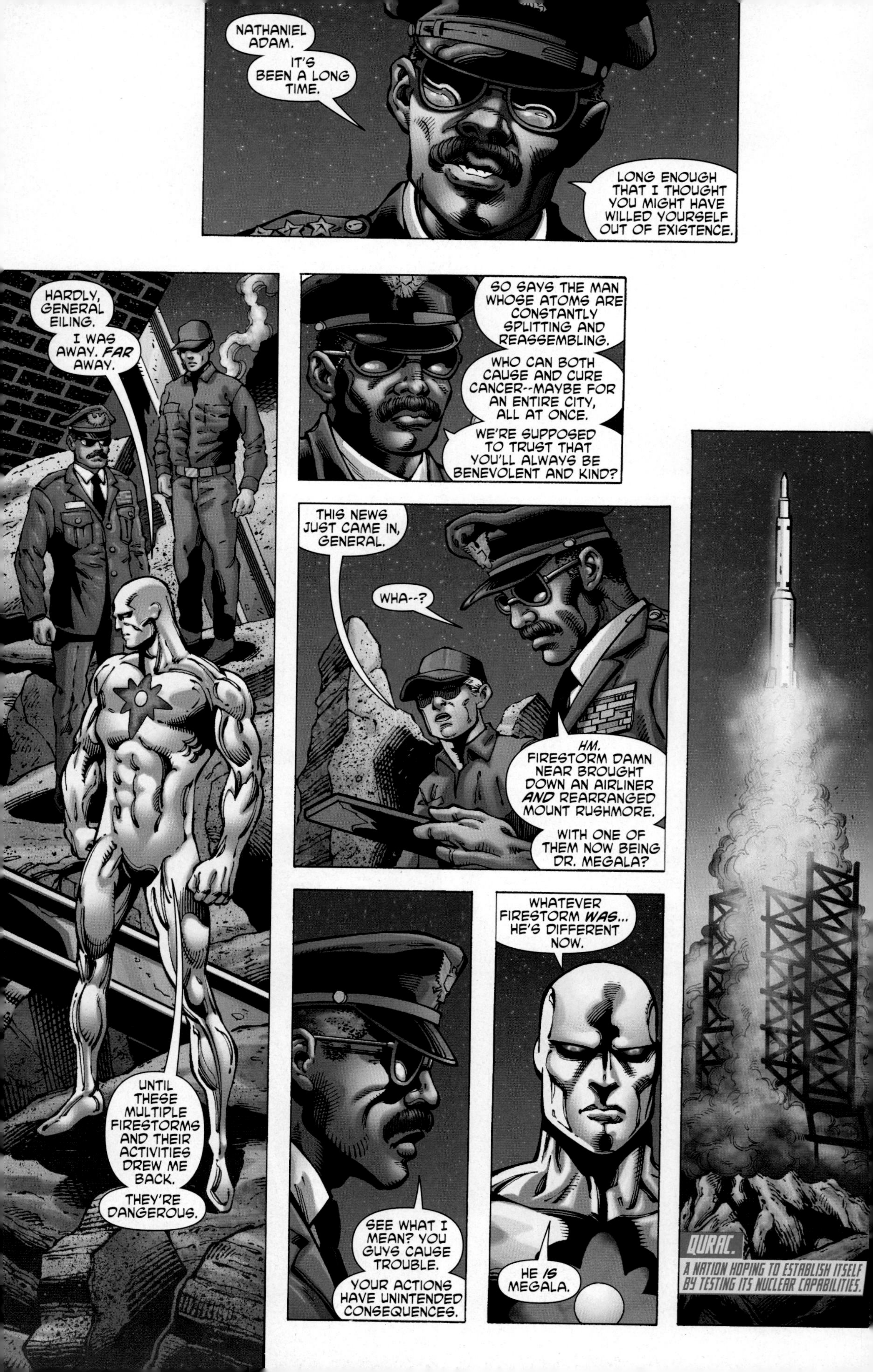

NATHANIEL ADAM. IT'S BEEN A LONG TIME.
LONG ENOUGH THAT I THOUGHT YOU MIGHT HAVE WILLED YOURSELF OUT OF EXISTENCE.
HARDLY, GENERAL EILING. I WAS AWAY. FAR AWAY.
UNTIL THESE MULTIPLE FIRESTORMS AND THEIR ACTIVITIES DREW ME BACK.
THEY'RE DANGEROUS.
SO SAYS THE MAN WHOSE ATOMS ARE CONSTANTLY SPLITTING AND REASSEMBLING.
WHO CAN BOTH CAUSE AND CURE CANCER--MAYBE FOR AN ENTIRE CITY, ALL AT ONCE.
WE'RE SUPPOSED TO TRUST THAT YOU'LL ALWAYS BE BENEVOLENT AND KIND?
THIS NEWS JUST CAME IN, GENERAL.
WHA--?
HM. FIRESTORM DAMN NEAR BROUGHT DOWN AN AIRLINER AND REARRANGED MOUNT RUSHMORE.
WITH ONE OF THEM NOW BEING DR. MEGALA?
WHATEVER FIRESTORM WAS... HE'S DIFFERENT NOW.
SEE WHAT I MEAN? YOU GUYS CAUSE TROUBLE.
YOUR ACTIONS HAVE UNINTENDED CONSEQUENCES.
HE IS MEGALA.
QURAC.
A NATION HOPING TO ESTABLISH ITSELF BY TESTING ITS NUCLEAR CAPABILITIES.

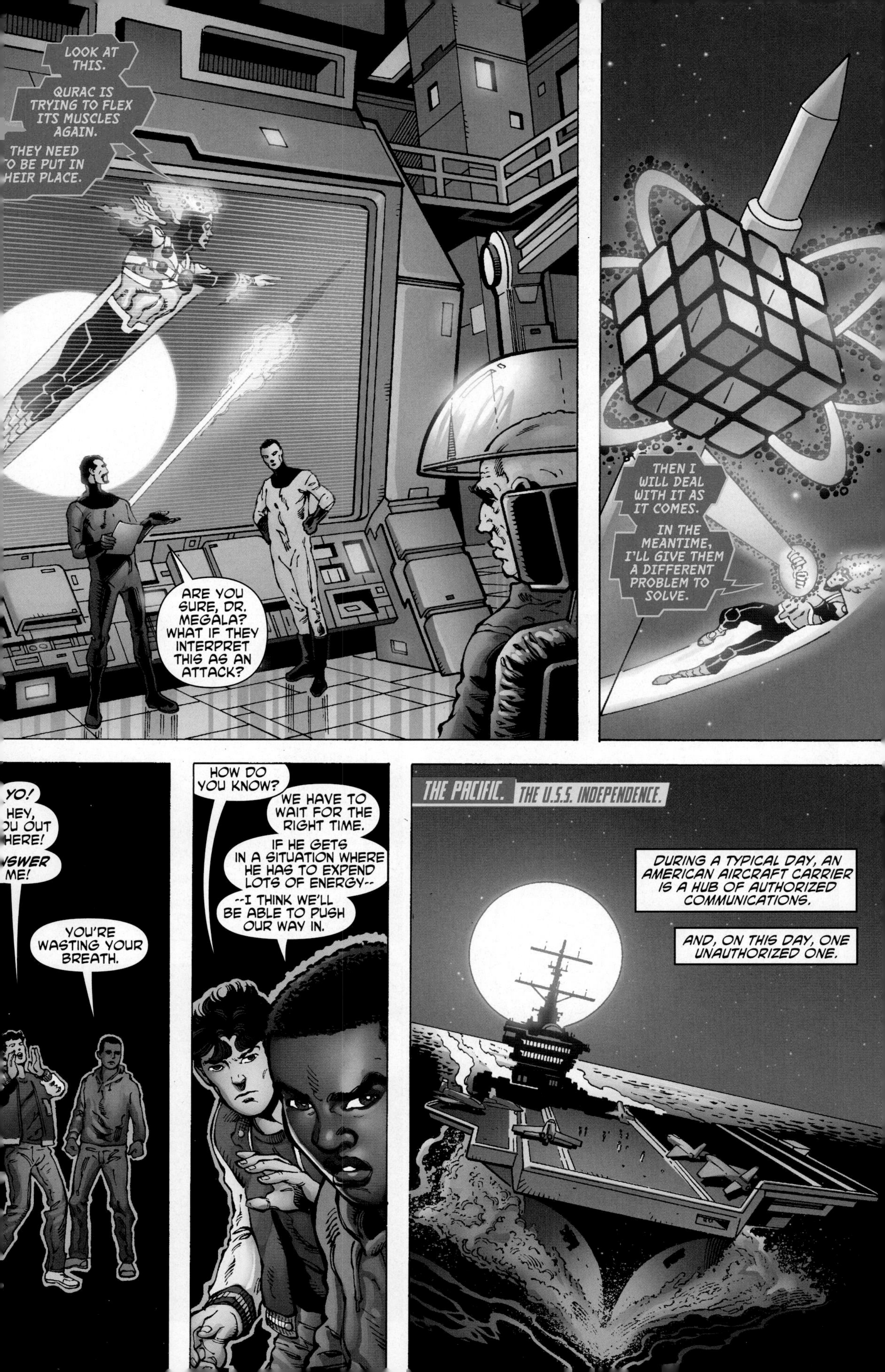
LOOK AT THIS.
QURAC IS TRYING TO FLEX ITS MUSCLES AGAIN.
THEY NEED TO BE PUT IN THEIR PLACE.
ARE YOU SURE, DR. MEGALA? WHAT IF THEY INTERPRET THIS AS AN ATTACK?
THEN I WILL DEAL WITH IT AS IT COMES.
IN THE MEANTIME, I'LL GIVE THEM A DIFFERENT PROBLEM TO SOLVE.
YO!
HEY, YOU OUT HERE!
ANSWER ME!
YOU'RE WASTING YOUR BREATH.
HOW DO YOU KNOW?
WE HAVE TO WAIT FOR THE RIGHT TIME.
IF HE GETS IN A SITUATION WHERE HE HAS TO EXPEND LOTS OF ENERGY--
--I THINK WE'LL BE ABLE TO PUSH OUR WAY IN.
THE PACIFIC. THE U.S.S. INDEPENDENCE.
DURING A TYPICAL DAY, AN AMERICAN AIRCRAFT CARRIER IS A HUB OF AUTHORIZED COMMUNICATIONS.
AND, ON THIS DAY, ONE UNAUTHORIZED ONE.

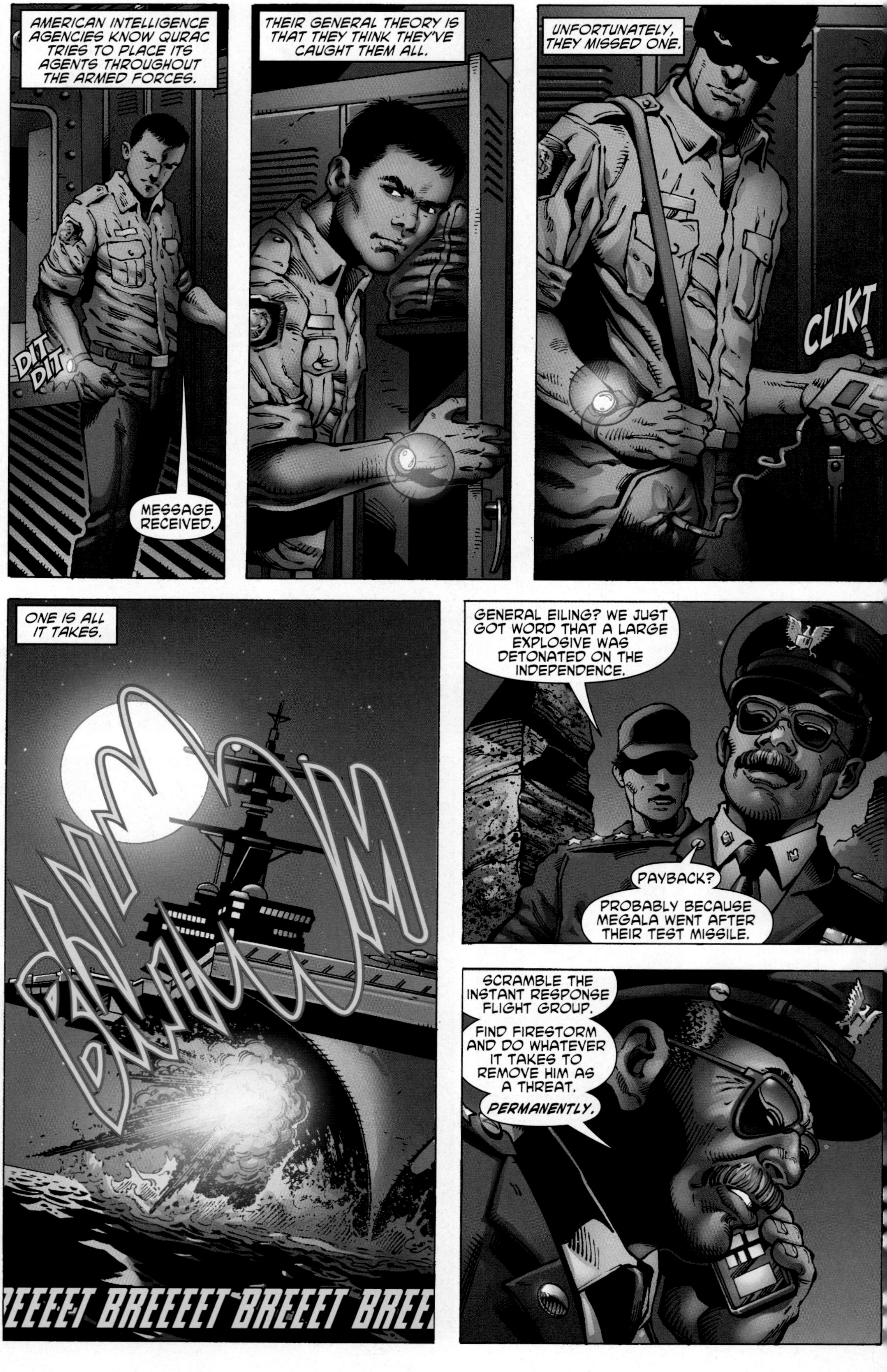

AMERICAN INTELLIGENCE AGENCIES KNOW QURAC TRIES TO PLACE ITS AGENTS THROUGHOUT THE ARMED FORCES.
DIT DIT
MESSAGE RECEIVED.
THEIR GENERAL THEORY IS THAT THEY THINK THEY'VE CAUGHT THEM ALL.
UNFORTUNATELY, THEY MISSED ONE.
CLIKT
ONE IS ALL IT TAKES.
BREEEET BREEET
GENERAL EILING? WE JUST GOT WORD THAT A LARGE EXPLOSIVE WAS DETONATED ON THE INDEPENDENCE.
PAYBACK?
PROBABLY BECAUSE MEGALA WENT AFTER THEIR TEST MISSILE.
SCRAMBLE THE INSTANT RESPONSE FLIGHT GROUP.
FIND FIRESTORM AND DO WHATEVER IT TAKES TO REMOVE HIM AS A THREAT.
PERMANENTLY.

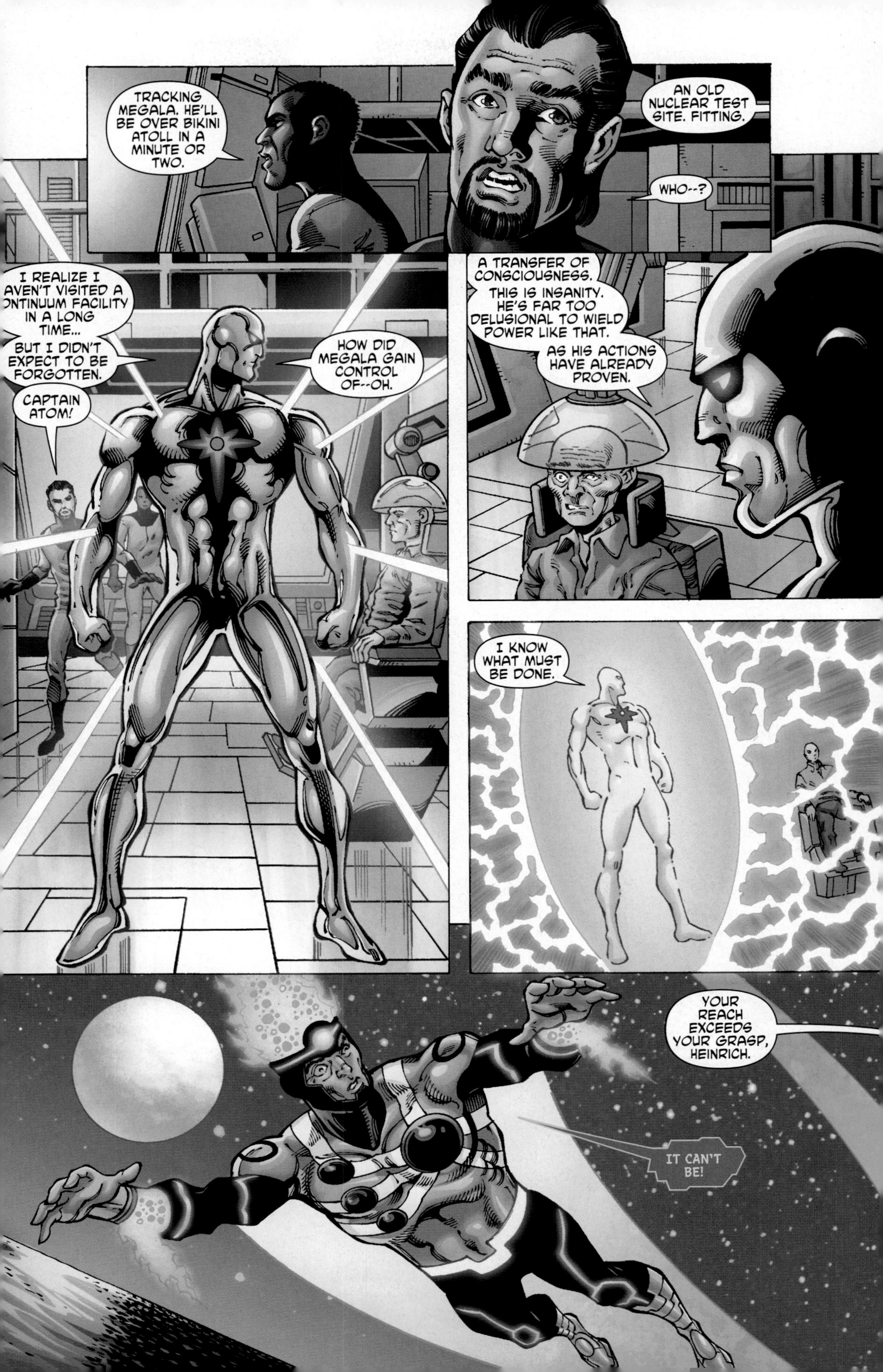
TRACKING MEGALA. HE'LL BE OVER BIKINI ATOLL IN A MINUTE OR TWO.
AN OLD NUCLEAR TEST SITE. FITTING.
WHO--?
I REALIZE I AVEN'T VISITED A ONTINUUM FACILITY IN A LONG TIME...
BUT I DIDN'T EXPECT TO BE FORGOTTEN.
CAPTAIN ATOM!
HOW DID MEGALA GAIN CONTROL OF--OH.
A TRANSFER OF CONSCIOUSNESS.
THIS IS INSANITY. HE'S FAR TOO DELUSIONAL TO WIELD POWER LIKE THAT.
AS HIS ACTIONS HAVE ALREADY PROVEN.
I KNOW WHAT MUST BE DONE.
YOUR REACH EXCEEDS YOUR GRASP, HEINRICH.
IT CAN'T BE!

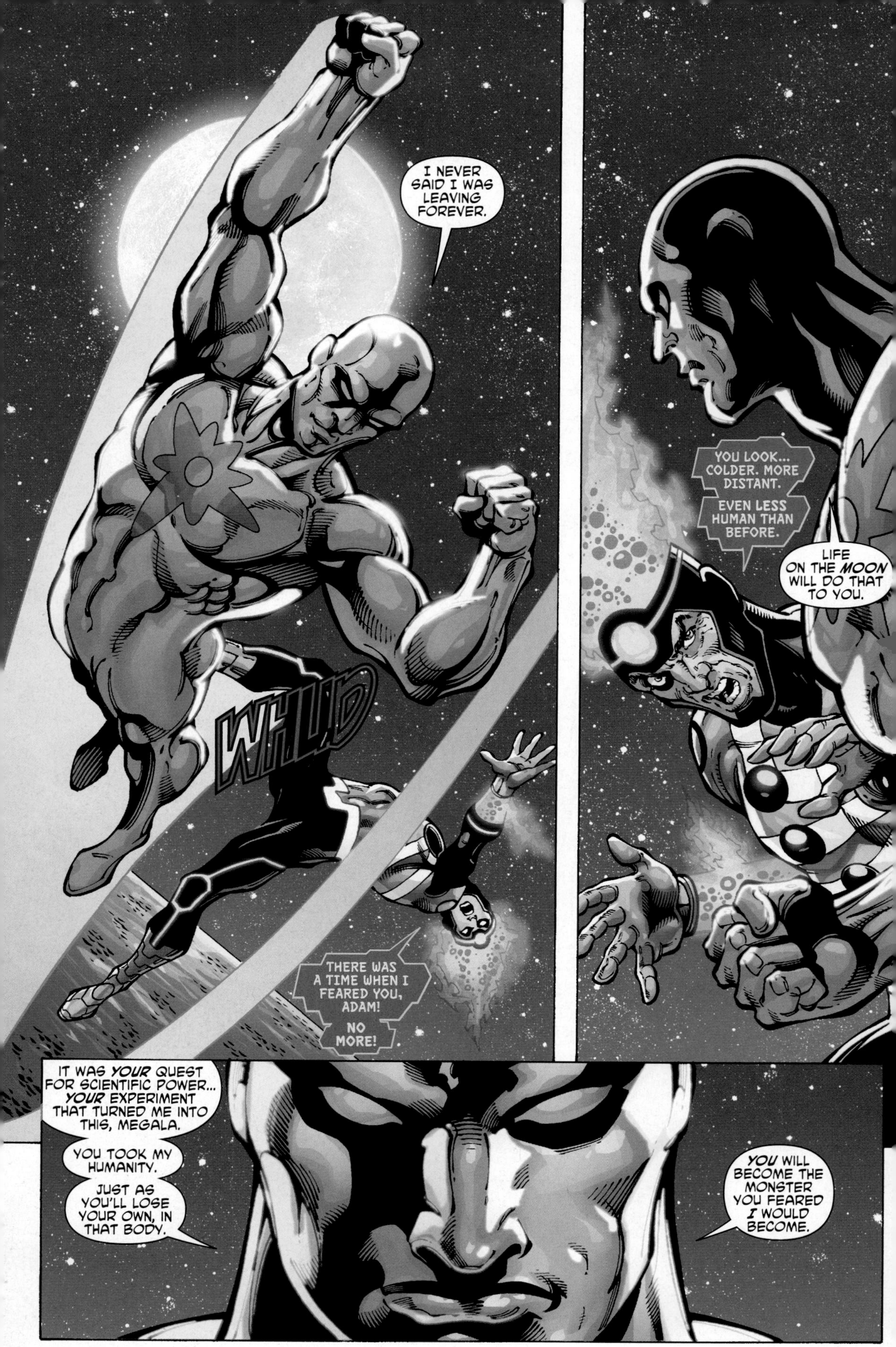
I NEVER SAID I WAS LEAVING FOREVER.
WHUD
THERE WAS A TIME WHEN I FEARED YOU, ADAM!
NO MORE!
YOU LOOK... COLDER. MORE DISTANT.
EVEN LESS HUMAN THAN BEFORE.
LIFE ON THE MOON WILL DO THAT TO YOU.
IT WAS YOUR QUEST FOR SCIENTIFIC POWER... YOUR EXPERIMENT THAT TURNED ME INTO THIS, MEGALA.
YOU TOOK MY HUMANITY.
JUST AS YOU'LL LOSE YOUR OWN, IN THAT BODY.
YOU WILL BECOME THE MONSTER YOU FEARED I WOULD BECOME.

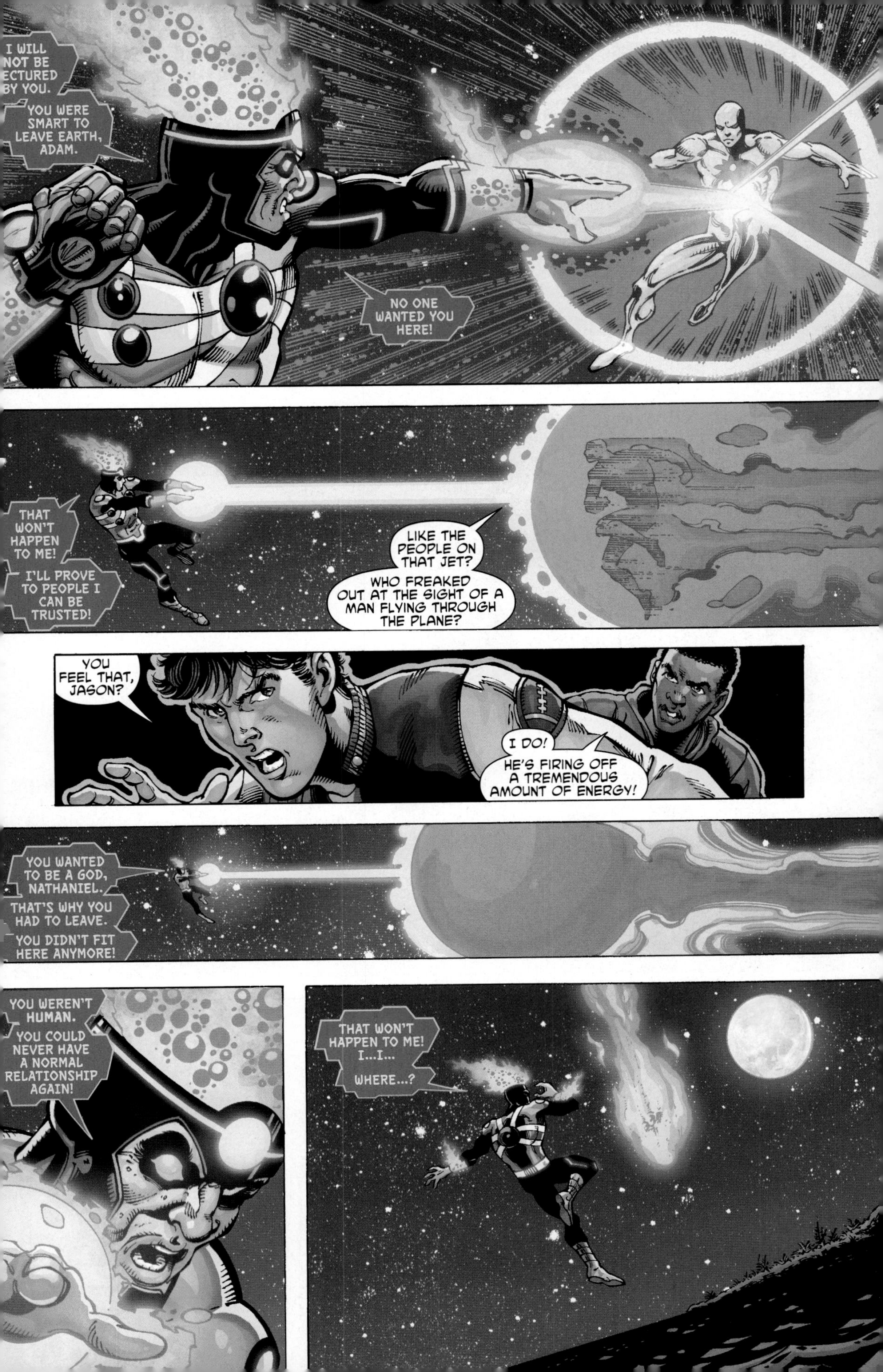
I WILL NOT BE LECTURED BY YOU.
YOU WERE SMART TO LEAVE EARTH, ADAM.
NO ONE WANTED YOU HERE!
THAT WON'T HAPPEN TO ME!
I'LL PROVE TO PEOPLE I CAN BE TRUSTED!
LIKE THE PEOPLE ON THAT JET?
WHO FREAKED OUT AT THE SIGHT OF A MAN FLYING THROUGH THE PLANE?
YOU FEEL THAT, JASON?
I DO!
HE'S FIRING OFF A TREMENDOUS AMOUNT OF ENERGY!
YOU WANTED TO BE A GOD, NATHANIEL.
THAT'S WHY YOU HAD TO LEAVE.
YOU DIDN'T FIT HERE ANYMORE!
YOU WEREN'T HUMAN.
YOU COULD NEVER HAVE A NORMAL RELATIONSHIP AGAIN!
THAT WON'T HAPPEN TO ME!
I...I...
WHERE...?

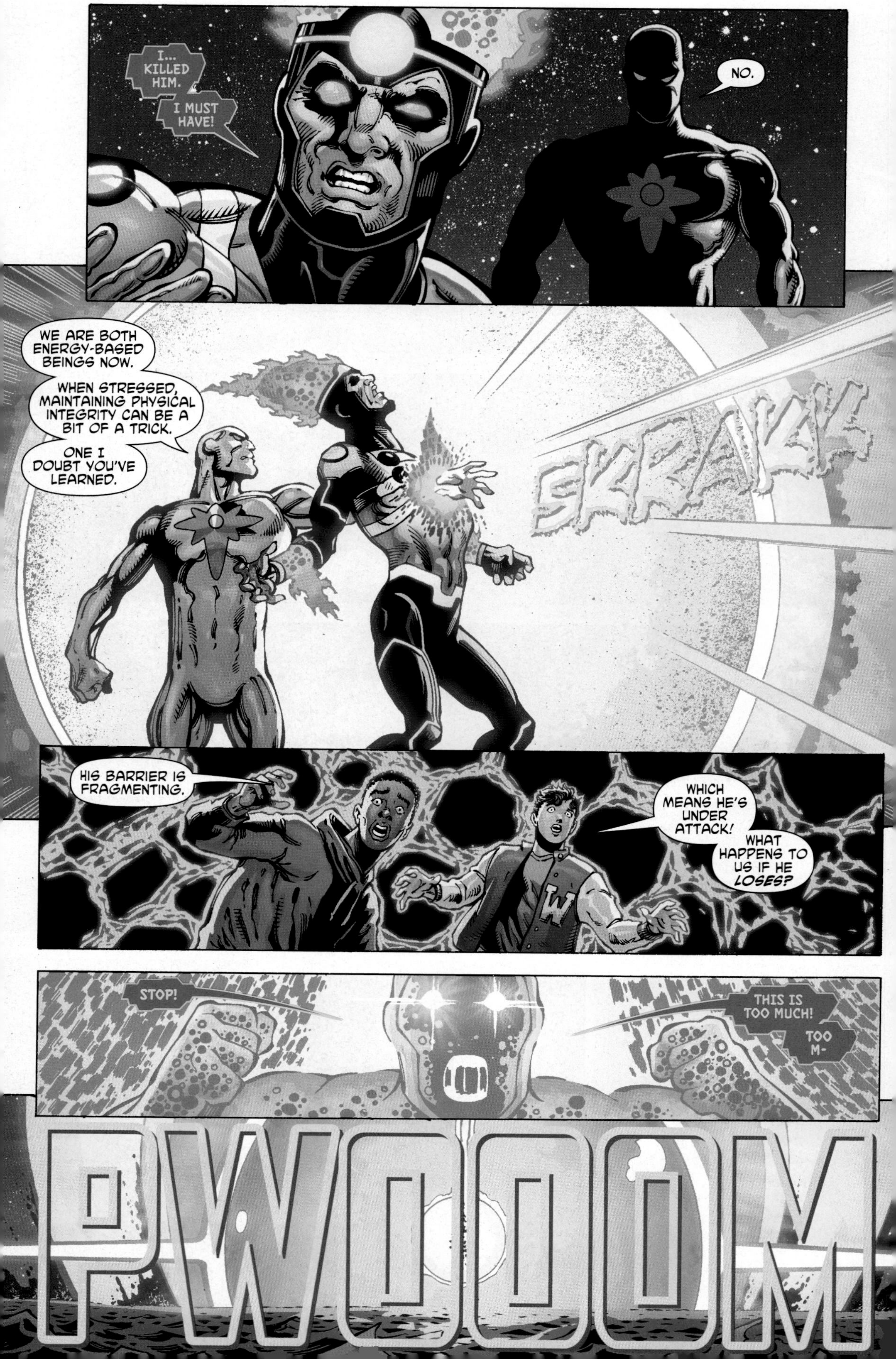
I... KILLED HIM.
I MUST HAVE!
NO.
WE ARE BOTH ENERGY-BASED BEINGS NOW.
WHEN STRESSED, MAINTAINING PHYSICAL INTEGRITY CAN BE A BIT OF A TRICK.
ONE I DOUBT YOU'VE LEARNED.
SKRAKK
HIS BARRIER IS FRAGMENTING.
WHICH MEANS HE'S UNDER ATTACK!
WHAT HAPPENS TO US IF HE *LOSES?*
STOP!
THIS IS TOO MUCH!
TOO M-
PWOOOM

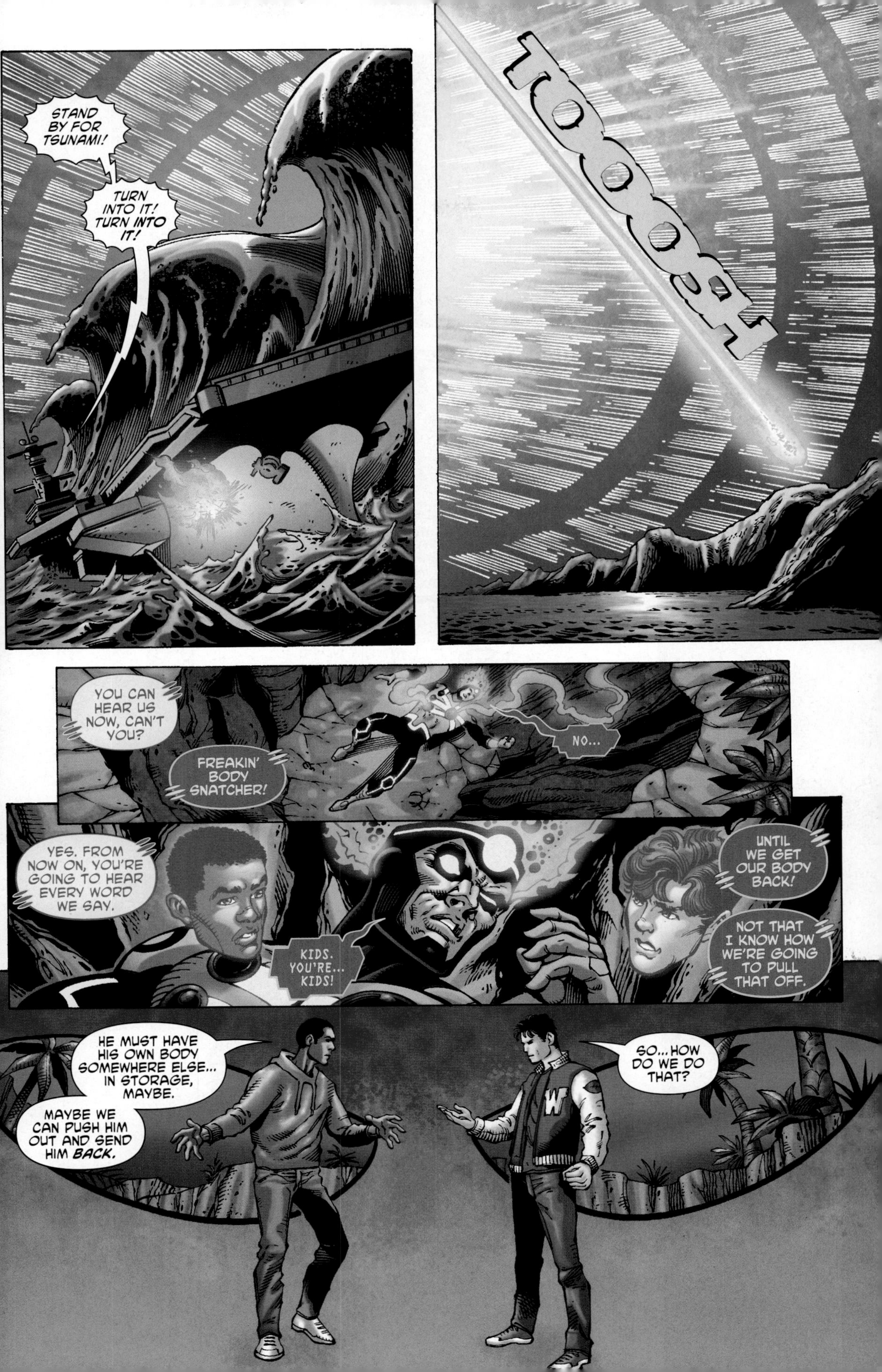
STAND BY FOR TSUNAMI!
TURN INTO IT! TURN INTO IT!
YOU CAN HEAR US NOW, CAN'T YOU?
FREAKIN' BODY SNATCHER!
NO...
YES. FROM NOW ON, YOU'RE GOING TO HEAR EVERY WORD WE SAY.
KIDS. YOU'RE... KIDS!
UNTIL WE GET OUR BODY BACK!
NOT THAT I KNOW HOW WE'RE GOING TO PULL THAT OFF.
HE MUST HAVE HIS OWN BODY SOMEWHERE ELSE... IN STORAGE, MAYBE.
MAYBE WE CAN PUSH HIM OUT AND SEND HIM BACK.
SO... HOW DO WE DO THAT?

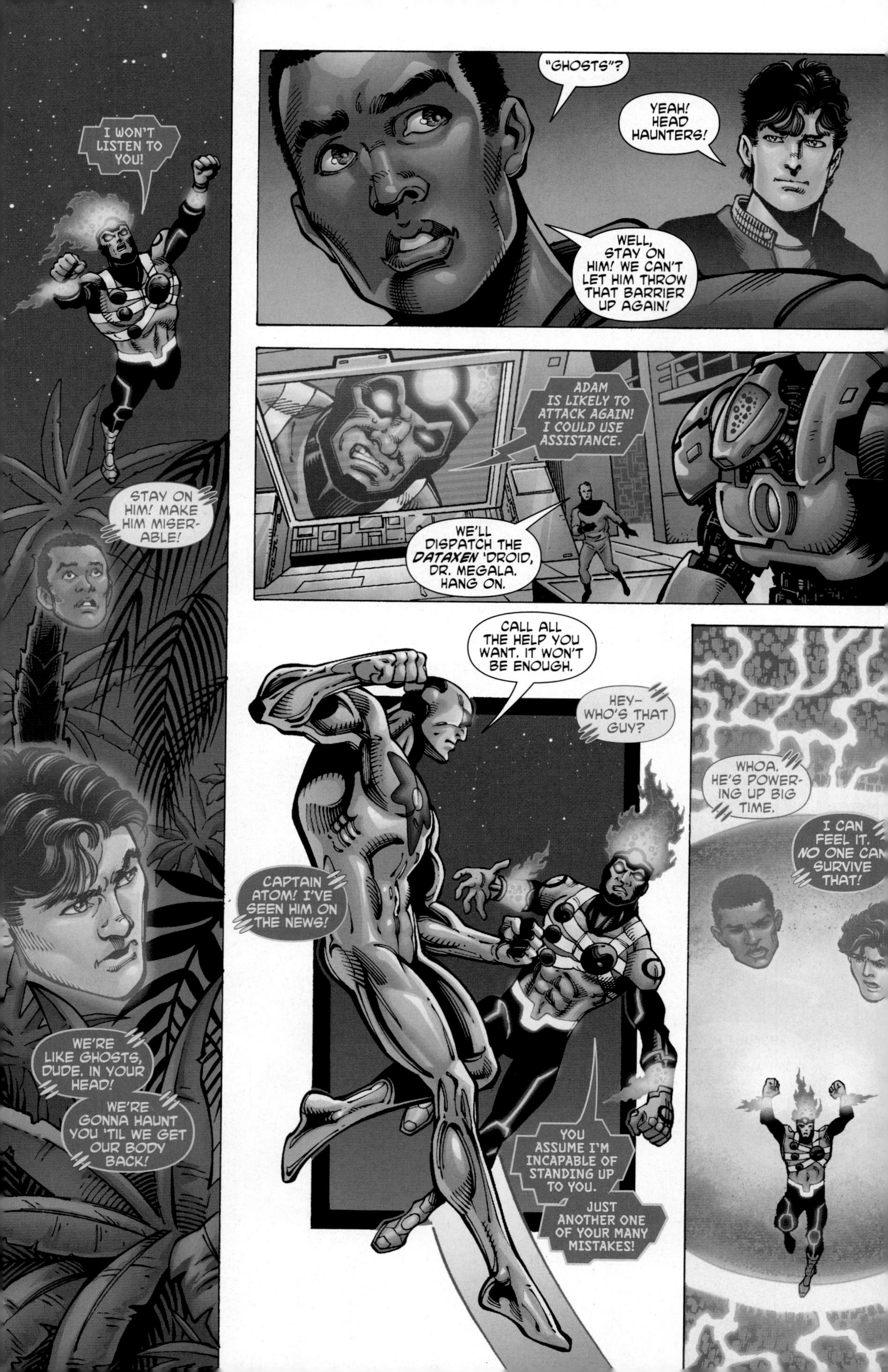
I WON'T LISTEN TO YOU!
STAY ON HIM! MAKE HIM MISER-ABLE!
WE'RE LIKE GHOSTS, DUDE, IN YOUR HEAD!
WE'RE GONNA HAUNT YOU 'TIL WE GET OUR BODY BACK!
"GHOSTS"?
YEAH! HEAD HAUNTERS!
WELL, STAY ON HIM! WE CAN'T LET HIM THROW THAT BARRIER UP AGAIN!
ADAM IS LIKELY TO ATTACK AGAIN! I COULD USE ASSISTANCE.
WE'LL DISPATCH THE DATAXEN 'DROID, DR. MEGALA. HANG ON.
CALL ALL THE HELP YOU WANT. IT WON'T BE ENOUGH.
HEY-WHO'S THAT GUY?
CAPTAIN ATOM! I'VE SEEN HIM ON THE NEWS!
YOU ASSUME I'M INCAPABLE OF STANDING UP TO YOU.
JUST ANOTHER ONE OF YOUR MANY MISTAKES!
WHOA. HE'S POWER-ING UP BIG TIME.
I CAN FEEL IT. NO ONE CAN SURVIVE THAT!

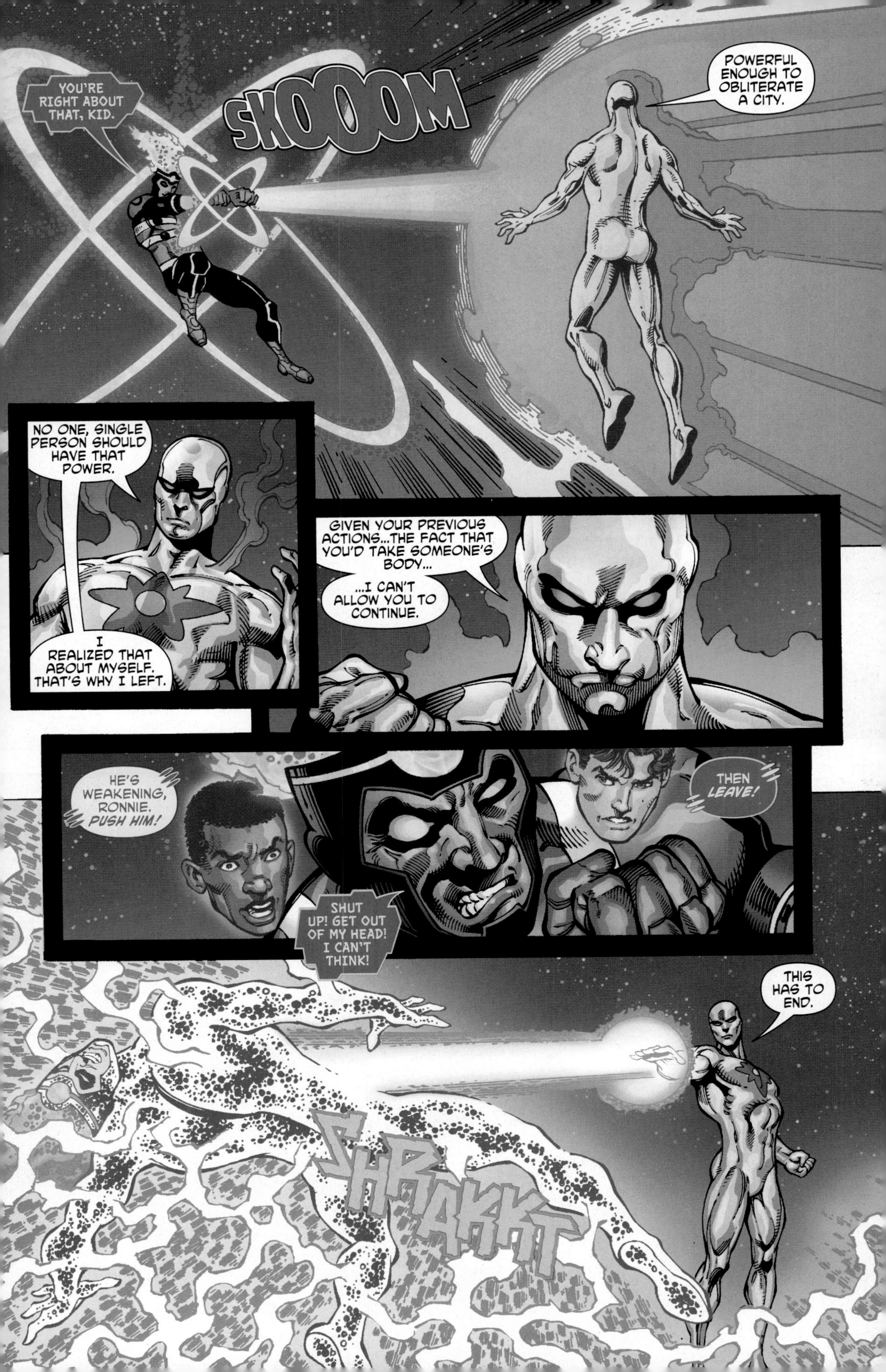
YOU'RE RIGHT ABOUT THAT, KID.
SKOOOM
POWERFUL ENOUGH TO OBLITERATE A CITY.
NO ONE, SINGLE PERSON SHOULD HAVE THAT POWER.
I REALIZED THAT ABOUT MYSELF. THAT'S WHY I LEFT.
GIVEN YOUR PREVIOUS ACTIONS...THE FACT THAT YOU'D TAKE SOMEONE'S BODY...
...I CAN'T ALLOW YOU TO CONTINUE.
HE'S WEAKENING, RONNIE. PUSH HIM!
THEN LEAVE!
SHUT UP! GET OUT OF MY HEAD! I CAN'T THINK!
THIS HAS TO END.
SHRAKKT

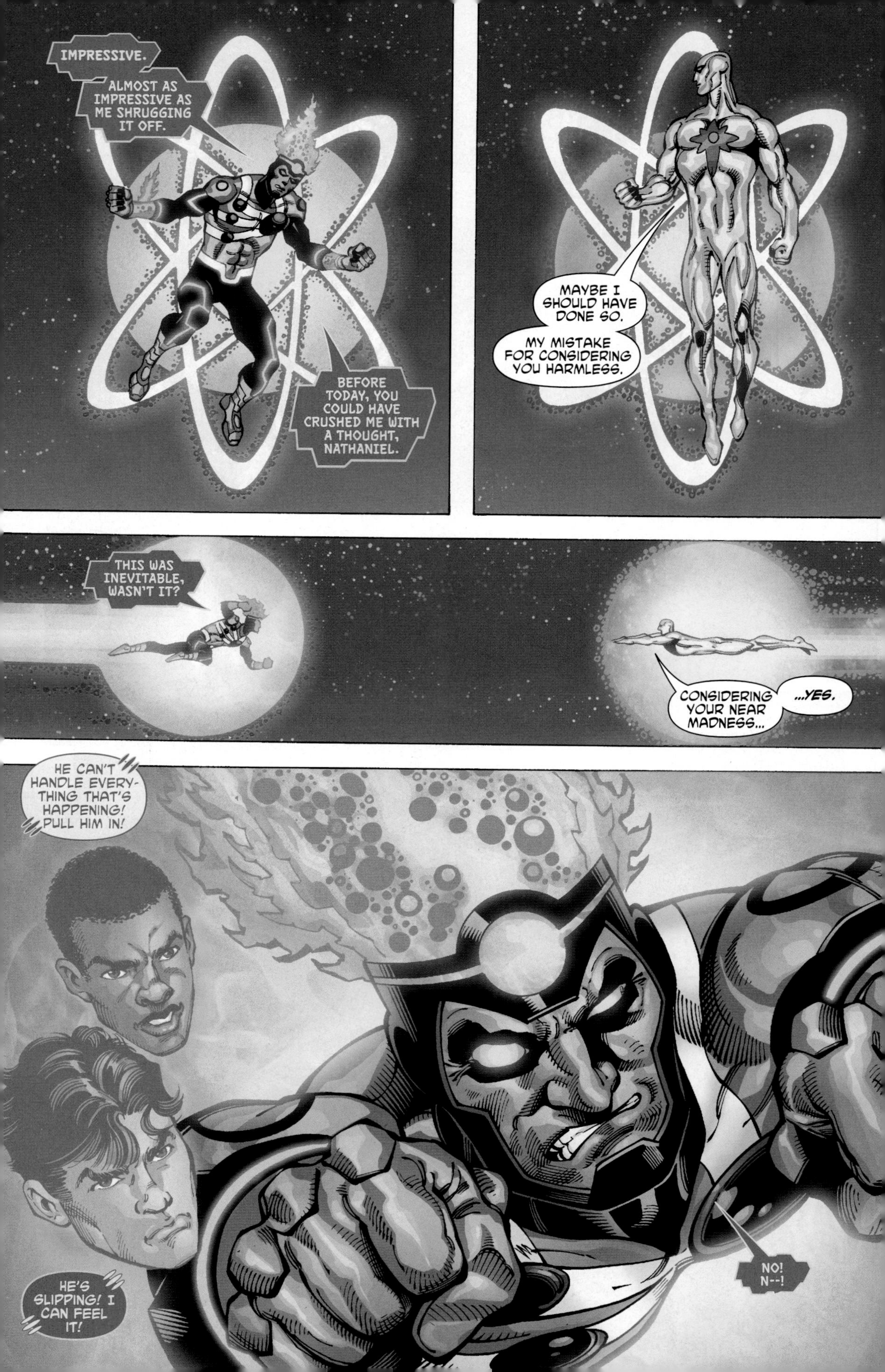
IMPRESSIVE.
ALMOST AS IMPRESSIVE AS ME SHRUGGING IT OFF.
BEFORE TODAY, YOU COULD HAVE CRUSHED ME WITH A THOUGHT, NATHANIEL.
MAYBE I SHOULD HAVE DONE SO.
MY MISTAKE FOR CONSIDERING YOU HARMLESS.
THIS WAS INEVITABLE, WASN'T IT?
CONSIDERING YOUR NEAR MADNESS...
...YES.
HE CAN'T HANDLE EVERY-THING THAT'S HAPPENING! PULL HIM IN!
HE'S SLIPPING! I CAN FEEL IT!
NO! N--!

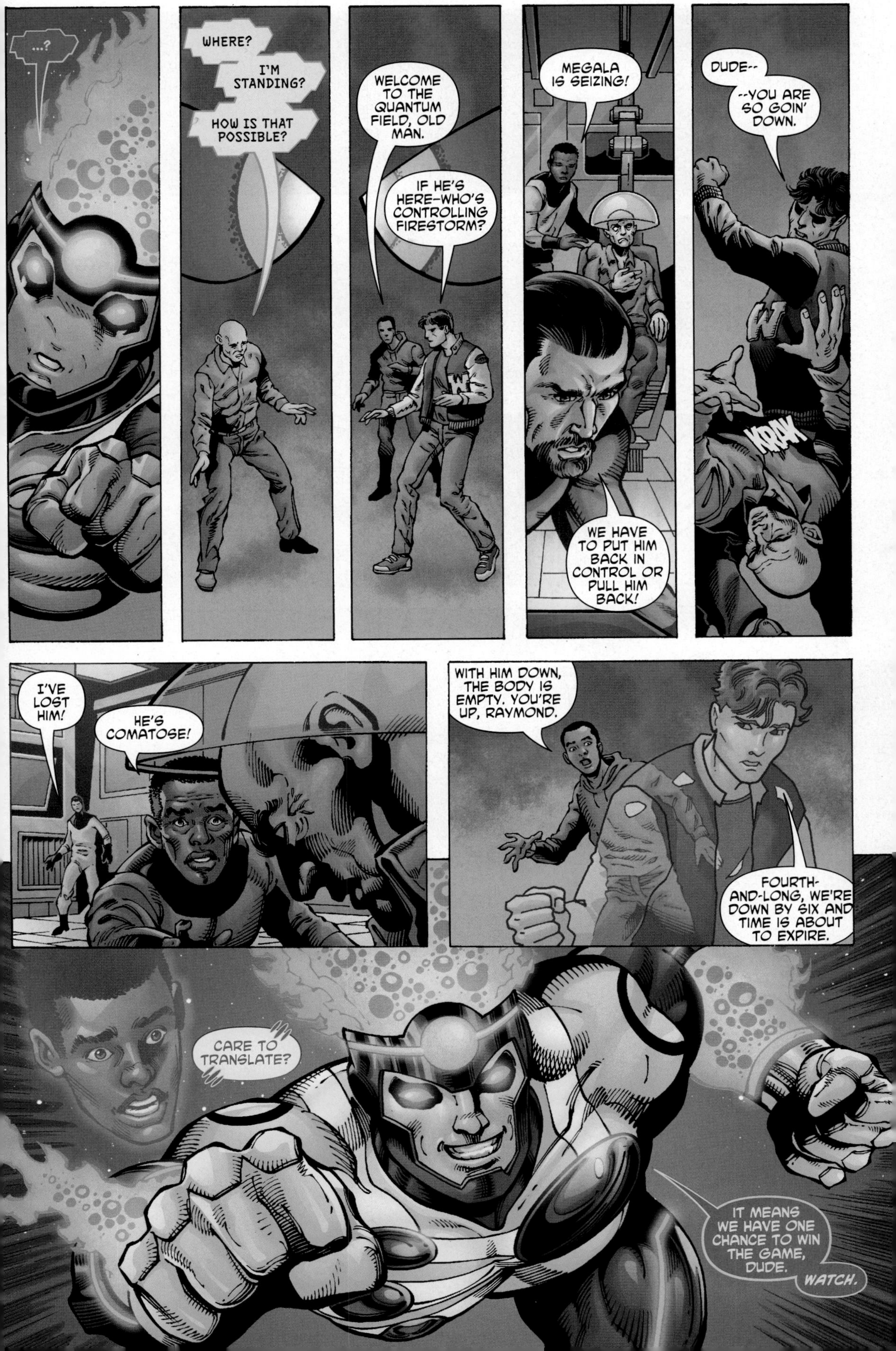
...?
WHERE?
I'M STANDING?
HOW IS THAT POSSIBLE?
WELCOME TO THE QUANTUM FIELD, OLD MAN.
IF HE'S HERE--WHO'S CONTROLLING FIRESTORM?
MEGALA IS SEIZING!
WE HAVE TO PUT HIM BACK IN CONTROL OR PULL HIM BACK!
DUDE--
--YOU ARE SO GOIN' DOWN.
KRAK
I'VE LOST HIM!
HE'S COMATOSE!
WITH HIM DOWN, THE BODY IS EMPTY. YOU'RE UP, RAYMOND.
FOURTH-AND-LONG, WE'RE DOWN BY SIX AND TIME IS ABOUT TO EXPIRE.
CARE TO TRANSLATE?
IT MEANS WE HAVE ONE CHANCE TO WIN THE GAME, DUDE.
WATCH.

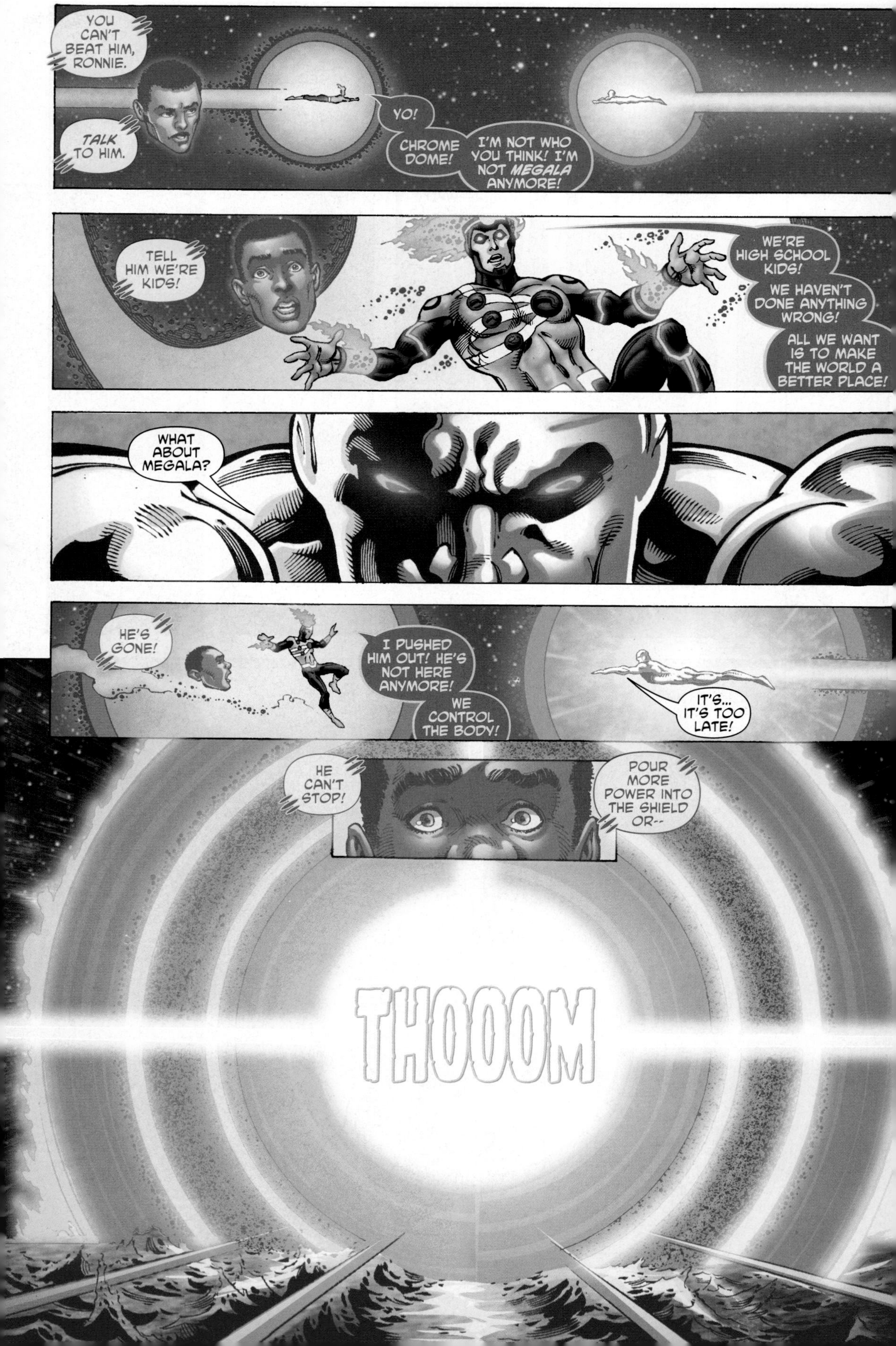
YOU CAN'T BEAT HIM, RONNIE.
TALK TO HIM.
YO!
CHROME DOME!
I'M NOT WHO YOU THINK! I'M NOT MEGALA ANYMORE!
TELL HIM WE'RE KIDS!
WE'RE HIGH SCHOOL KIDS!
WE HAVEN'T DONE ANYTHING WRONG!
ALL WE WANT IS TO MAKE THE WORLD A BETTER PLACE!
WHAT ABOUT MEGALA?
HE'S GONE!
I PUSHED HIM OUT! HE'S NOT HERE ANYMORE!
WE CONTROL THE BODY!
IT'S... IT'S TOO LATE!
HE CAN'T STOP!
POUR MORE POWER INTO THE SHIELD OR--
THOOOM

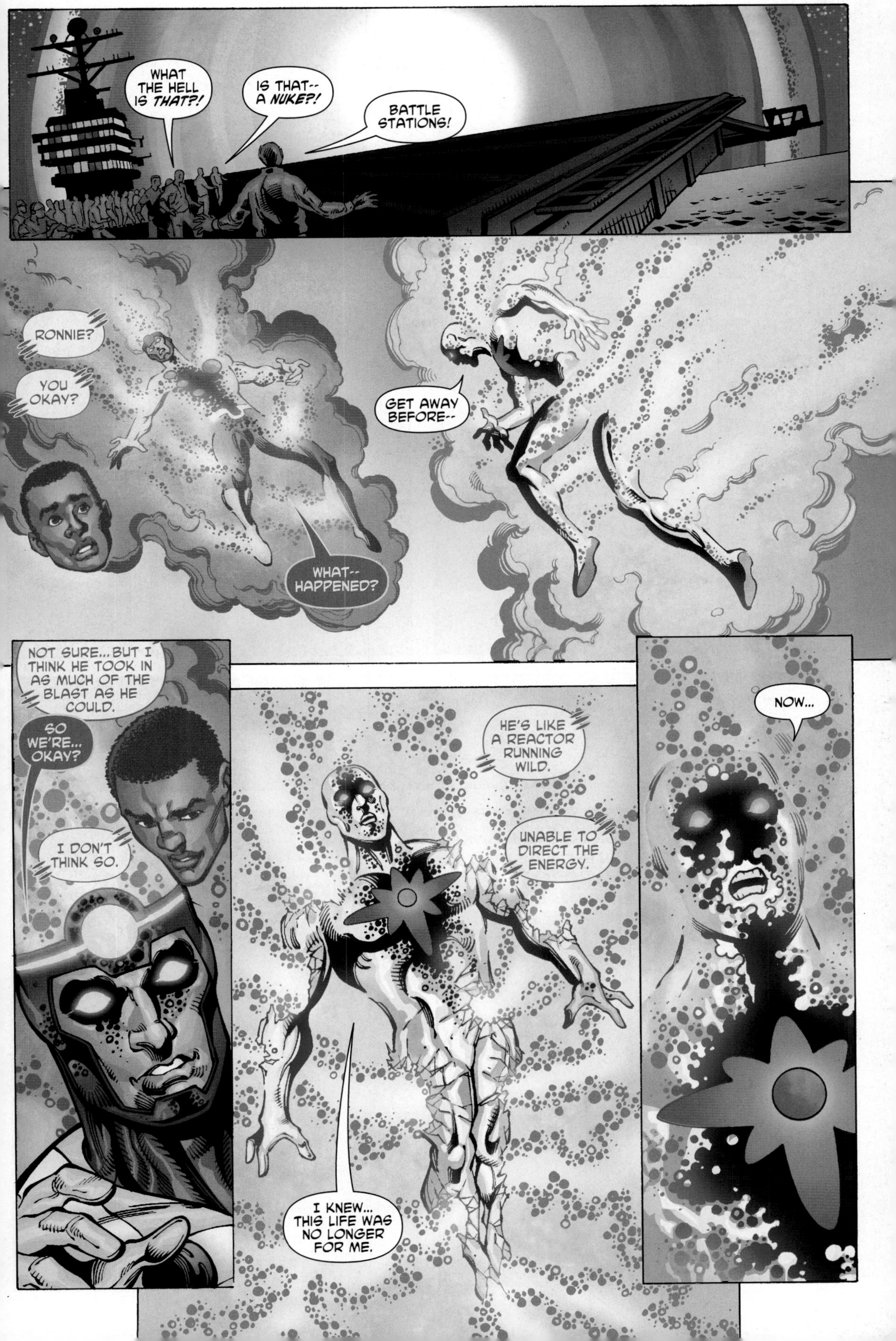
WHAT THE HELL IS *THAT?!*
IS THAT-- A *NUKE?!*
BATTLE STATIONS!
RONNIE?
YOU OKAY?
WHAT-- HAPPENED?
GET AWAY BEFORE--
NOT SURE... BUT I THINK HE TOOK IN AS MUCH OF THE BLAST AS HE COULD.
SO WE'RE... OKAY?
I DON'T THINK SO.
HE'S LIKE A REACTOR RUNNING WILD.
UNABLE TO DIRECT THE ENERGY.
I KNEW... THIS LIFE WAS NO LONGER FOR ME.
NOW...

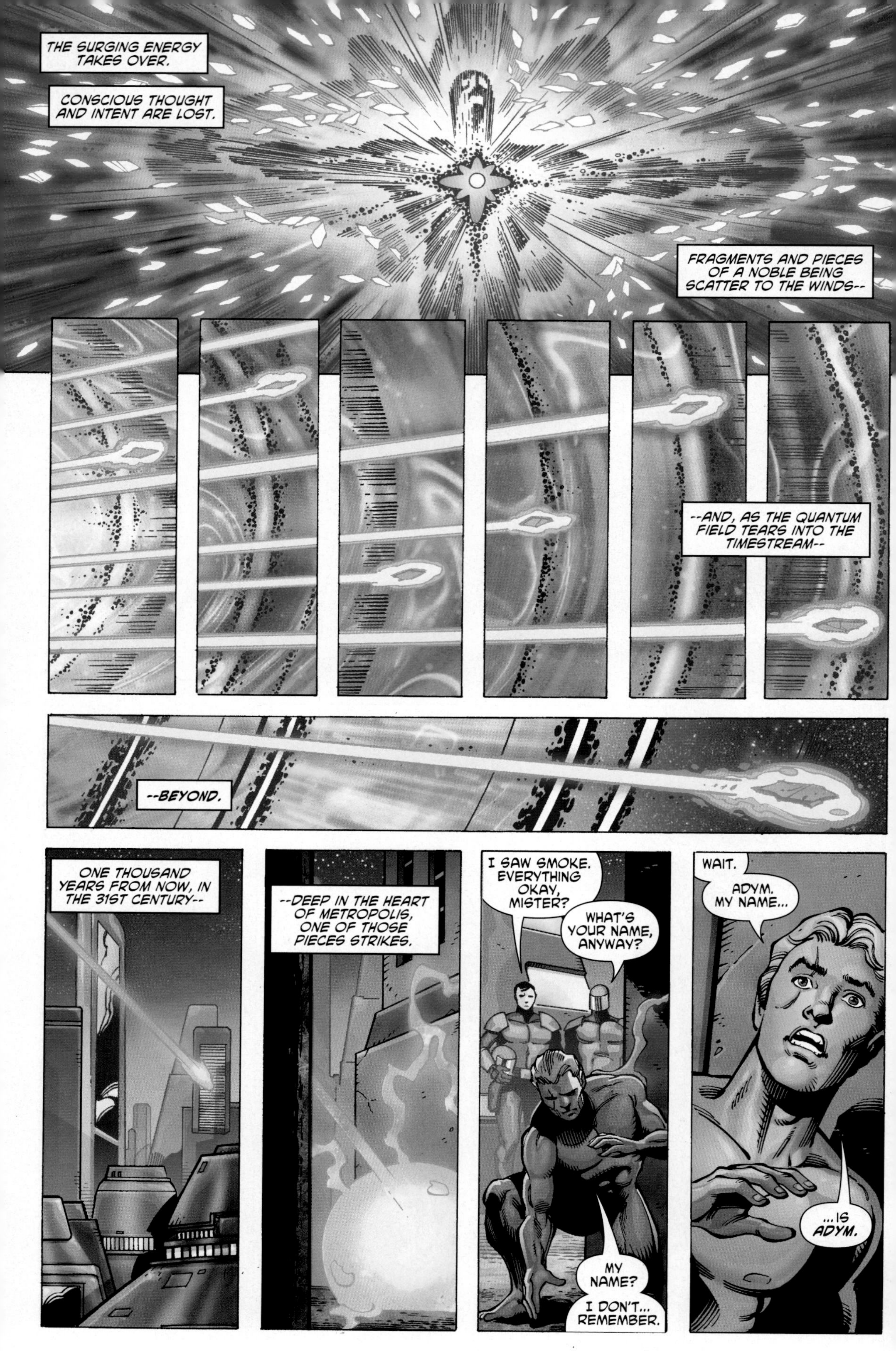
THE SURGING ENERGY TAKES OVER.
CONSCIOUS THOUGHT AND INTENT ARE LOST.
FRAGMENTS AND PIECES OF A NOBLE BEING SCATTER TO THE WINDS--
--AND, AS THE QUANTUM FIELD TEARS INTO THE TIMESTREAM--
--BEYOND.
ONE THOUSAND YEARS FROM NOW, IN THE 31ST CENTURY--
--DEEP IN THE HEART OF METROPOLIS, ONE OF THOSE PIECES STRIKES.
I SAW SMOKE. EVERYTHING OKAY, MISTER?
WHAT'S YOUR NAME, ANYWAY?
MY NAME?
I DON'T... REMEMBER.
WAIT.
ADYM. MY NAME...
...IS ADYM.

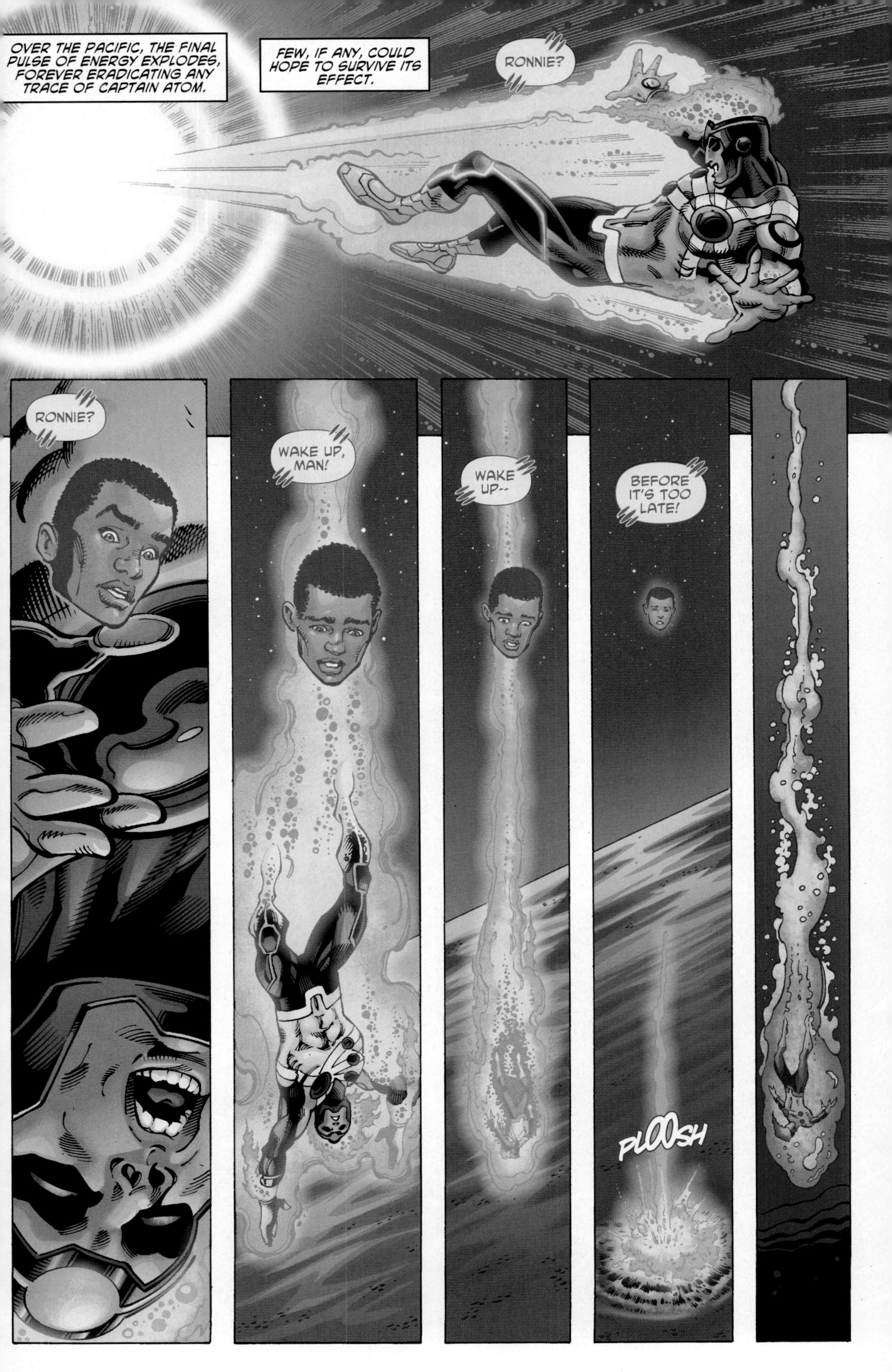
OVER THE PACIFIC, THE FINAL PULSE OF ENERGY EXPLODES, FOREVER ERADICATING ANY TRACE OF CAPTAIN ATOM.
FEW, IF ANY, COULD HOPE TO SURVIVE ITS EFFECT.
RONNIE?
RONNIE?
WAKE UP, MAN!
WAKE UP--
BEFORE IT'S TOO LATE!
PLOOSH

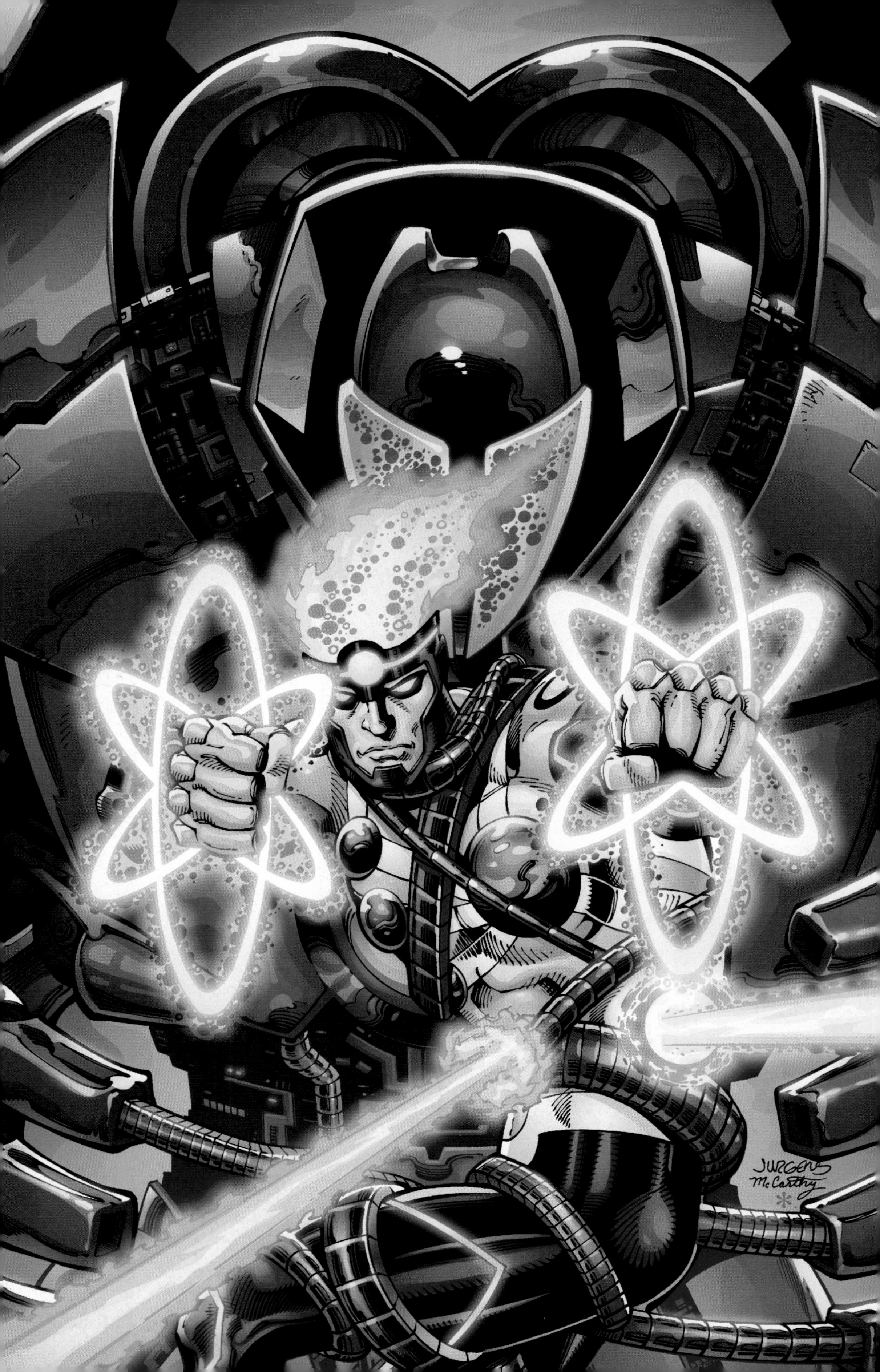
JURGENS
McCarthy

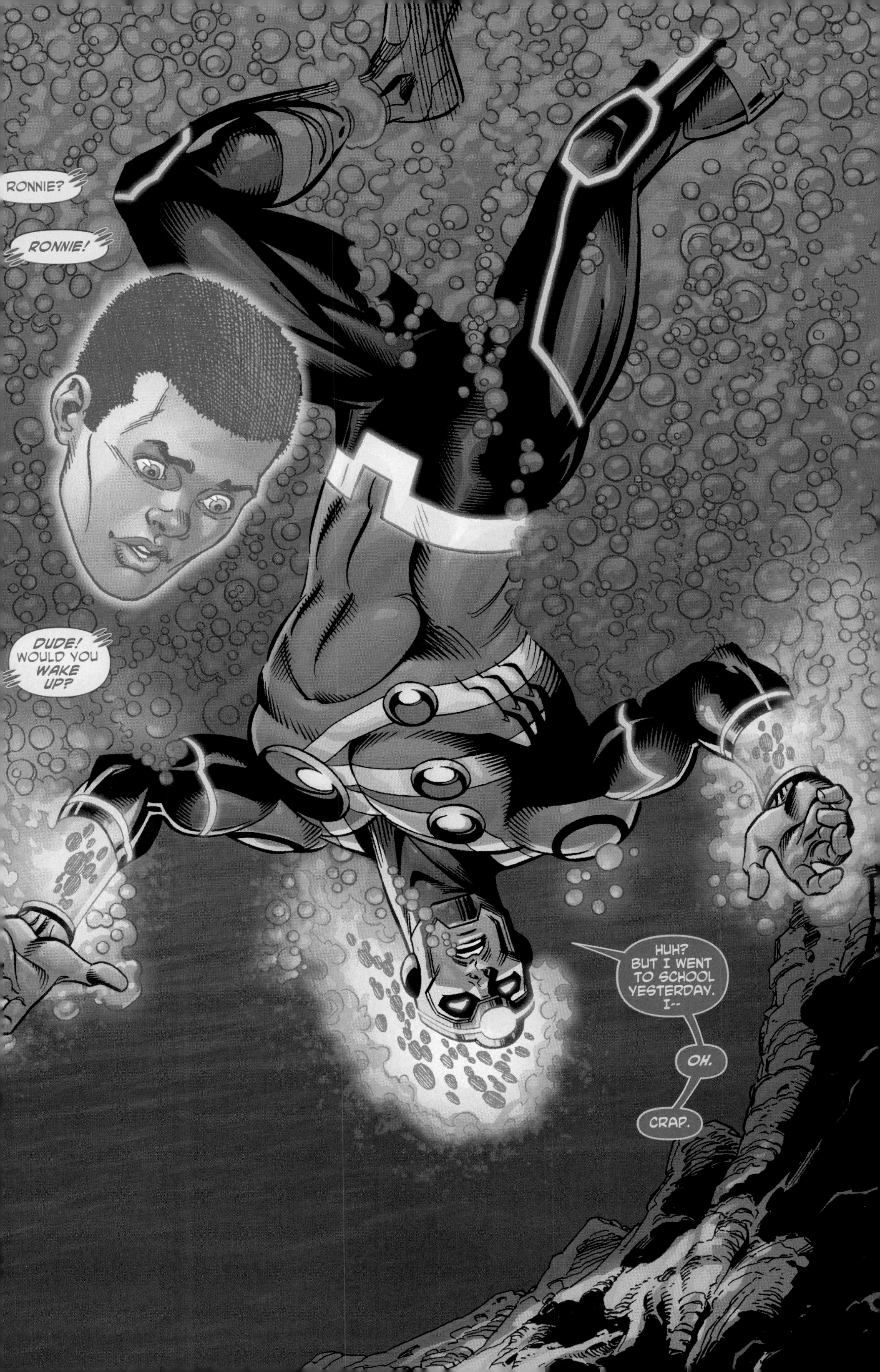
RONNIE?
RONNIE!
DUDE! WOULD YOU WAKE UP?
HUH? BUT I WENT TO SCHOOL YESTERDAY. I--
OH.
CRAP.

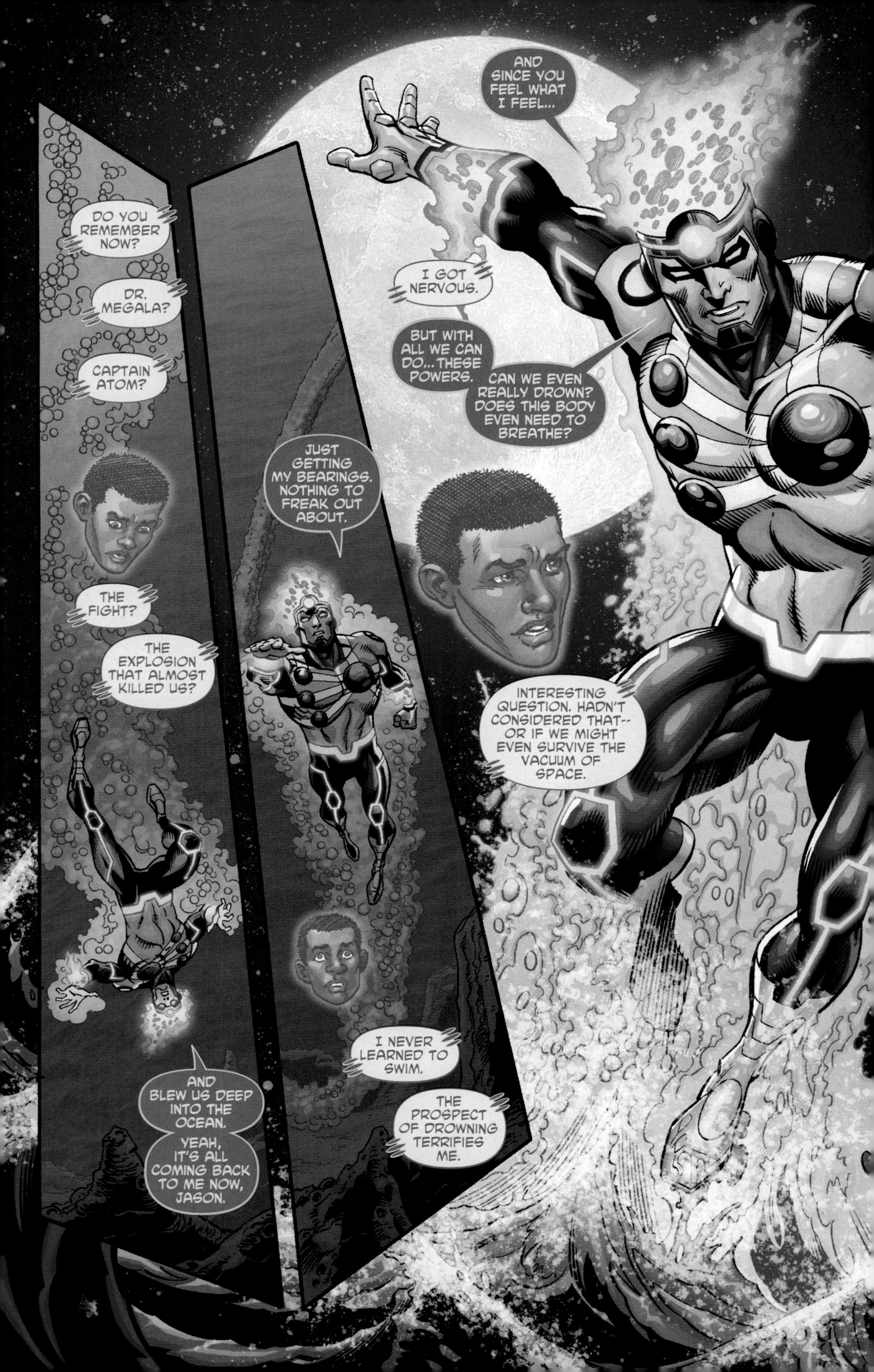
DO YOU REMEMBER NOW?
DR. MEGALA?
CAPTAIN ATOM?
THE FIGHT?
THE EXPLOSION THAT ALMOST KILLED US?
AND BLEW US DEEP INTO THE OCEAN.
YEAH, IT'S ALL COMING BACK TO ME NOW, JASON.
JUST GETTING MY BEARINGS. NOTHING TO FREAK OUT ABOUT.
I NEVER LEARNED TO SWIM.
THE PROSPECT OF DROWNING TERRIFIES ME.
AND SINCE YOU FEEL WHAT I FEEL...
I GOT NERVOUS.
BUT WITH ALL WE CAN DO...THESE POWERS.
CAN WE EVEN REALLY DROWN? DOES THIS BODY EVEN NEED TO BREATHE?
INTERESTING QUESTION. HADN'T CONSIDERED THAT-- OR IF WE MIGHT EVEN SURVIVE THE VACUUM OF SPACE.

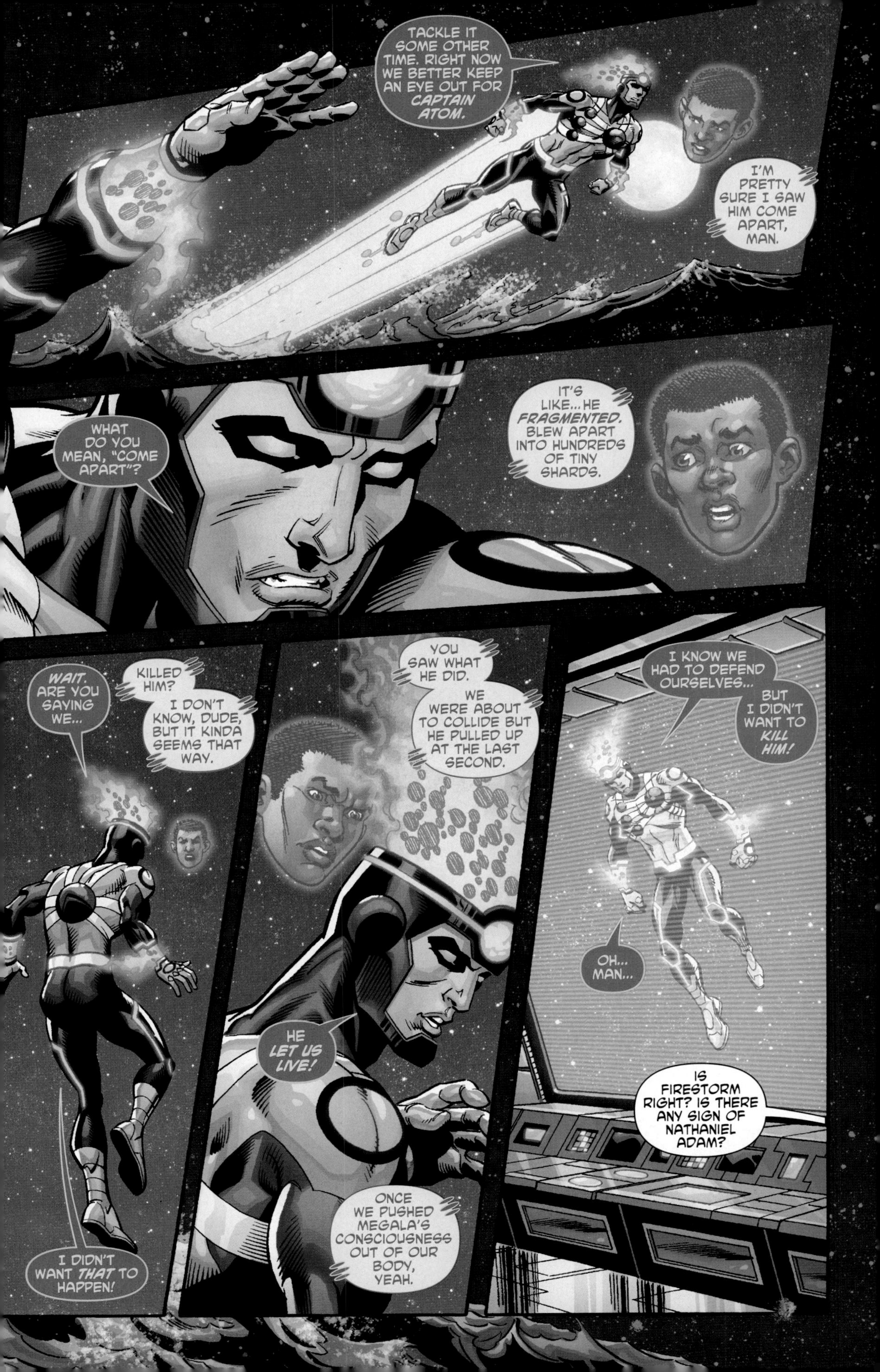
TACKLE IT SOME OTHER TIME. RIGHT NOW WE BETTER KEEP AN EYE OUT FOR CAPTAIN ATOM.
I'M PRETTY SURE I SAW HIM COME APART, MAN.
WHAT DO YOU MEAN, "COME APART"?
IT'S LIKE... HE FRAGMENTED. BLEW APART INTO HUNDREDS OF TINY SHARDS.
WAIT. ARE YOU SAYING WE...
KILLED HIM?
I DON'T KNOW, DUDE, BUT IT KINDA SEEMS THAT WAY.
I DIDN'T WANT THAT TO HAPPEN!
YOU SAW WHAT HE DID.
WE WERE ABOUT TO COLLIDE BUT HE PULLED UP AT THE LAST SECOND.
HE LET US LIVE!
ONCE WE PUSHED MEGALA'S CONSCIOUSNESS OUT OF OUR BODY, YEAH.
I KNOW WE HAD TO DEFEND OURSELVES...
BUT I DIDN'T WANT TO KILL HIM!
OH... MAN...
IS FIRESTORM RIGHT? IS THERE ANY SIGN OF NATHANIEL ADAM?

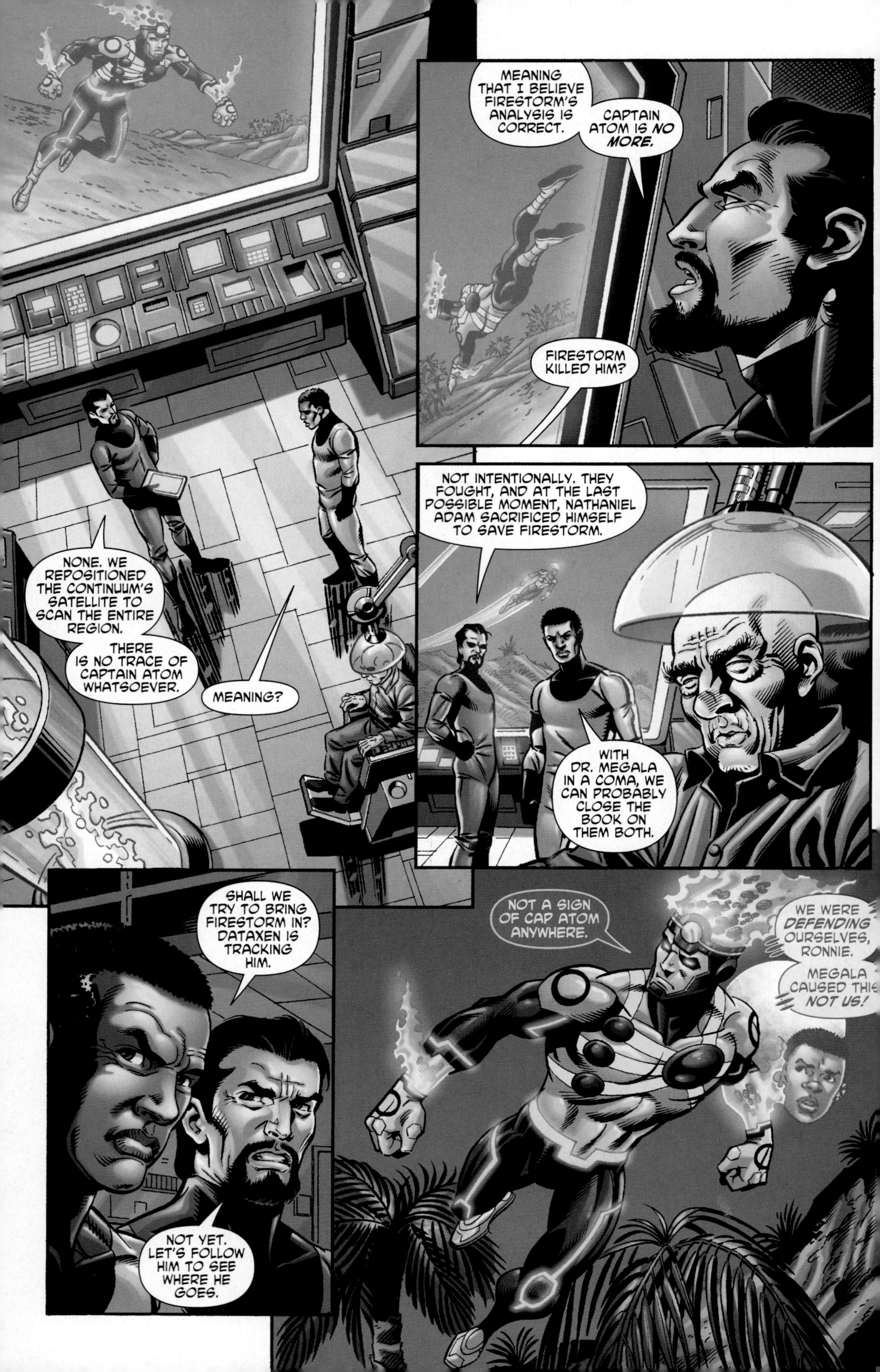
NONE. WE REPOSITIONED THE CONTINUUM'S SATELLITE TO SCAN THE ENTIRE REGION.
THERE IS NO TRACE OF CAPTAIN ATOM WHATSOEVER.
MEANING?
MEANING THAT I BELIEVE FIRESTORM'S ANALYSIS IS CORRECT.
CAPTAIN ATOM IS *NO MORE.*
FIRESTORM KILLED HIM?
NOT INTENTIONALLY. THEY FOUGHT, AND AT THE LAST POSSIBLE MOMENT, NATHANIEL ADAM SACRIFICED HIMSELF TO SAVE FIRESTORM.
WITH DR. MEGALA IN A COMA, WE CAN PROBABLY CLOSE THE BOOK ON THEM BOTH.
SHALL WE TRY TO BRING FIRESTORM IN? DATAXEN IS TRACKING HIM.
NOT YET. LET'S FOLLOW HIM TO SEE WHERE HE GOES.
NOT A SIGN OF CAP ATOM ANYWHERE.
WE WERE *DEFENDING* OURSELVES, RONNIE.
MEGALA CAUSED THIS *NOT US!*

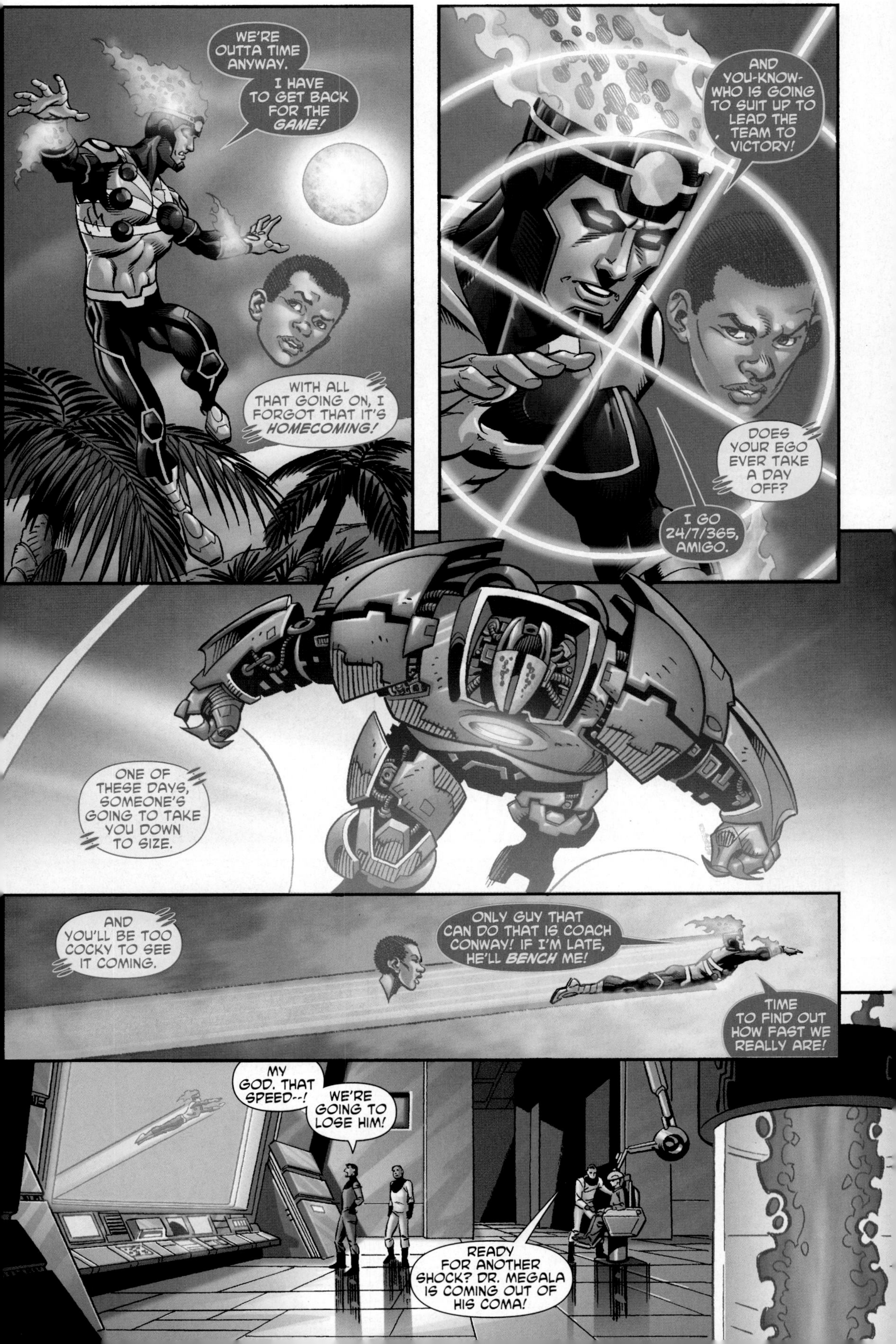
WE'RE OUTTA TIME ANYWAY.
I HAVE TO GET BACK FOR THE *GAME!*
WITH ALL THAT GOING ON, I FORGOT THAT IT'S *HOMECOMING!*
AND YOU-KNOW-WHO IS GOING TO SUIT UP TO LEAD THE TEAM TO VICTORY!
DOES YOUR EGO EVER TAKE A DAY OFF?
I GO 24/7/365, AMIGO.
ONE OF THESE DAYS, SOMEONE'S GOING TO TAKE YOU DOWN TO SIZE.
AND YOU'LL BE TOO COCKY TO SEE IT COMING.
ONLY GUY THAT CAN DO THAT IS COACH CONWAY! IF I'M LATE, HE'LL *BENCH* ME!
TIME TO FIND OUT HOW FAST WE REALLY ARE!
MY GOD. THAT SPEED--!
WE'RE GOING TO LOSE HIM!
READY FOR ANOTHER SHOCK? DR. MEGALA IS COMING OUT OF HIS COMA!

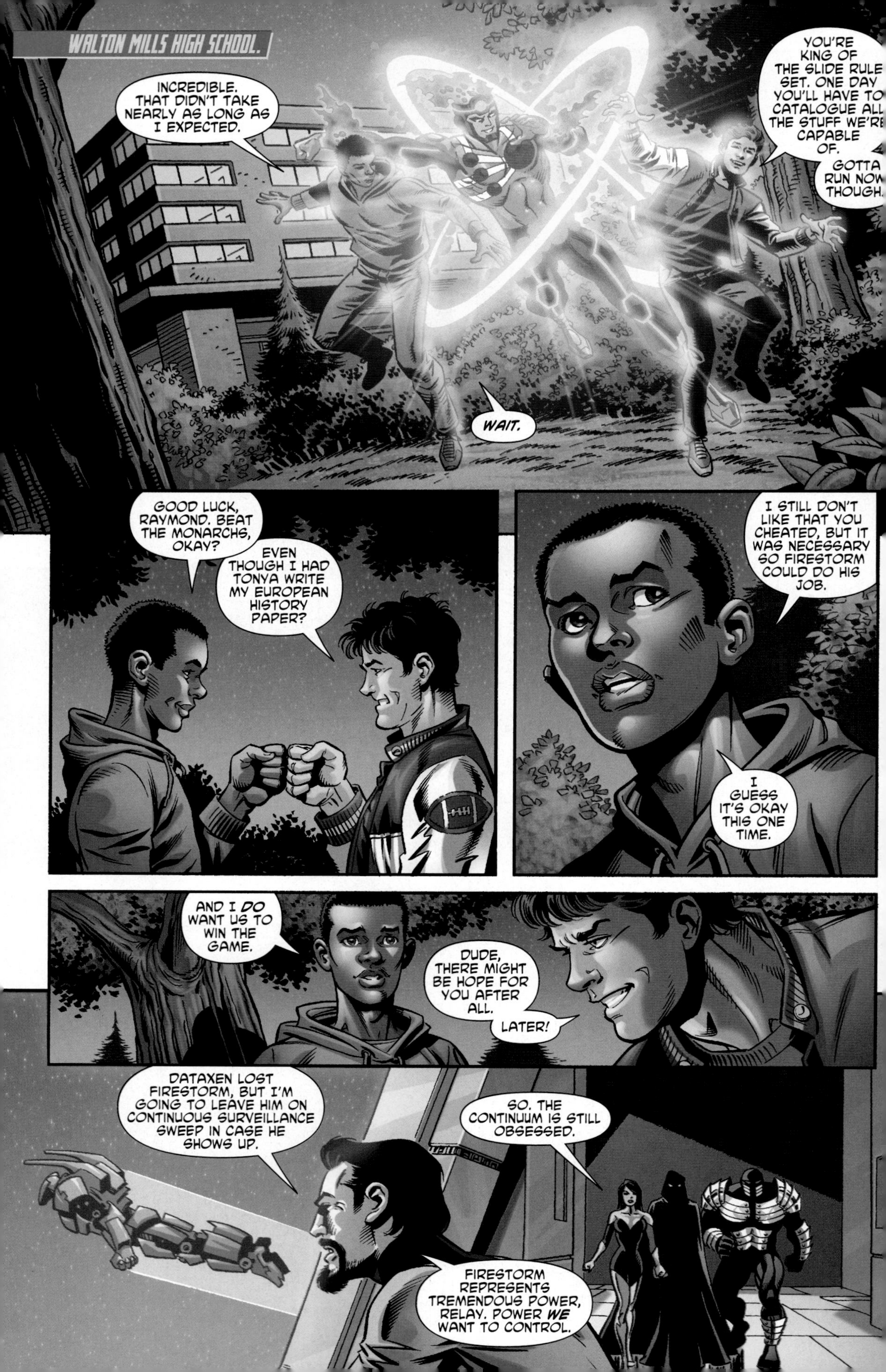
WALTON MILLS HIGH SCHOOL.
INCREDIBLE. THAT DIDN'T TAKE NEARLY AS LONG AS I EXPECTED.
YOU'RE KING OF THE SLIDE RULE SET. ONE DAY YOU'LL HAVE TO CATALOGUE ALL THE STUFF WE'RE CAPABLE OF.
GOTTA RUN NOW THOUGH.
WAIT.
GOOD LUCK, RAYMOND. BEAT THE MONARCHS, OKAY?
EVEN THOUGH I HAD TONYA WRITE MY EUROPEAN HISTORY PAPER?
I STILL DON'T LIKE THAT YOU CHEATED, BUT IT WAS NECESSARY SO FIRESTORM COULD DO HIS JOB.
I GUESS IT'S OKAY THIS ONE TIME.
AND I DO WANT US TO WIN THE GAME.
DUDE, THERE MIGHT BE HOPE FOR YOU AFTER ALL.
LATER!
DATAXEN LOST FIRESTORM, BUT I'M GOING TO LEAVE HIM ON CONTINUOUS SURVEILLANCE SWEEP IN CASE HE SHOWS UP.
SO. THE CONTINUUM IS STILL OBSESSED.
FIRESTORM REPRESENTS TREMENDOUS POWER, RELAY. POWER WE WANT TO CONTROL.

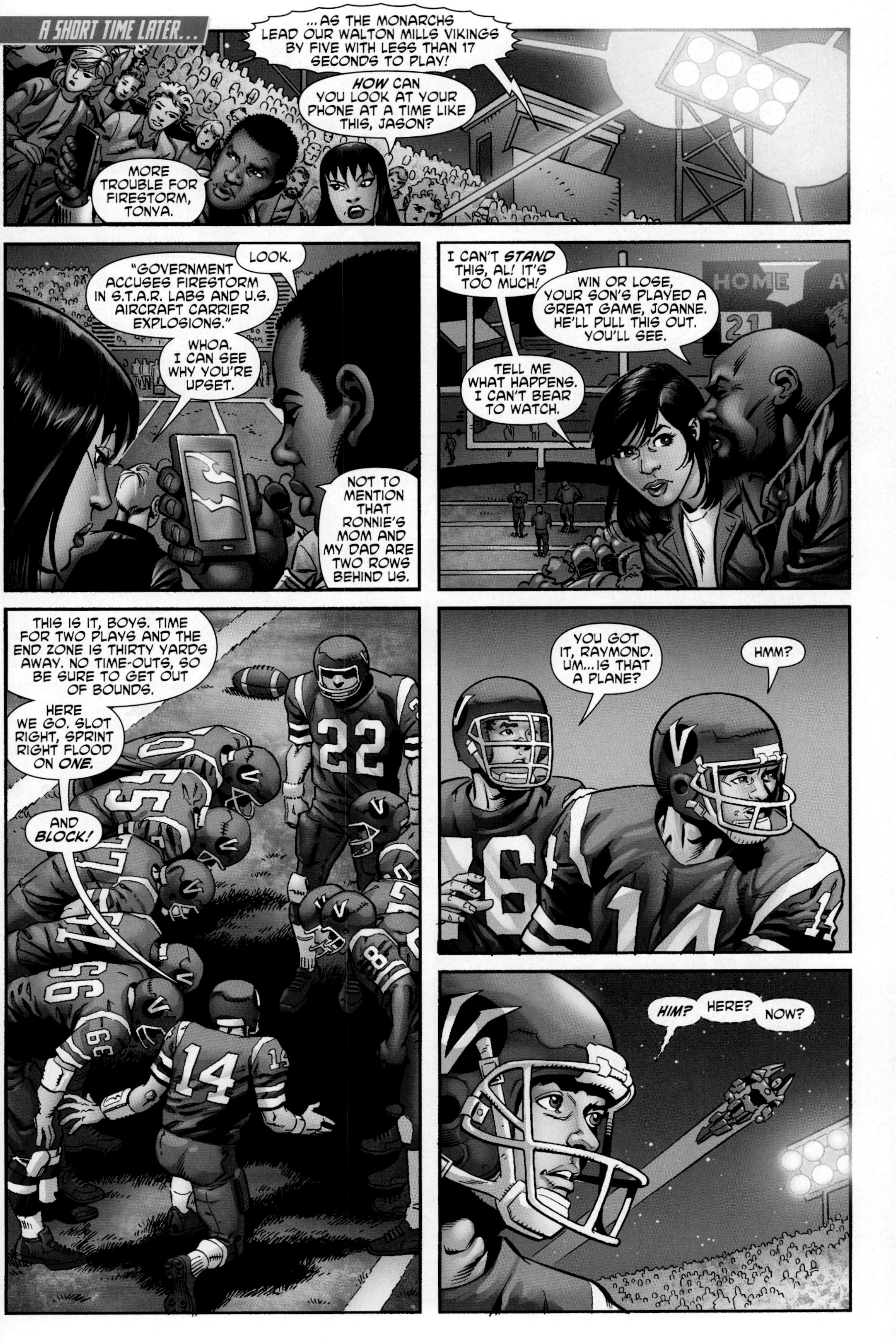
A SHORT TIME LATER...
...AS THE MONARCHS LEAD OUR WALTON MILLS VIKINGS BY FIVE WITH LESS THAN 17 SECONDS TO PLAY!
HOW CAN YOU LOOK AT YOUR PHONE AT A TIME LIKE THIS, JASON?
MORE TROUBLE FOR FIRESTORM, TONYA.
LOOK.
"GOVERNMENT ACCUSES FIRESTORM IN S.T.A.R. LABS AND U.S. AIRCRAFT CARRIER EXPLOSIONS."
WHOA. I CAN SEE WHY YOU'RE UPSET.
NOT TO MENTION THAT RONNIE'S MOM AND MY DAD ARE TWO ROWS BEHIND US.
I CAN'T STAND THIS, AL! IT'S TOO MUCH!
WIN OR LOSE, YOUR SON'S PLAYED A GREAT GAME, JOANNE. HE'LL PULL THIS OUT. YOU'LL SEE.
TELL ME WHAT HAPPENS. I CAN'T BEAR TO WATCH.
HOME
21
THIS IS IT, BOYS. TIME FOR TWO PLAYS AND THE END ZONE IS THIRTY YARDS AWAY. NO TIME-OUTS, SO BE SURE TO GET OUT OF BOUNDS.
HERE WE GO. SLOT RIGHT, SPRINT RIGHT FLOOD ON ONE.
AND BLOCK!
YOU GOT IT, RAYMOND. UM...IS THAT A PLANE?
HMM?
HIM?
HERE?
NOW?

BLACK 88!

I'M GONNA GUT YOU LIKE A FISH, RAYMOND.

BLACK 88!

GO!

THAT WAS DATAXEN THAT JUST FLEW OVER!

HOW DOES HE KNOW YOU'RE HERE?

NO IDEA, BUT IF HE ATTACKS, A LOT OF PEOPLE ARE GOING TO GET HURT!

WE NEED FIRESTORM!

NOW? HOW--?

RAYMOND-TO-WASHINGTON OUT-OF-BOUNDS FOR 18 YARDS AND A FIRST DOWN! THE CLOCK STOPS WITH SIX SECONDS LEFT TO PLAY!

NICE WORK, BOYS. WE SCORE HERE AND WE WIN.

JET, Y MOTION, DRAG LEFT ON ONE!

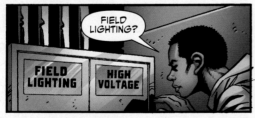

FIELD LIGHTING?

FIELD LIGHTING

HIGH VOLTAGE

SEEMS EXCESSIVE.

BUT SOMETIMES YOU GOTTA DO WHAT YOU GOTTA DO.

KEEP 'EM OFF ME!

CAN'T HOLD 'EM ANY LONGER! THROW IT!

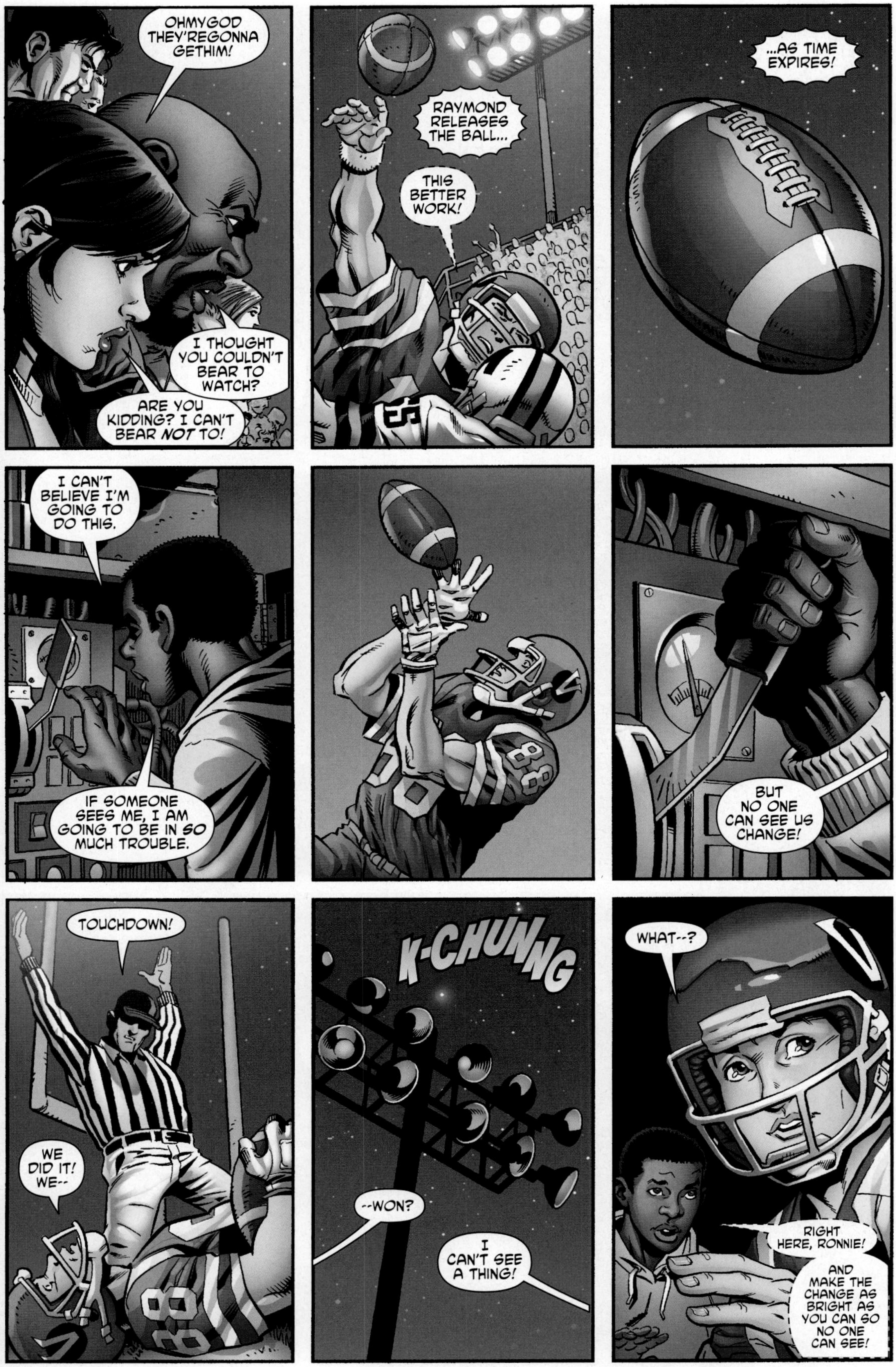
OHMYGOD THEY'REGONNA GETHIM!
I THOUGHT YOU COULDN'T BEAR TO WATCH?
ARE YOU KIDDING? I CAN'T BEAR *NOT* TO!
RAYMOND RELEASES THE BALL...
THIS BETTER WORK!
...AS TIME EXPIRES!
I CAN'T BELIEVE I'M GOING TO DO THIS.
IF SOMEONE SEES ME, I AM GOING TO BE IN *SO* MUCH TROUBLE.
BUT NO ONE CAN SEE US CHANGE!
TOUCHDOWN!
WE DID IT! WE--
K-CHUNNG
--WON?
I CAN'T SEE A THING!
WHAT--?
RIGHT HERE, RONNIE!
AND MAKE THE CHANGE AS BRIGHT AS YOU CAN SO NO ONE CAN SEE!

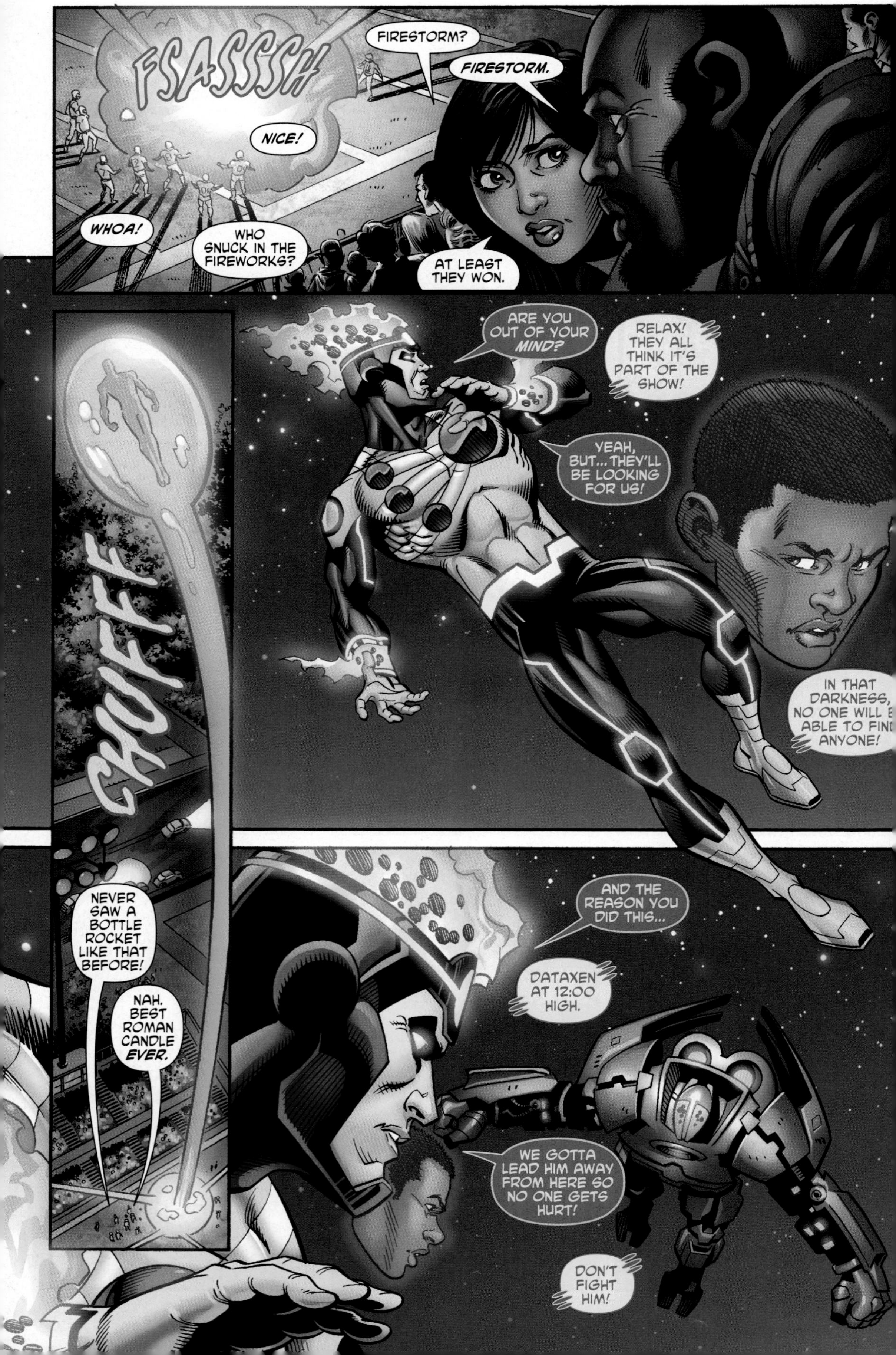
FSASSSH
FIRESTORM?
FIRESTORM.
NICE!
WHOA!
WHO SNUCK IN THE FIREWORKS?
AT LEAST THEY WON.
CHUFFF
ARE YOU OUT OF YOUR MIND?
RELAX! THEY ALL THINK IT'S PART OF THE SHOW!
YEAH, BUT...THEY'LL BE LOOKING FOR US!
IN THAT DARKNESS, NO ONE WILL BE ABLE TO FIND ANYONE!
NEVER SAW A BOTTLE ROCKET LIKE THAT BEFORE!
NAH. BEST ROMAN CANDLE EVER.
AND THE REASON YOU DID THIS...
DATAXEN AT 12:00 HIGH.
WE GOTTA LEAD HIM AWAY FROM HERE SO NO ONE GETS HURT!
DON'T FIGHT HIM!

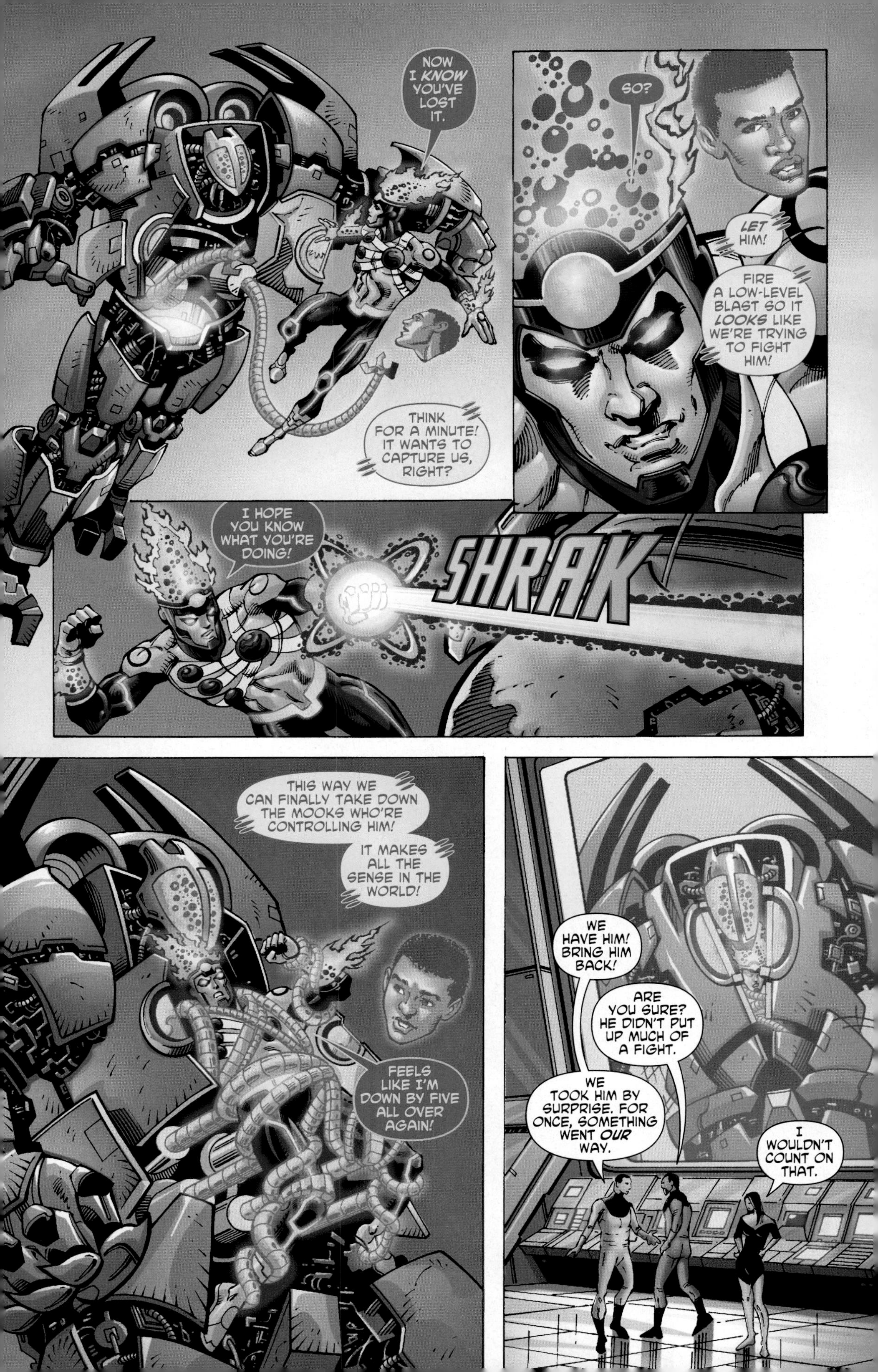
NOW I *KNOW* YOU'VE LOST IT.
THINK FOR A MINUTE! IT WANTS TO CAPTURE US, RIGHT?
SO?
LET HIM!
FIRE A LOW-LEVEL BLAST SO IT *LOOKS* LIKE WE'RE TRYING TO FIGHT HIM!
I HOPE YOU KNOW WHAT YOU'RE DOING!
SHRAK
THIS WAY WE CAN FINALLY TAKE DOWN THE MOOKS WHO'RE CONTROLLING HIM!
IT MAKES ALL THE SENSE IN THE WORLD!
FEELS LIKE I'M DOWN BY FIVE ALL OVER AGAIN!
WE HAVE HIM! BRING HIM BACK!
ARE YOU SURE? HE DIDN'T PUT UP MUCH OF A FIGHT.
WE TOOK HIM BY SURPRISE. FOR ONCE, SOMETHING WENT *OUR* WAY.
I WOULDN'T COUNT ON THAT.

OW.

THE QUANTUM ENERGY IN THESE CABLES *HURTS*.

HANG IN THERE AND DON'T FIGHT IT.

IF YOU DO, THEY'LL ONLY INCREASE INTENSITY.

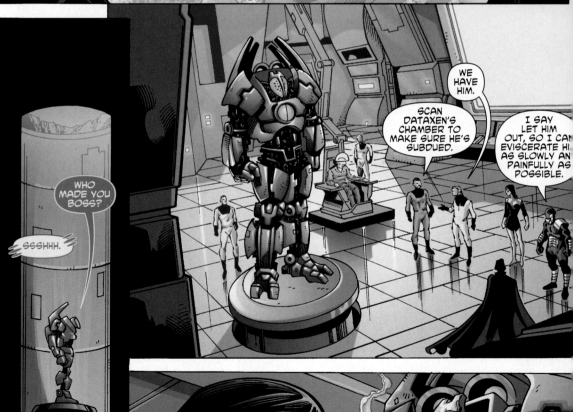

WE HAVE HIM.

SCAN DATAXEN'S CHAMBER TO MAKE SURE HE'S SUBDUED.

I SAY LET HIM OUT, SO I CAN EVISCERATE HIM AS SLOWLY AND PAINFULLY AS POSSIBLE.

WHO MADE YOU BOSS?

SSSHHH.

DON'T WORRY, SKULL CRUSHER. I BELIEVE YOU'RE ABOUT TO GET YOUR WISH.

HEY... WHAT'S WITH THE SMOKE?

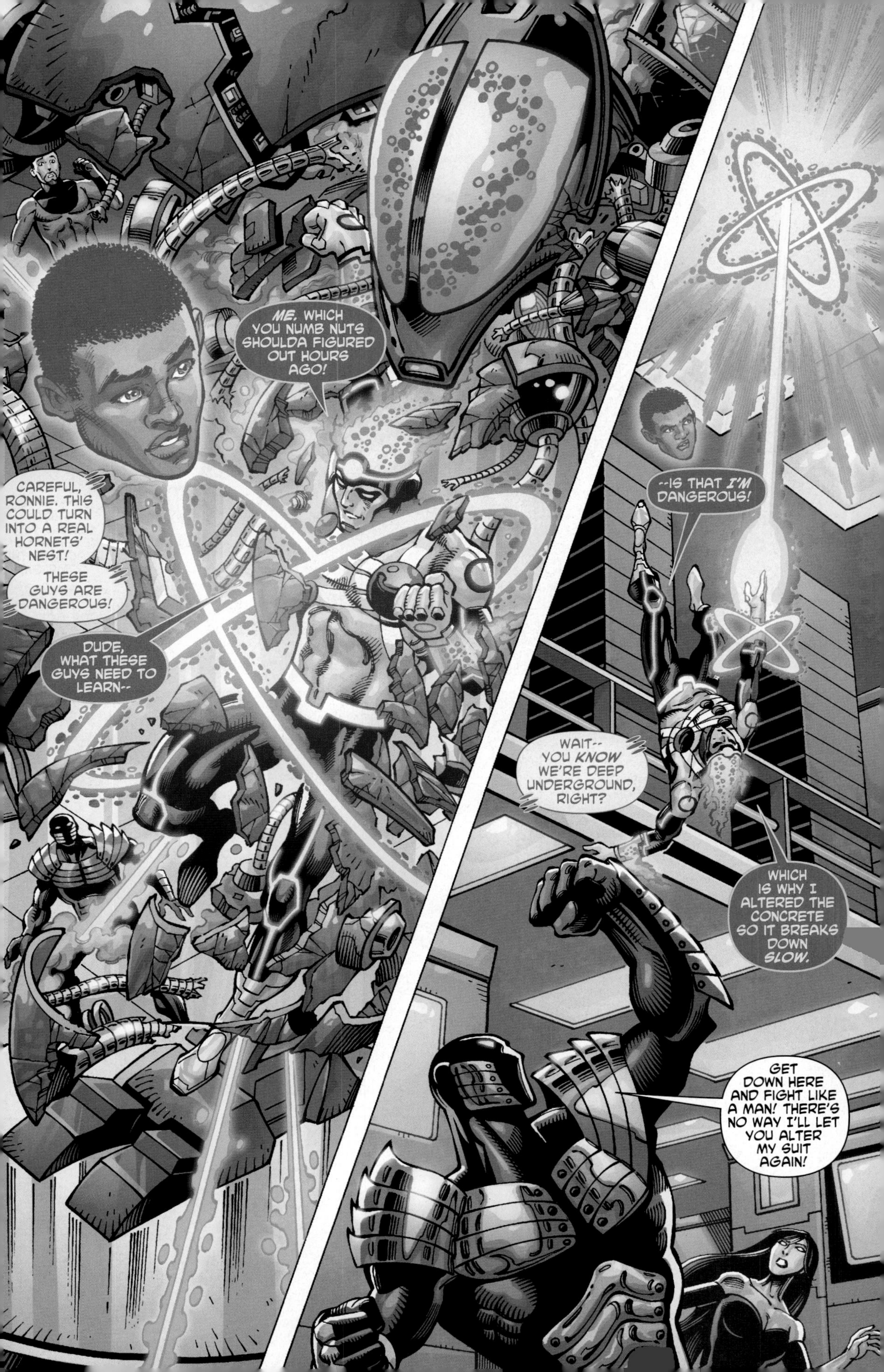
ME, WHICH YOU NUMB NUTS SHOULDA FIGURED OUT HOURS AGO!
CAREFUL, RONNIE. THIS COULD TURN INTO A REAL HORNETS' NEST!
THESE GUYS ARE DANGEROUS!
DUDE, WHAT THESE GUYS NEED TO LEARN--
--IS THAT I'M DANGEROUS!
WAIT-- YOU KNOW WE'RE DEEP UNDERGROUND, RIGHT?
WHICH IS WHY I ALTERED THE CONCRETE SO IT BREAKS DOWN SLOW.
GET DOWN HERE AND FIGHT LIKE A MAN! THERE'S NO WAY I'LL LET YOU ALTER MY SUIT AGAIN!

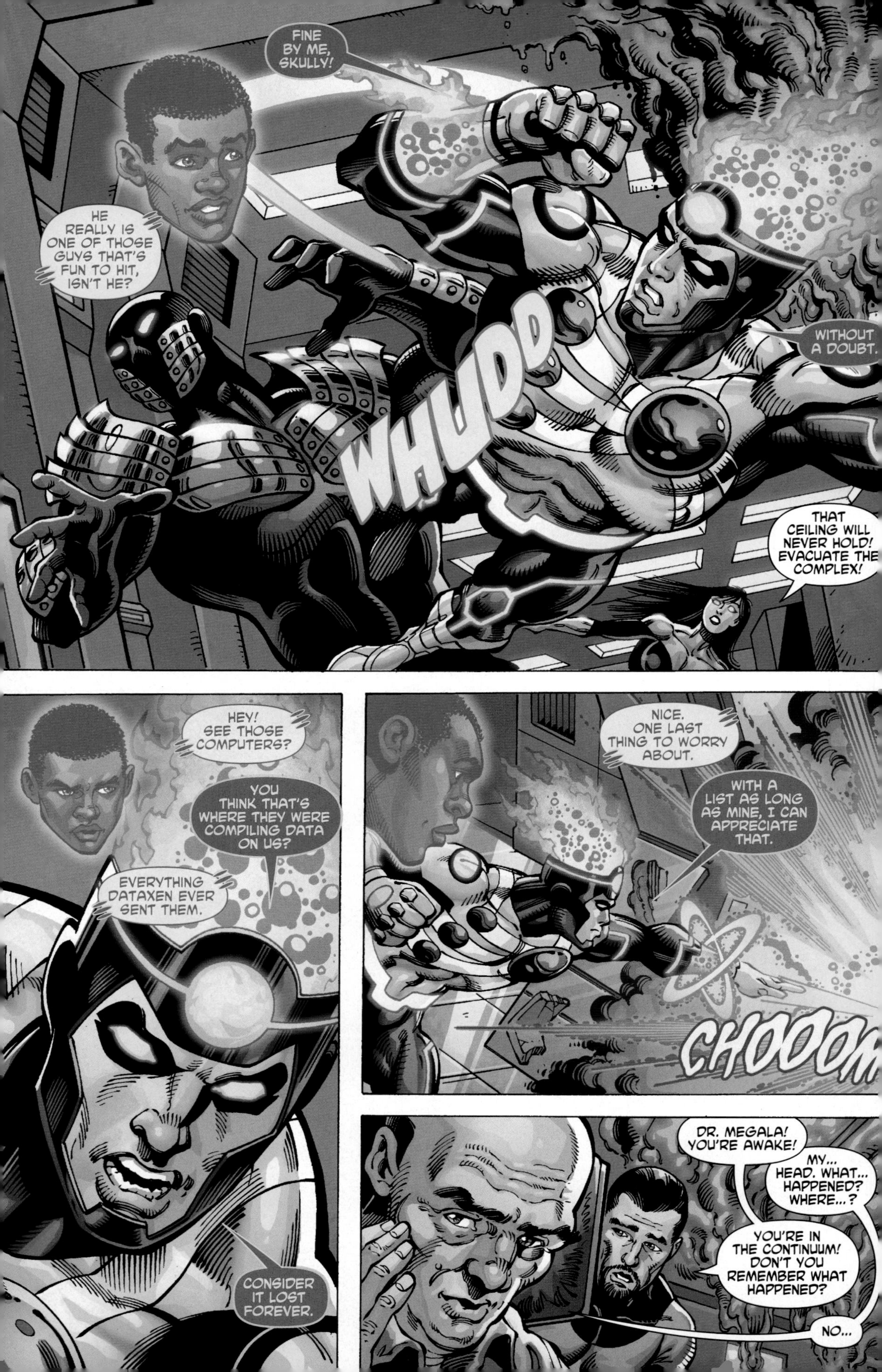
FINE BY ME, SKULLY!
HE REALLY IS ONE OF THOSE GUYS THAT'S FUN TO HIT, ISN'T HE?
WHUDD
WITHOUT A DOUBT.
THAT CEILING WILL NEVER HOLD! EVACUATE THE COMPLEX!
HEY! SEE THOSE COMPUTERS?
YOU THINK THAT'S WHERE THEY WERE COMPILING DATA ON US?
EVERYTHING DATAXEN EVER SENT THEM.
CONSIDER IT LOST FOREVER.
NICE. ONE LAST THING TO WORRY ABOUT.
WITH A LIST AS LONG AS MINE, I CAN APPRECIATE THAT.
CHOOOM
DR. MEGALA! YOU'RE AWAKE!
MY... HEAD. WHAT... HAPPENED? WHERE...?
YOU'RE IN THE CONTINUUM! DON'T YOU REMEMBER WHAT HAPPENED?
NO...

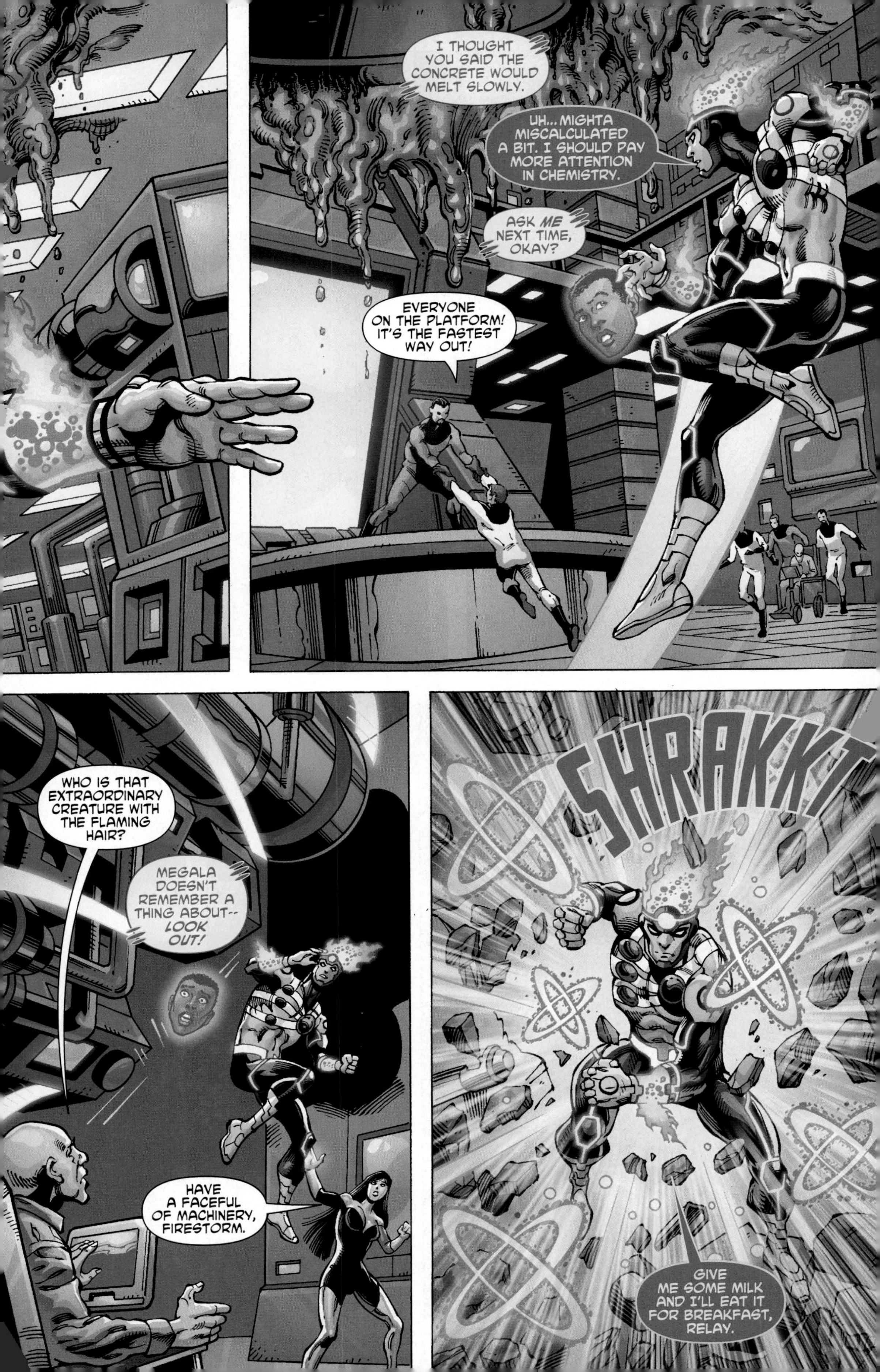
I THOUGHT YOU SAID THE CONCRETE WOULD MELT SLOWLY.
UH... MIGHTA MISCALCULATED A BIT. I SHOULD PAY MORE ATTENTION IN CHEMISTRY.
ASK *ME* NEXT TIME, OKAY?
EVERYONE ON THE PLATFORM! IT'S THE FASTEST WAY OUT!
WHO IS THAT EXTRAORDINARY CREATURE WITH THE FLAMING HAIR?
MEGALA DOESN'T REMEMBER A THING ABOUT-- *LOOK OUT!*
HAVE A FACEFUL OF MACHINERY, FIRESTORM.
SHRAKKT
GIVE ME SOME MILK AND I'LL EAT IT FOR BREAKFAST, RELAY.

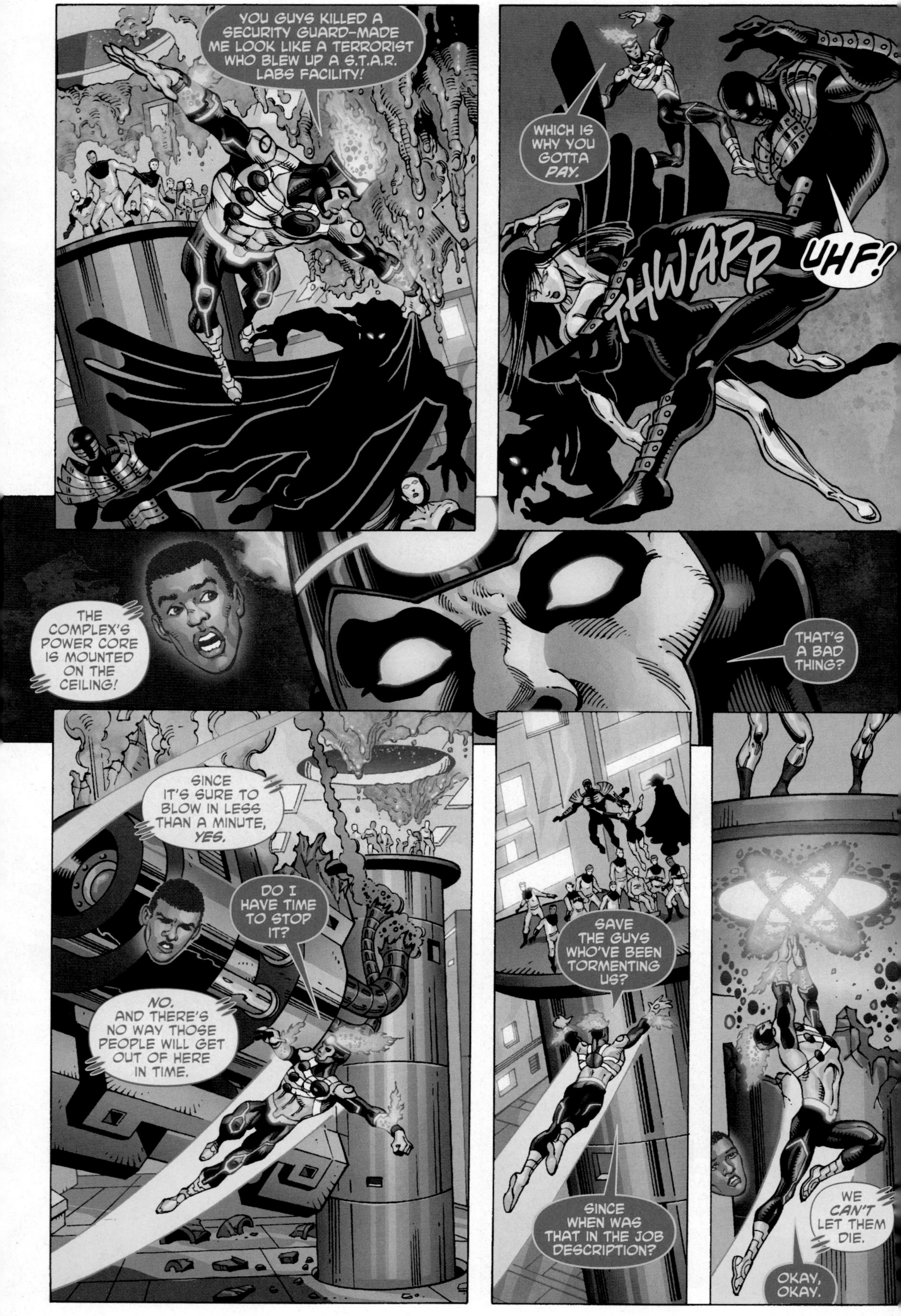
YOU GUYS KILLED A SECURITY GUARD—MADE ME LOOK LIKE A TERRORIST WHO BLEW UP A S.T.A.R. LABS FACILITY!
WHICH IS WHY YOU GOTTA PAY.
THWAPP
UHF!
THE COMPLEX'S POWER CORE IS MOUNTED ON THE CEILING!
THAT'S A BAD THING?
SINCE IT'S SURE TO BLOW IN LESS THAN A MINUTE, YES.
DO I HAVE TIME TO STOP IT?
NO. AND THERE'S NO WAY THOSE PEOPLE WILL GET OUT OF HERE IN TIME.
SAVE THE GUYS WHO'VE BEEN TORMENTING US?
SINCE WHEN WAS THAT IN THE JOB DESCRIPTION?
WE CAN'T LET THEM DIE.
OKAY, OKAY.

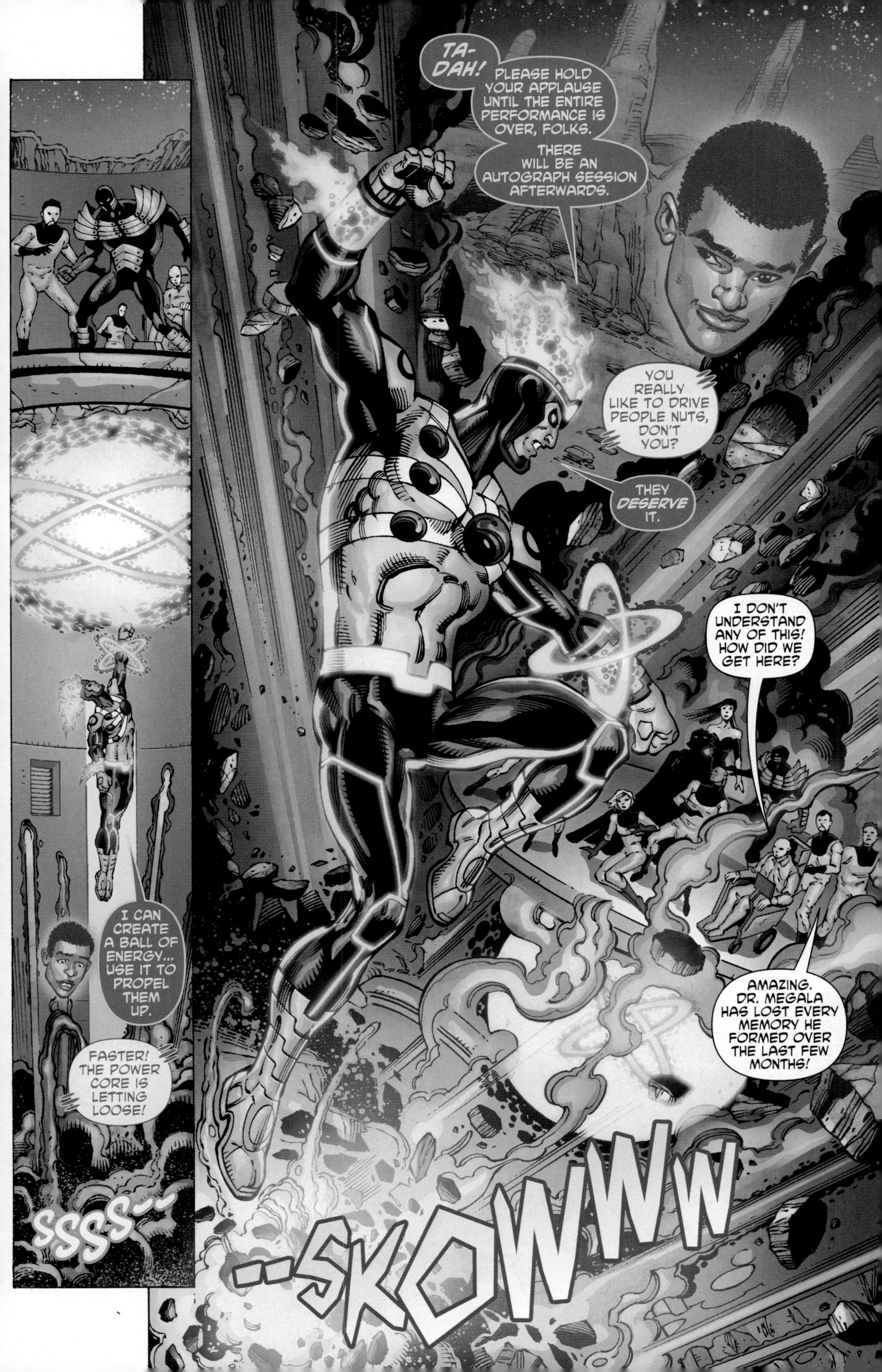
I CAN CREATE A BALL OF ENERGY... USE IT TO PROPEL THEM UP.
FASTER! THE POWER CORE IS LETTING LOOSE!
SSSS--
TA-DAH!
PLEASE HOLD YOUR APPLAUSE UNTIL THE ENTIRE PERFORMANCE IS OVER, FOLKS.
THERE WILL BE AN AUTOGRAPH SESSION AFTERWARDS.
YOU REALLY LIKE TO DRIVE PEOPLE NUTS, DON'T YOU?
THEY DESERVE IT.
I DON'T UNDERSTAND ANY OF THIS! HOW DID WE GET HERE?
AMAZING. DR. MEGALA HAS LOST EVERY MEMORY HE FORMED OVER THE LAST FEW MONTHS!
--SKOWWWW

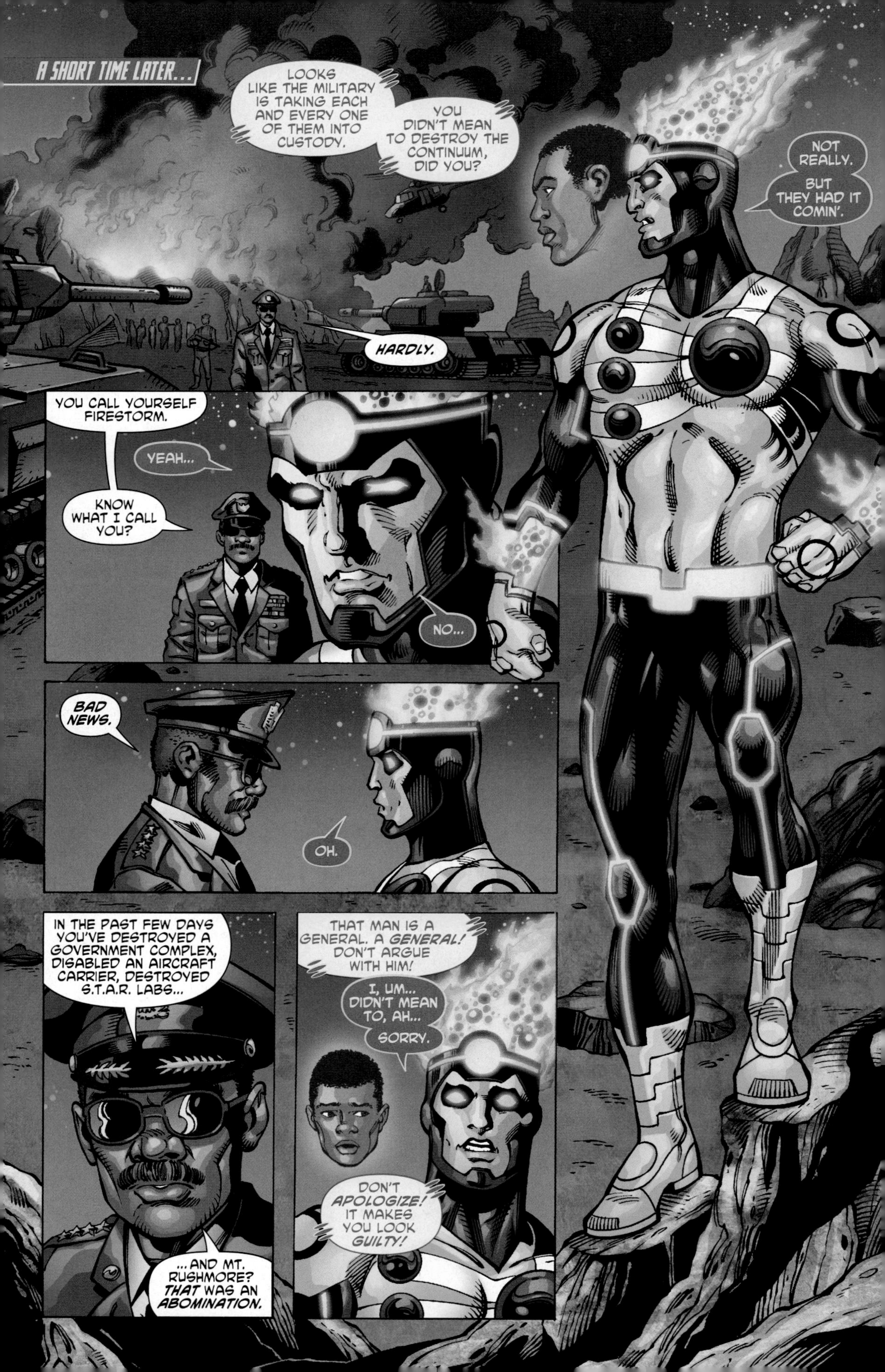
A SHORT TIME LATER...
LOOKS LIKE THE MILITARY IS TAKING EACH AND EVERY ONE OF THEM INTO CUSTODY.
YOU DIDN'T MEAN TO DESTROY THE CONTINUUM, DID YOU?
NOT REALLY. BUT THEY HAD IT COMIN'.
HARDLY.
YOU CALL YOURSELF FIRESTORM.
YEAH...
KNOW WHAT I CALL YOU?
NO...
BAD NEWS.
OH.
IN THE PAST FEW DAYS YOU'VE DESTROYED A GOVERNMENT COMPLEX, DISABLED AN AIRCRAFT CARRIER, DESTROYED S.T.A.R. LABS...
...AND MT. RUSHMORE? THAT WAS AN ABOMINATION.
THAT MAN IS A GENERAL. A GENERAL! DON'T ARGUE WITH HIM!
I, UM... DIDN'T MEAN TO, AH...
SORRY.
DON'T APOLOGIZE! IT MAKES YOU LOOK GUILTY!

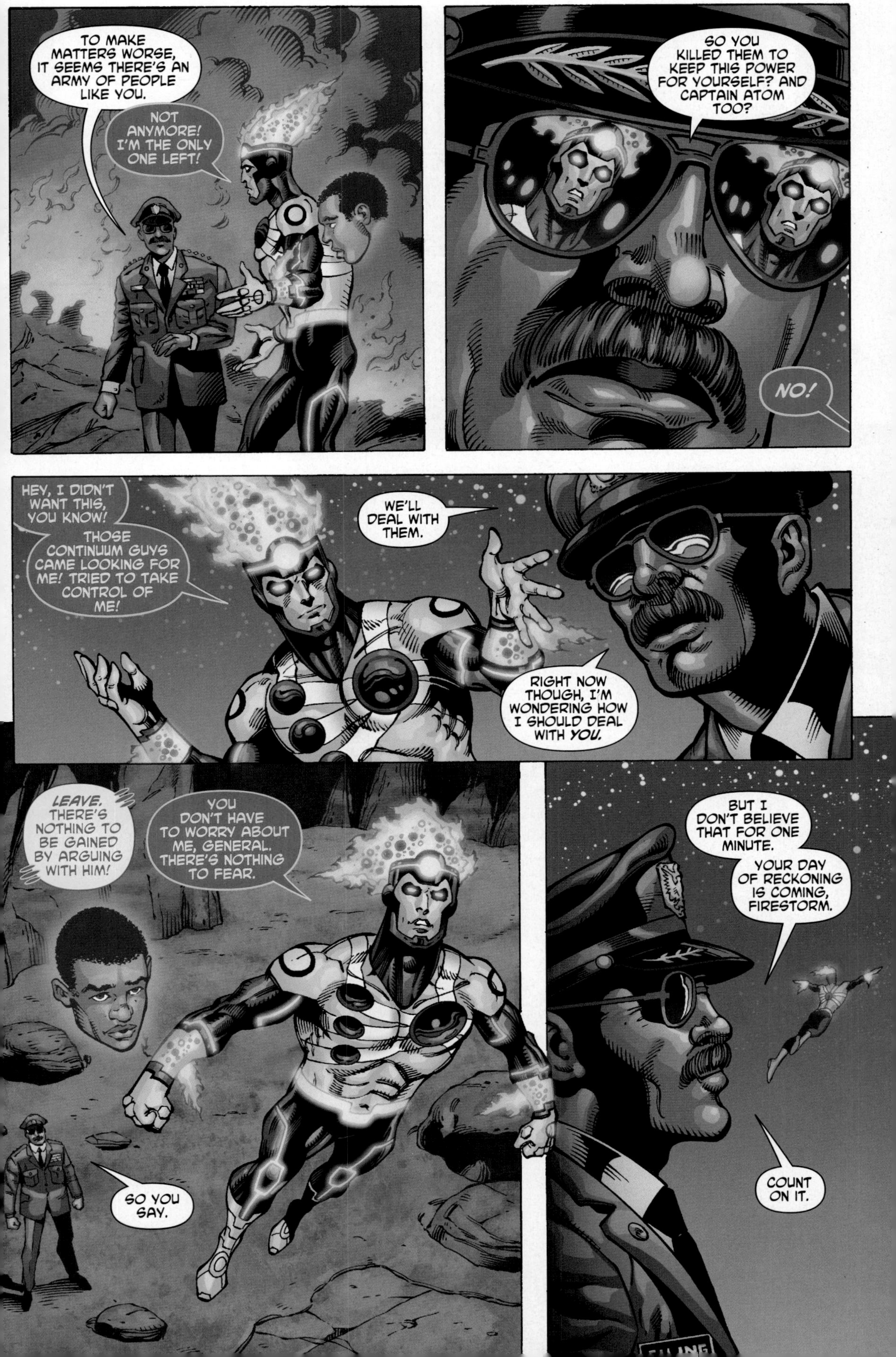

TO MAKE MATTERS WORSE, IT SEEMS THERE'S AN ARMY OF PEOPLE LIKE YOU.
NOT ANYMORE! I'M THE ONLY ONE LEFT!
SO YOU KILLED THEM TO KEEP THIS POWER FOR YOURSELF? AND CAPTAIN ATOM TOO?
NO!
HEY, I DIDN'T WANT THIS, YOU KNOW!
THOSE CONTINUUM GUYS CAME LOOKING FOR ME! TRIED TO TAKE CONTROL OF ME!
WE'LL DEAL WITH THEM.
RIGHT NOW THOUGH, I'M WONDERING HOW I SHOULD DEAL WITH *YOU.*
LEAVE. THERE'S NOTHING TO BE GAINED BY ARGUING WITH HIM!
YOU DON'T HAVE TO WORRY ABOUT ME, GENERAL. THERE'S NOTHING TO FEAR.
SO YOU SAY.
BUT I DON'T BELIEVE THAT FOR ONE MINUTE.
YOUR DAY OF RECKONING IS COMING, FIRESTORM.
COUNT ON IT.

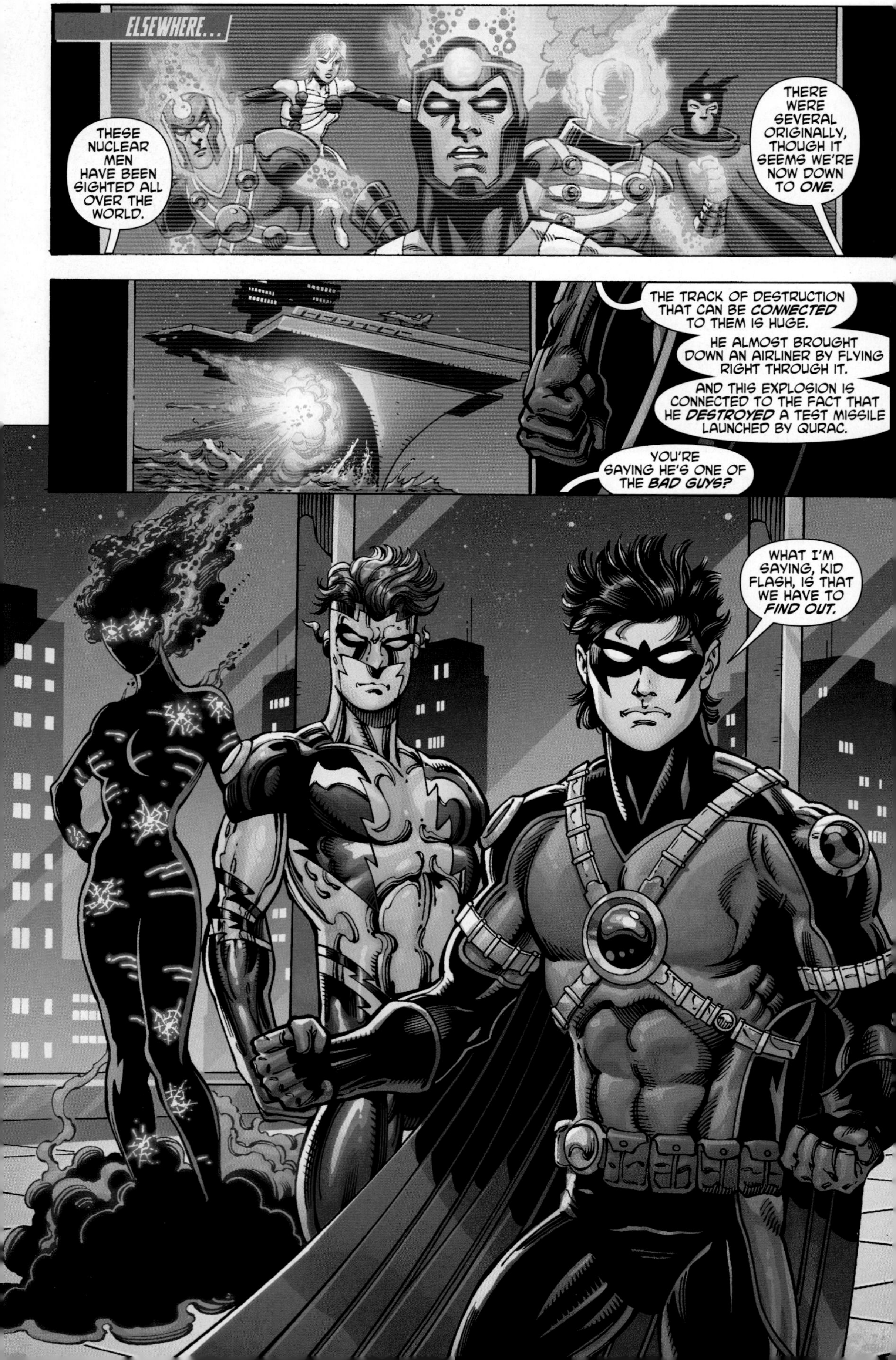
ELSEWHERE...
THESE NUCLEAR MEN HAVE BEEN SIGHTED ALL OVER THE WORLD.
THERE WERE SEVERAL ORIGINALLY, THOUGH IT SEEMS WE'RE NOW DOWN TO ONE.
THE TRACK OF DESTRUCTION THAT CAN BE CONNECTED TO THEM IS HUGE.
HE ALMOST BROUGHT DOWN AN AIRLINER BY FLYING RIGHT THROUGH IT.
AND THIS EXPLOSION IS CONNECTED TO THE FACT THAT HE DESTROYED A TEST MISSILE LAUNCHED BY QURAC.
YOU'RE SAYING HE'S ONE OF THE BAD GUYS?
WHAT I'M SAYING, KID FLASH, IS THAT WE HAVE TO FIND OUT.

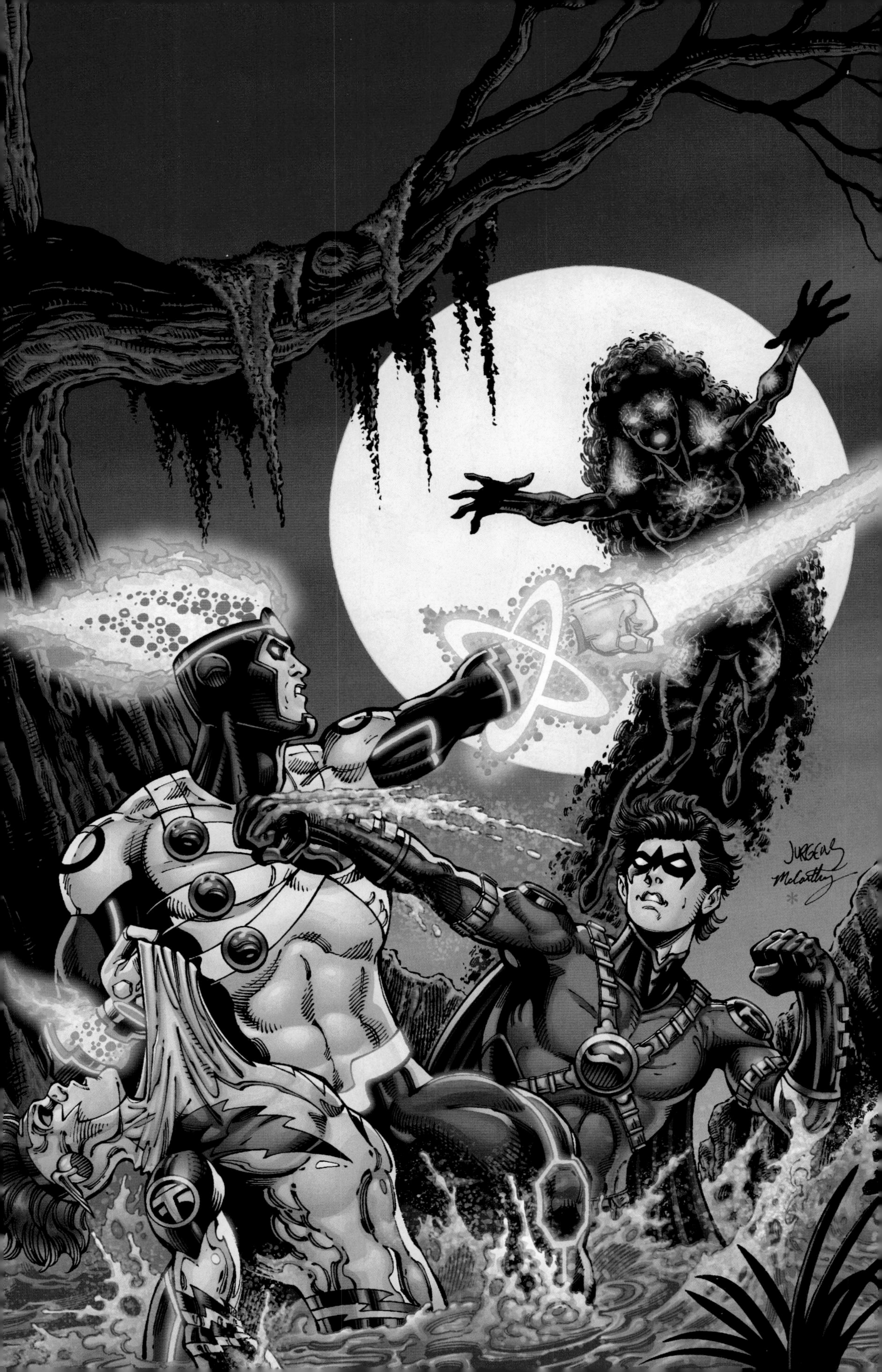

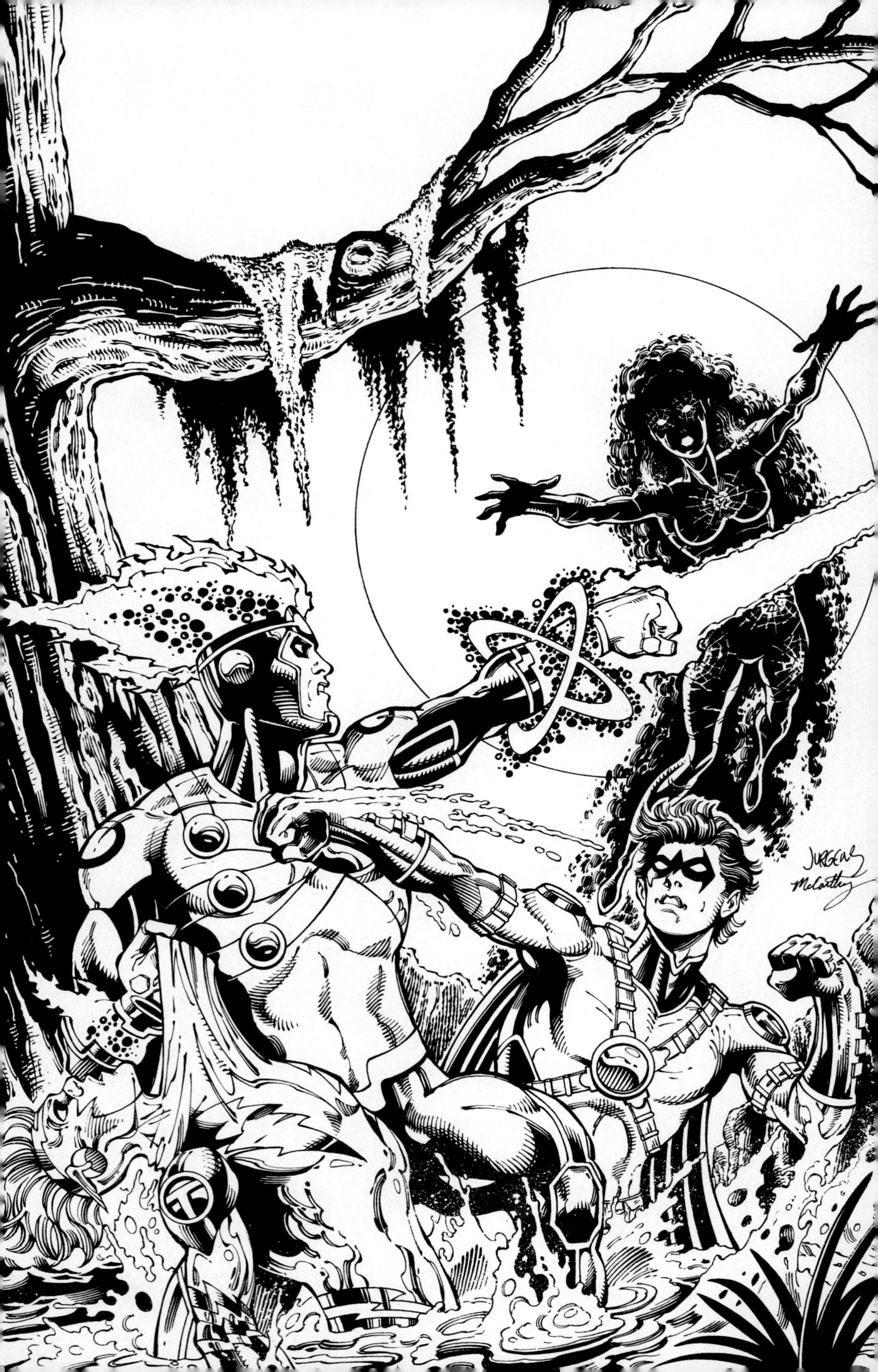
JURGENS
McCarthy

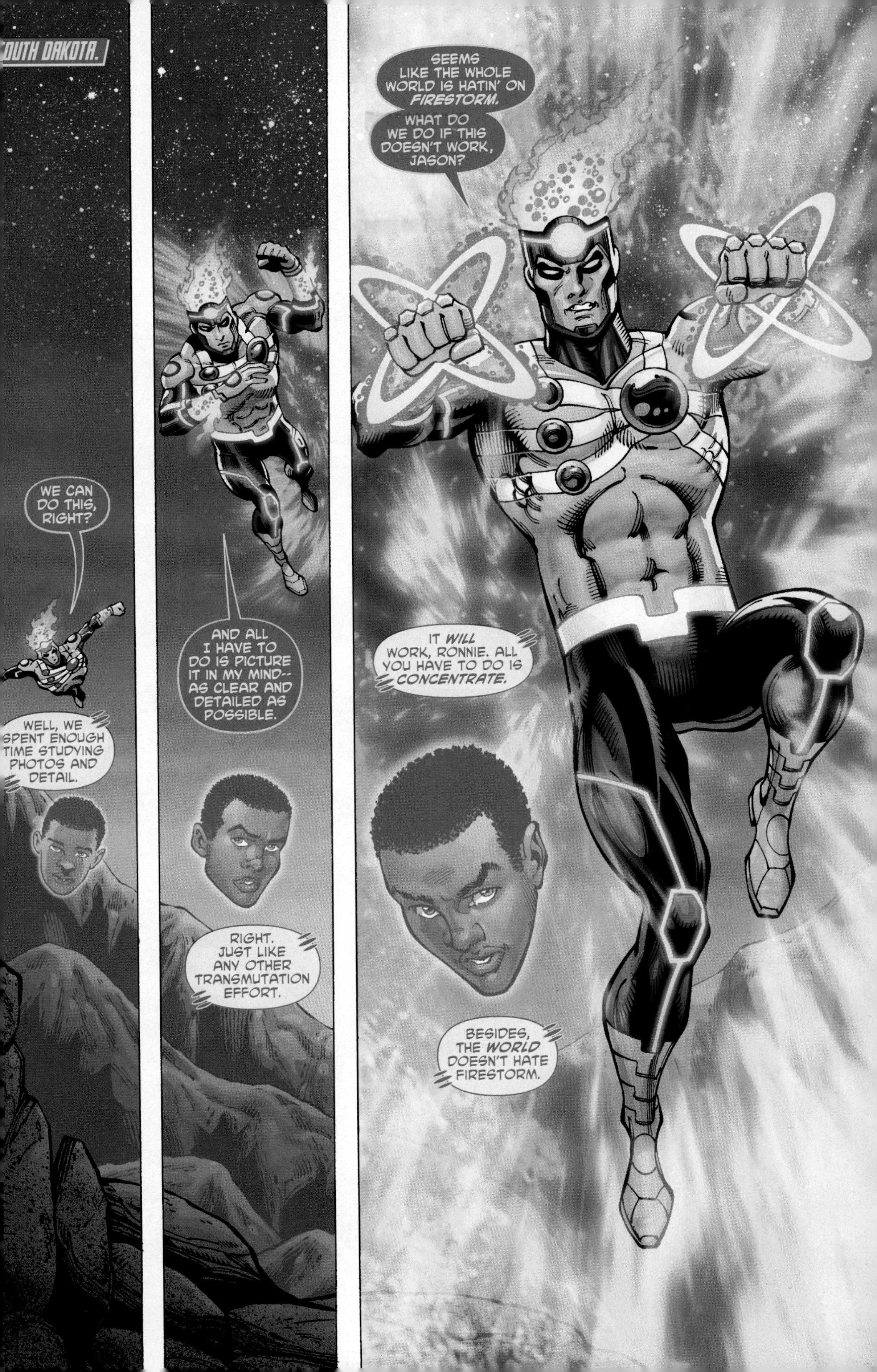
SOUTH DAKOTA.
WE CAN DO THIS, RIGHT?
WELL, WE SPENT ENOUGH TIME STUDYING PHOTOS AND DETAIL.
AND ALL I HAVE TO DO IS PICTURE IT IN MY MIND-- AS CLEAR AND DETAILED AS POSSIBLE.
RIGHT. JUST LIKE ANY OTHER TRANSMUTATION EFFORT.
SEEMS LIKE THE WHOLE WORLD IS HATIN' ON FIRESTORM.
WHAT DO WE DO IF THIS DOESN'T WORK, JASON?
IT WILL WORK, RONNIE. ALL YOU HAVE TO DO IS CONCENTRATE.
BESIDES, THE WORLD DOESN'T HATE FIRESTORM.

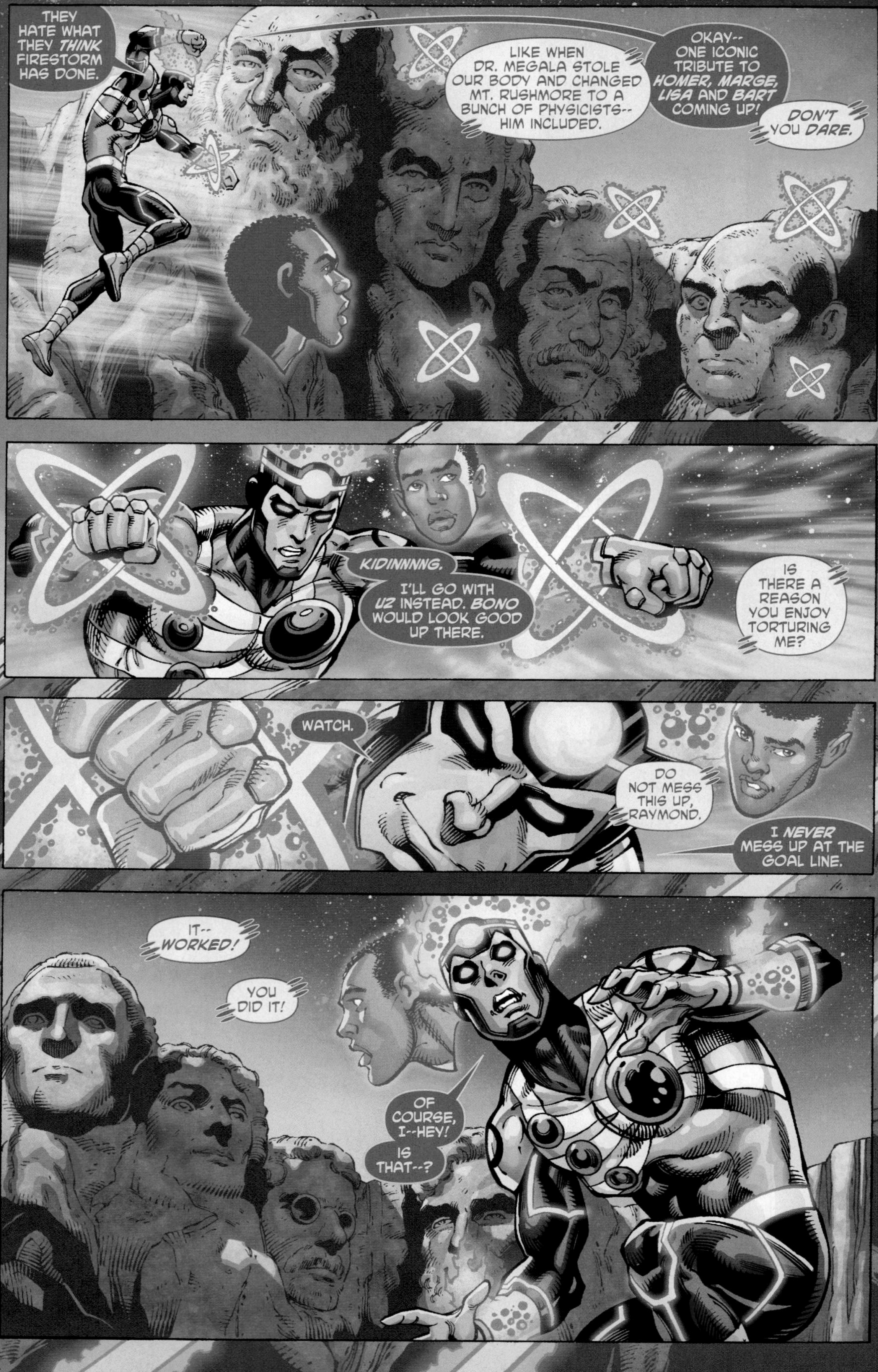
THEY HATE WHAT THEY *THINK* FIRESTORM HAS DONE.
LIKE WHEN DR. MEGALA STOLE OUR BODY AND CHANGED MT. RUSHMORE TO A BUNCH OF PHYSICISTS-- HIM INCLUDED.
OKAY-- ONE ICONIC TRIBUTE TO *HOMER, MARGE, LISA* AND *BART* COMING UP!
DON'T YOU *DARE.*
KIDINNNNG.
I'LL GO WITH *U2* INSTEAD. *BONO* WOULD LOOK GOOD UP THERE.
IS THERE A REASON YOU ENJOY TORTURING ME?
WATCH.
DO NOT MESS THIS UP, RAYMOND.
I *NEVER* MESS UP AT THE GOAL LINE.
IT-- *WORKED!*
YOU DID IT!
OF COURSE, I--HEY!
IS THAT--?

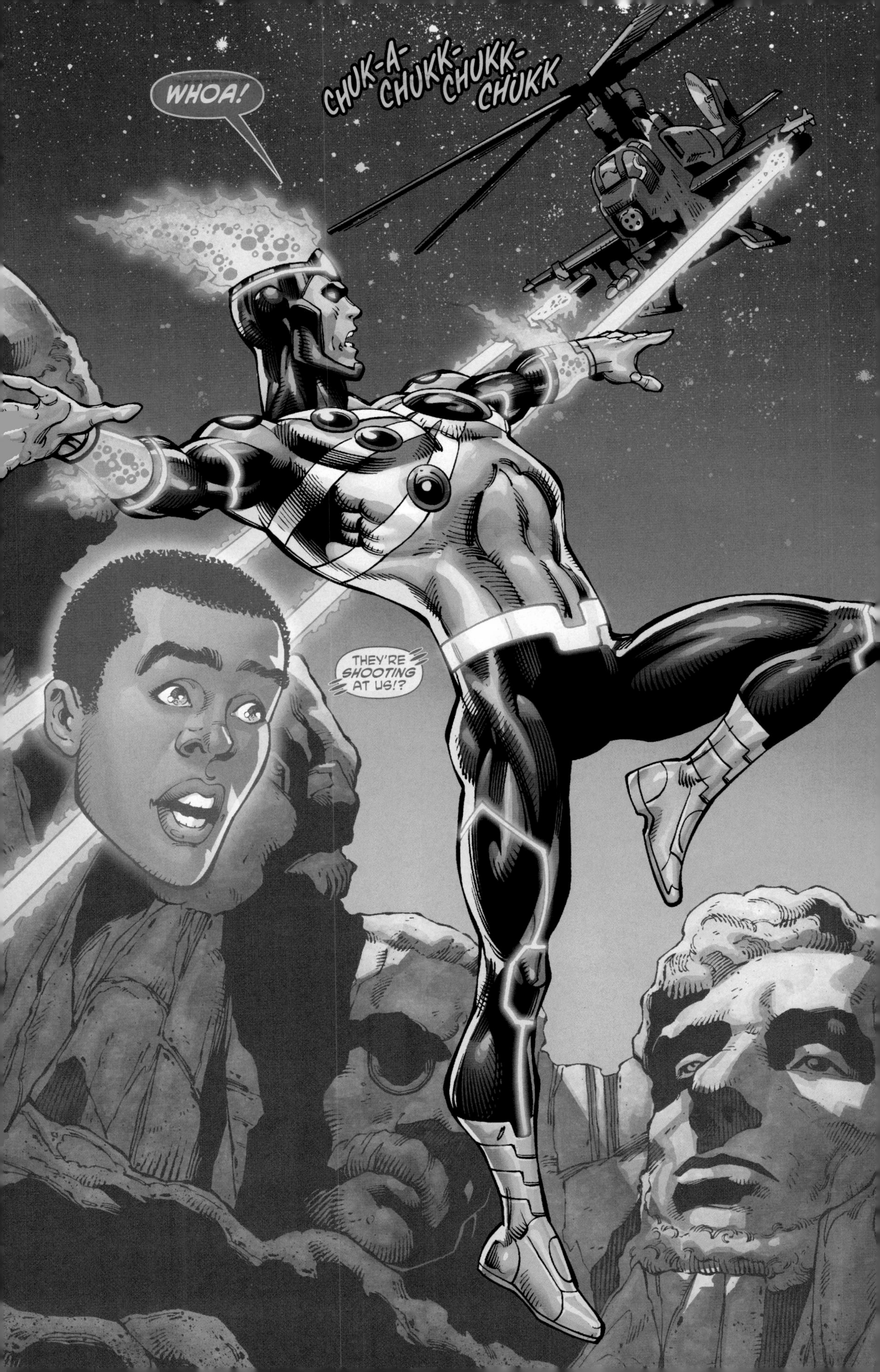
WHOA!
CHUK-A-CHUKK-CHUKK-CHUKK
THEY'RE SHOOTING AT US!?

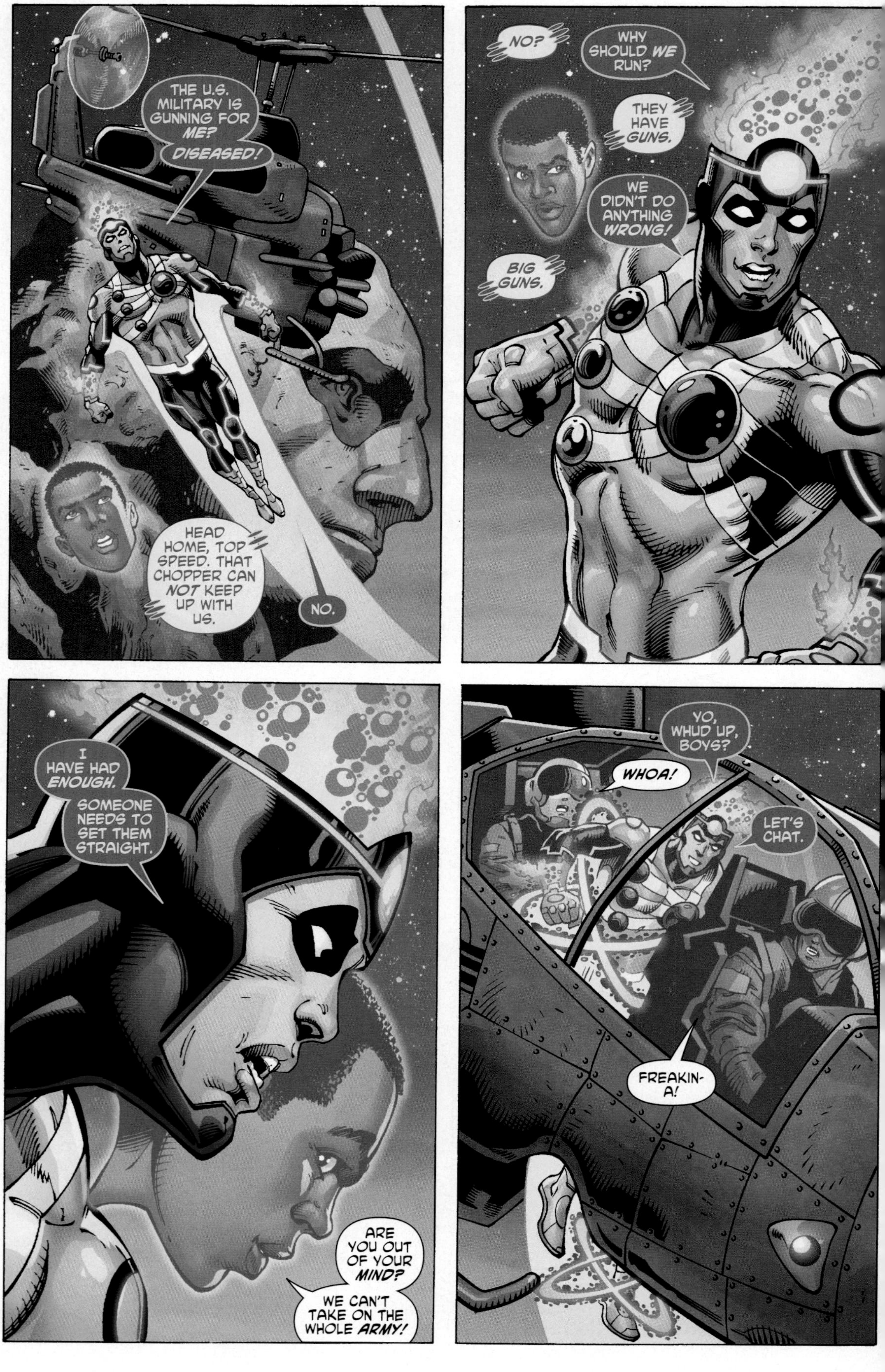
THE U.S. MILITARY IS GUNNING FOR ME? DISEASED!
HEAD HOME, TOP SPEED. THAT CHOPPER CAN NOT KEEP UP WITH US.
NO.
NO?
WHY SHOULD WE RUN?
THEY HAVE GUNS.
WE DIDN'T DO ANYTHING WRONG!
BIG GUNS.
I HAVE HAD ENOUGH.
SOMEONE NEEDS TO SET THEM STRAIGHT.
ARE YOU OUT OF YOUR MIND?
WE CAN'T TAKE ON THE WHOLE ARMY!
YO, WHUD UP, BOYS?
WHOA!
LET'S CHAT.
FREAKIN-A!

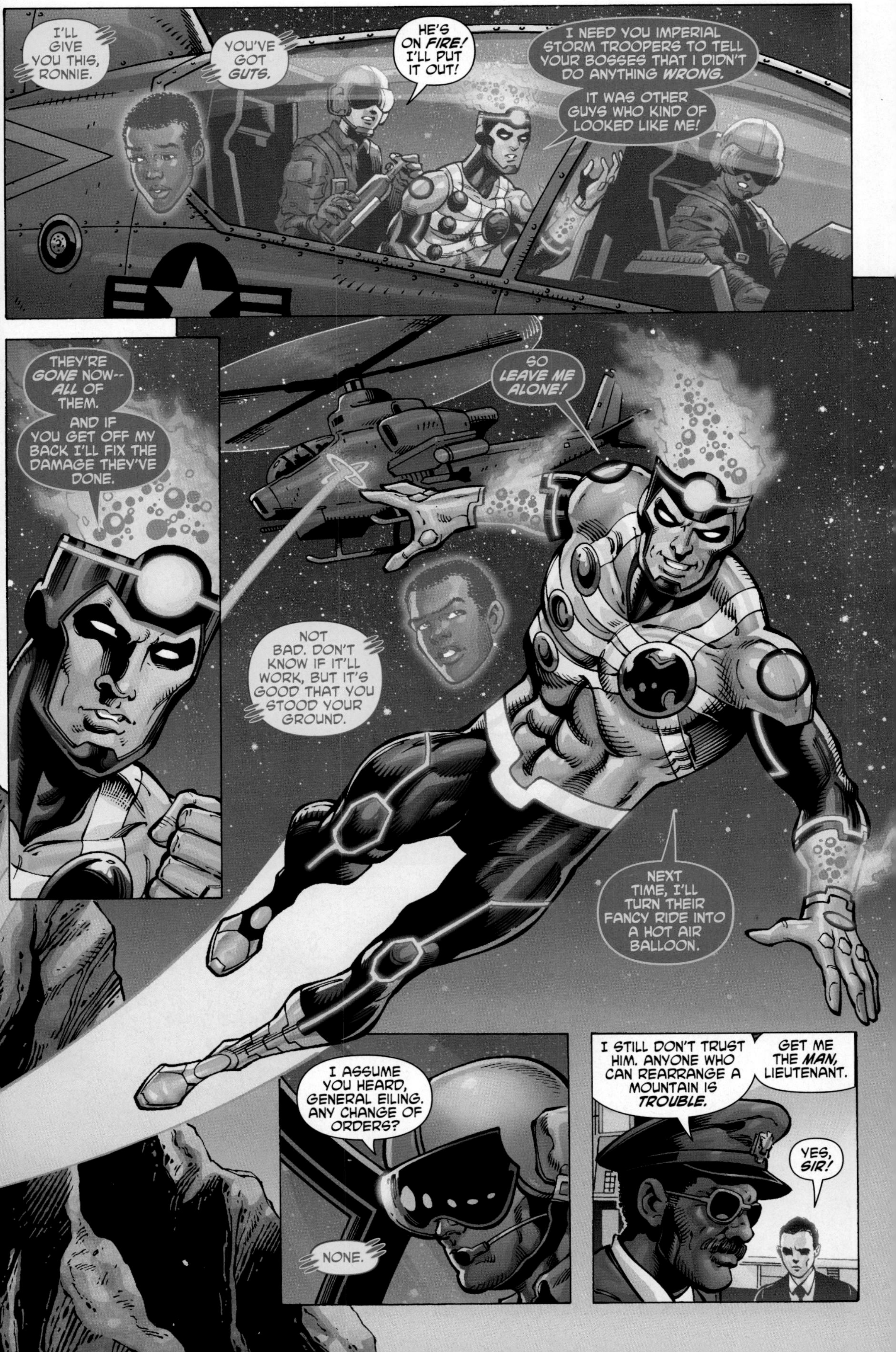
I'LL GIVE YOU THIS, RONNIE.
YOU'VE GOT GUTS.
HE'S ON FIRE! I'LL PUT IT OUT!
I NEED YOU IMPERIAL STORM TROOPERS TO TELL YOUR BOSSES THAT I DIDN'T DO ANYTHING WRONG.
IT WAS OTHER GUYS WHO KIND OF LOOKED LIKE ME!
THEY'RE GONE NOW-- ALL OF THEM.
AND IF YOU GET OFF MY BACK I'LL FIX THE DAMAGE THEY'VE DONE.
SO LEAVE ME ALONE!
NOT BAD. DON'T KNOW IF IT'LL WORK, BUT IT'S GOOD THAT YOU STOOD YOUR GROUND.
NEXT TIME, I'LL TURN THEIR FANCY RIDE INTO A HOT AIR BALLOON.
I ASSUME YOU HEARD, GENERAL EILING. ANY CHANGE OF ORDERS?
NONE.
I STILL DON'T TRUST HIM. ANYONE WHO CAN REARRANGE A MOUNTAIN IS TROUBLE.
GET ME THE MAN, LIEUTENANT.
YES, SIR!

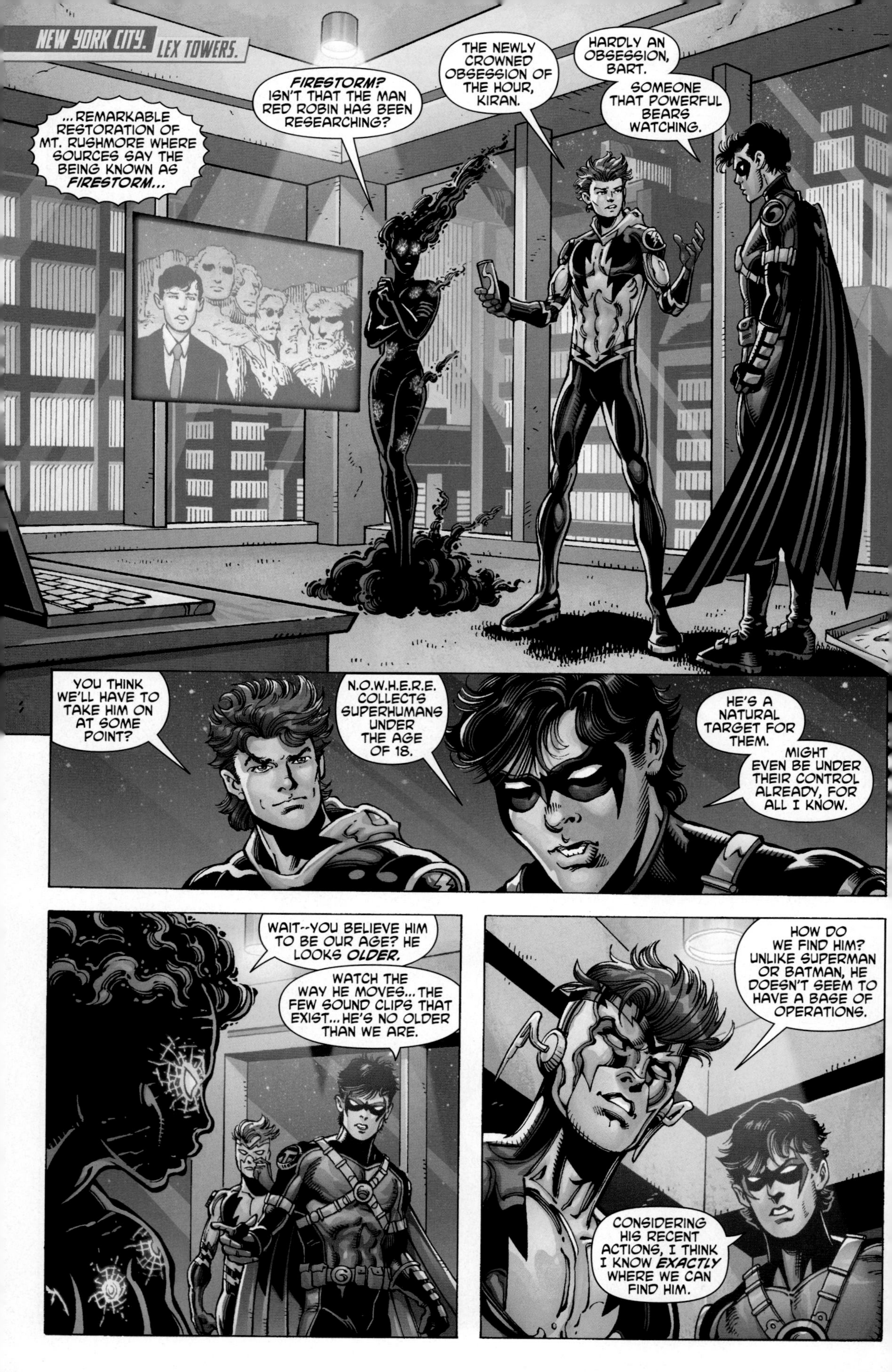
NEW YORK CITY.
LEX TOWERS.
...REMARKABLE RESTORATION OF MT. RUSHMORE WHERE SOURCES SAY THE BEING KNOWN AS *FIRESTORM*...
FIRESTORM? ISN'T THAT THE MAN RED ROBIN HAS BEEN RESEARCHING?
THE NEWLY CROWNED OBSESSION OF THE HOUR, KIRAN.
HARDLY AN OBSESSION, BART.
SOMEONE THAT POWERFUL BEARS WATCHING.
YOU THINK WE'LL HAVE TO TAKE HIM ON AT SOME POINT?
N.O.W.H.E.R.E. COLLECTS SUPERHUMANS UNDER THE AGE OF 18.
HE'S A NATURAL TARGET FOR THEM.
MIGHT EVEN BE UNDER THEIR CONTROL ALREADY, FOR ALL I KNOW.
WAIT--YOU BELIEVE HIM TO BE OUR AGE? HE LOOKS *OLDER.*
WATCH THE WAY HE MOVES... THE FEW SOUND CLIPS THAT EXIST... HE'S NO OLDER THAN WE ARE.
HOW DO WE FIND HIM? UNLIKE SUPERMAN OR BATMAN, HE DOESN'T SEEM TO HAVE A BASE OF OPERATIONS.
CONSIDERING HIS RECENT ACTIONS, I THINK I KNOW *EXACTLY* WHERE WE CAN FIND HIM.

JUST A QUICK STOP BEFORE WE HEAD OUT AGAIN. I'M *HUNGRY*.

YOU'RE *ALWAYS* HUNGRY.

THOUGH I AM TOO, COME TO THINK OF IT.

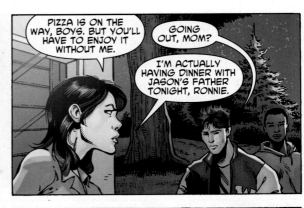

PIZZA IS ON THE WAY, BOYS. BUT YOU'LL HAVE TO ENJOY IT WITHOUT ME.

GOING OUT, MOM?

I'M ACTUALLY HAVING DINNER WITH JASON'S FATHER TONIGHT, RONNIE.

HE'S A SPECIAL MAN, JASON. YOU'RE LUCKY TO HAVE HIM FOR A FATHER.

UM... YEAH.

TONYA IS WAITING FOR YOU BOYS IN THE REC ROOM.

ABOUT TIME YOU GOT BACK! YOU WON'T *BELIEVE* WHAT HAPPENED!

GOOD OR BAD?

WELL... THAT'S KIND OF COMPLICATED.

THEN IT'S BAD. COMPLICATED IS *NEVER* GOOD.

REMEMBER THAT EUROPEAN HISTORY PAPER I WROTE FOR YOU SO FIRESTORM COULD TAKE CARE OF BUSINESS?

MRS. SCHMIDT FOUND OUT, DIDN'T SHE? I'M *DOOMED*.

NO! SHE LOVED IT SO MUCH SHE SUBMITTED IT TO THE YOUNG SCHOLARS COMPETITION!

IT *WON!* FIRST *PLACE!*

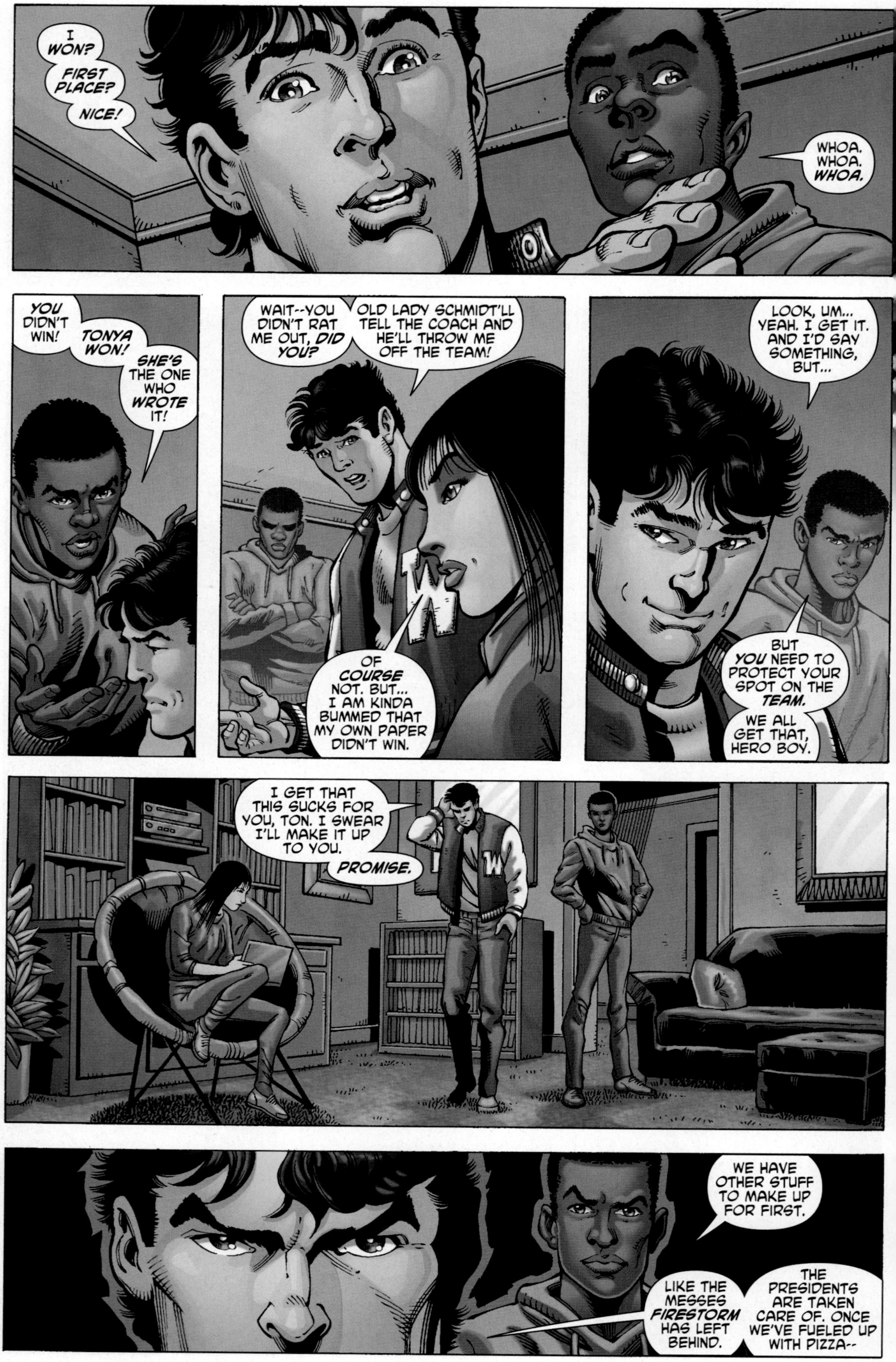
I WON? FIRST PLACE? NICE!
WHOA. WHOA. WHOA.
YOU DIDN'T WIN! TONYA WON! SHE'S THE ONE WHO WROTE IT!
WAIT--YOU DIDN'T RAT ME OUT, DID YOU?
OLD LADY SCHMIDT'LL TELL THE COACH AND HE'LL THROW ME OFF THE TEAM!
OF COURSE NOT. BUT... I AM KINDA BUMMED THAT MY OWN PAPER DIDN'T WIN.
LOOK, UM... YEAH. I GET IT. AND I'D SAY SOMETHING, BUT...
BUT YOU NEED TO PROTECT YOUR SPOT ON THE TEAM.
WE ALL GET THAT, HERO BOY.
I GET THAT THIS SUCKS FOR YOU, TON. I SWEAR I'LL MAKE IT UP TO YOU.
PROMISE.
WE HAVE OTHER STUFF TO MAKE UP FOR FIRST.
LIKE THE MESSES FIRESTORM HAS LEFT BEHIND.
THE PRESIDENTS ARE TAKEN CARE OF. ONCE WE'VE FUELED UP WITH PIZZA--

"--WE'RE OFF TO S.T.A.R. LABS."

IT WASN'T OUR FAULT IT BLEW UP.

TRUE. JUST THE BYPRODUCT OF US TRYING TO ESCAPE THE CREEPS WHO ATTACKED US THERE.

BUT IF WE CAN FIX IT, JOHNNY LAW WILL GET OFF OUR BACKS.

EXACTLY. THERE ARE ENOUGH REAL SUPER VILLAINS FOR THEM TO WORRY ABOUT.

POLICE LINE DO NOT

RE-FORMING A MOUNTAIN SCULPTURE IS ONE THING. RECONSTRUCTING AN ENTIRE BUILDING? I DON'T KNOW ABOUT THIS, RONNIE.

CROSS | POLICE LINE DO NOT CROSS POLICE LIN

LINE DO NOT CROSS POLICE / LINE D

WHAT CAN BE SO HARD?

LIKE YOU SAID BEFORE-- ALL I HAVE TO DO IS PICTURE IT IN MY MIND AND--VOILA! GOOD AS--

--NEW?!

WHADDAYA KNOW? *RED ROBIN* WAS RIGHT AGAIN!

'COURSE, IT'S NOT LIKE HE'S EVER *WRONG.*

LET'S SEE YOUR HAIR BURN NOW, FIREBOY.

SPLASSSH

WHO THE HELL--?

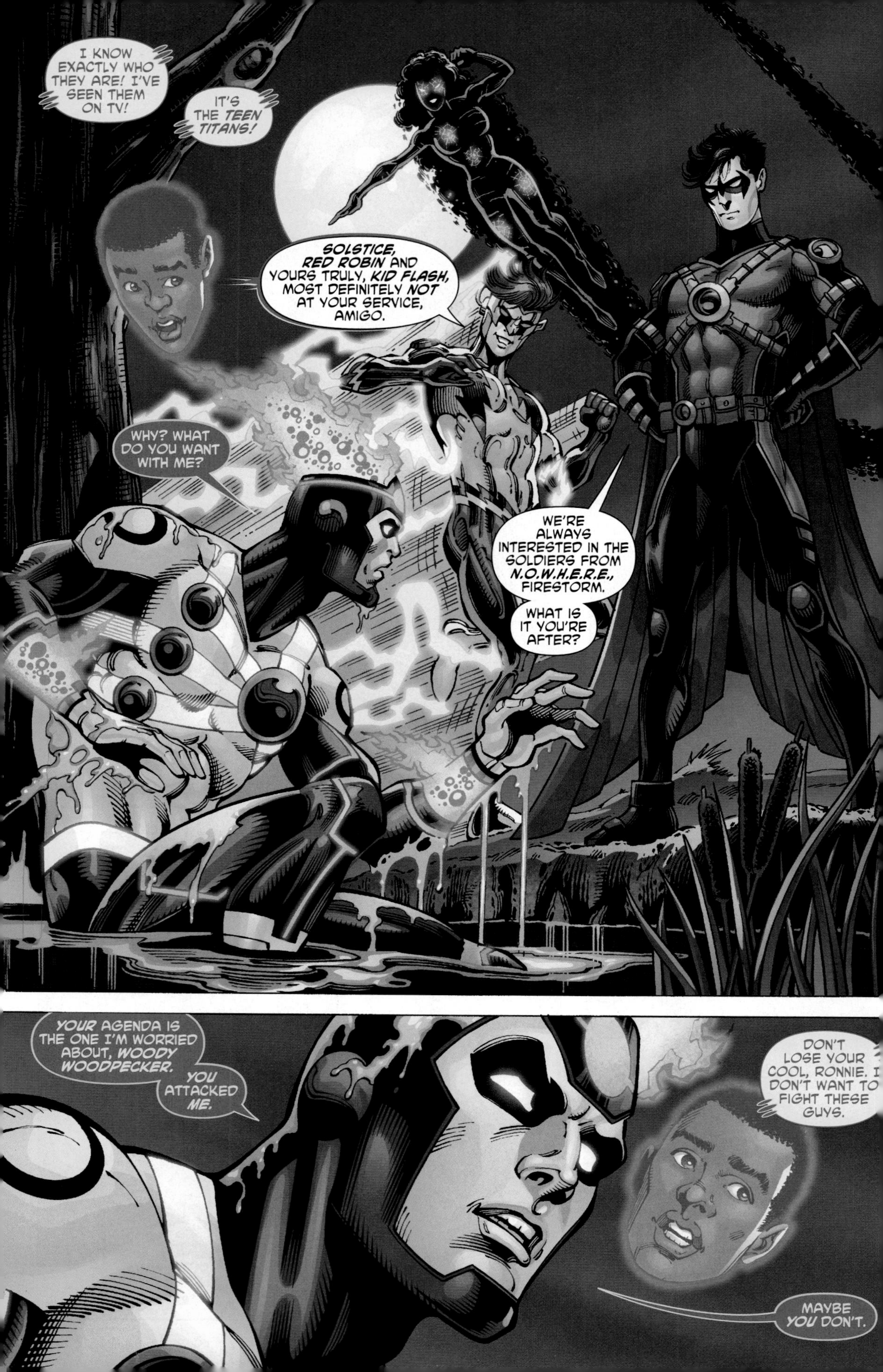
I KNOW EXACTLY WHO THEY ARE! I'VE SEEN THEM ON TV!
IT'S THE TEEN TITANS!
SOLSTICE, RED ROBIN AND YOURS TRULY, KID FLASH, MOST DEFINITELY NOT AT YOUR SERVICE, AMIGO.
WHY? WHAT DO YOU WANT WITH ME?
WE'RE ALWAYS INTERESTED IN THE SOLDIERS FROM N.O.W.H.E.R.E., FIRESTORM.
WHAT IS IT YOU'RE AFTER?
YOUR AGENDA IS THE ONE I'M WORRIED ABOUT, WOODY WOODPECKER.
YOU ATTACKED ME.
DON'T LOSE YOUR COOL, RONNIE. I DON'T WANT TO FIGHT THESE GUYS.
MAYBE YOU DON'T.

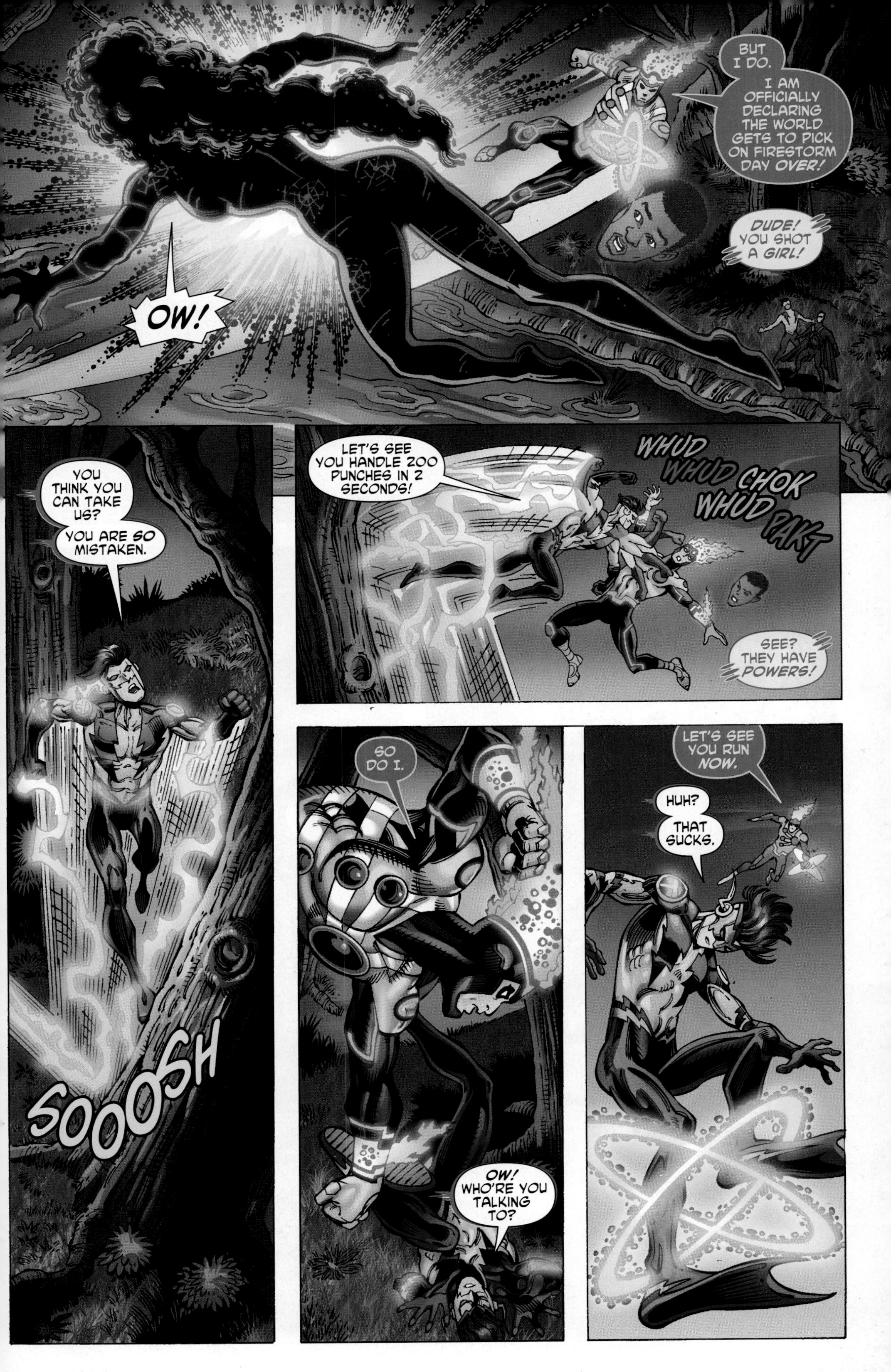
BUT I DO.
I AM OFFICIALLY DECLARING THE WORLD GETS TO PICK ON FIRESTORM DAY OVER!
DUDE! YOU SHOT A GIRL!
OW!
YOU THINK YOU CAN TAKE US?
YOU ARE SO MISTAKEN.
SOOOSH
LET'S SEE YOU HANDLE 200 PUNCHES IN 2 SECONDS!
WHUD WHUD CHOK WHUD PAKT
SEE? THEY HAVE POWERS!
SO DO I.
OW! WHO'RE YOU TALKING TO?
LET'S SEE YOU RUN NOW.
HUH?
THAT SUCKS.

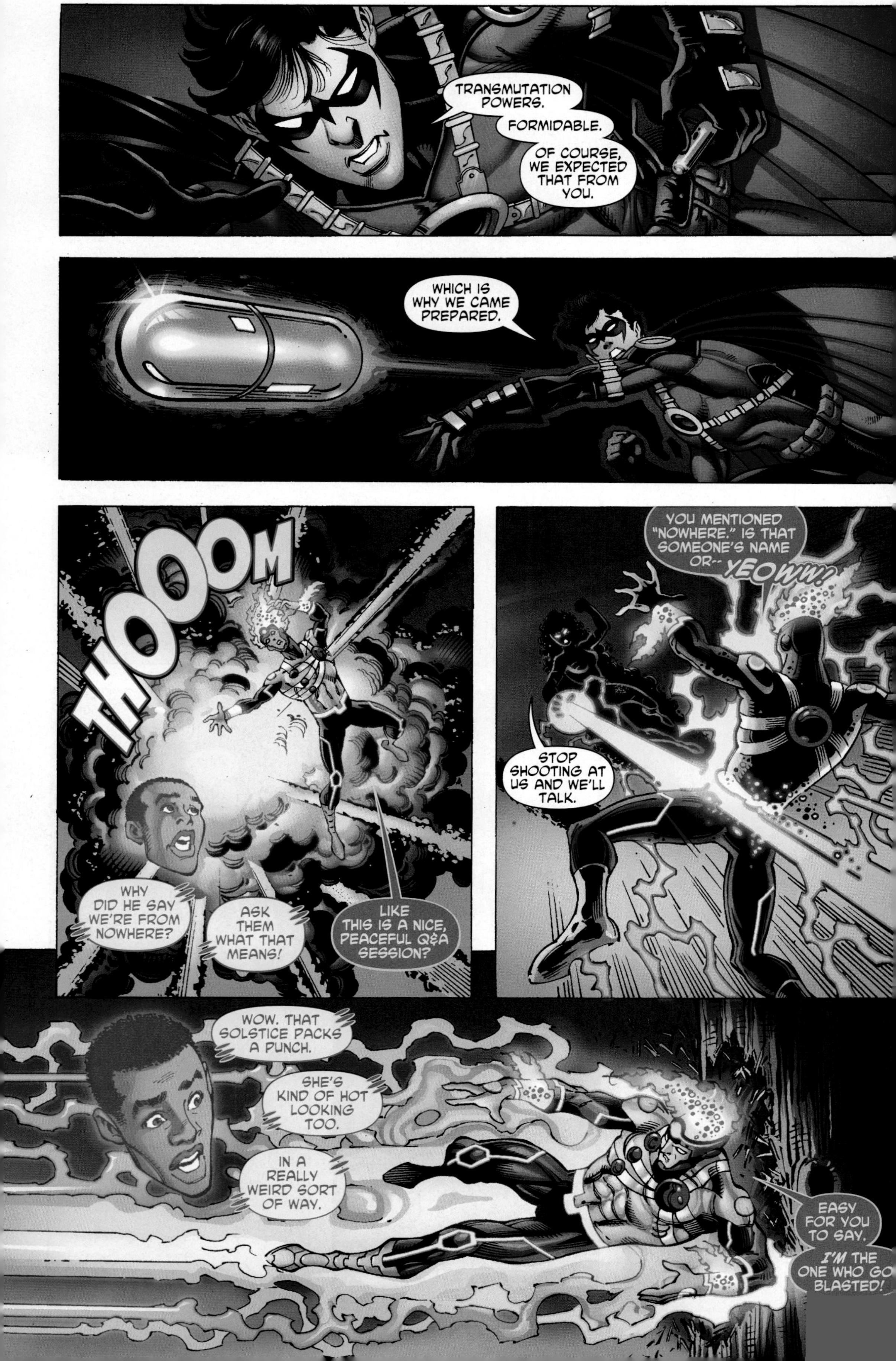
TRANSMUTATION POWERS.
FORMIDABLE.
OF COURSE, WE EXPECTED THAT FROM YOU.
WHICH IS WHY WE CAME PREPARED.
THOOOM
WHY DID HE SAY WE'RE FROM NOWHERE?
ASK THEM WHAT THAT MEANS!
LIKE THIS IS A NICE, PEACEFUL Q&A SESSION?
YOU MENTIONED "NOWHERE." IS THAT SOMEONE'S NAME OR-- YEOWW!
STOP SHOOTING AT US AND WE'LL TALK.
WOW. THAT SOLSTICE PACKS A PUNCH.
SHE'S KIND OF HOT LOOKING TOO.
IN A REALLY WEIRD SORT OF WAY.
EASY FOR YOU TO SAY.
I'M THE ONE WHO GO BLASTED!

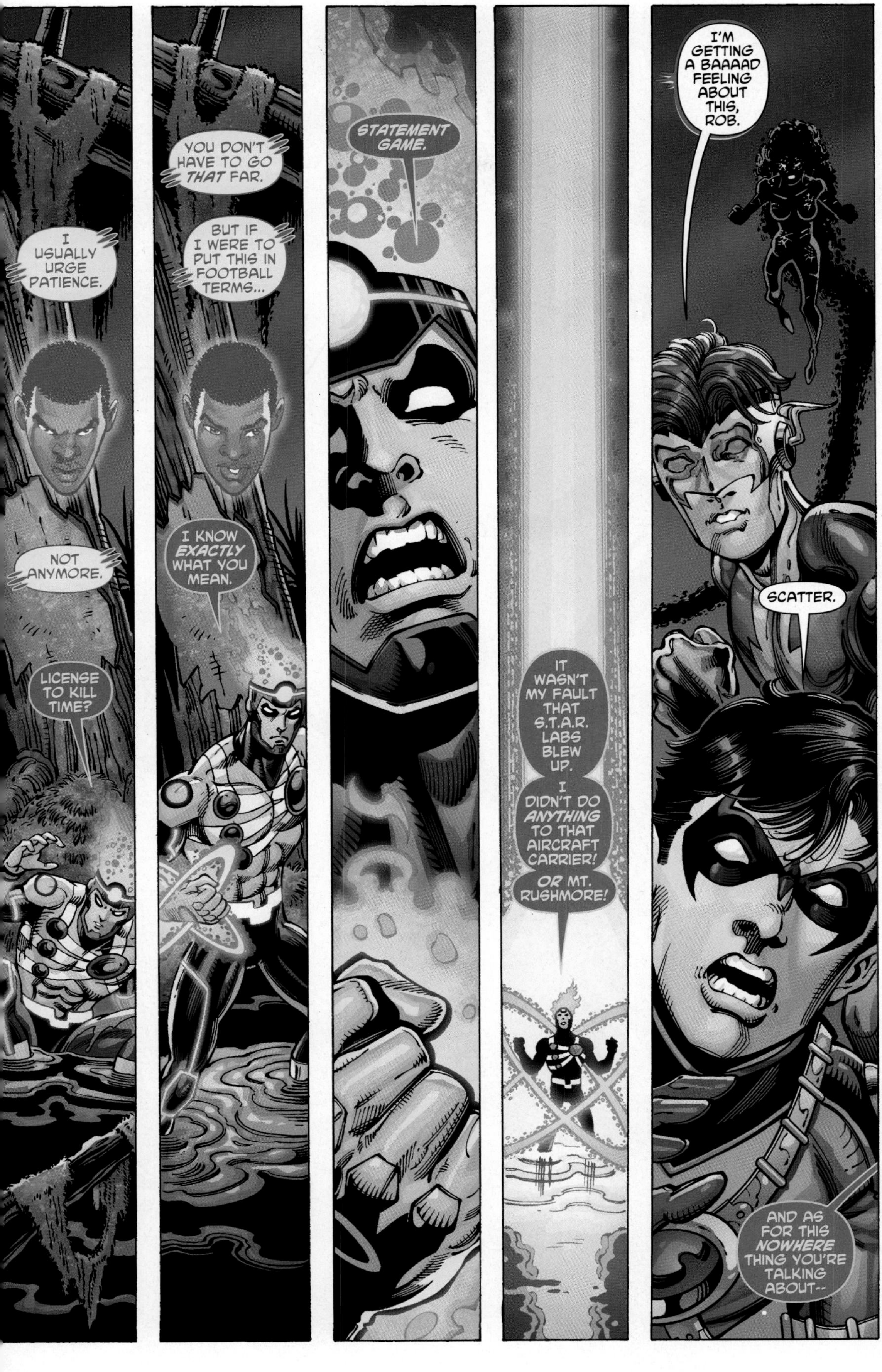
I USUALLY URGE PATIENCE.
NOT ANYMORE.
LICENSE TO KILL TIME?
YOU DON'T HAVE TO GO *THAT* FAR.
BUT IF I WERE TO PUT THIS IN FOOTBALL TERMS...
I KNOW *EXACTLY* WHAT YOU MEAN.
STATEMENT GAME.
IT WASN'T MY FAULT THAT S.T.A.R. LABS BLEW UP.
I DIDN'T DO *ANYTHING* TO THAT AIRCRAFT CARRIER!
OR MT. RUSHMORE!
I'M GETTING A BAAAAD FEELING ABOUT THIS, ROB.
SCATTER.
AND AS FOR THIS *NOWHERE* THING YOU'RE TALKING ABOUT--

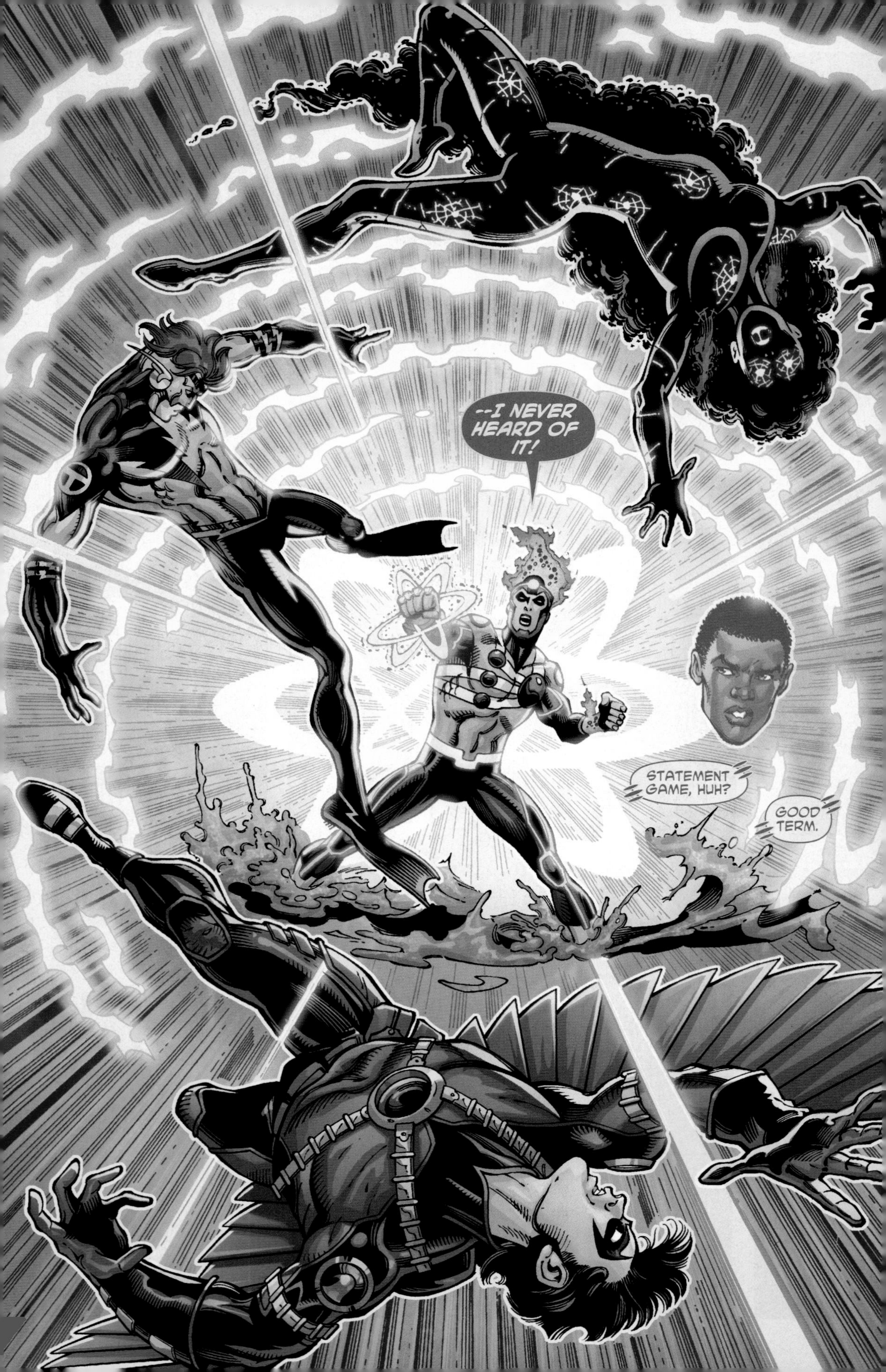
--I NEVER HEARD OF IT!
STATEMENT GAME, HUH?
GOOD TERM.

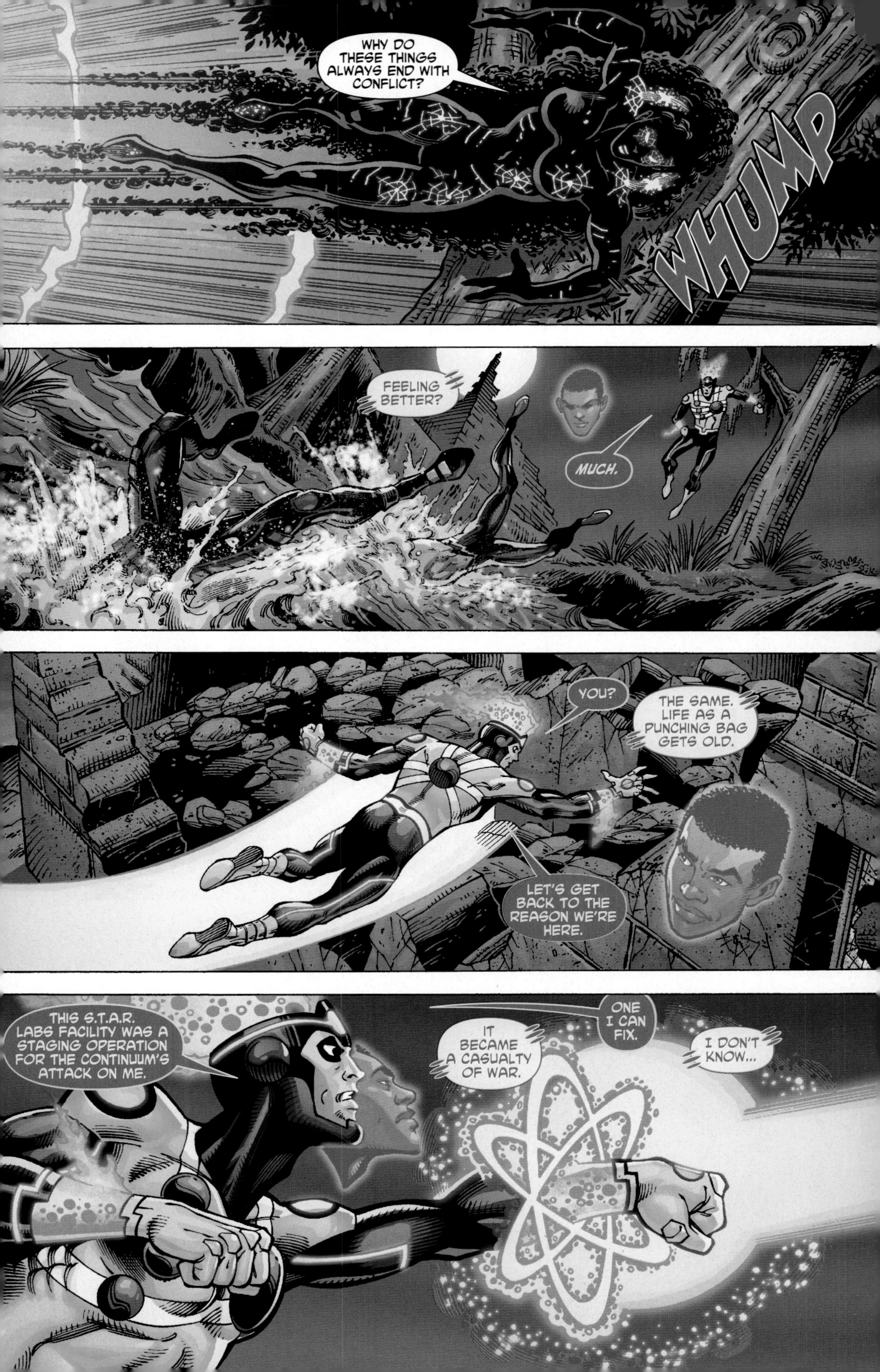
WHY DO THESE THINGS ALWAYS END WITH CONFLICT?
WHUMP
FEELING BETTER?
MUCH.
YOU?
THE SAME. LIFE AS A PUNCHING BAG GETS OLD.
LET'S GET BACK TO THE REASON WE'RE HERE.
THIS S.T.A.R. LABS FACILITY WAS A STAGING OPERATION FOR THE CONTINUUM'S ATTACK ON ME.
IT BECAME A CASUALTY OF WAR.
ONE I CAN FIX.
I DON'T KNOW...

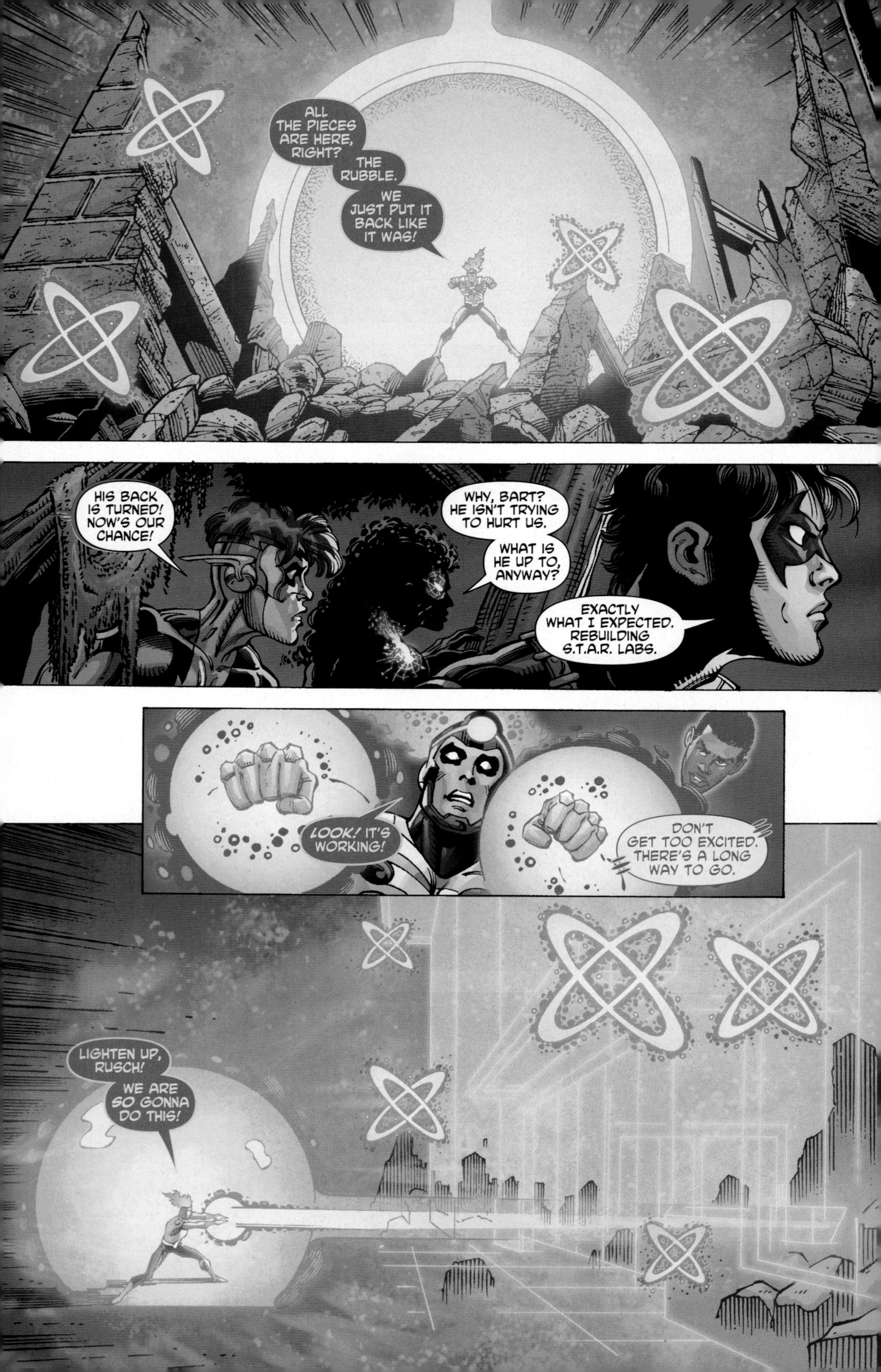
ALL THE PIECES ARE HERE, RIGHT?
THE RUBBLE.
WE JUST PUT IT BACK LIKE IT WAS!
HIS BACK IS TURNED! NOW'S OUR CHANCE!
WHY, BART? HE ISN'T TRYING TO HURT US.
WHAT IS HE UP TO, ANYWAY?
EXACTLY WHAT I EXPECTED. REBUILDING S.T.A.R. LABS.
LOOK! IT'S WORKING!
DON'T GET TOO EXCITED. THERE'S A LONG WAY TO GO.
LIGHTEN UP, RUSCH!
WE ARE SO GONNA DO THIS!

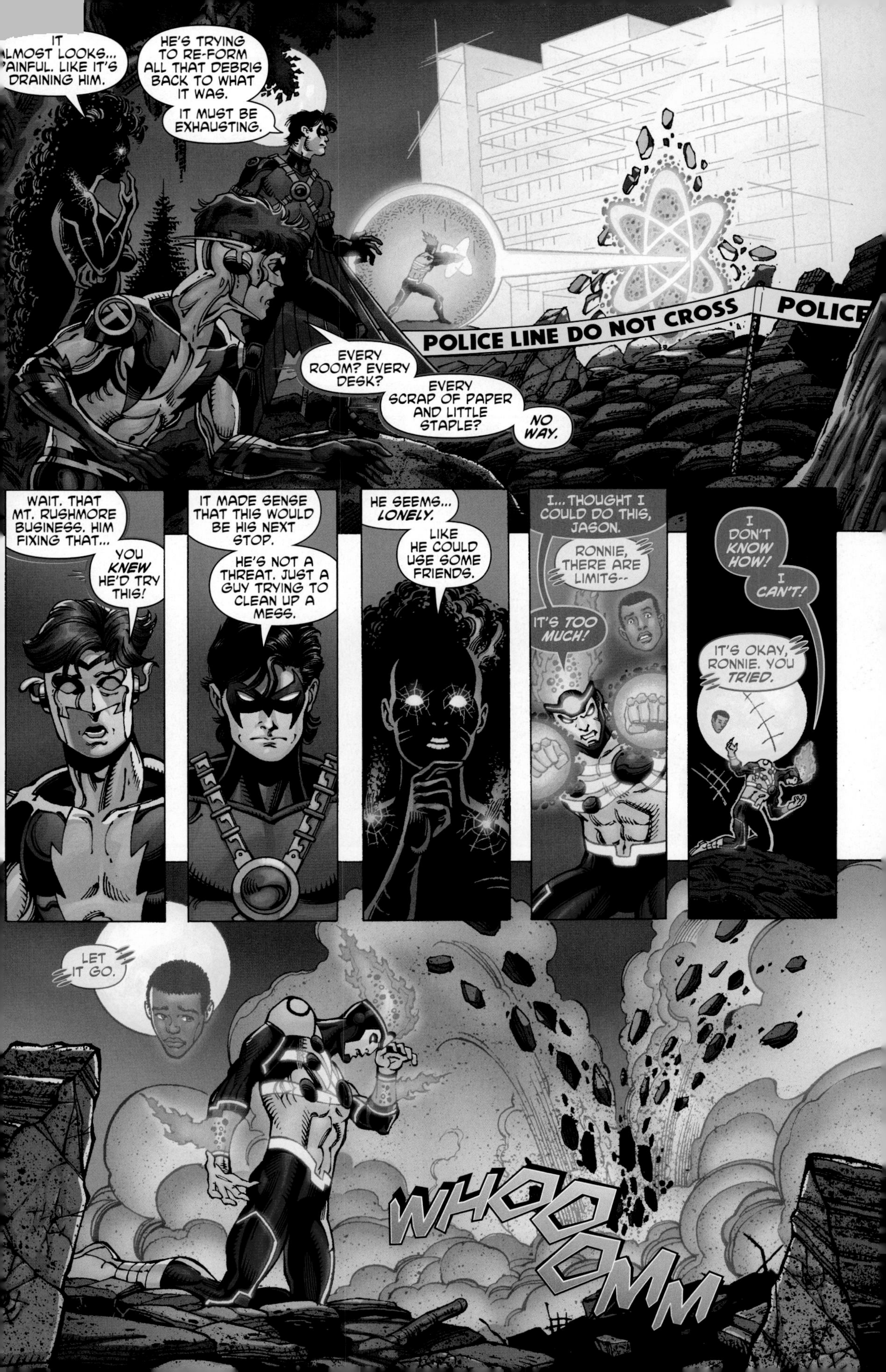
IT ALMOST LOOKS... PAINFUL. LIKE IT'S DRAINING HIM.
HE'S TRYING TO RE-FORM ALL THAT DEBRIS BACK TO WHAT IT WAS.
IT MUST BE EXHAUSTING.
POLICE LINE DO NOT CROSS
POLICE
EVERY ROOM? EVERY DESK?
EVERY SCRAP OF PAPER AND LITTLE STAPLE?
NO WAY.
WAIT. THAT MT. RUSHMORE BUSINESS. HIM FIXING THAT...
YOU KNEW HE'D TRY THIS!
IT MADE SENSE THAT THIS WOULD BE HIS NEXT STOP.
HE'S NOT A THREAT. JUST A GUY TRYING TO CLEAN UP A MESS.
HE SEEMS... LONELY.
LIKE HE COULD USE SOME FRIENDS.
I... THOUGHT I COULD DO THIS, JASON.
RONNIE, THERE ARE LIMITS--
IT'S TOO MUCH!
I DON'T KNOW HOW!
I CAN'T!
IT'S OKAY, RONNIE. YOU TRIED.
LET IT GO.
WHOOOMM

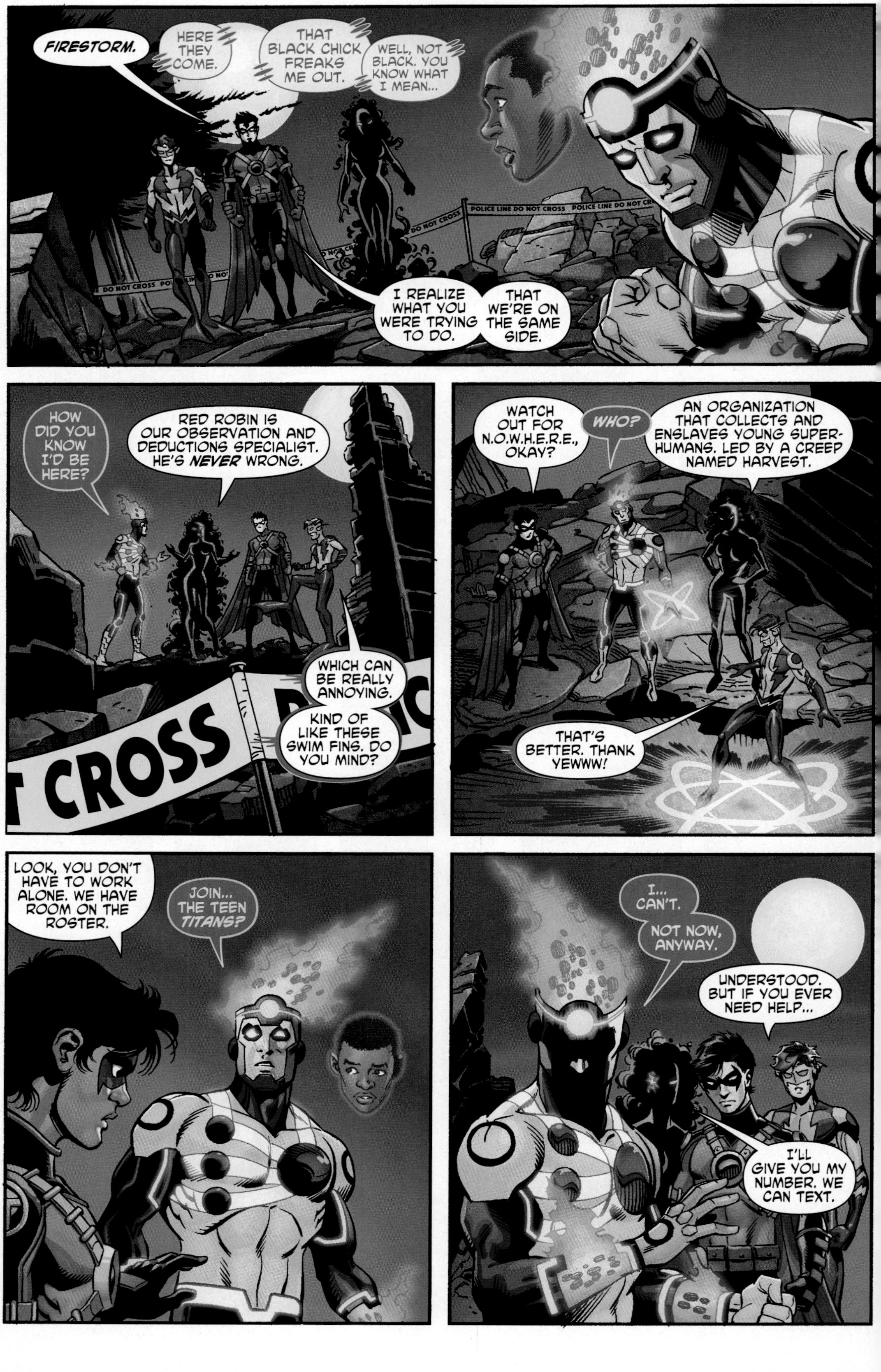
FIRESTORM.
HERE THEY COME.
THAT BLACK CHICK FREAKS ME OUT.
WELL, NOT BLACK. YOU KNOW WHAT I MEAN...
POLICE LINE DO NOT CROSS
I REALIZE WHAT YOU WERE TRYING TO DO.
THAT WE'RE ON THE SAME SIDE.
HOW DID YOU KNOW I'D BE HERE?
RED ROBIN IS OUR OBSERVATION AND DEDUCTIONS SPECIALIST. HE'S NEVER WRONG.
WHICH CAN BE REALLY ANNOYING.
KIND OF LIKE THESE SWIM FINS. DO YOU MIND?
CROSS
WATCH OUT FOR N.O.W.H.E.R.E., OKAY?
WHO?
AN ORGANIZATION THAT COLLECTS AND ENSLAVES YOUNG SUPER-HUMANS. LED BY A CREEP NAMED HARVEST.
THAT'S BETTER. THANK YEWWW!
LOOK, YOU DON'T HAVE TO WORK ALONE. WE HAVE ROOM ON THE ROSTER.
JOIN... THE TEEN TITANS?
I... CAN'T.
NOT NOW, ANYWAY.
UNDERSTOOD. BUT IF YOU EVER NEED HELP...
I'LL GIVE YOU MY NUMBER. WE CAN TEXT.

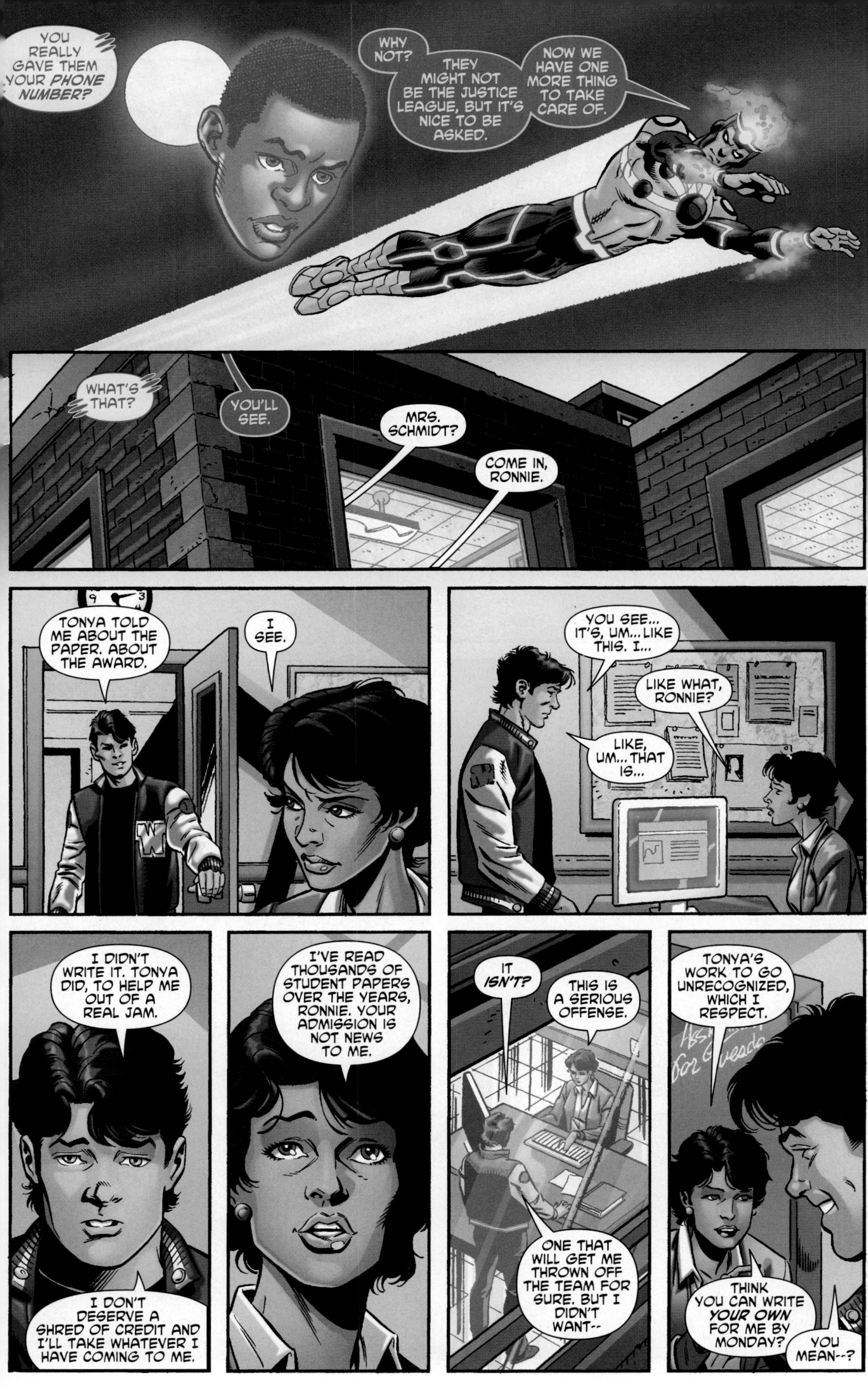
YOU REALLY GAVE THEM YOUR *PHONE NUMBER?*
WHY NOT?
THEY MIGHT NOT BE THE JUSTICE LEAGUE, BUT IT'S NICE TO BE ASKED.
NOW WE HAVE ONE MORE THING TO TAKE CARE OF.
WHAT'S THAT?
YOU'LL SEE.
MRS. SCHMIDT?
COME IN, RONNIE.
TONYA TOLD ME ABOUT THE PAPER. ABOUT THE AWARD.
I SEE.
YOU SEE... IT'S, UM... LIKE THIS. I...
LIKE WHAT, RONNIE?
LIKE, UM... THAT IS...
I DIDN'T WRITE IT. TONYA DID, TO HELP ME OUT OF A REAL JAM.
I DON'T DESERVE A SHRED OF CREDIT AND I'LL TAKE WHATEVER I HAVE COMING TO ME.
I'VE READ THOUSANDS OF STUDENT PAPERS OVER THE YEARS, RONNIE. YOUR ADMISSION IS NOT NEWS TO ME.
IT *ISN'T?*
THIS IS A SERIOUS OFFENSE.
ONE THAT WILL GET ME THROWN OFF THE TEAM FOR SURE. BUT I DIDN'T WANT--
TONYA'S WORK TO GO UNRECOGNIZED, WHICH I RESPECT.
THINK YOU CAN WRITE *YOUR OWN* FOR ME BY MONDAY?
YOU MEAN--?

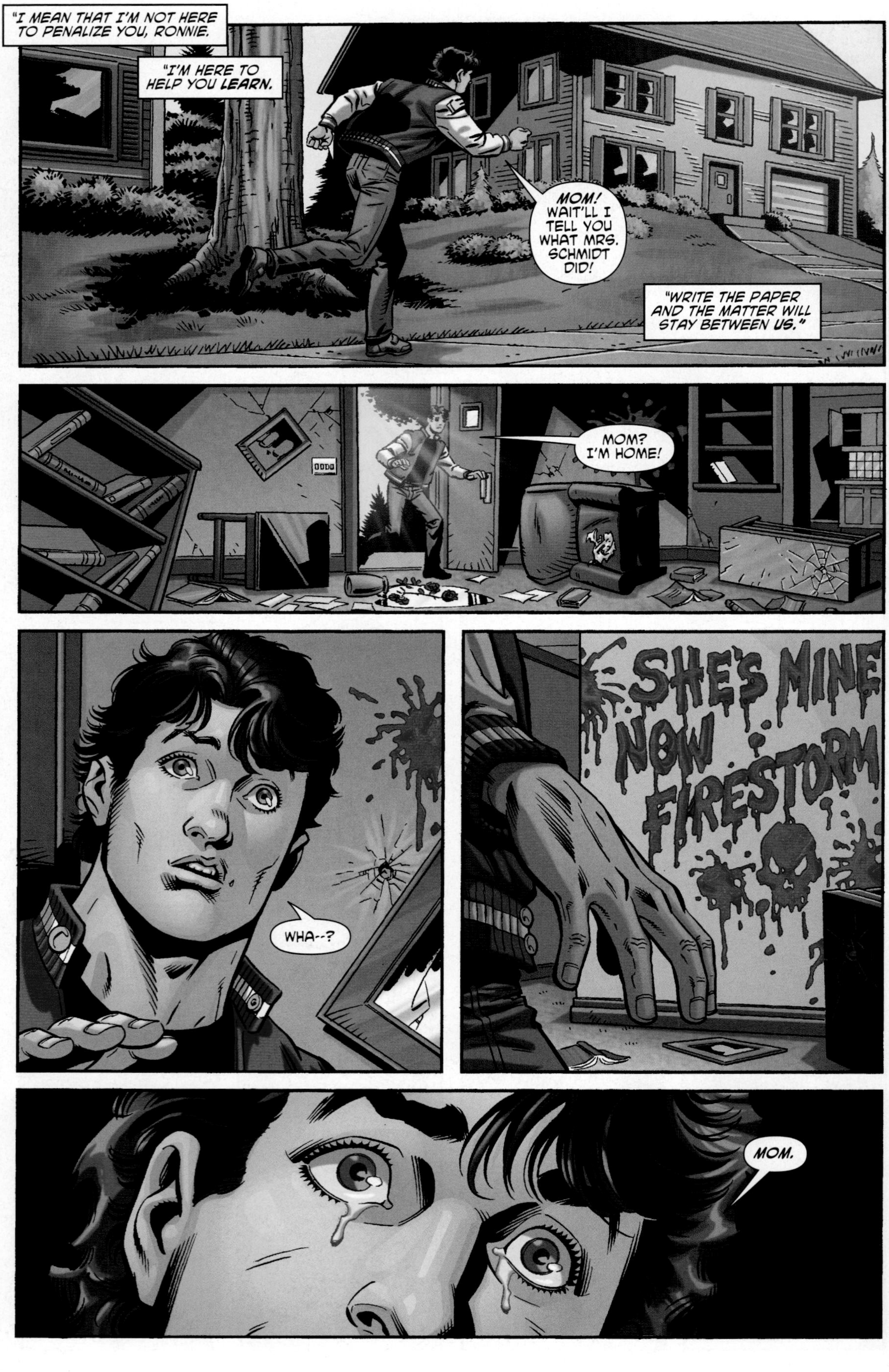
"I MEAN THAT I'M NOT HERE TO PENALIZE YOU, RONNIE.
"I'M HERE TO HELP YOU LEARN.
MOM! WAIT'LL I TELL YOU WHAT MRS. SCHMIDT DID!
"WRITE THE PAPER AND THE MATTER WILL STAY BETWEEN US."
MOM? I'M HOME!
WHA--?
SHE'S MINE NOW FIRESTORM
MOM.

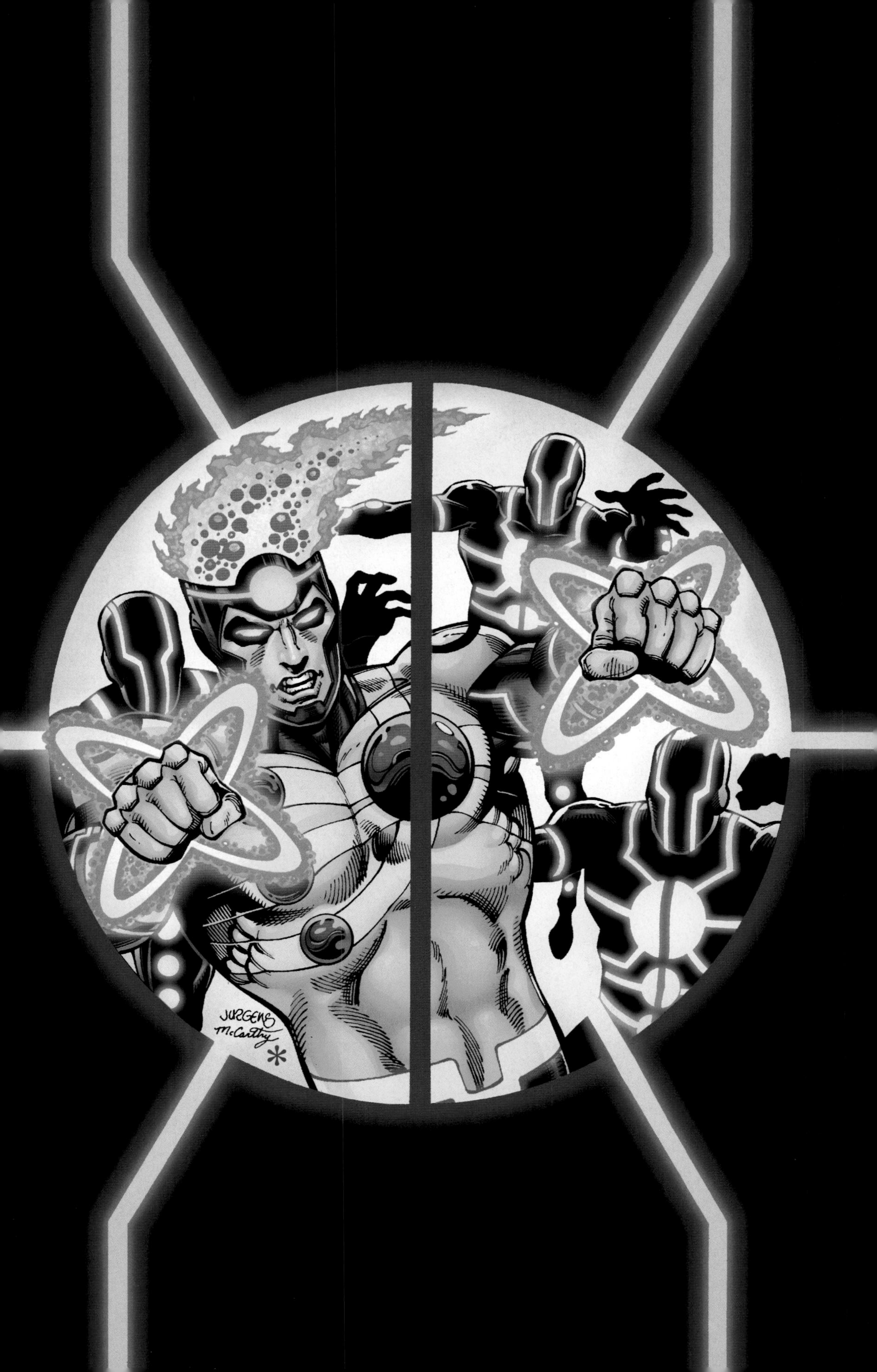
JURGENS
McCarthy

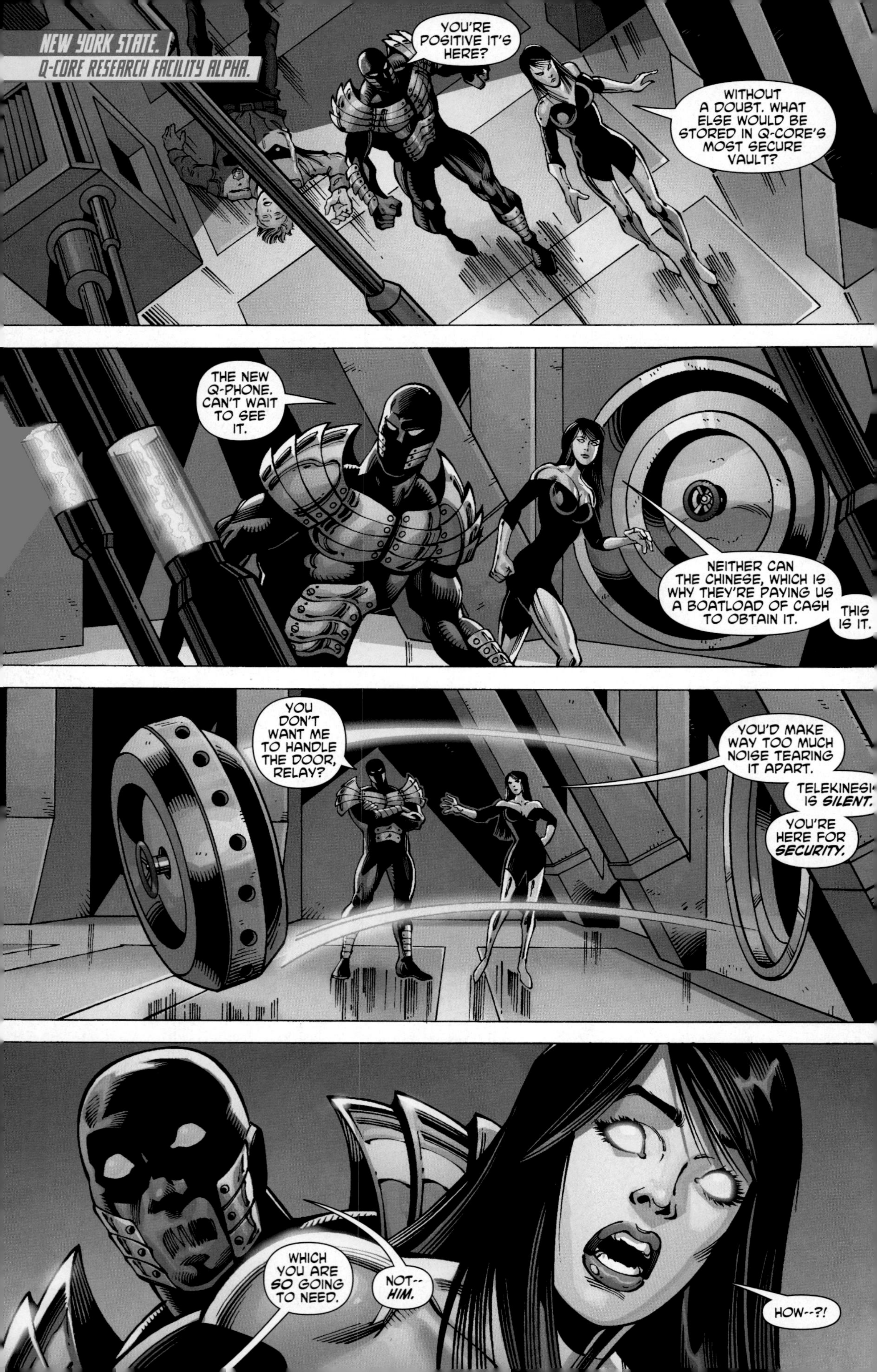
NEW YORK STATE.
Q-CORE RESEARCH FACILITY ALPHA.
YOU'RE POSITIVE IT'S HERE?
WITHOUT A DOUBT. WHAT ELSE WOULD BE STORED IN Q-CORE'S MOST SECURE VAULT?
THE NEW Q-PHONE. CAN'T WAIT TO SEE IT.
NEITHER CAN THE CHINESE, WHICH IS WHY THEY'RE PAYING US A BOATLOAD OF CASH TO OBTAIN IT.
THIS IS IT.
YOU DON'T WANT ME TO HANDLE THE DOOR, RELAY?
YOU'D MAKE WAY TOO MUCH NOISE TEARING IT APART.
TELEKINESI IS SILENT.
YOU'RE HERE FOR SECURITY.
WHICH YOU ARE SO GOING TO NEED.
NOT-- HIM.
HOW--?!

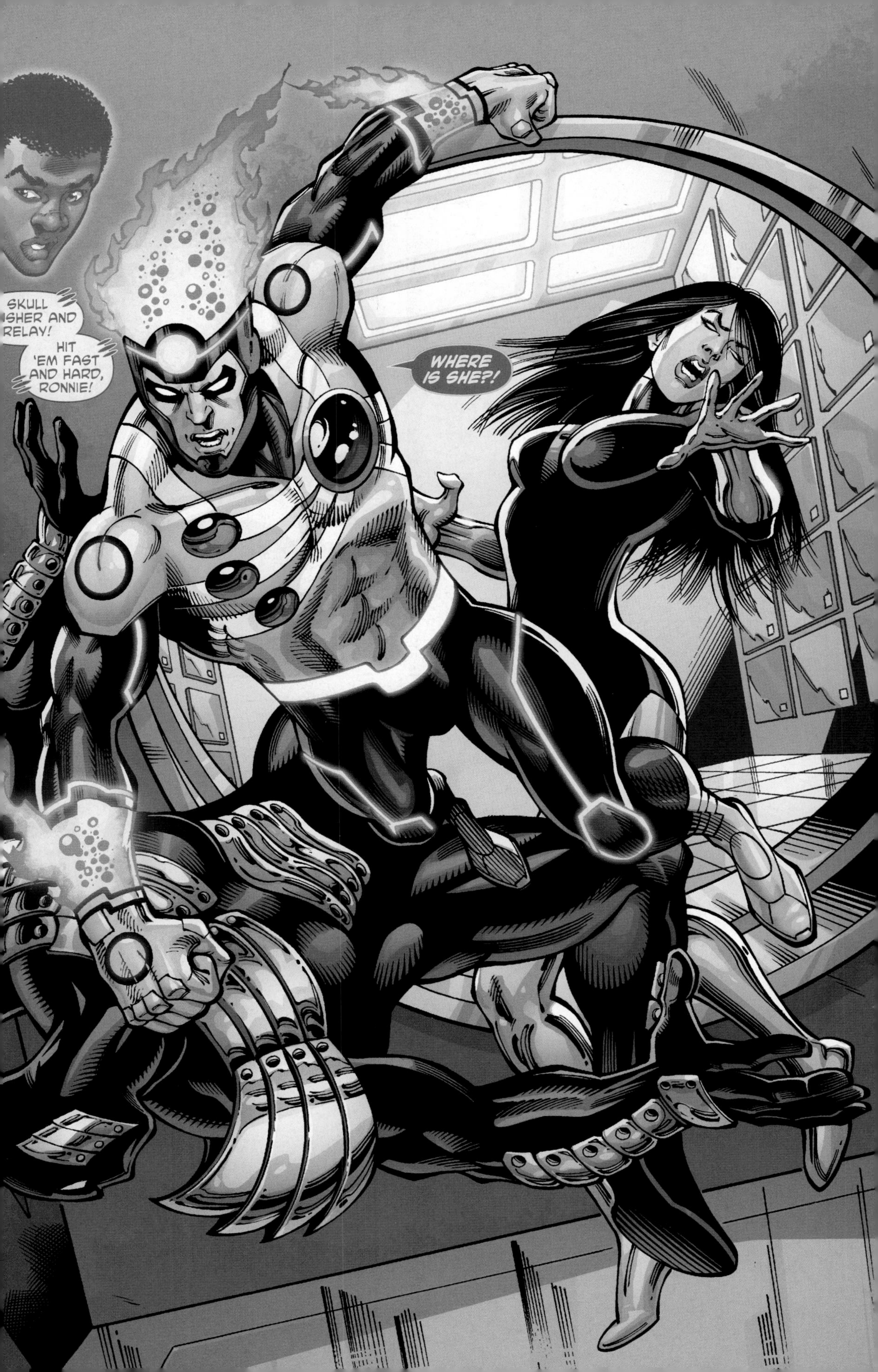
SKULL SHER AND RELAY!
HIT 'EM FAST AND HARD, RONNIE!
WHERE IS SHE?!

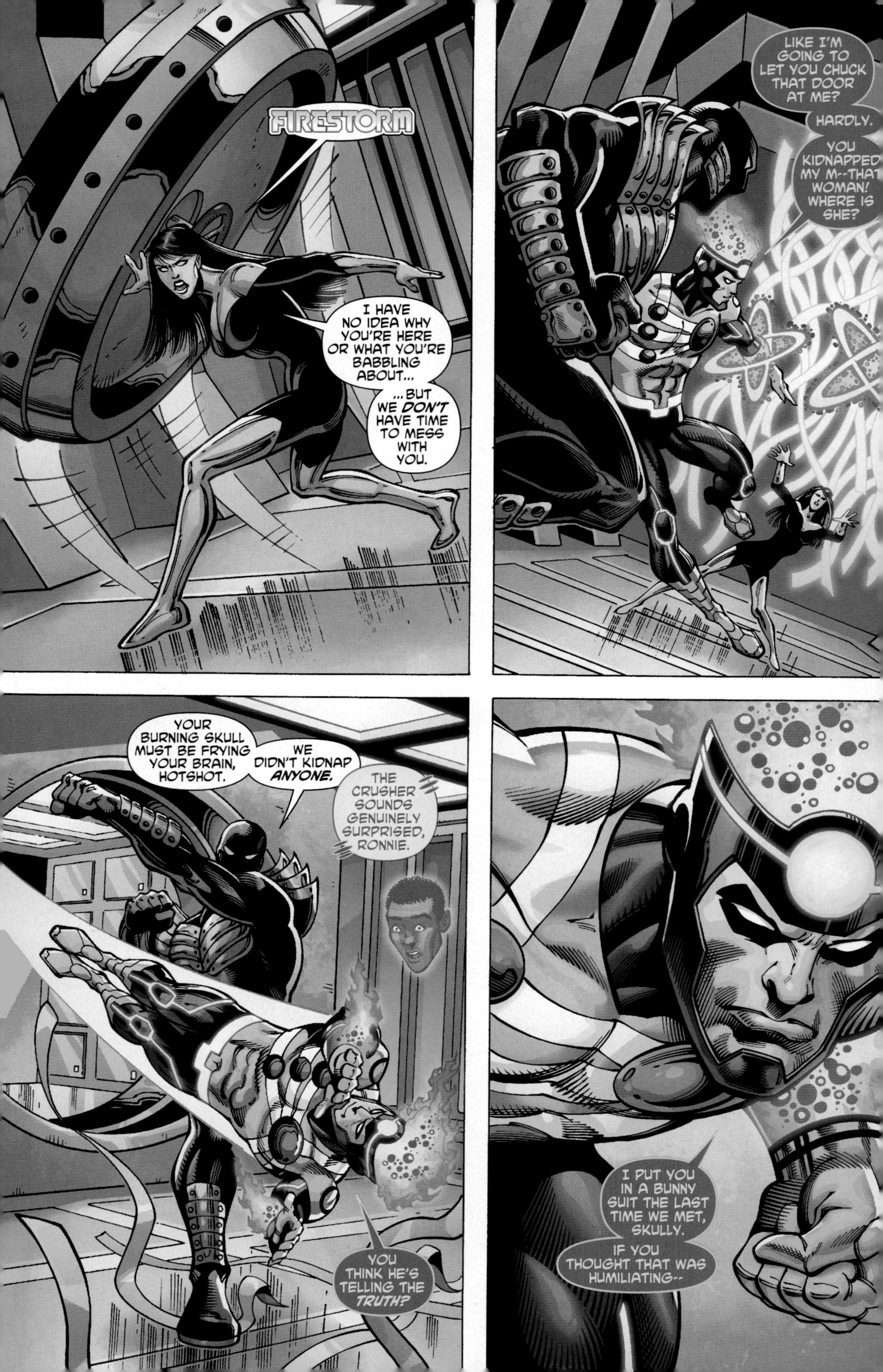
FIRESTORM
I HAVE NO IDEA WHY YOU'RE HERE OR WHAT YOU'RE BABBLING ABOUT...
...BUT WE DON'T HAVE TIME TO MESS WITH YOU.
LIKE I'M GOING TO LET YOU CHUCK THAT DOOR AT ME?
HARDLY.
YOU KIDNAPPED MY M--THAT WOMAN! WHERE IS SHE?
YOUR BURNING SKULL MUST BE FRYING YOUR BRAIN, HOTSHOT.
WE DIDN'T KIDNAP ANYONE.
THE CRUSHER SOUNDS GENUINELY SURPRISED, RONNIE.
YOU THINK HE'S TELLING THE TRUTH?
I PUT YOU IN A BUNNY SUIT THE LAST TIME WE MET, SKULLY.
IF YOU THOUGHT THAT WAS HUMILIATING--

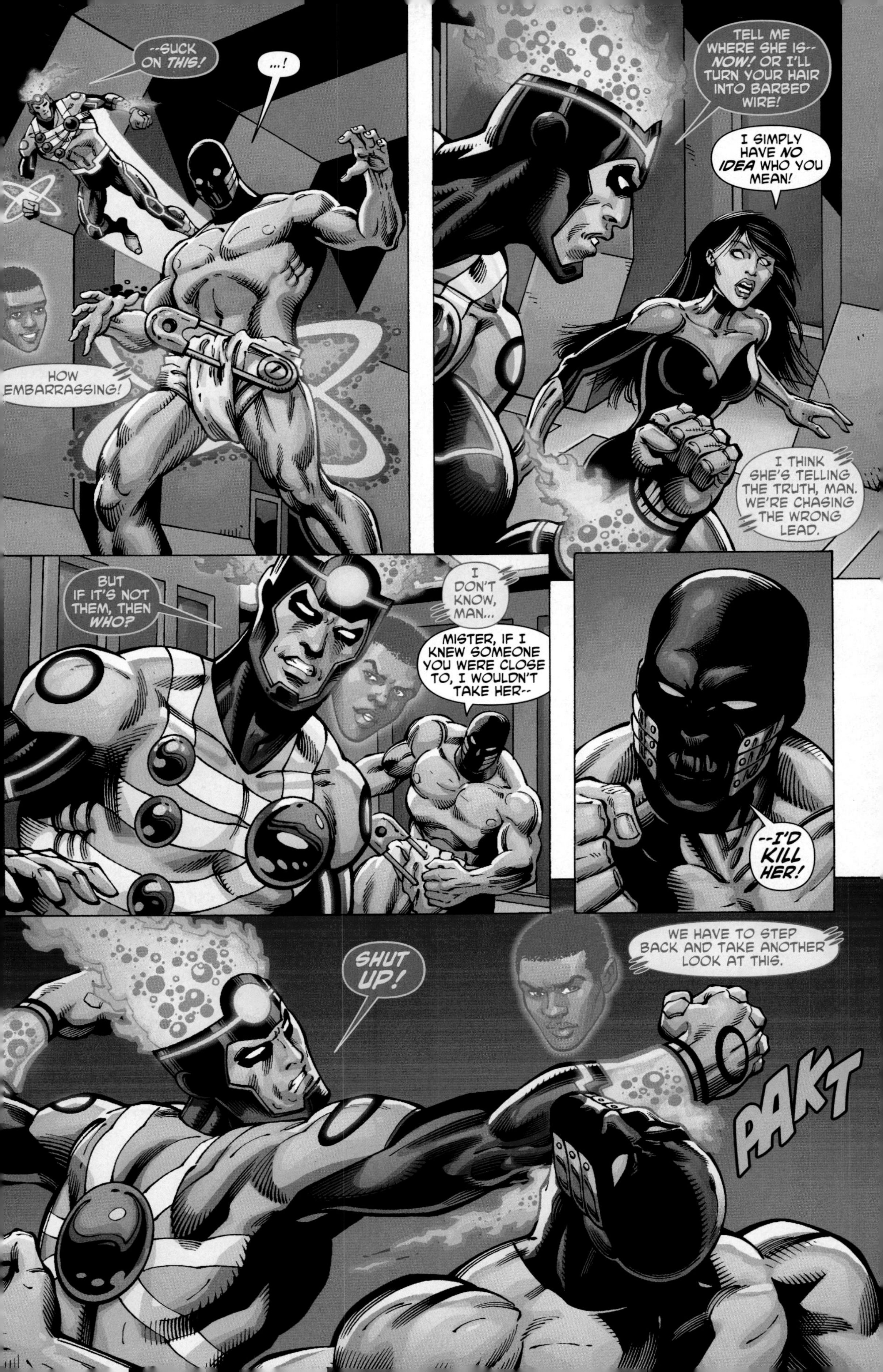
--SUCK ON THIS!
...!
HOW EMBARRASSING!
TELL ME WHERE SHE IS-- NOW! OR I'LL TURN YOUR HAIR INTO BARBED WIRE!
I SIMPLY HAVE NO IDEA WHO YOU MEAN!
I THINK SHE'S TELLING THE TRUTH, MAN. WE'RE CHASING THE WRONG LEAD.
BUT IF IT'S NOT THEM, THEN WHO?
I DON'T KNOW, MAN...
MISTER, IF I KNEW SOMEONE YOU WERE CLOSE TO, I WOULDN'T TAKE HER--
--I'D KILL HER!
SHUT UP!
WE HAVE TO STEP BACK AND TAKE ANOTHER LOOK AT THIS.
PAKT

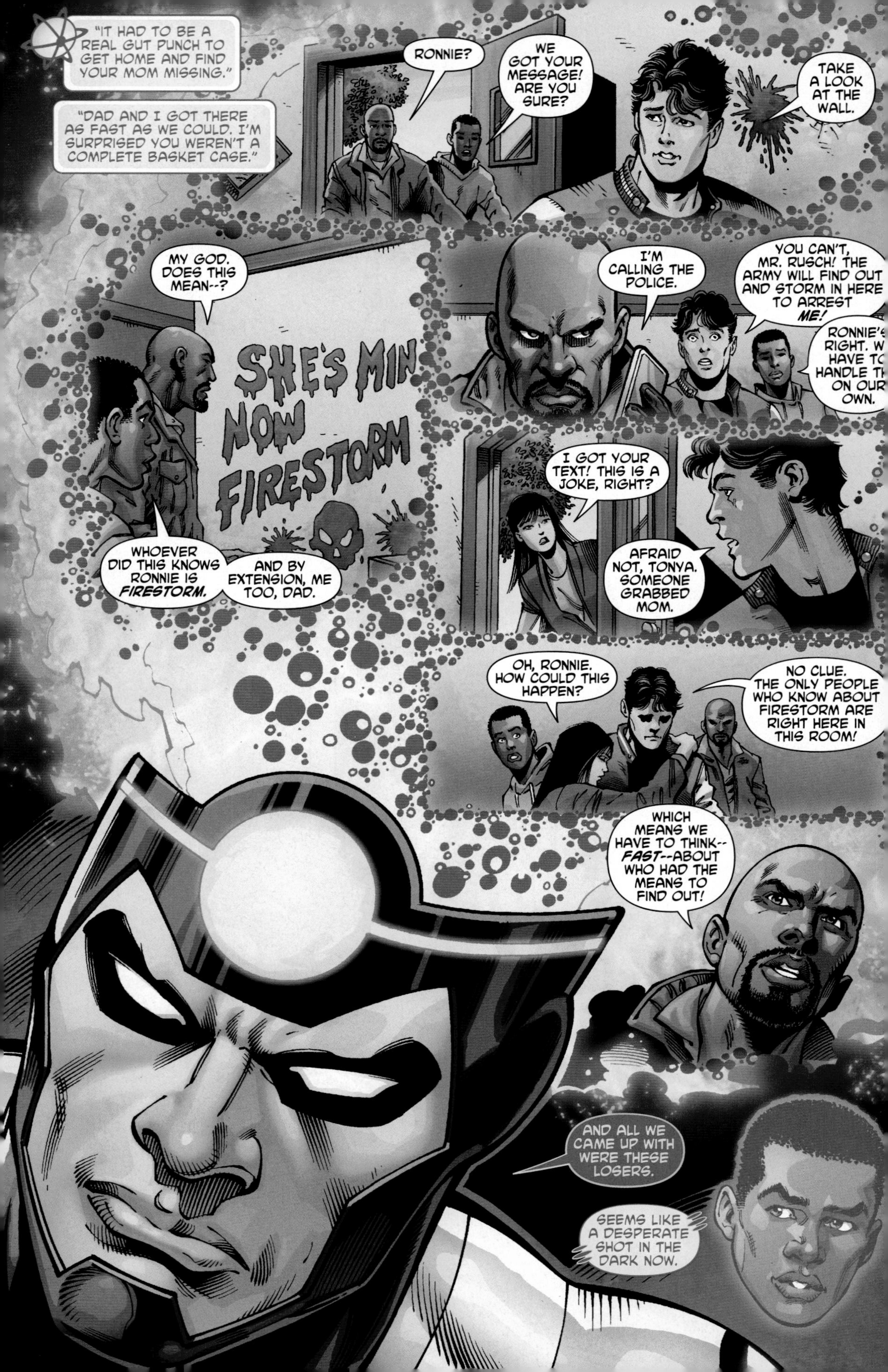
"IT HAD TO BE A REAL GUT PUNCH TO GET HOME AND FIND YOUR MOM MISSING."
"DAD AND I GOT THERE AS FAST AS WE COULD. I'M SURPRISED YOU WEREN'T A COMPLETE BASKET CASE."
RONNIE?
WE GOT YOUR MESSAGE! ARE YOU SURE?
TAKE A LOOK AT THE WALL.
MY GOD. DOES THIS MEAN--?
SHE'S MIN NOW FIRESTORM
WHOEVER DID THIS KNOWS RONNIE IS FIRESTORM.
AND BY EXTENSION, ME TOO, DAD.
I'M CALLING THE POLICE.
YOU CAN'T, MR. RUSCH! THE ARMY WILL FIND OUT AND STORM IN HERE TO ARREST ME!
I GOT YOUR TEXT! THIS IS A JOKE, RIGHT?
AFRAID NOT, TONYA. SOMEONE GRABBED MOM.
OH, RONNIE. HOW COULD THIS HAPPEN?
NO CLUE. THE ONLY PEOPLE WHO KNOW ABOUT FIRESTORM ARE RIGHT HERE IN THIS ROOM!
WHICH MEANS WE HAVE TO THINK-- FAST--ABOUT WHO HAD THE MEANS TO FIND OUT!
AND ALL WE CAME UP WITH WERE THESE LOSERS.
SEEMS LIKE A DESPERATE SHOT IN THE DARK NOW.

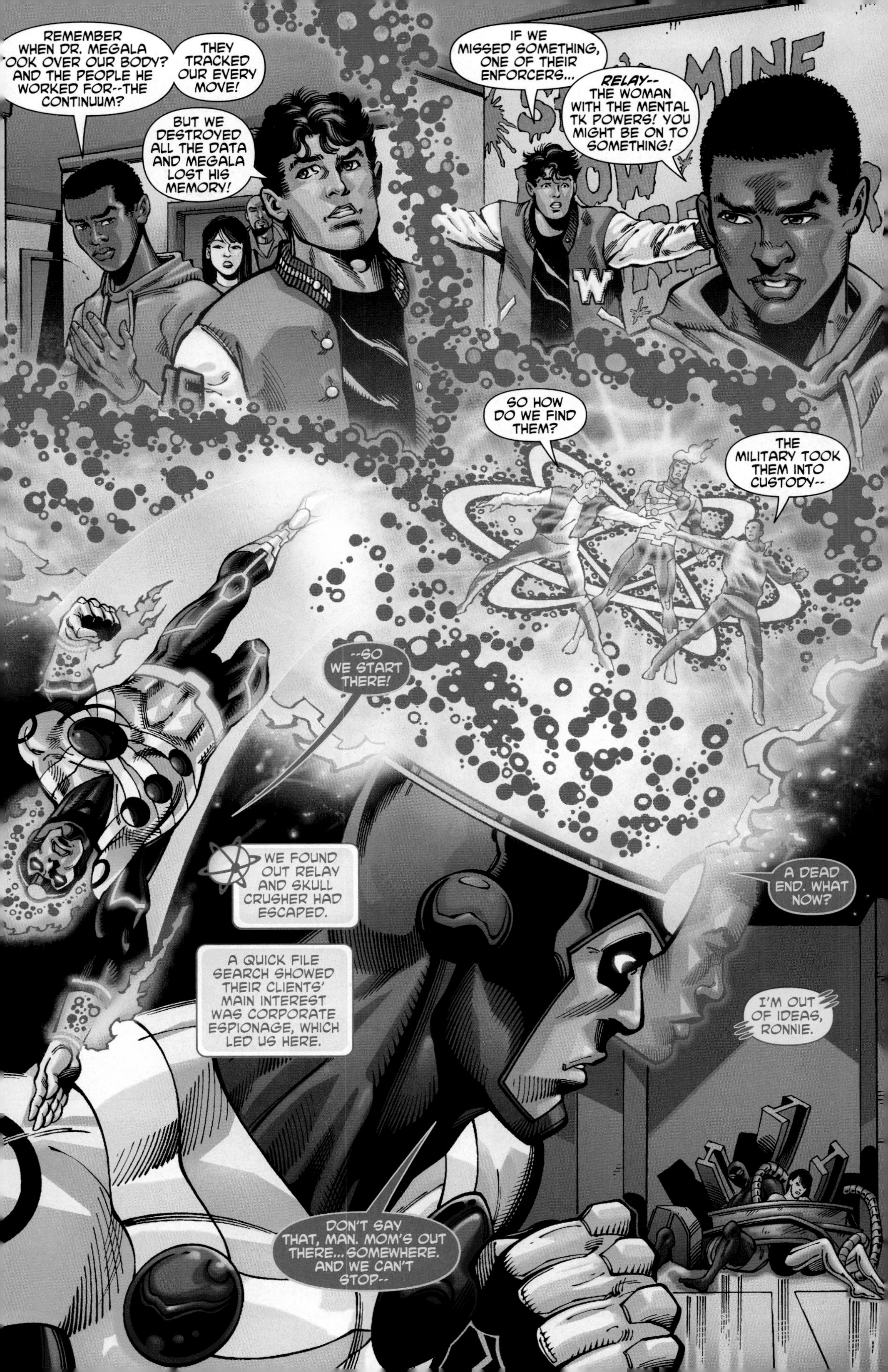
REMEMBER WHEN DR. MEGALA TOOK OVER OUR BODY? AND THE PEOPLE HE WORKED FOR--THE CONTINUUM?
THEY TRACKED OUR EVERY MOVE!
BUT WE DESTROYED ALL THE DATA AND MEGALA LOST HIS MEMORY!
IF WE MISSED SOMETHING, ONE OF THEIR ENFORCERS...
RELAY-- THE WOMAN WITH THE MENTAL TK POWERS! YOU MIGHT BE ON TO SOMETHING!
SO HOW DO WE FIND THEM?
THE MILITARY TOOK THEM INTO CUSTODY--
--SO WE START THERE!
WE FOUND OUT RELAY AND SKULL CRUSHER HAD ESCAPED.
A QUICK FILE SEARCH SHOWED THEIR CLIENTS' MAIN INTEREST WAS CORPORATE ESPIONAGE, WHICH LED US HERE.
A DEAD END. WHAT NOW?
I'M OUT OF IDEAS, RONNIE.
DON'T SAY THAT, MAN. MOM'S OUT THERE...SOMEWHERE. AND WE CAN'T STOP--

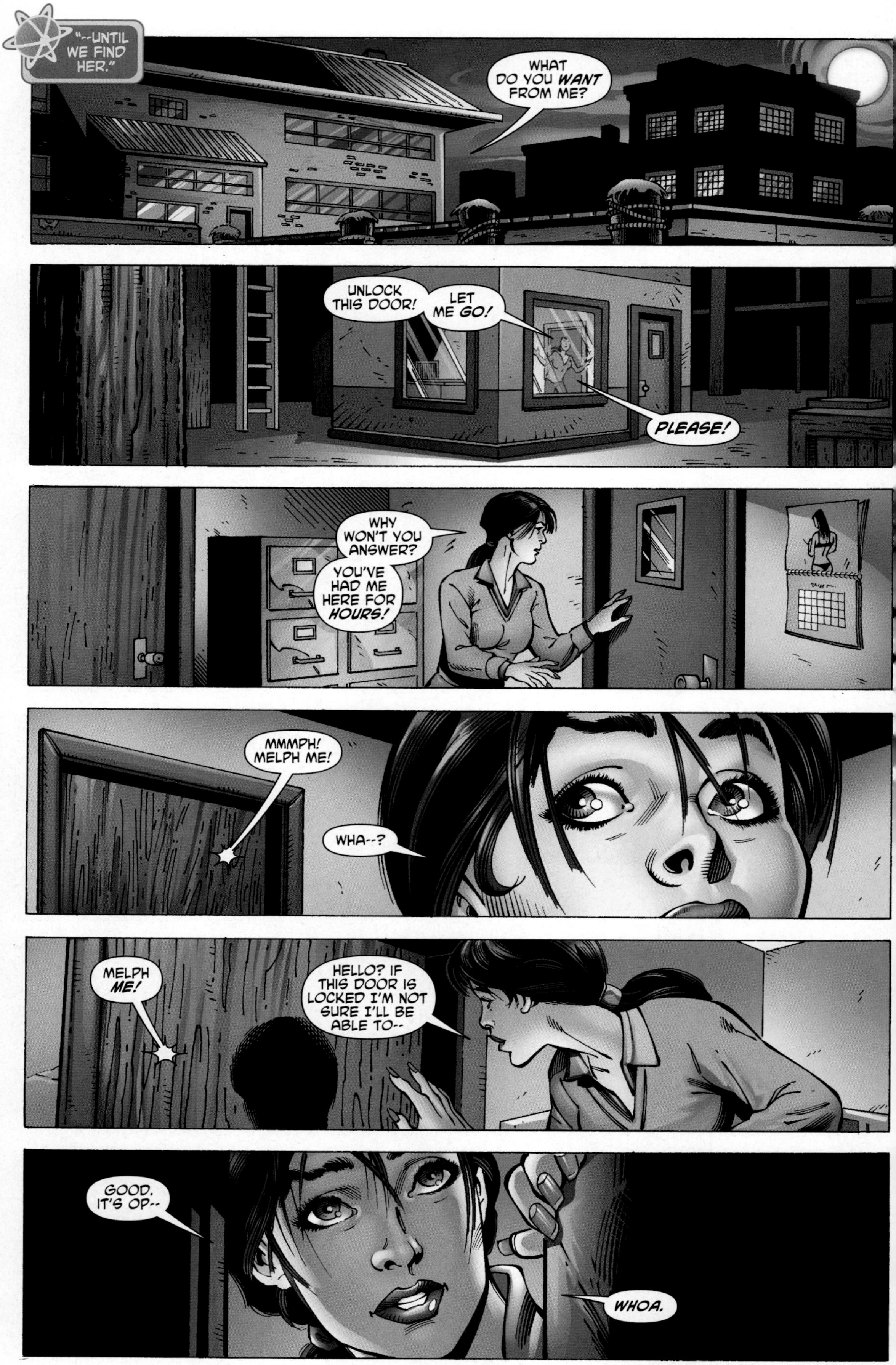
"--UNTIL WE FIND HER."
WHAT DO YOU WANT FROM ME?
UNLOCK THIS DOOR!
LET ME GO!
PLEASE!
WHY WON'T YOU ANSWER?
YOU'VE HAD ME HERE FOR HOURS!
MMMPH! MELPH ME!
WHA--?
MELPH ME!
HELLO? IF THIS DOOR IS LOCKED I'M NOT SURE I'LL BE ABLE TO--
GOOD. IT'S OP--
WHOA.

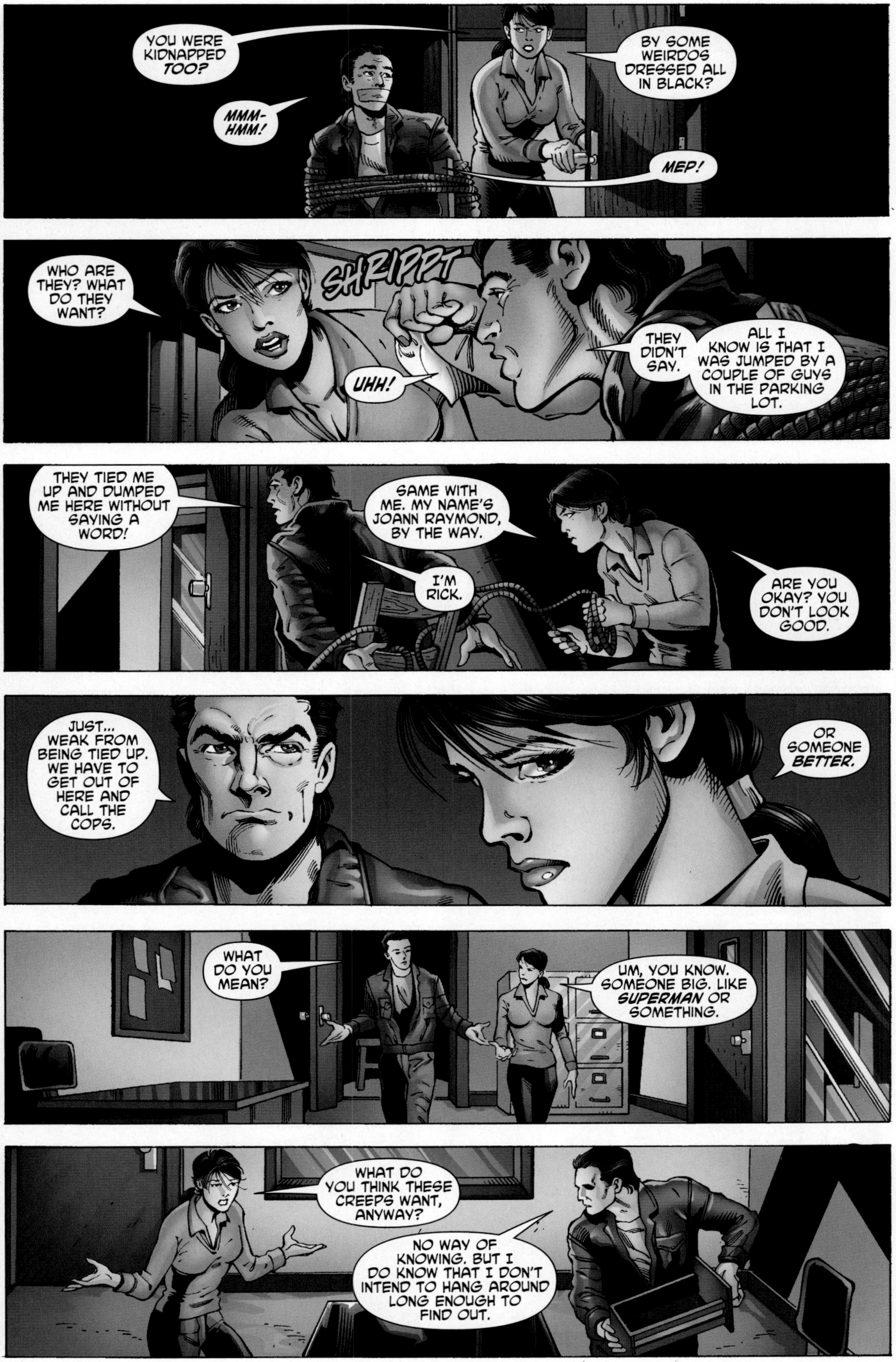
YOU WERE KIDNAPPED TOO?
BY SOME WEIRDOS DRESSED ALL IN BLACK?
MMM-HMM!
MEP!
WHO ARE THEY? WHAT DO THEY WANT?
SHRIPPT
UHH!
THEY DIDN'T SAY.
ALL I KNOW IS THAT I WAS JUMPED BY A COUPLE OF GUYS IN THE PARKING LOT.
THEY TIED ME UP AND DUMPED ME HERE WITHOUT SAYING A WORD!
SAME WITH ME. MY NAME'S JOANN RAYMOND, BY THE WAY.
I'M RICK.
ARE YOU OKAY? YOU DON'T LOOK GOOD.
JUST... WEAK FROM BEING TIED UP. WE HAVE TO GET OUT OF HERE AND CALL THE COPS.
OR SOMEONE BETTER.
WHAT DO YOU MEAN?
UM, YOU KNOW. SOMEONE BIG. LIKE SUPERMAN OR SOMETHING.
WHAT DO YOU THINK THESE CREEPS WANT, ANYWAY?
NO WAY OF KNOWING. BUT I DO KNOW THAT I DON'T INTEND TO HANG AROUND LONG ENOUGH TO FIND OUT.

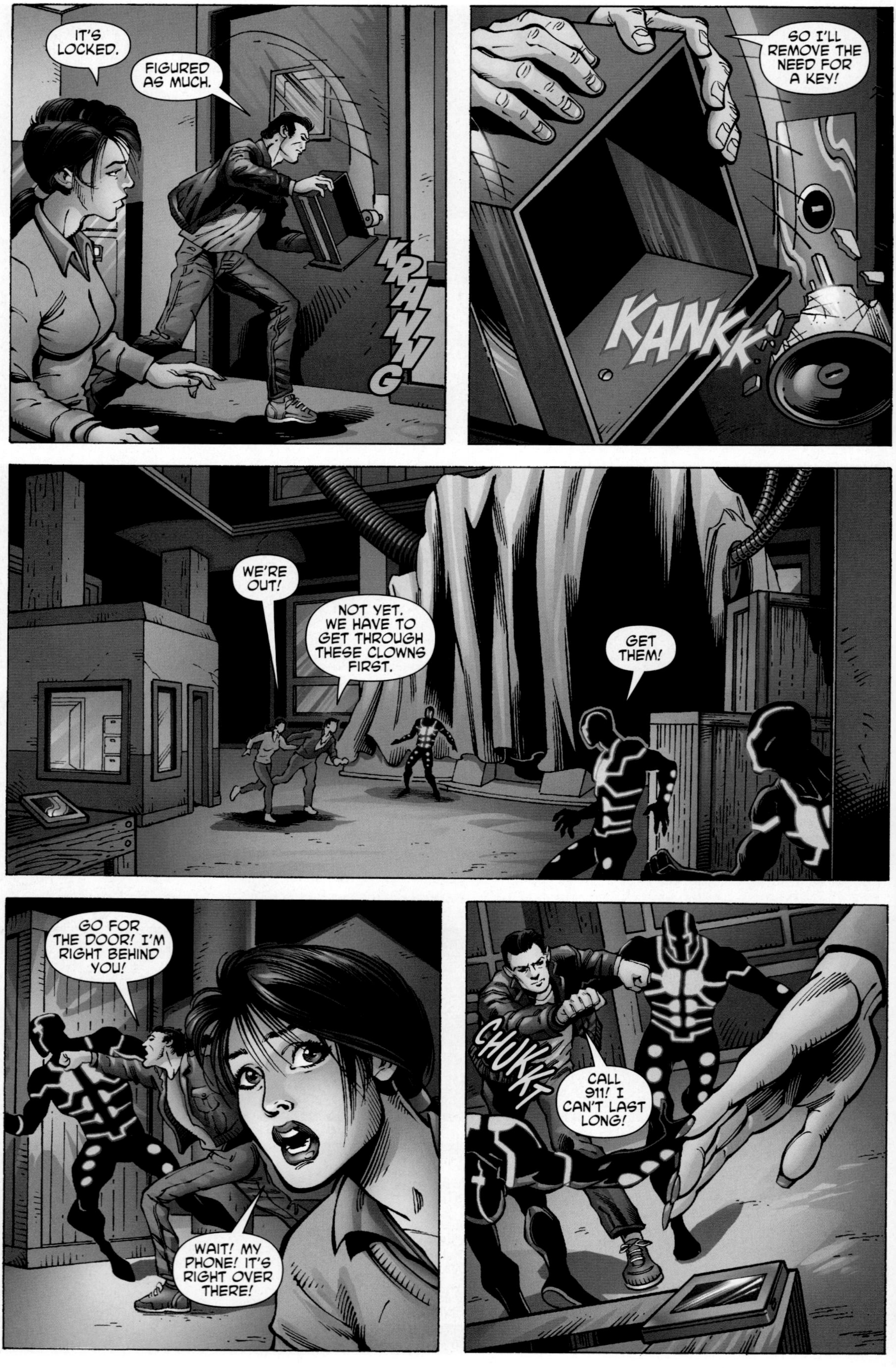
IT'S LOCKED.
FIGURED AS MUCH.
KRANNNG
SO I'LL REMOVE THE NEED FOR A KEY!
KANKK
WE'RE OUT!
NOT YET. WE HAVE TO GET THROUGH THESE CLOWNS FIRST.
GET THEM!
GO FOR THE DOOR! I'M RIGHT BEHIND YOU!
WAIT! MY PHONE! IT'S RIGHT OVER THERE!
CHUKKT
CALL 911! I CAN'T LAST LONG!

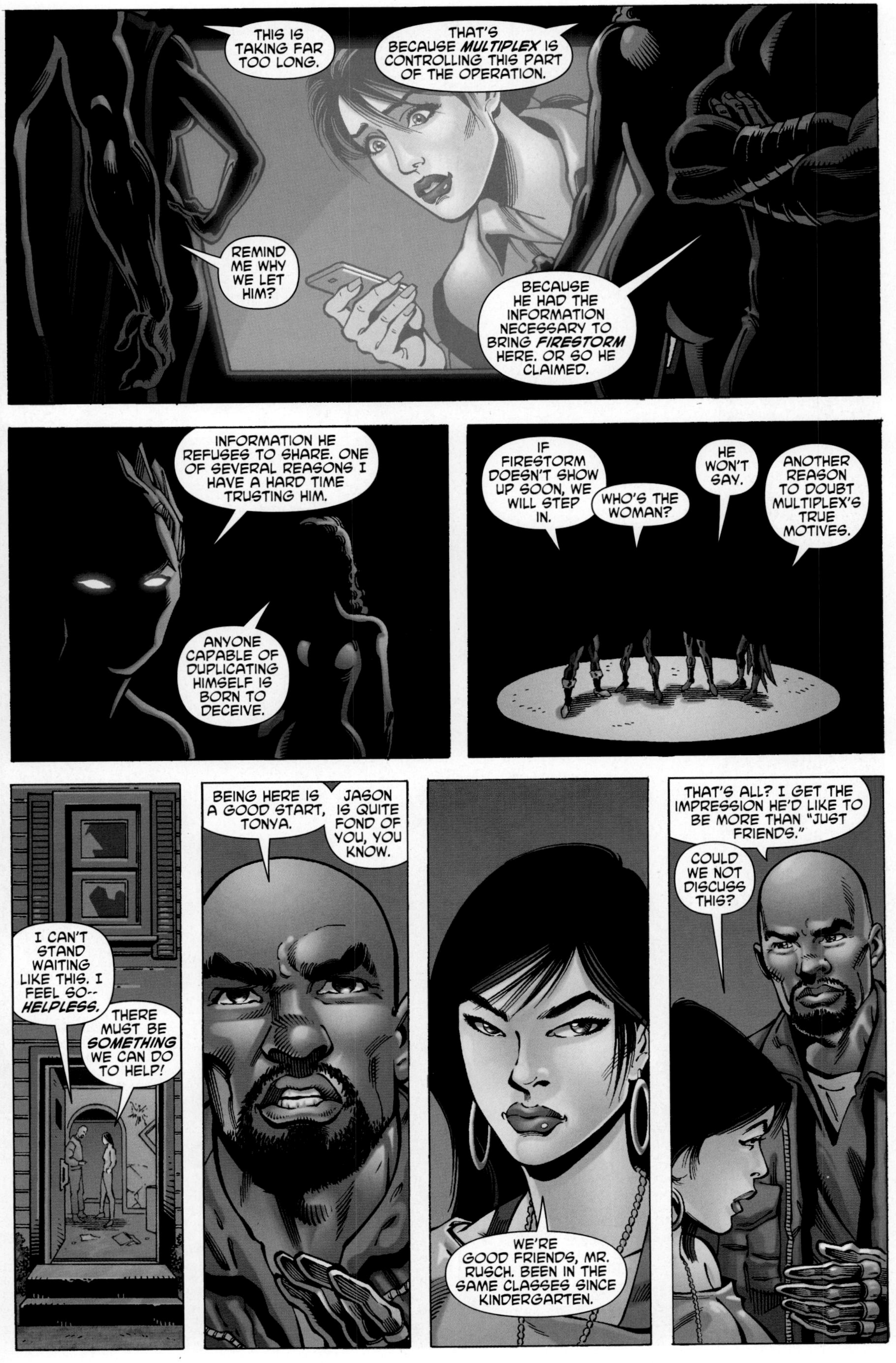
THIS IS TAKING FAR TOO LONG.
THAT'S BECAUSE MULTIPLEX IS CONTROLLING THIS PART OF THE OPERATION.
REMIND ME WHY WE LET HIM?
BECAUSE HE HAD THE INFORMATION NECESSARY TO BRING FIRESTORM HERE. OR SO HE CLAIMED.
INFORMATION HE REFUSES TO SHARE. ONE OF SEVERAL REASONS I HAVE A HARD TIME TRUSTING HIM.
ANYONE CAPABLE OF DUPLICATING HIMSELF IS BORN TO DECEIVE.
IF FIRESTORM DOESN'T SHOW UP SOON, WE WILL STEP IN.
WHO'S THE WOMAN?
HE WON'T SAY.
ANOTHER REASON TO DOUBT MULTIPLEX'S TRUE MOTIVES.
I CAN'T STAND WAITING LIKE THIS. I FEEL SO-- HELPLESS.
THERE MUST BE SOMETHING WE CAN DO TO HELP!
BEING HERE IS A GOOD START, TONYA.
JASON IS QUITE FOND OF YOU, YOU KNOW.
WE'RE GOOD FRIENDS, MR. RUSCH. BEEN IN THE SAME CLASSES SINCE KINDERGARTEN.
THAT'S ALL? I GET THE IMPRESSION HE'D LIKE TO BE MORE THAN "JUST FRIENDS."
COULD WE NOT DISCUSS THIS?

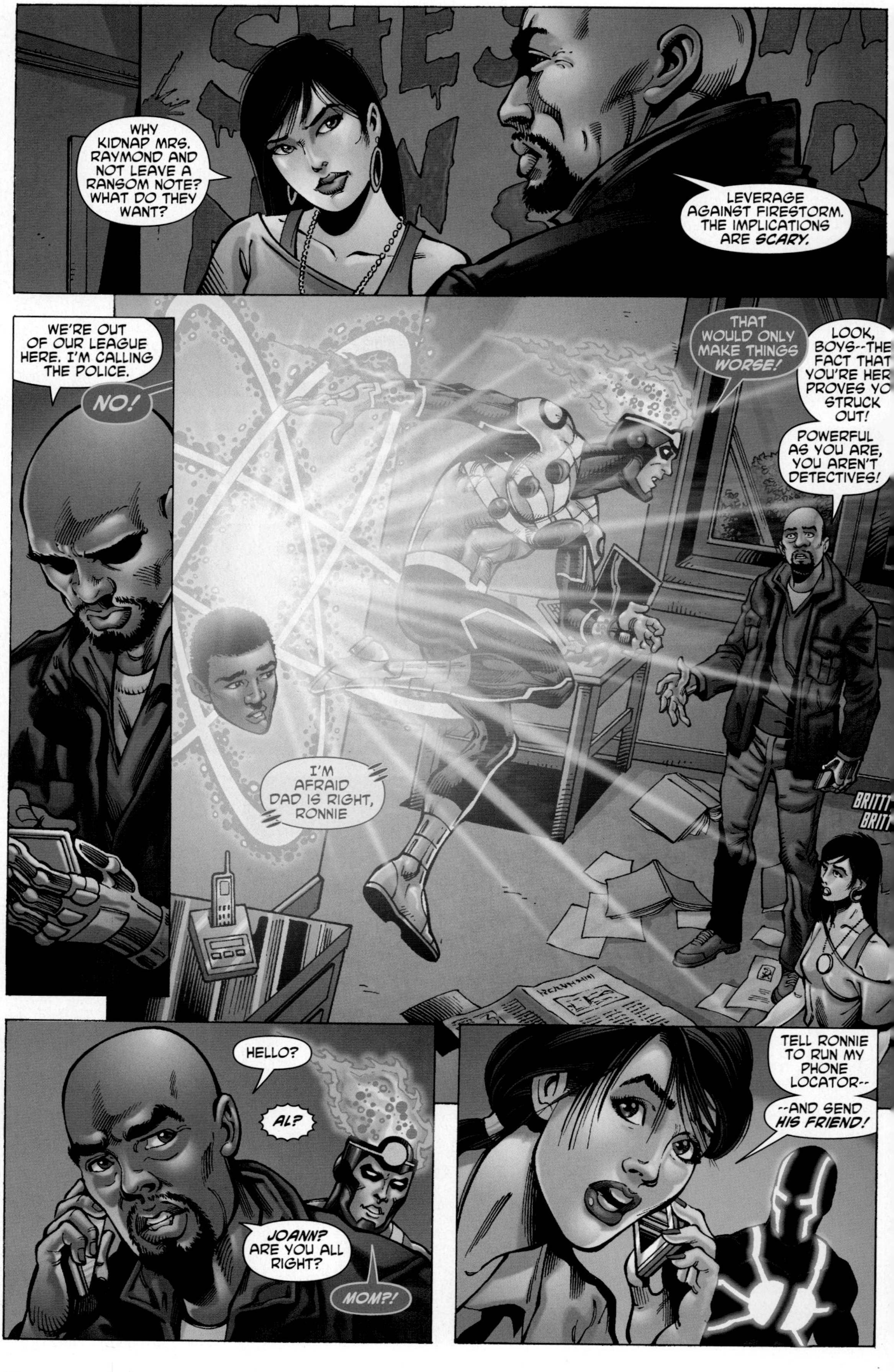
WHY KIDNAP MRS. RAYMOND AND NOT LEAVE A RANSOM NOTE? WHAT DO THEY WANT?
LEVERAGE AGAINST FIRESTORM. THE IMPLICATIONS ARE *SCARY.*
WE'RE OUT OF OUR LEAGUE HERE. I'M CALLING THE POLICE.
NO!
THAT WOULD ONLY MAKE THINGS *WORSE!*
LOOK, BOYS--THE FACT THAT YOU'RE HER PROVES YO STRUCK OUT!
POWERFUL AS YOU ARE, YOU AREN'T DETECTIVES!
I'M AFRAID DAD IS RIGHT, RONNIE
BRITT BRITT
HELLO?
AL?
JOANN? ARE YOU ALL RIGHT?
MOM?!
TELL RONNIE TO RUN MY PHONE LOCATOR--
--AND SEND *HIS FRIEND!*

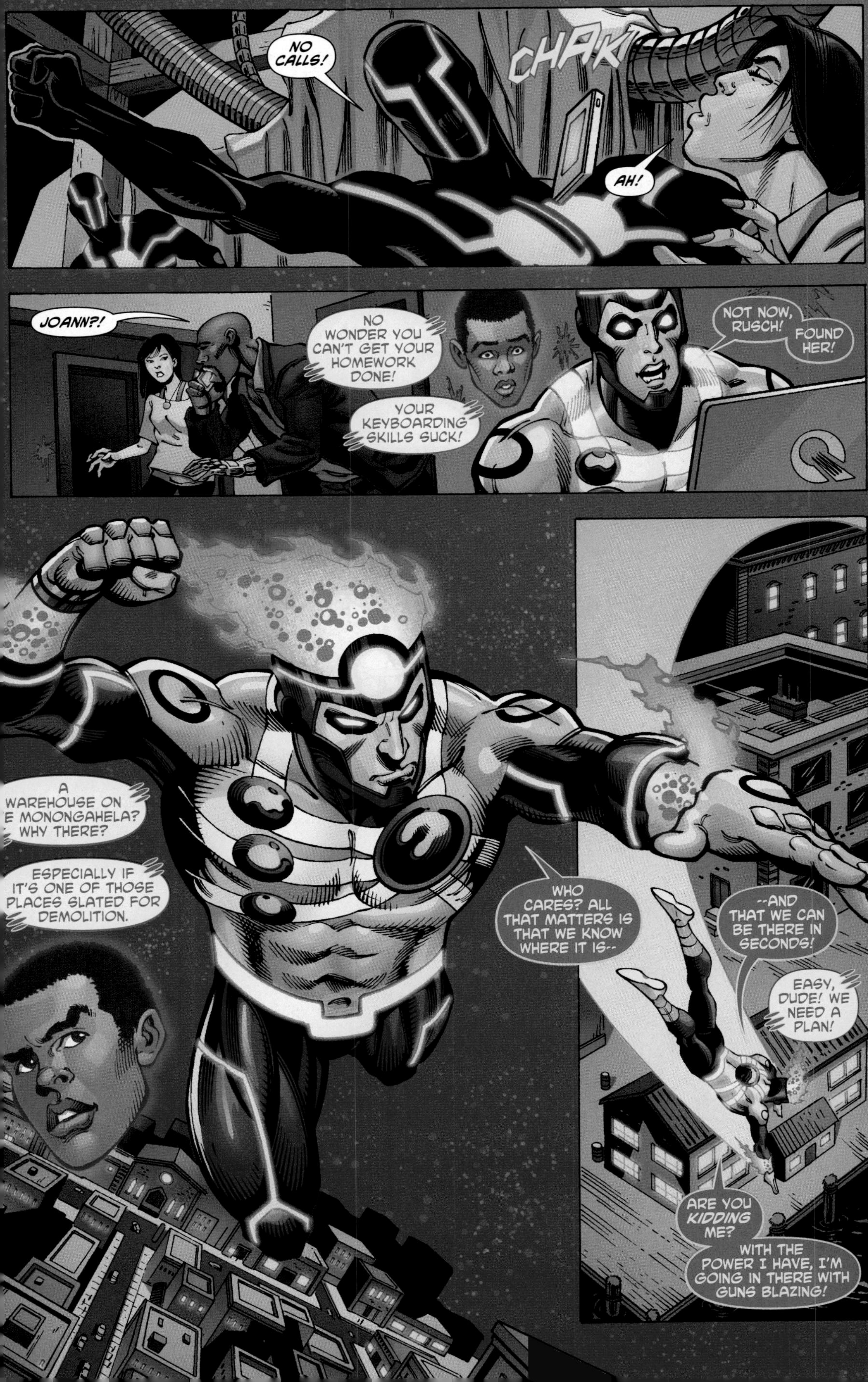
NO CALLS!
CHAK!
AH!
JOANN?!
NO WONDER YOU CAN'T GET YOUR HOMEWORK DONE!
YOUR KEYBOARDING SKILLS SUCK!
NOT NOW, RUSCH!
FOUND HER!
A WAREHOUSE ON E MONONGAHELA? WHY THERE?
ESPECIALLY IF IT'S ONE OF THOSE PLACES SLATED FOR DEMOLITION.
WHO CARES? ALL THAT MATTERS IS THAT WE KNOW WHERE IT IS--
--AND THAT WE CAN BE THERE IN SECONDS!
EASY, DUDE! WE NEED A PLAN!
ARE YOU *KIDDING* ME?
WITH THE POWER I HAVE, I'M GOING IN THERE WITH GUNS BLAZING!

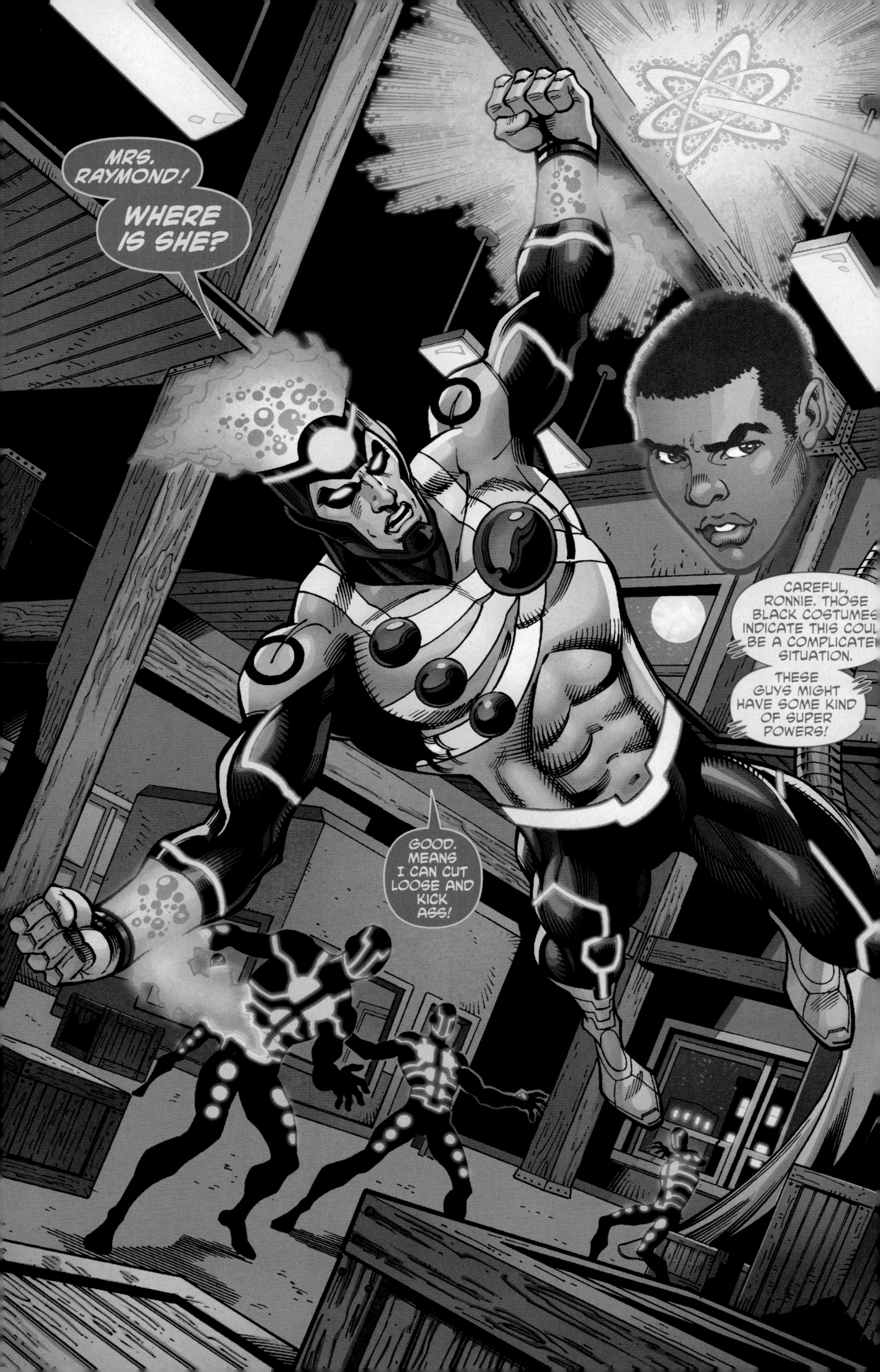
MRS. RAYMOND!
WHERE IS SHE?
CAREFUL, RONNIE. THOSE BLACK COSTUMES INDICATE THIS COUL BE A COMPLICATE SITUATION.
THESE GUYS MIGHT HAVE SOME KIND OF SUPER POWERS!
GOOD. MEANS I CAN CUT LOOSE AND KICK ASS!

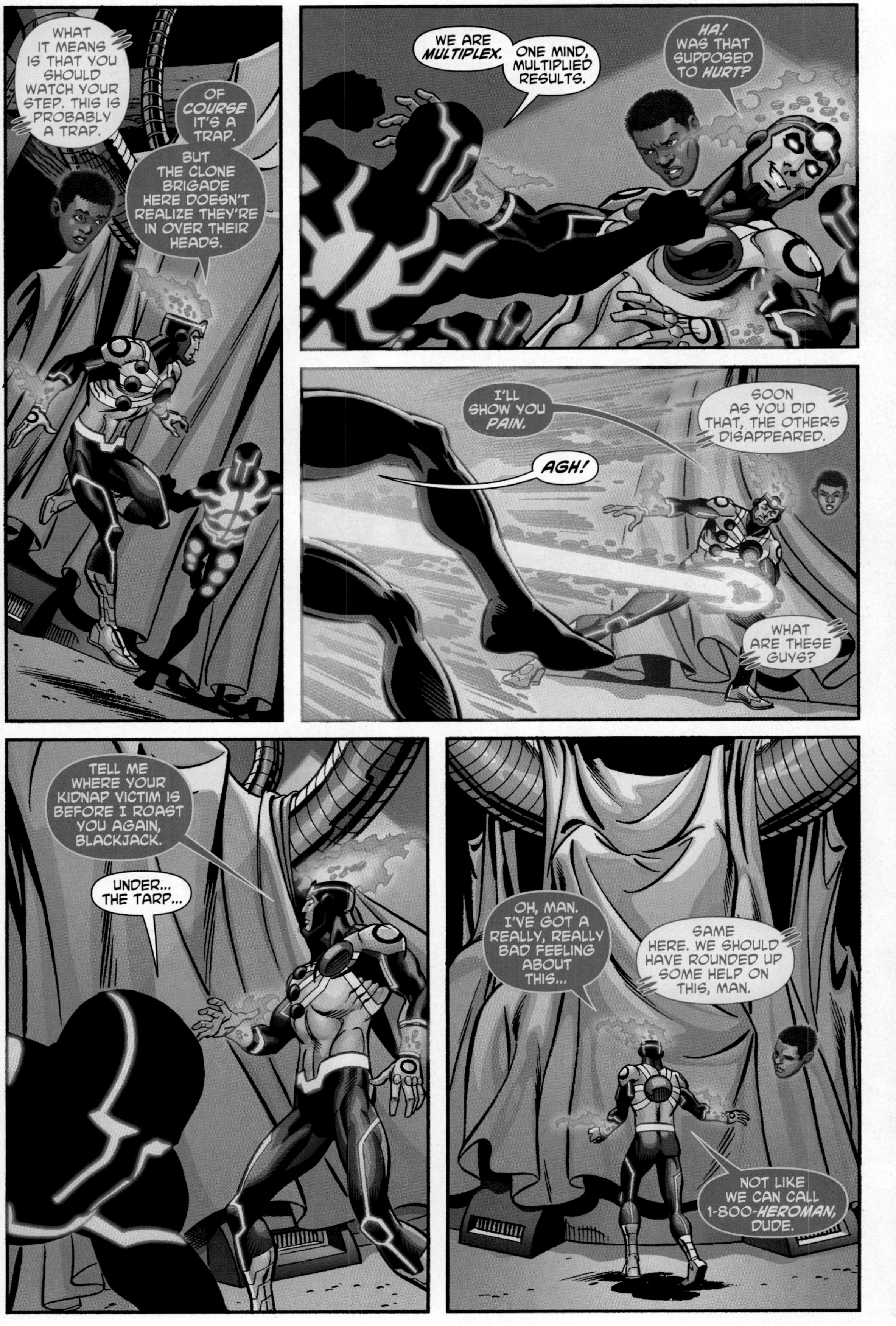
WHAT IT MEANS IS THAT YOU SHOULD WATCH YOUR STEP. THIS IS PROBABLY A TRAP.
OF COURSE IT'S A TRAP.
BUT THE CLONE BRIGADE HERE DOESN'T REALIZE THEY'RE IN OVER THEIR HEADS.
WE ARE MULTIPLEX.
ONE MIND, MULTIPLIED RESULTS.
HA! WAS THAT SUPPOSED TO HURT?
I'LL SHOW YOU PAIN.
SOON AS YOU DID THAT, THE OTHERS DISAPPEARED.
AGH!
WHAT ARE THESE GUYS?
TELL ME WHERE YOUR KIDNAP VICTIM IS BEFORE I ROAST YOU AGAIN, BLACKJACK.
UNDER... THE TARP...
OH, MAN. I'VE GOT A REALLY, REALLY BAD FEELING ABOUT THIS...
SAME HERE. WE SHOULD HAVE ROUNDED UP SOME HELP ON THIS, MAN.
NOT LIKE WE CAN CALL 1-800-HEROMAN, DUDE.

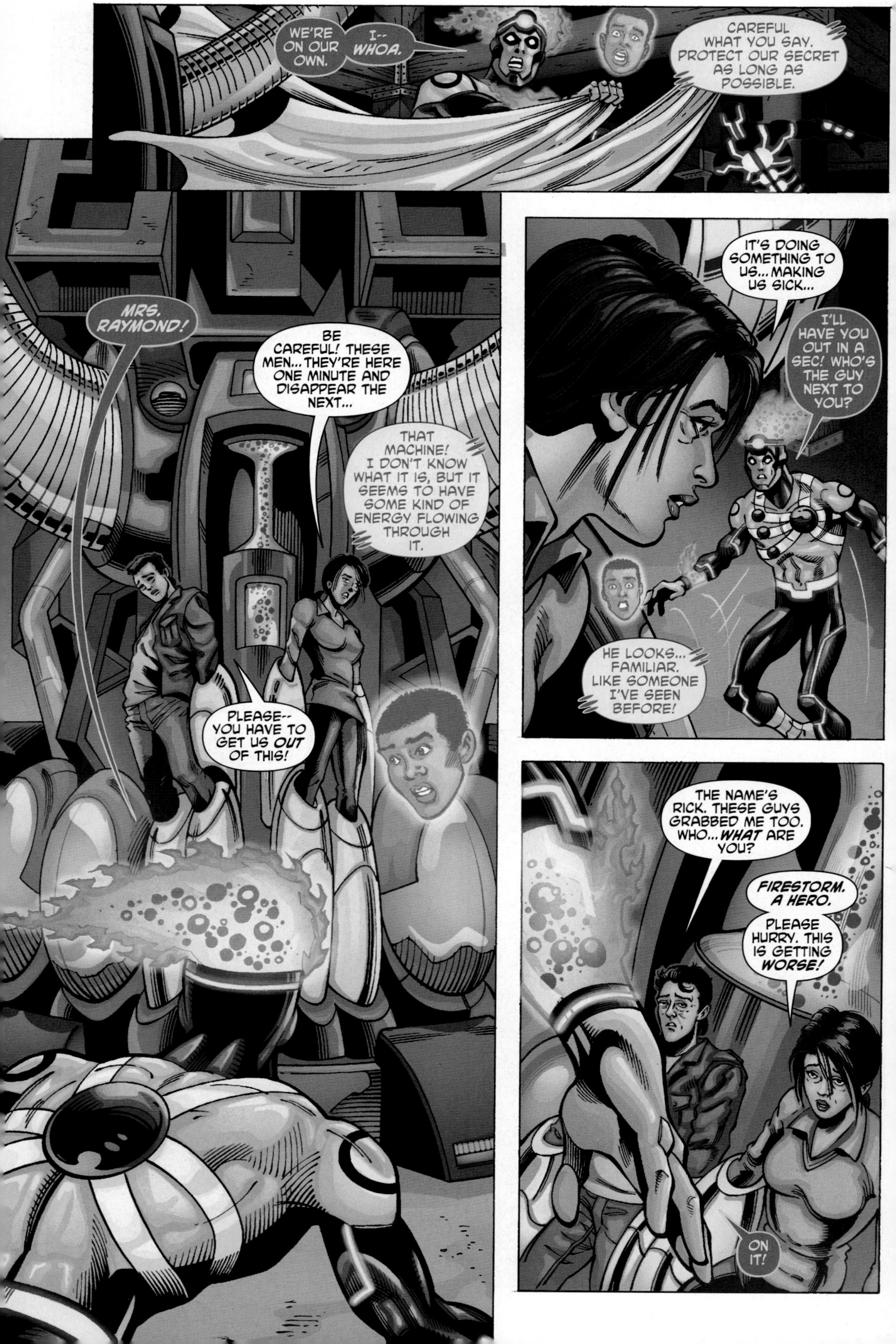
WE'RE ON OUR OWN.
I-- WHOA.
CAREFUL WHAT YOU SAY. PROTECT OUR SECRET AS LONG AS POSSIBLE.
MRS. RAYMOND!
BE CAREFUL! THESE MEN... THEY'RE HERE ONE MINUTE AND DISAPPEAR THE NEXT...
THAT MACHINE! I DON'T KNOW WHAT IT IS, BUT IT SEEMS TO HAVE SOME KIND OF ENERGY FLOWING THROUGH IT.
PLEASE-- YOU HAVE TO GET US OUT OF THIS!
IT'S DOING SOMETHING TO US... MAKING US SICK...
I'LL HAVE YOU OUT IN A SEC! WHO'S THE GUY NEXT TO YOU?
HE LOOKS... FAMILIAR. LIKE SOMEONE I'VE SEEN BEFORE!
THE NAME'S RICK. THESE GUYS GRABBED ME TOO. WHO... WHAT ARE YOU?
FIRESTORM. A HERO.
PLEASE HURRY. THIS IS GETTING WORSE!
ON IT!

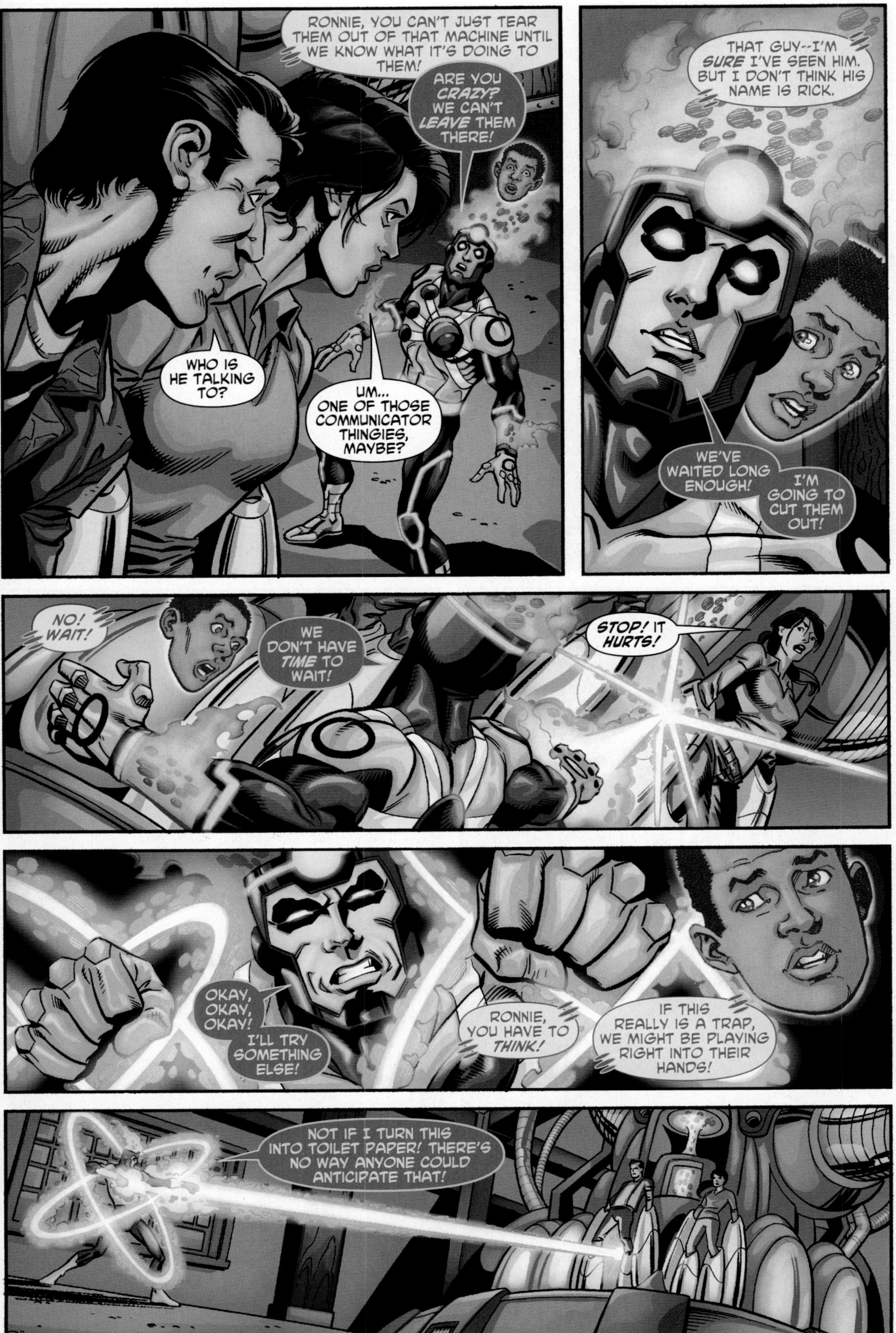
RONNIE, YOU CAN'T JUST TEAR THEM OUT OF THAT MACHINE UNTIL WE KNOW WHAT IT'S DOING TO THEM!
ARE YOU CRAZY? WE CAN'T LEAVE THEM THERE!
WHO IS HE TALKING TO?
UM... ONE OF THOSE COMMUNICATOR THINGIES, MAYBE?
THAT GUY--I'M SURE I'VE SEEN HIM. BUT I DON'T THINK HIS NAME IS RICK.
WE'VE WAITED LONG ENOUGH!
I'M GOING TO CUT THEM OUT!
NO! WAIT!
WE DON'T HAVE TIME TO WAIT!
STOP! IT HURTS!
OKAY, OKAY, OKAY!
I'LL TRY SOMETHING ELSE!
RONNIE, YOU HAVE TO THINK!
IF THIS REALLY IS A TRAP, WE MIGHT BE PLAYING RIGHT INTO THEIR HANDS!
NOT IF I TURN THIS INTO TOILET PAPER! THERE'S NO WAY ANYONE COULD ANTICIPATE THAT!

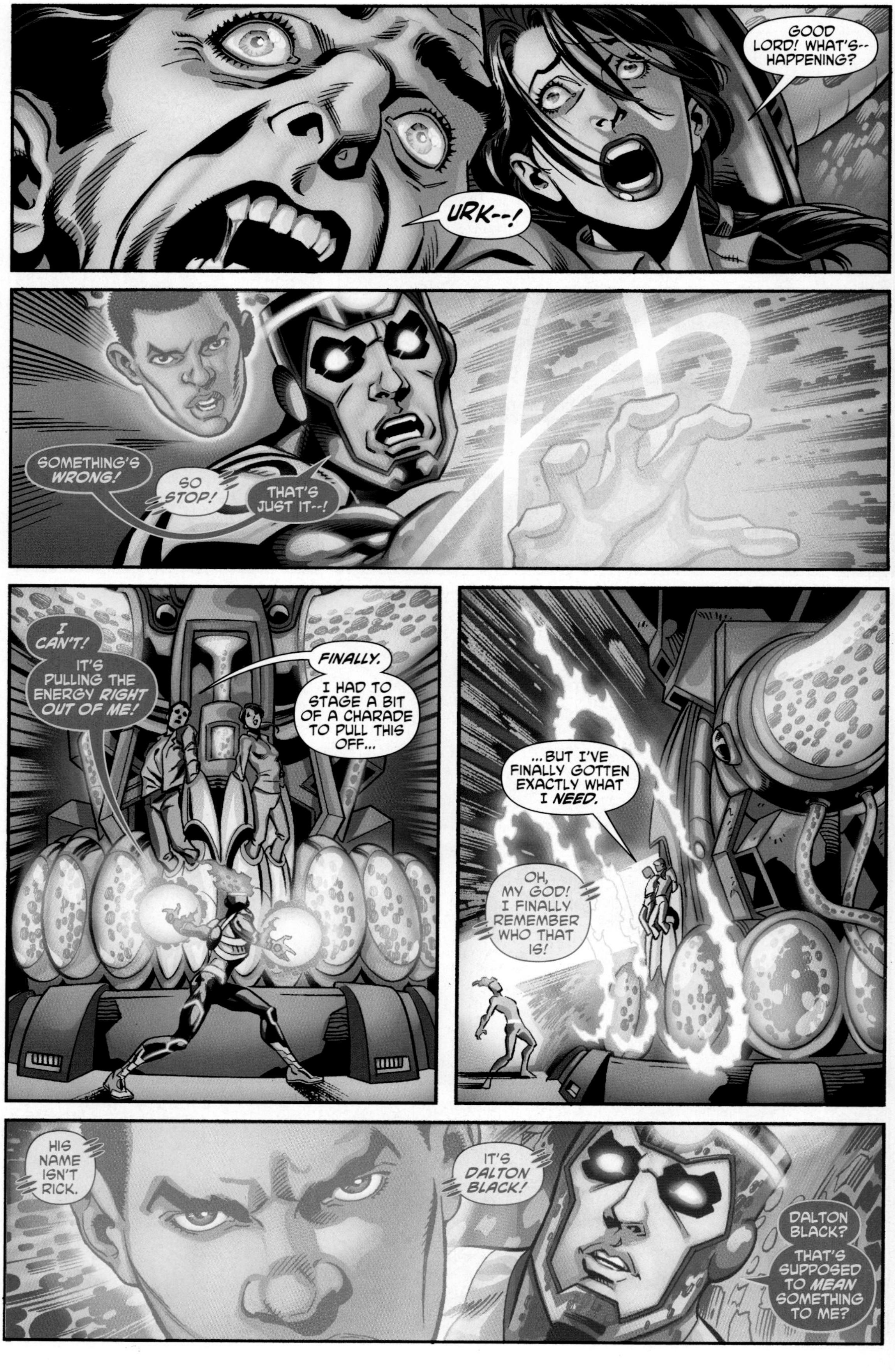
GOOD LORD! WHAT'S-- HAPPENING?
URK--!
SOMETHING'S WRONG!
SO STOP!
THAT'S JUST IT--!
I CAN'T!
IT'S PULLING THE ENERGY RIGHT OUT OF ME!
FINALLY.
I HAD TO STAGE A BIT OF A CHARADE TO PULL THIS OFF...
...BUT I'VE FINALLY GOTTEN EXACTLY WHAT I NEED.
OH, MY GOD! I FINALLY REMEMBER WHO THAT IS!
HIS NAME ISN'T RICK.
IT'S DALTON BLACK!
DALTON BLACK?
THAT'S SUPPOSED TO MEAN SOMETHING TO ME?

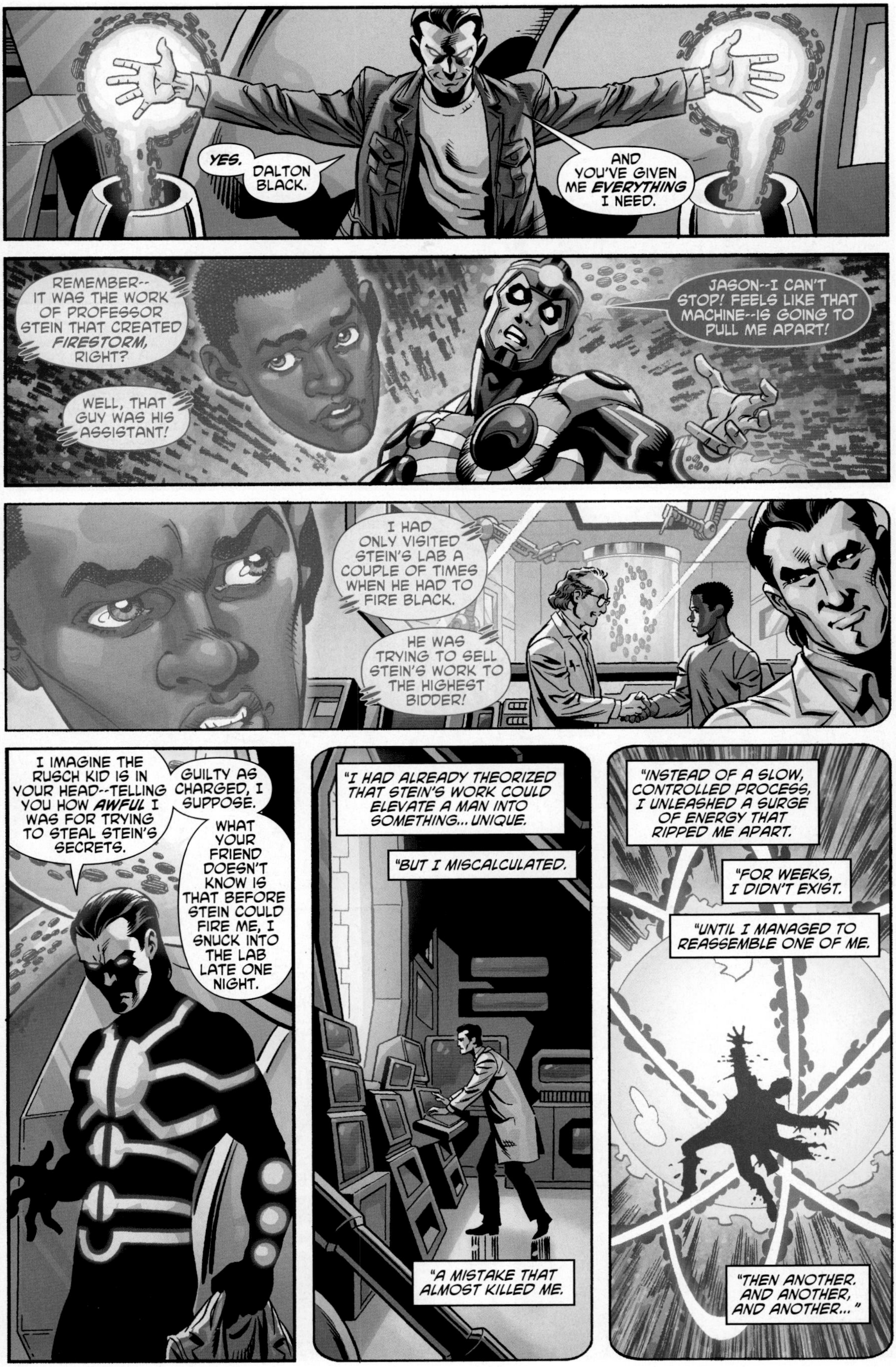
YES. DALTON BLACK.
AND YOU'VE GIVEN ME EVERYTHING I NEED.
REMEMBER-- IT WAS THE WORK OF PROFESSOR STEIN THAT CREATED FIRESTORM, RIGHT?
WELL, THAT GUY WAS HIS ASSISTANT!
JASON--I CAN'T STOP! FEELS LIKE THAT MACHINE--IS GOING TO PULL ME APART!
I HAD ONLY VISITED STEIN'S LAB A COUPLE OF TIMES WHEN HE HAD TO FIRE BLACK.
HE WAS TRYING TO SELL STEIN'S WORK TO THE HIGHEST BIDDER!
I IMAGINE THE RUSCH KID IS IN YOUR HEAD--TELLING YOU HOW AWFUL I WAS FOR TRYING TO STEAL STEIN'S SECRETS.
GUILTY AS CHARGED, I SUPPOSE.
WHAT YOUR FRIEND DOESN'T KNOW IS THAT BEFORE STEIN COULD FIRE ME, I SNUCK INTO THE LAB LATE ONE NIGHT.
"I HAD ALREADY THEORIZED THAT STEIN'S WORK COULD ELEVATE A MAN INTO SOMETHING... UNIQUE.
"BUT I MISCALCULATED.
"A MISTAKE THAT ALMOST KILLED ME.
"INSTEAD OF A SLOW, CONTROLLED PROCESS, I UNLEASHED A SURGE OF ENERGY THAT RIPPED ME APART.
"FOR WEEKS, I DIDN'T EXIST.
"UNTIL I MANAGED TO REASSEMBLE ONE OF ME.
"THEN ANOTHER. AND ANOTHER. AND ANOTHER..."

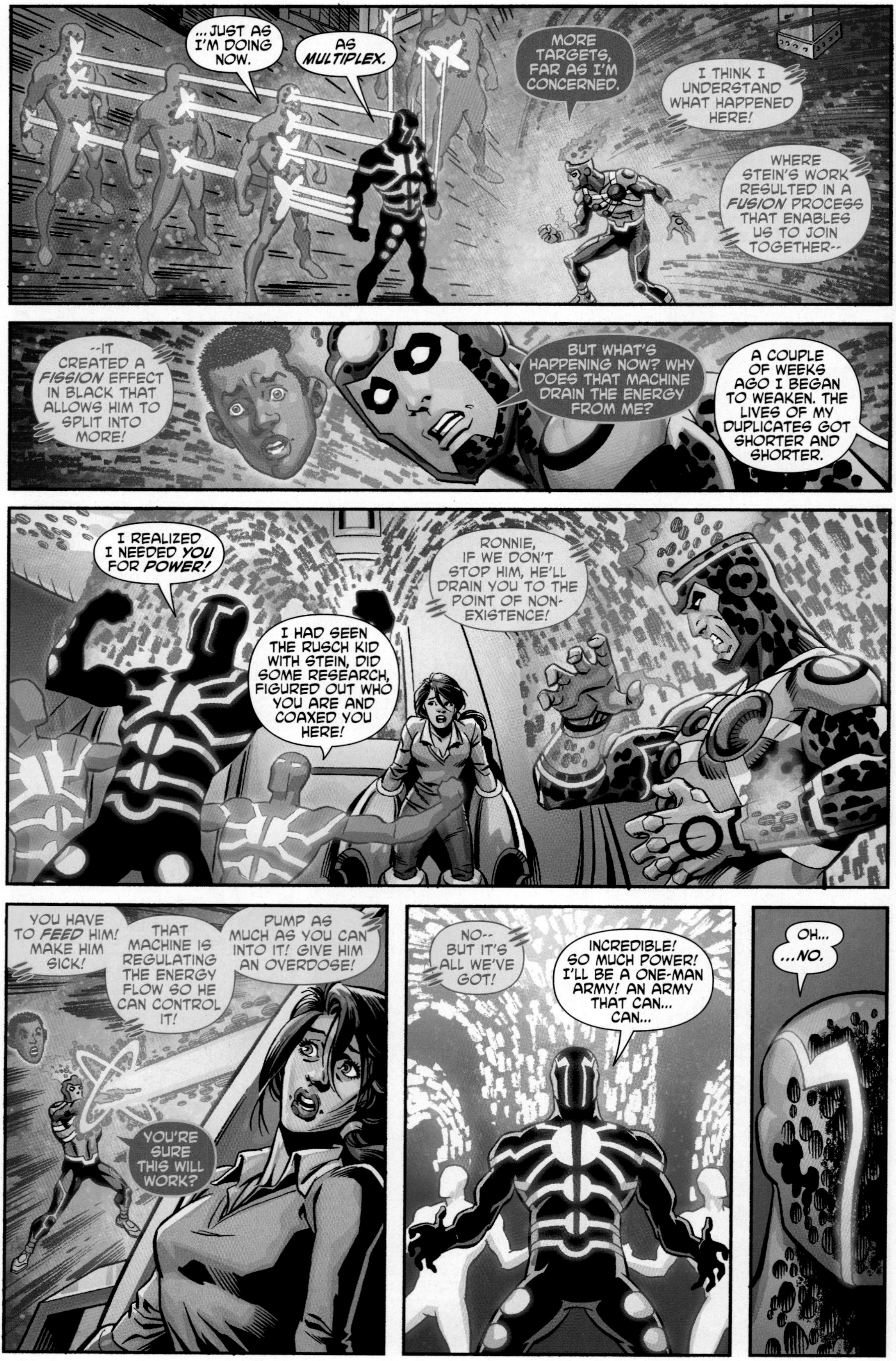
...JUST AS I'M DOING NOW.
AS MULTIPLEX.
MORE TARGETS, FAR AS I'M CONCERNED.
I THINK I UNDERSTAND WHAT HAPPENED HERE!
WHERE STEIN'S WORK RESULTED IN A FUSION PROCESS THAT ENABLES US TO JOIN TOGETHER--
--IT CREATED A FISSION EFFECT IN BLACK THAT ALLOWS HIM TO SPLIT INTO MORE!
BUT WHAT'S HAPPENING NOW? WHY DOES THAT MACHINE DRAIN THE ENERGY FROM ME?
A COUPLE OF WEEKS AGO I BEGAN TO WEAKEN. THE LIVES OF MY DUPLICATES GOT SHORTER AND SHORTER.
I REALIZED I NEEDED YOU FOR POWER!
I HAD SEEN THE RUSCH KID WITH STEIN, DID SOME RESEARCH, FIGURED OUT WHO YOU ARE AND COAXED YOU HERE!
RONNIE, IF WE DON'T STOP HIM, HE'LL DRAIN YOU TO THE POINT OF NON-EXISTENCE!
YOU HAVE TO FEED HIM! MAKE HIM SICK!
THAT MACHINE IS REGULATING THE ENERGY FLOW SO HE CAN CONTROL IT!
PUMP AS MUCH AS YOU CAN INTO IT! GIVE HIM AN OVERDOSE!
YOU'RE SURE THIS WILL WORK?
NO-- BUT IT'S ALL WE'VE GOT!
INCREDIBLE! SO MUCH POWER! I'LL BE A ONE-MAN ARMY! AN ARMY THAT CAN... CAN...
OH... ...NO.

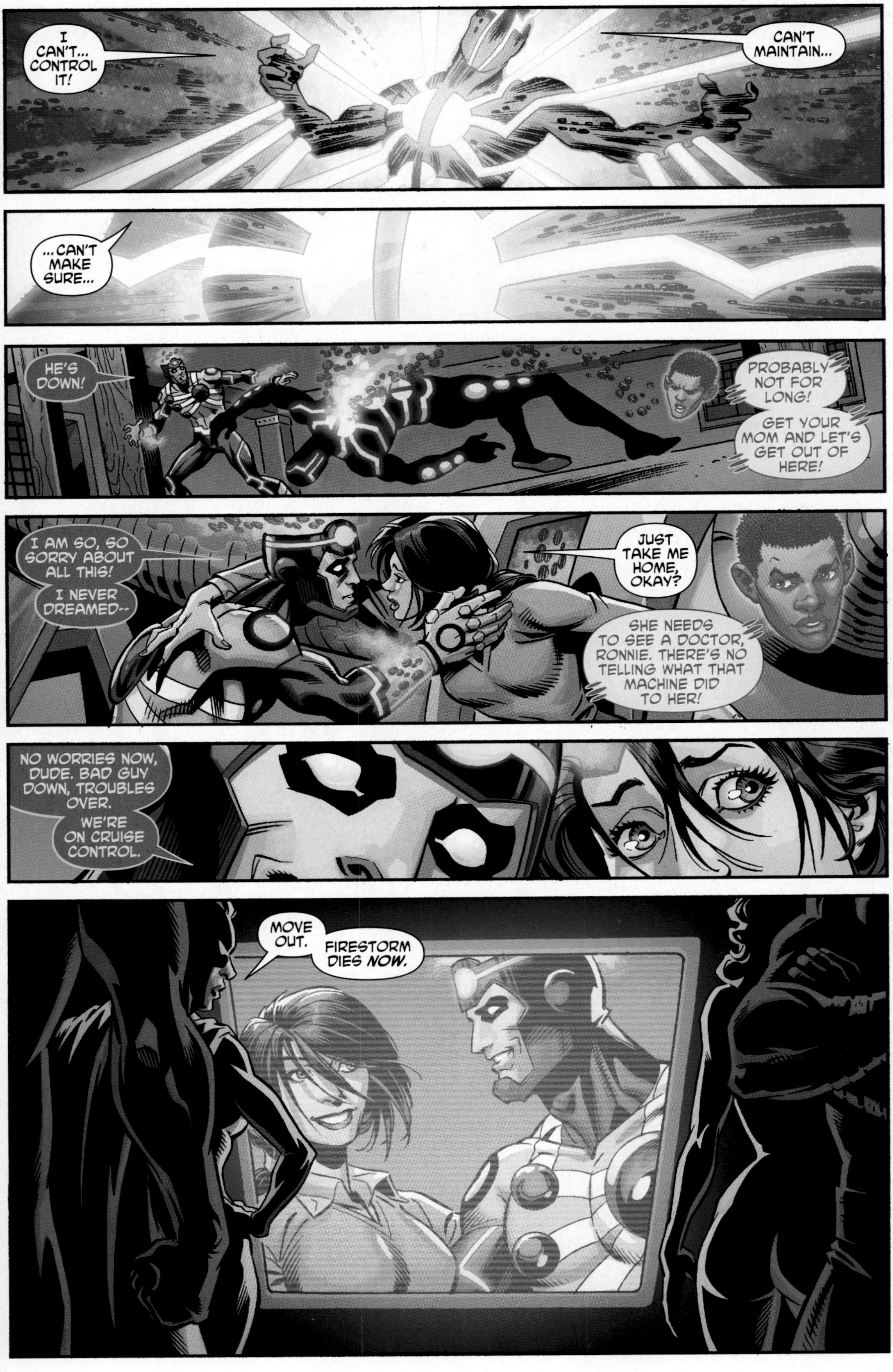
I CAN'T... CONTROL IT!
CAN'T MAINTAIN...
...CAN'T MAKE SURE...
HE'S DOWN!
PROBABLY NOT FOR LONG!
GET YOUR MOM AND LET'S GET OUT OF HERE!
I AM SO, SO SORRY ABOUT ALL THIS!
I NEVER DREAMED--
JUST TAKE ME HOME, OKAY?
SHE NEEDS TO SEE A DOCTOR, RONNIE. THERE'S NO TELLING WHAT THAT MACHINE DID TO HER!
NO WORRIES NOW, DUDE. BAD GUY DOWN, TROUBLES OVER.
WE'RE ON CRUISE CONTROL.
MOVE OUT.
FIRESTORM DIES NOW.

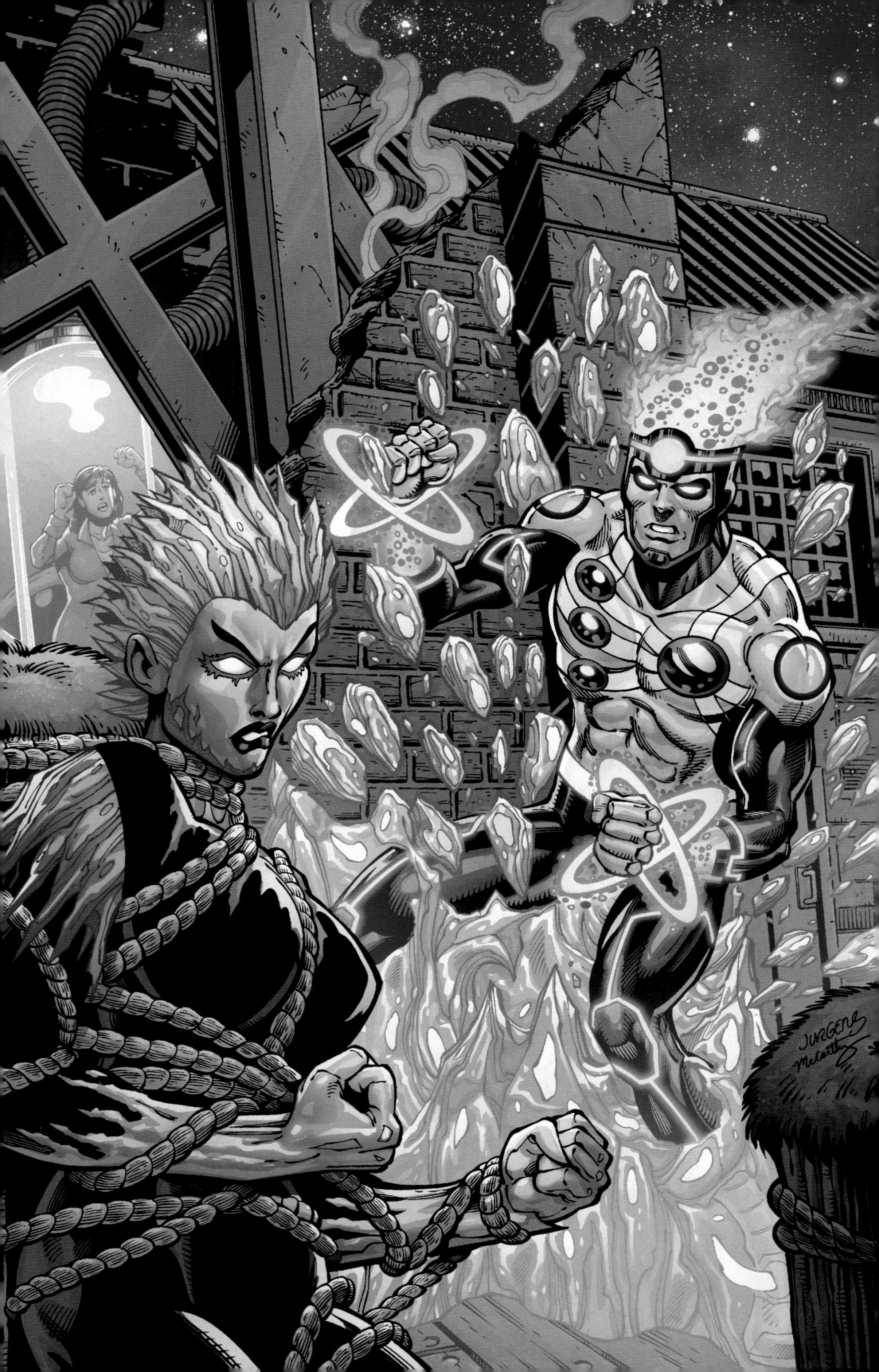

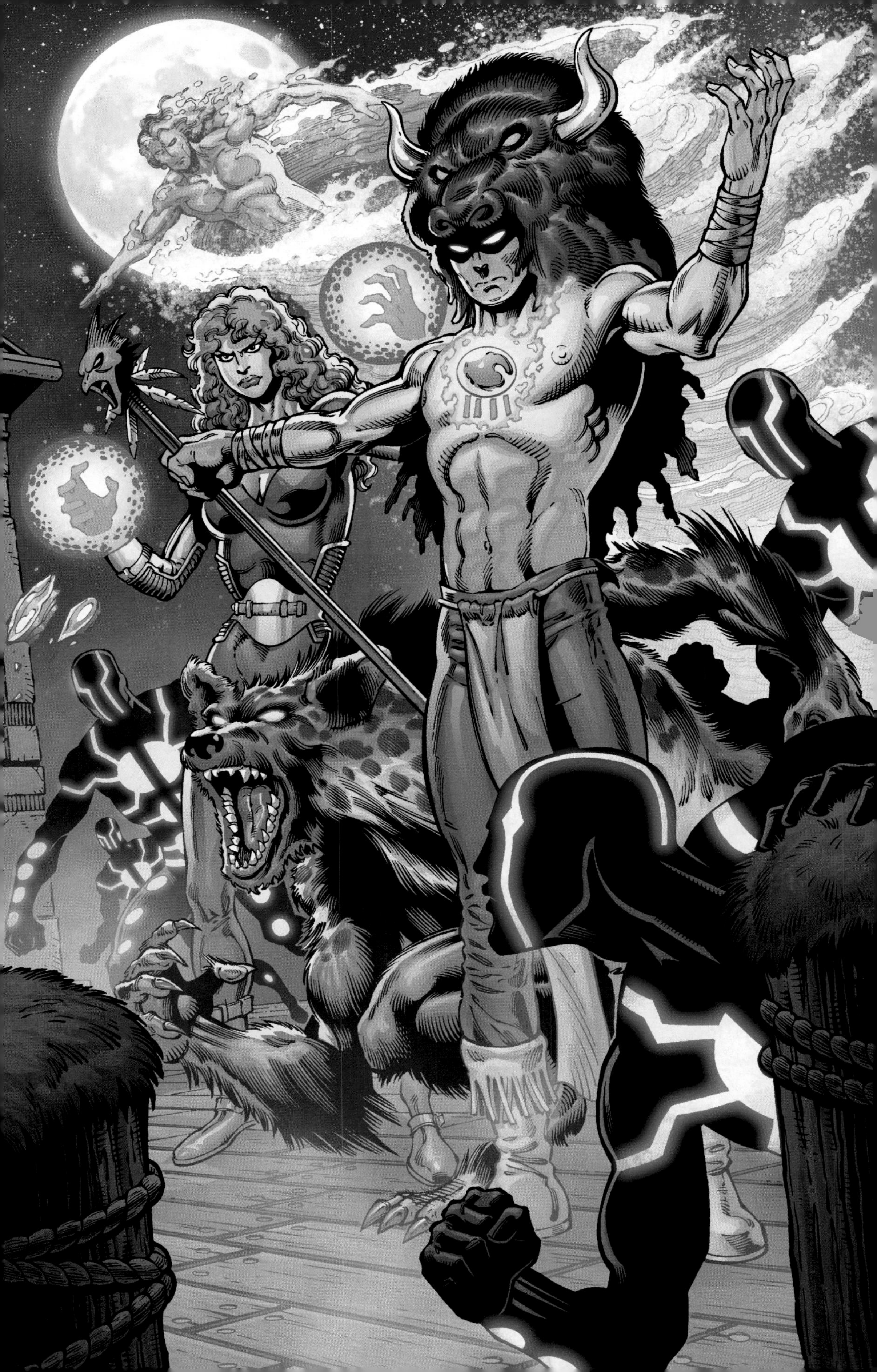

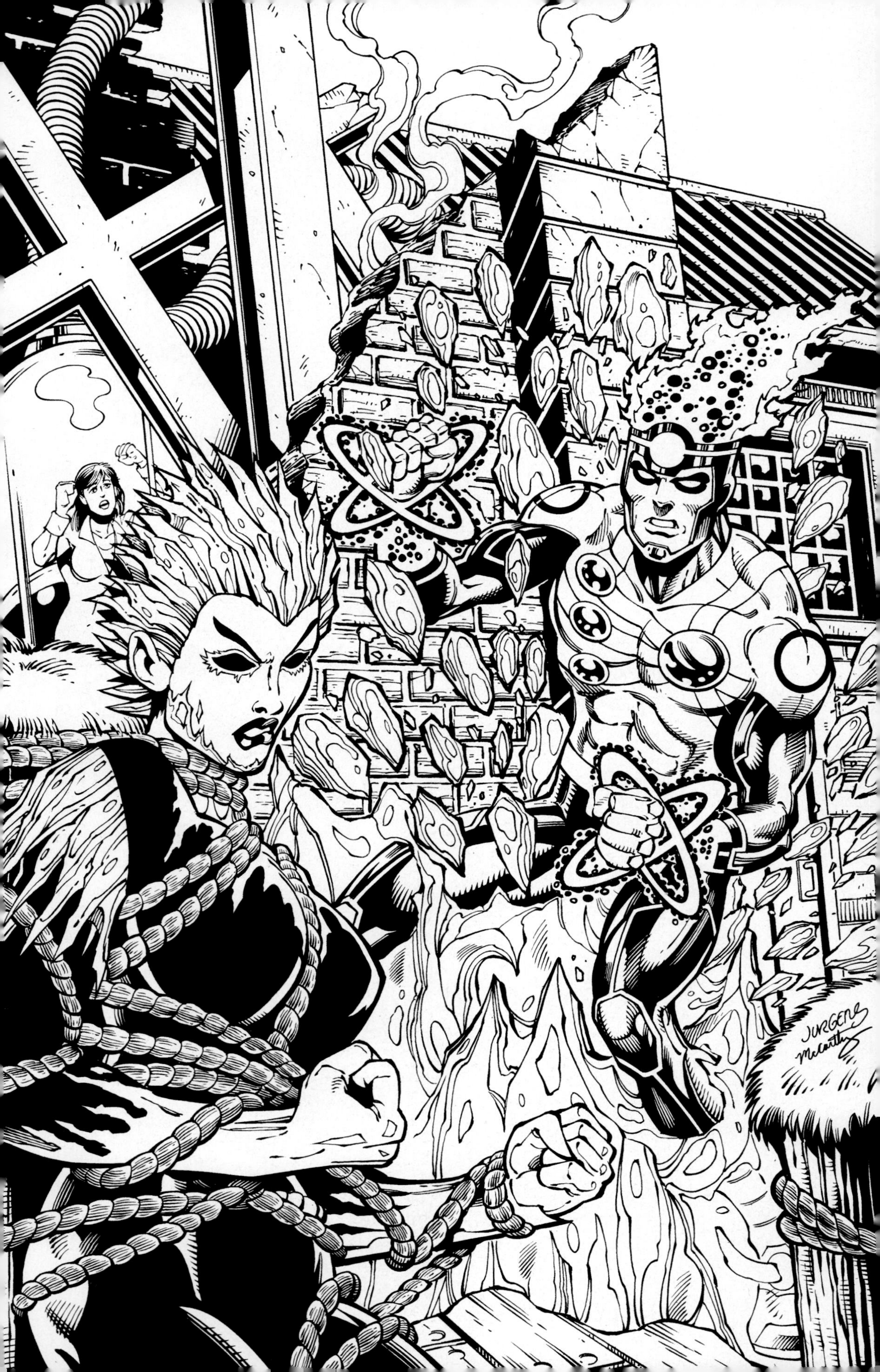
JURGENS
McCarthy

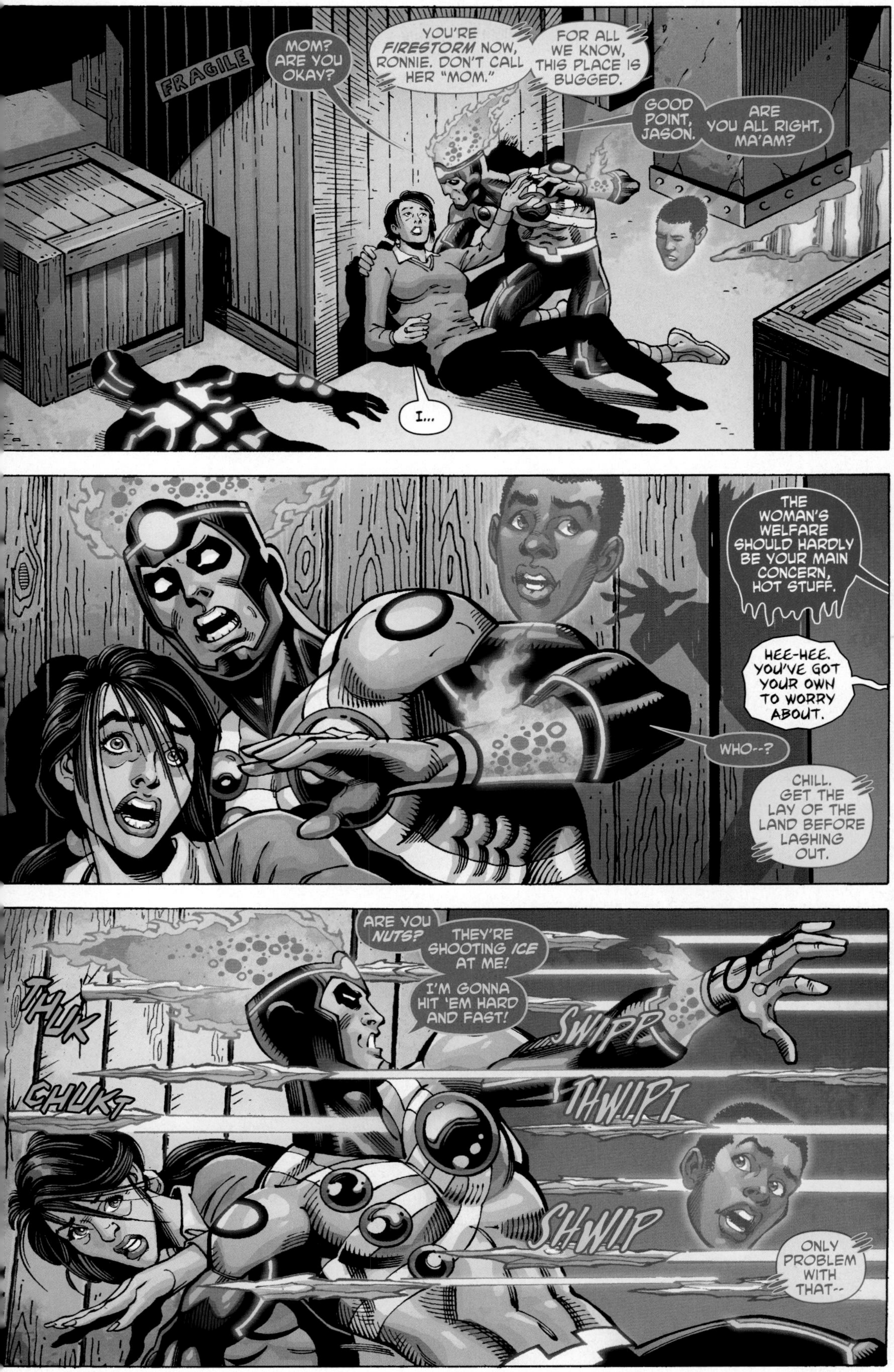
FRAGILE
MOM? ARE YOU OKAY?
YOU'RE FIRESTORM NOW, RONNIE. DON'T CALL HER "MOM."
FOR ALL WE KNOW, THIS PLACE IS BUGGED.
GOOD POINT, JASON.
ARE YOU ALL RIGHT, MA'AM?
I...
THE WOMAN'S WELFARE SHOULD HARDLY BE YOUR MAIN CONCERN, HOT STUFF.
HEE-HEE. YOU'VE GOT YOUR OWN TO WORRY ABOUT.
WHO--?
CHILL. GET THE LAY OF THE LAND BEFORE LASHING OUT.
ARE YOU NUTS?
THEY'RE SHOOTING ICE AT ME!
I'M GONNA HIT 'EM HARD AND FAST!
THUK
SWIPP
CHUKT
THWIPT
SHWIP
ONLY PROBLEM WITH THAT--

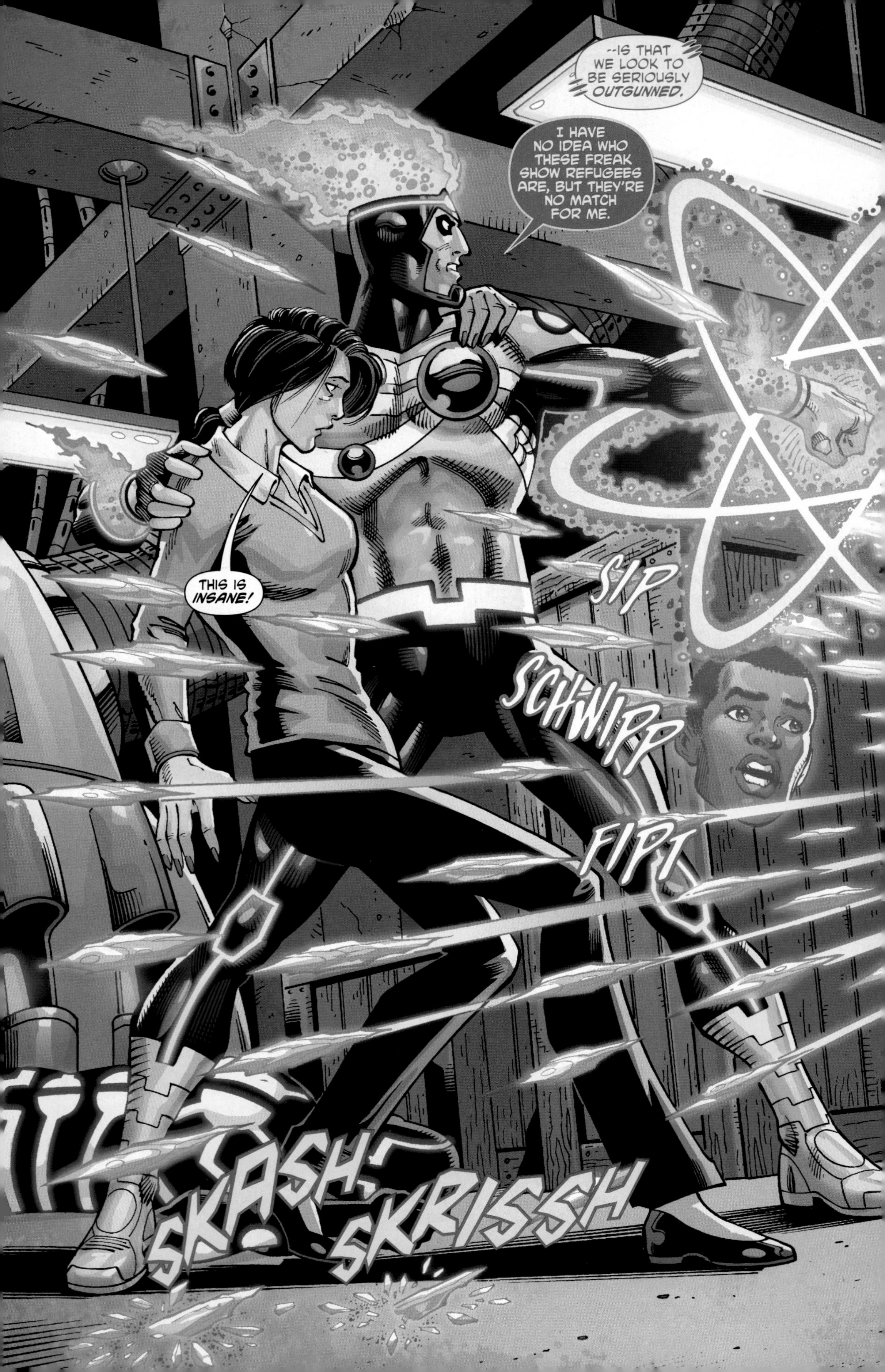
--IS THAT WE LOOK TO BE SERIOUSLY OUTGUNNED.
I HAVE NO IDEA WHO THESE FREAK SHOW REFUGEES ARE, BUT THEY'RE NO MATCH FOR ME.
THIS IS INSANE!
SIP
SCHWIPP
FIPT
SKASH
SKRISSH

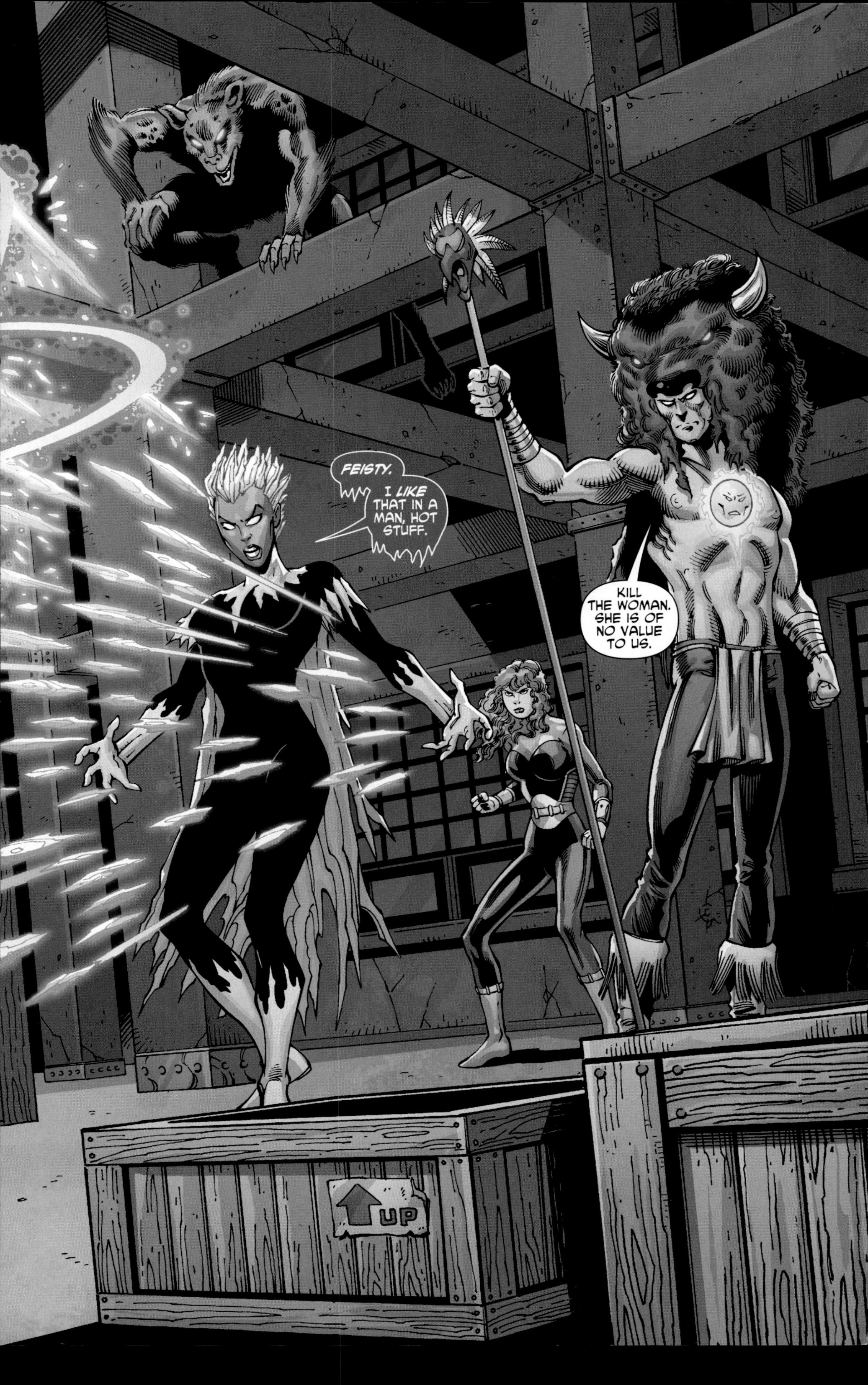
FEISTY.
I LIKE THAT IN A MAN, HOT STUFF.
KILL THE WOMAN. SHE IS OF NO VALUE TO US.
UP

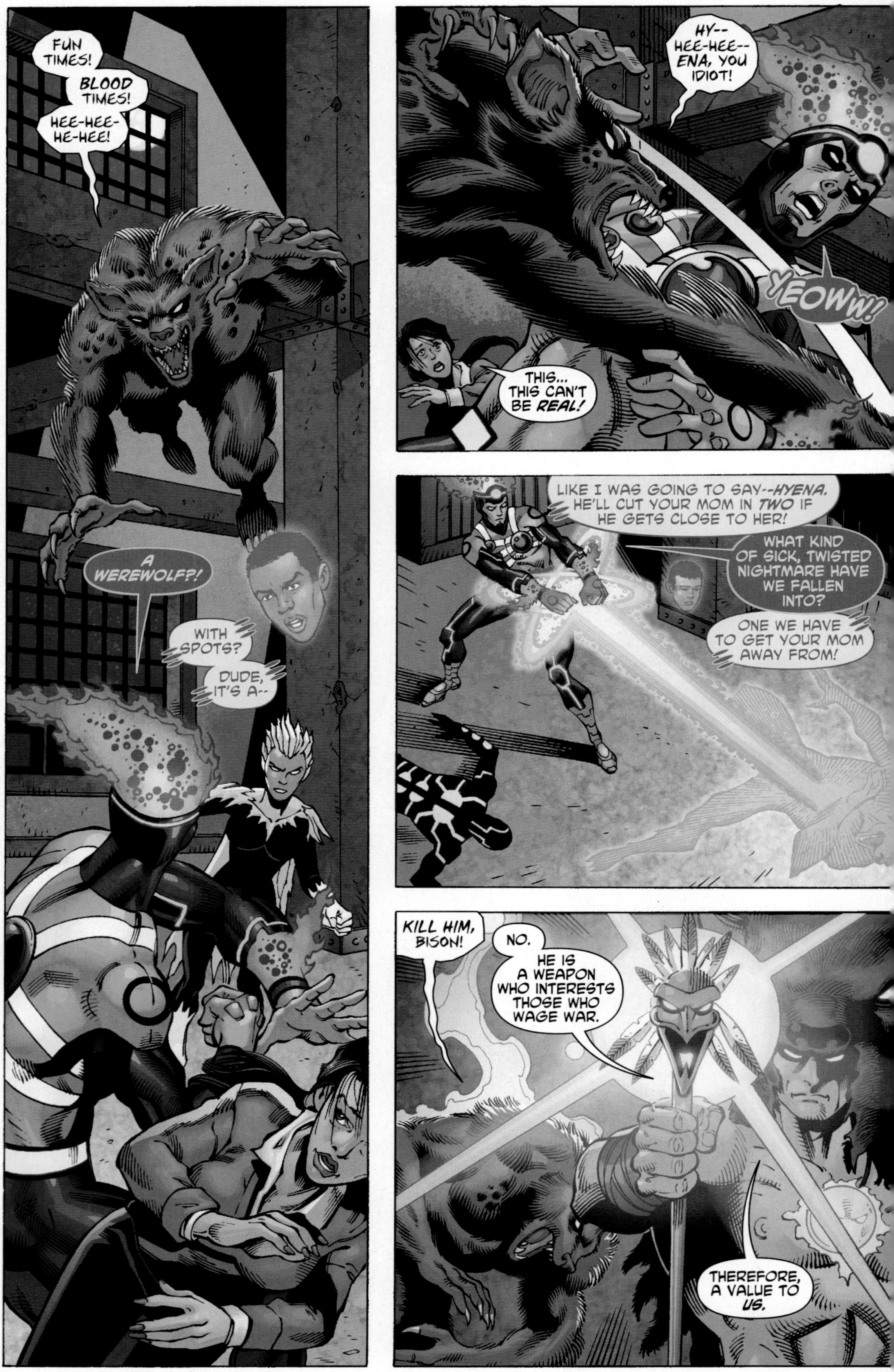
FUN TIMES!
BLOOD TIMES!
HEE-HEE-HE-HEE!
A WEREWOLF?!
WITH SPOTS?
DUDE, IT'S A--
HY--HEE-HEE--ENA, YOU IDIOT!
YEOWW!
THIS... THIS CAN'T BE REAL!
LIKE I WAS GOING TO SAY--HYENA. HE'LL CUT YOUR MOM IN TWO IF HE GETS CLOSE TO HER!
WHAT KIND OF SICK, TWISTED NIGHTMARE HAVE WE FALLEN INTO?
ONE WE HAVE TO GET YOUR MOM AWAY FROM!
KILL HIM, BISON!
NO.
HE IS A WEAPON WHO INTERESTS THOSE WHO WAGE WAR.
THEREFORE, A VALUE TO US.

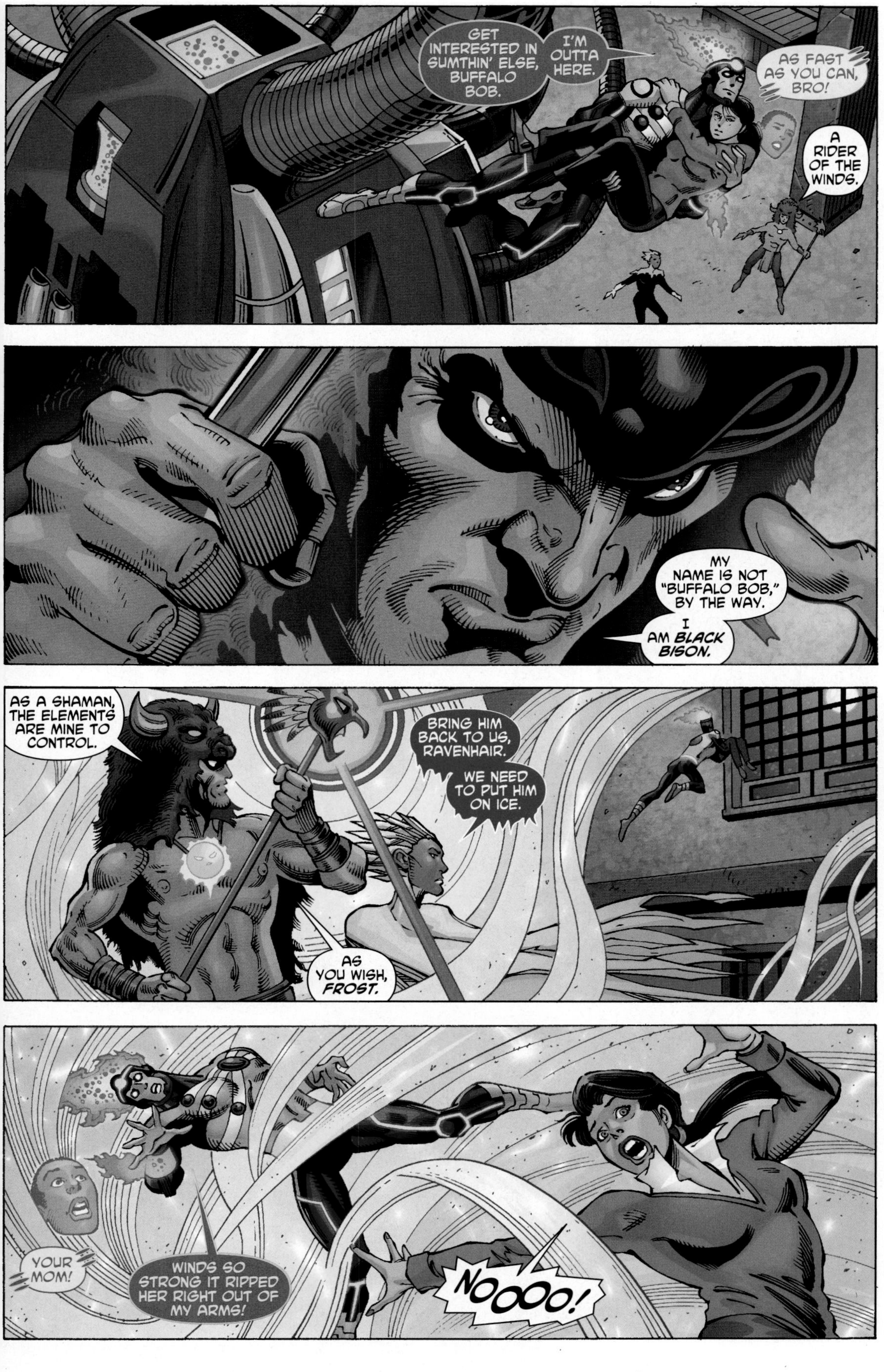
GET INTERESTED IN SUMTHIN' ELSE, BUFFALO BOB.
I'M OUTTA HERE.
AS FAST AS YOU CAN, BRO!
A RIDER OF THE WINDS.
MY NAME IS NOT "BUFFALO BOB," BY THE WAY.
I AM BLACK BISON.
AS A SHAMAN, THE ELEMENTS ARE MINE TO CONTROL.
BRING HIM BACK TO US, RAVENHAIR.
WE NEED TO PUT HIM ON ICE.
AS YOU WISH, FROST.
YOUR MOM!
WINDS SO STRONG IT RIPPED HER RIGHT OUT OF MY ARMS!
NOOOO!

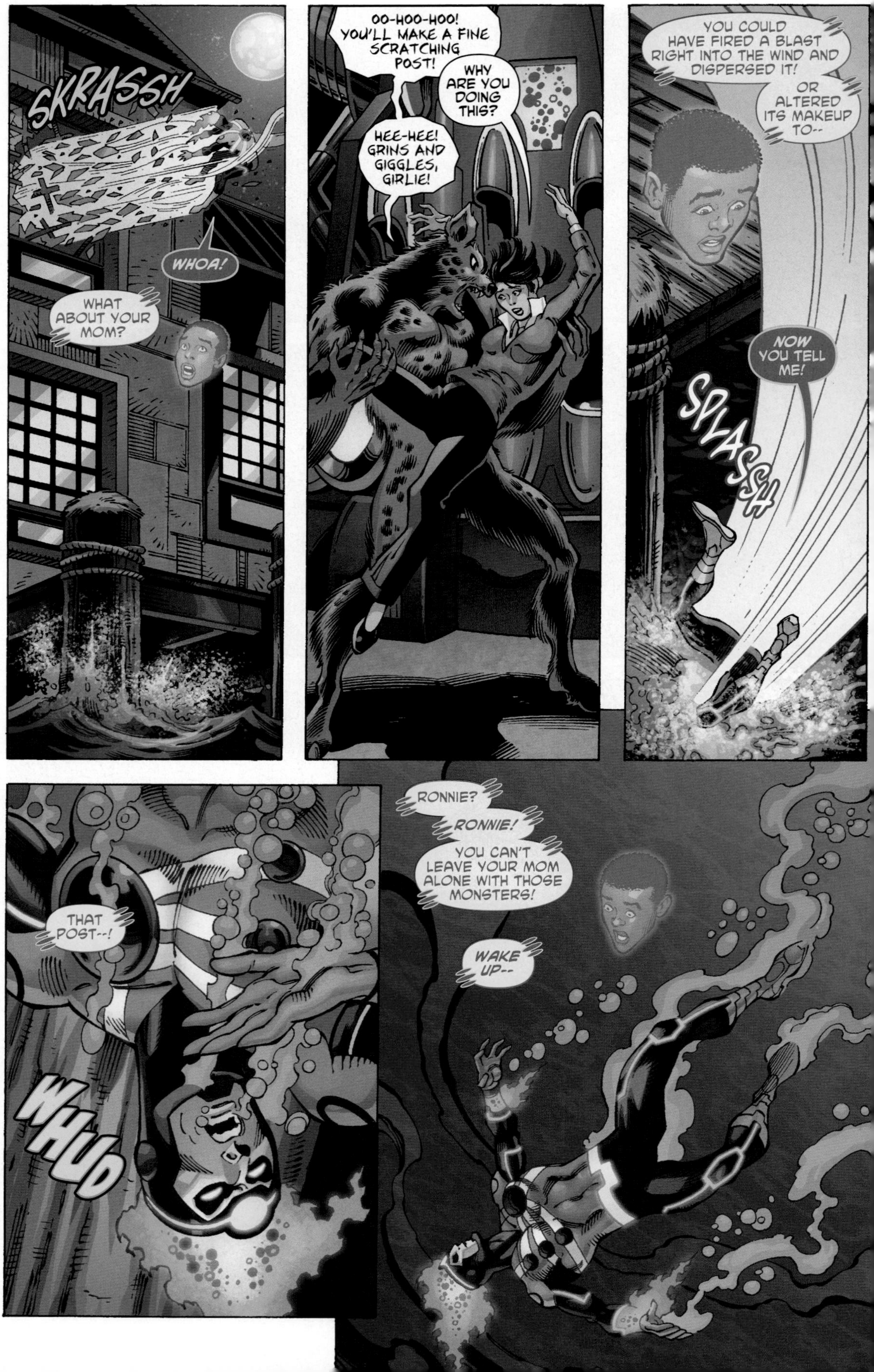
SKRASSH
WHOA!
WHAT ABOUT YOUR MOM?
OO-HOO-HOO! YOU'LL MAKE A FINE SCRATCHING POST!
WHY ARE YOU DOING THIS?
HEE-HEE! GRINS AND GIGGLES, GIRLIE!
YOU COULD HAVE FIRED A BLAST RIGHT INTO THE WIND AND DISPERSED IT!
OR ALTERED ITS MAKEUP TO--
NOW YOU TELL ME!
SPLASSH
THAT POST--!
WHUD
RONNIE?
RONNIE!
YOU CAN'T LEAVE YOUR MOM ALONE WITH THOSE MONSTERS!
WAKE UP--

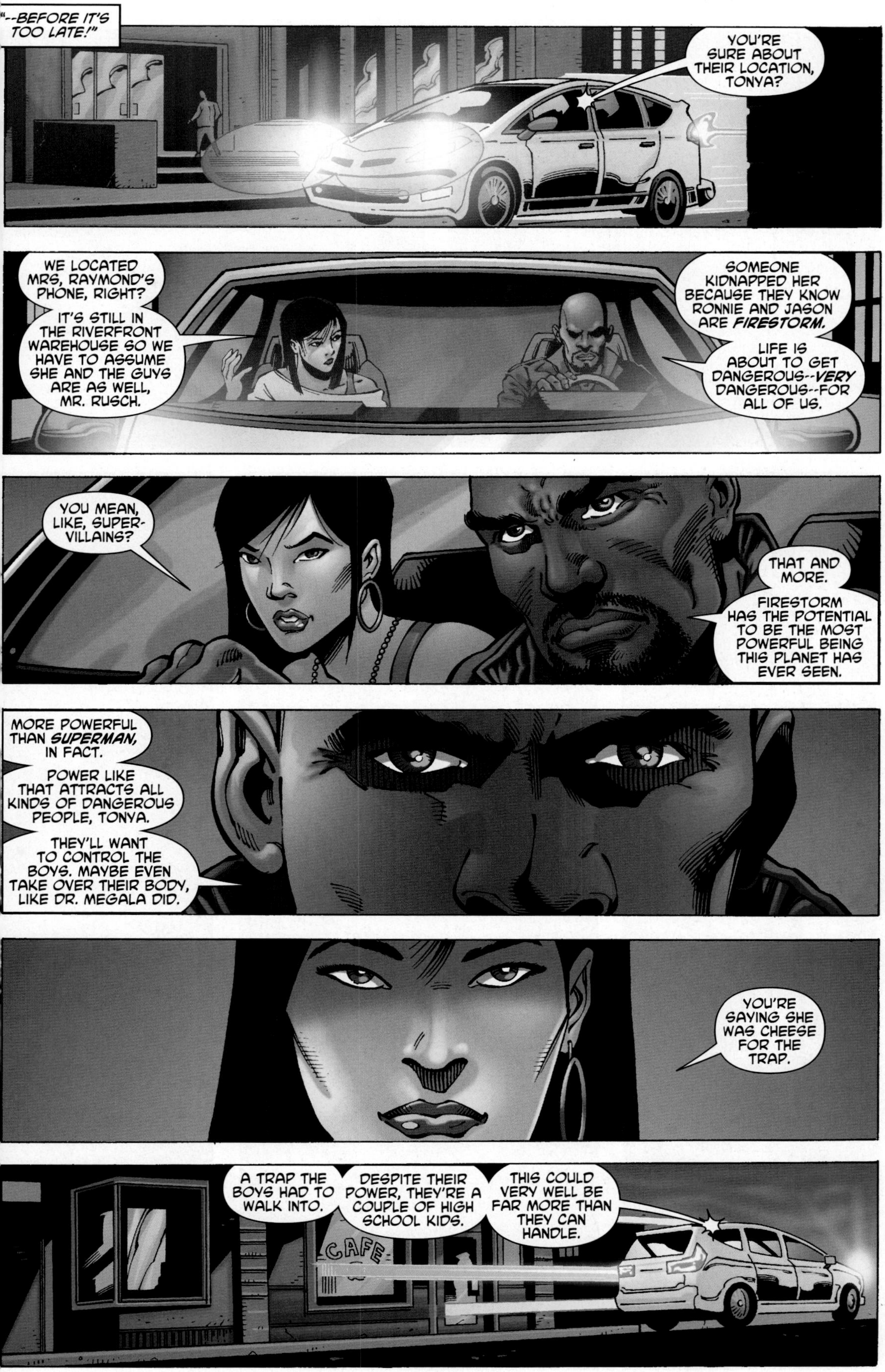
"--BEFORE IT'S TOO LATE!"
YOU'RE SURE ABOUT THEIR LOCATION, TONYA?
WE LOCATED MRS. RAYMOND'S PHONE, RIGHT?
IT'S STILL IN THE RIVERFRONT WAREHOUSE SO WE HAVE TO ASSUME SHE AND THE GUYS ARE AS WELL, MR. RUSCH.
SOMEONE KIDNAPPED HER BECAUSE THEY KNOW RONNIE AND JASON ARE FIRESTORM.
LIFE IS ABOUT TO GET DANGEROUS--VERY DANGEROUS--FOR ALL OF US.
YOU MEAN, LIKE, SUPER-VILLAINS?
THAT AND MORE.
FIRESTORM HAS THE POTENTIAL TO BE THE MOST POWERFUL BEING THIS PLANET HAS EVER SEEN.
MORE POWERFUL THAN SUPERMAN, IN FACT.
POWER LIKE THAT ATTRACTS ALL KINDS OF DANGEROUS PEOPLE, TONYA.
THEY'LL WANT TO CONTROL THE BOYS. MAYBE EVEN TAKE OVER THEIR BODY, LIKE DR. MEGALA DID.
YOU'RE SAYING SHE WAS CHEESE FOR THE TRAP.
A TRAP THE BOYS HAD TO WALK INTO.
DESPITE THEIR POWER, THEY'RE A COUPLE OF HIGH SCHOOL KIDS.
THIS COULD VERY WELL BE FAR MORE THAN THEY CAN HANDLE.
CAFE

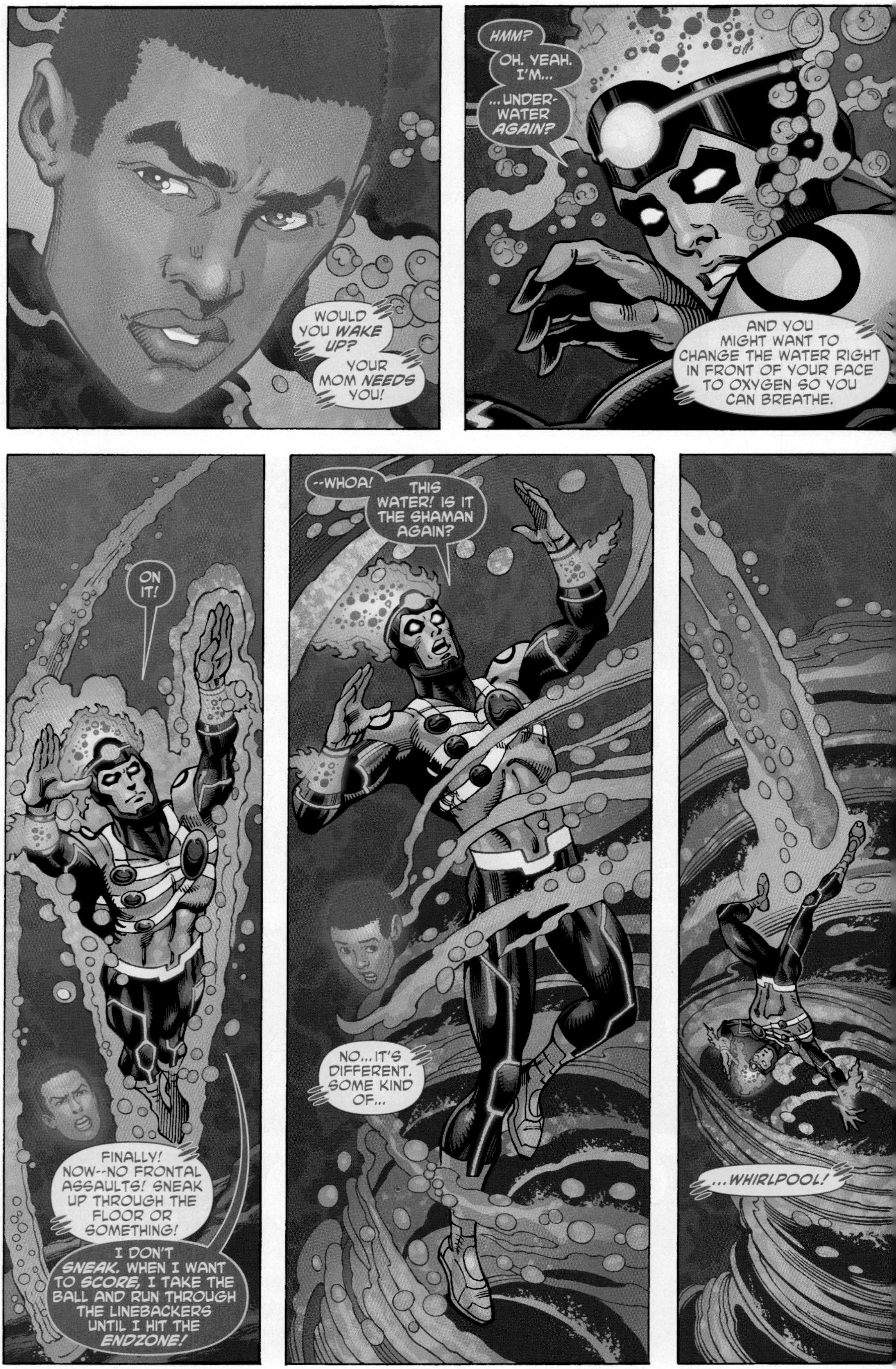
WOULD YOU WAKE UP? YOUR MOM NEEDS YOU!
HMM?
OH. YEAH. I'M...
...UNDER-WATER AGAIN?
AND YOU MIGHT WANT TO CHANGE THE WATER RIGHT IN FRONT OF YOUR FACE TO OXYGEN SO YOU CAN BREATHE.
ON IT!
FINALLY! NOW--NO FRONTAL ASSAULTS! SNEAK UP THROUGH THE FLOOR OR SOMETHING!
I DON'T SNEAK. WHEN I WANT TO SCORE, I TAKE THE BALL AND RUN THROUGH THE LINEBACKERS UNTIL I HIT THE ENDZONE!
--WHOA!
THIS WATER! IS IT THE SHAMAN AGAIN?
NO... IT'S DIFFERENT. SOME KIND OF...
...WHIRLPOOL!

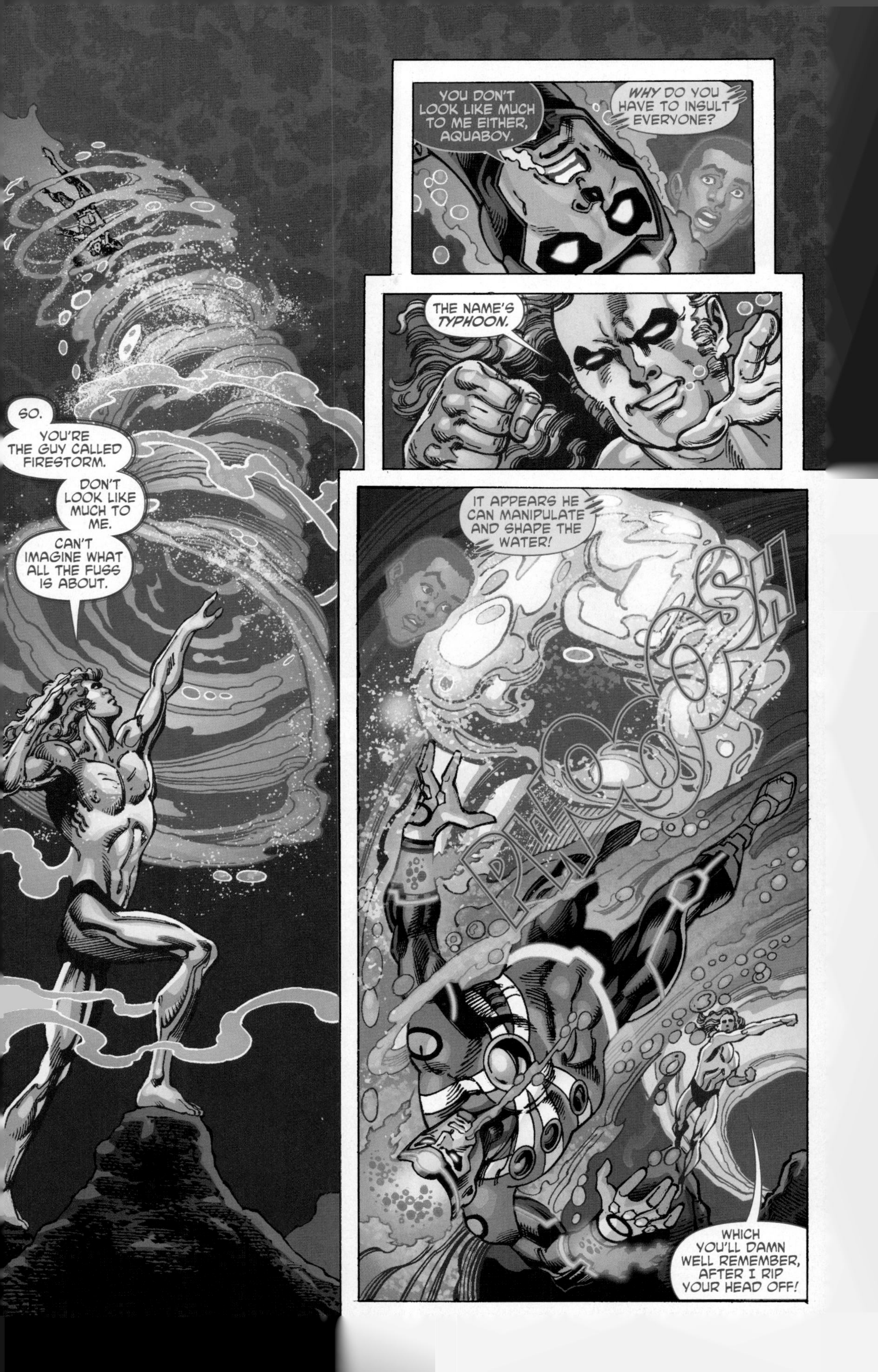
SO.
YOU'RE THE GUY CALLED FIRESTORM.
DON'T LOOK LIKE MUCH TO ME.
CAN'T IMAGINE WHAT ALL THE FUSS IS ABOUT.
YOU DON'T LOOK LIKE MUCH TO ME EITHER, AQUABOY.
WHY DO YOU HAVE TO INSULT EVERYONE?
THE NAME'S TYPHOON.
IT APPEARS HE CAN MANIPULATE AND SHAPE THE WATER!
SHOOOOSH
WHICH YOU'LL DAMN WELL REMEMBER, AFTER I RIP YOUR HEAD OFF!

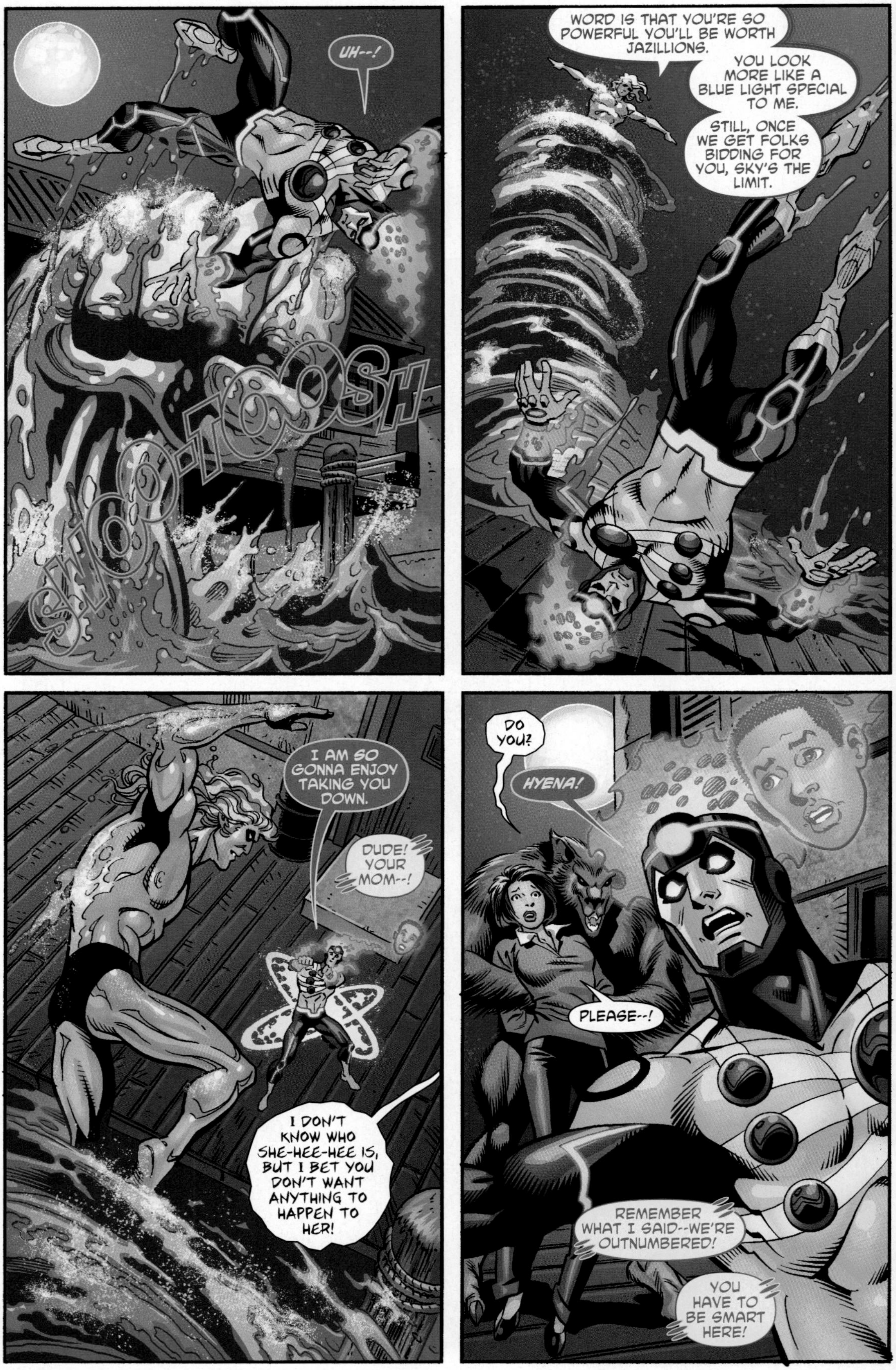
UH--!
SWOOP-TOOSH
WORD IS THAT YOU'RE SO POWERFUL YOU'LL BE WORTH JAZILLIONS.
YOU LOOK MORE LIKE A BLUE LIGHT SPECIAL TO ME.
STILL, ONCE WE GET FOLKS BIDDING FOR YOU, SKY'S THE LIMIT.
I AM SO GONNA ENJOY TAKING YOU DOWN.
DUDE! YOUR MOM--!
I DON'T KNOW WHO SHE-HEE-HEE IS, BUT I BET YOU DON'T WANT ANYTHING TO HAPPEN TO HER!
DO YOU?
HYENA!
PLEASE--!
REMEMBER WHAT I SAID--WE'RE OUTNUMBERED!
YOU HAVE TO BE SMART HERE!

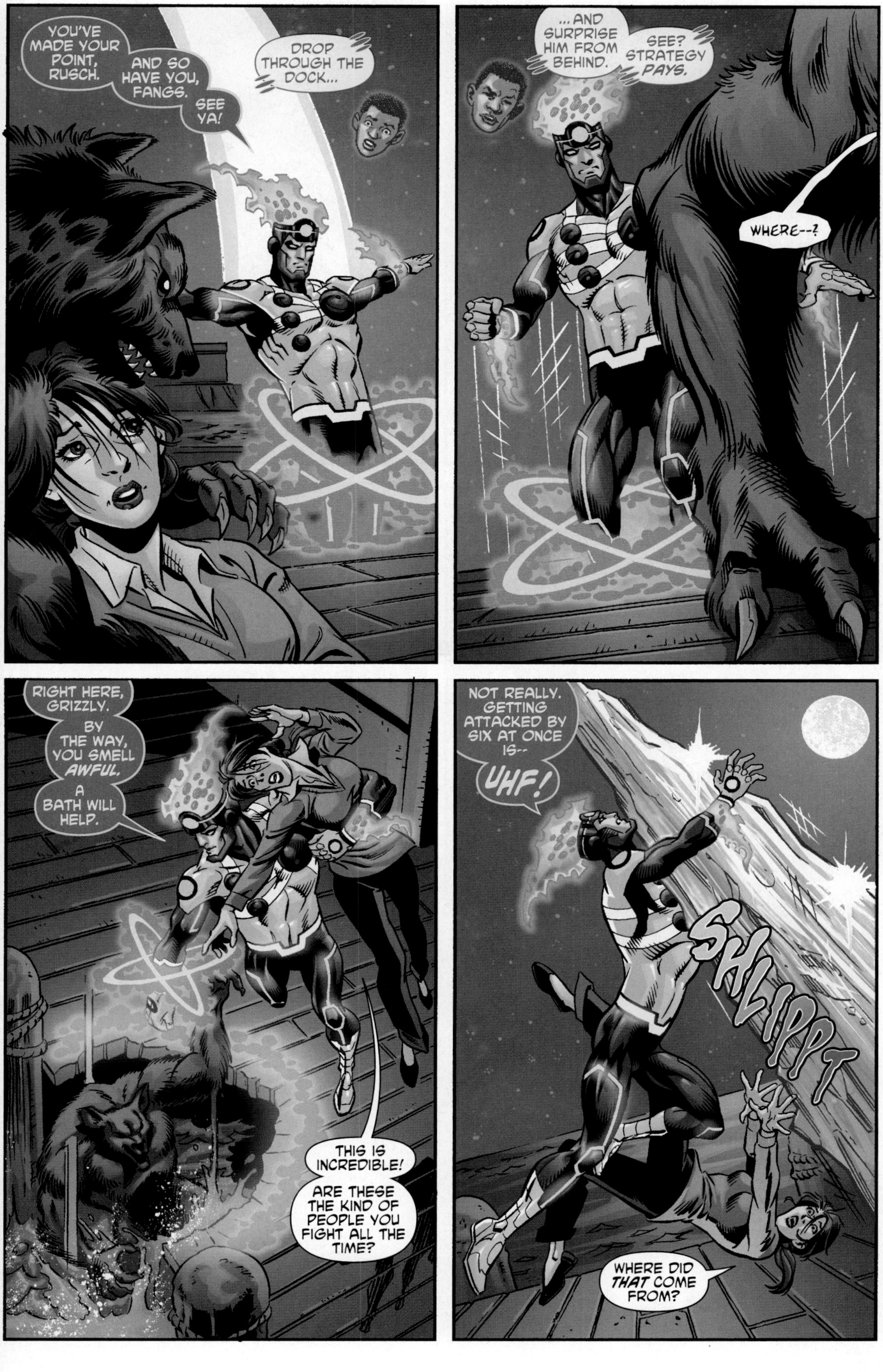
YOU'VE MADE YOUR POINT, RUSCH.
AND SO HAVE YOU, FANGS.
SEE YA!
DROP THROUGH THE DOCK...
...AND SURPRISE HIM FROM BEHIND.
SEE? STRATEGY PAYS.
WHERE--?
RIGHT HERE, GRIZZLY.
BY THE WAY, YOU SMELL AWFUL.
A BATH WILL HELP.
THIS IS INCREDIBLE!
ARE THESE THE KIND OF PEOPLE YOU FIGHT ALL THE TIME?
NOT REALLY. GETTING ATTACKED BY SIX AT ONCE IS--
UHF!
SHLIPPT
WHERE DID THAT COME FROM?

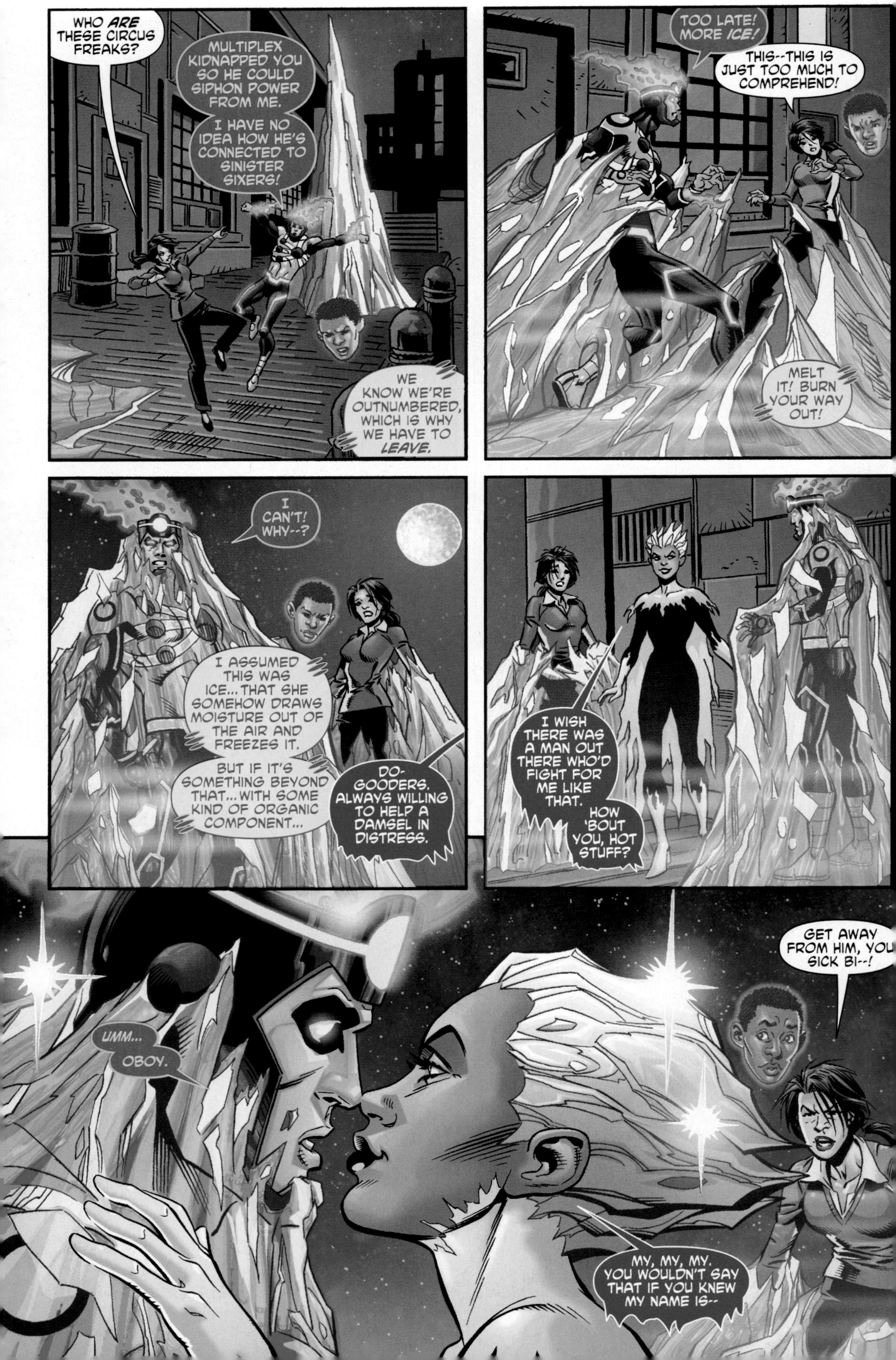

WHO *ARE* THESE CIRCUS FREAKS?
MULTIPLEX KIDNAPPED YOU SO HE COULD SIPHON POWER FROM ME.
I HAVE NO IDEA HOW HE'S CONNECTED TO SINISTER SIXERS!
WE KNOW WE'RE OUTNUMBERED, WHICH IS WHY WE HAVE TO *LEAVE.*
TOO LATE! MORE *ICE!*
THIS--THIS IS JUST TOO MUCH TO COMPREHEND!
MELT IT! BURN YOUR WAY OUT!
I CAN'T! WHY--?
I ASSUMED THIS WAS ICE... THAT SHE SOMEHOW DRAWS MOISTURE OUT OF THE AIR AND FREEZES IT.
BUT IF IT'S SOMETHING BEYOND THAT... WITH SOME KIND OF ORGANIC COMPONENT...
DO-GOODERS. ALWAYS WILLING TO HELP A DAMSEL IN DISTRESS.
I WISH THERE WAS A MAN OUT THERE WHO'D FIGHT FOR ME LIKE THAT.
HOW 'BOUT YOU, HOT STUFF?
UMM...
OBOY.
GET AWAY FROM HIM, YOU SICK BI--!
MY, MY, MY. YOU WOULDN'T SAY THAT IF YOU KNEW MY NAME IS--

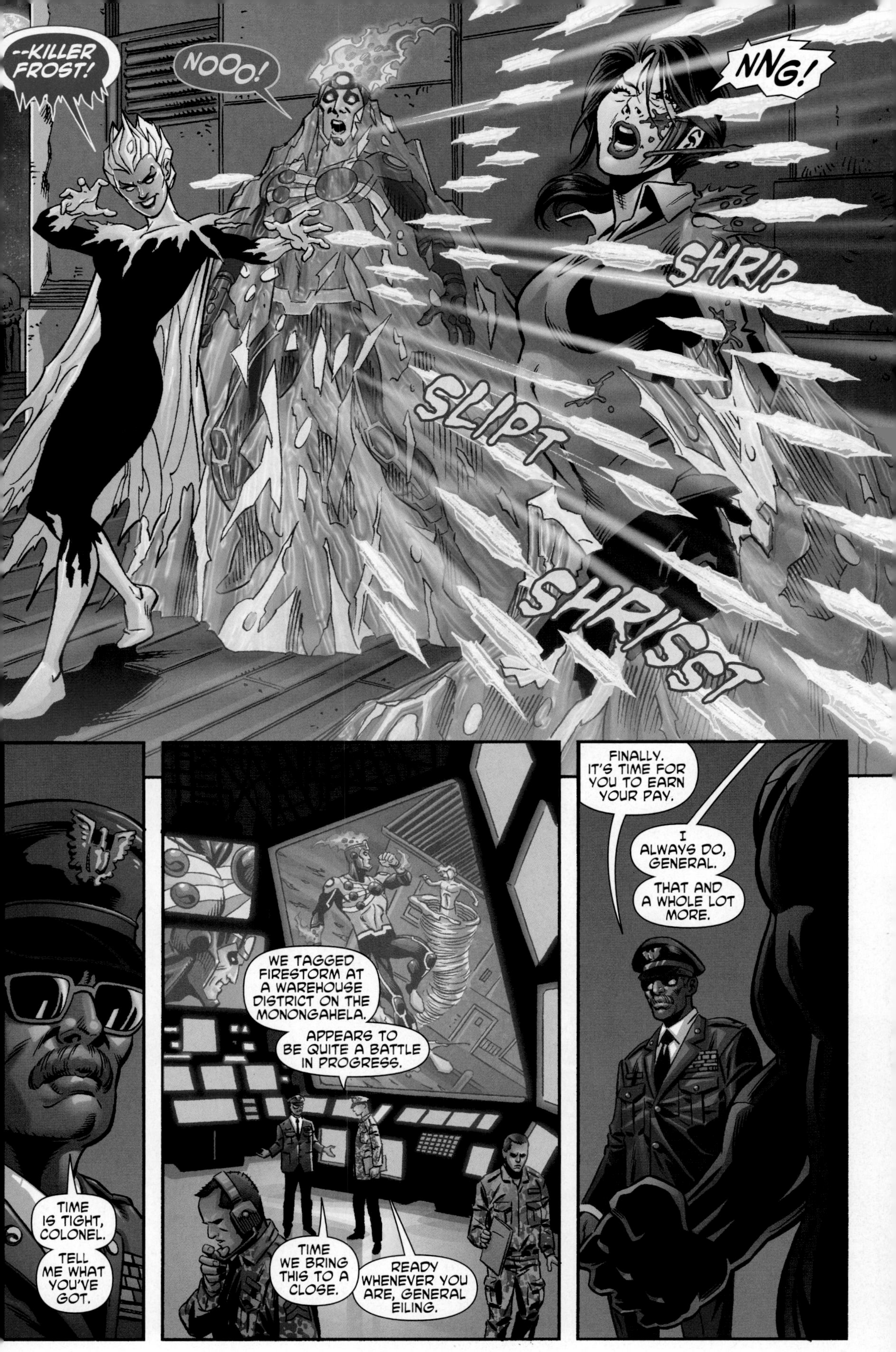
--KILLER FROST!
NOOO!
NNG!
SHRIP
SLIPT
SHRISST
TIME IS TIGHT, COLONEL.
TELL ME WHAT YOU'VE GOT.
WE TAGGED FIRESTORM AT A WAREHOUSE DISTRICT ON THE MONONGAHELA.
APPEARS TO BE QUITE A BATTLE IN PROGRESS.
TIME WE BRING THIS TO A CLOSE.
READY WHENEVER YOU ARE, GENERAL EILING.
FINALLY. IT'S TIME FOR YOU TO EARN YOUR PAY.
I ALWAYS DO, GENERAL.
THAT AND A WHOLE LOT MORE.

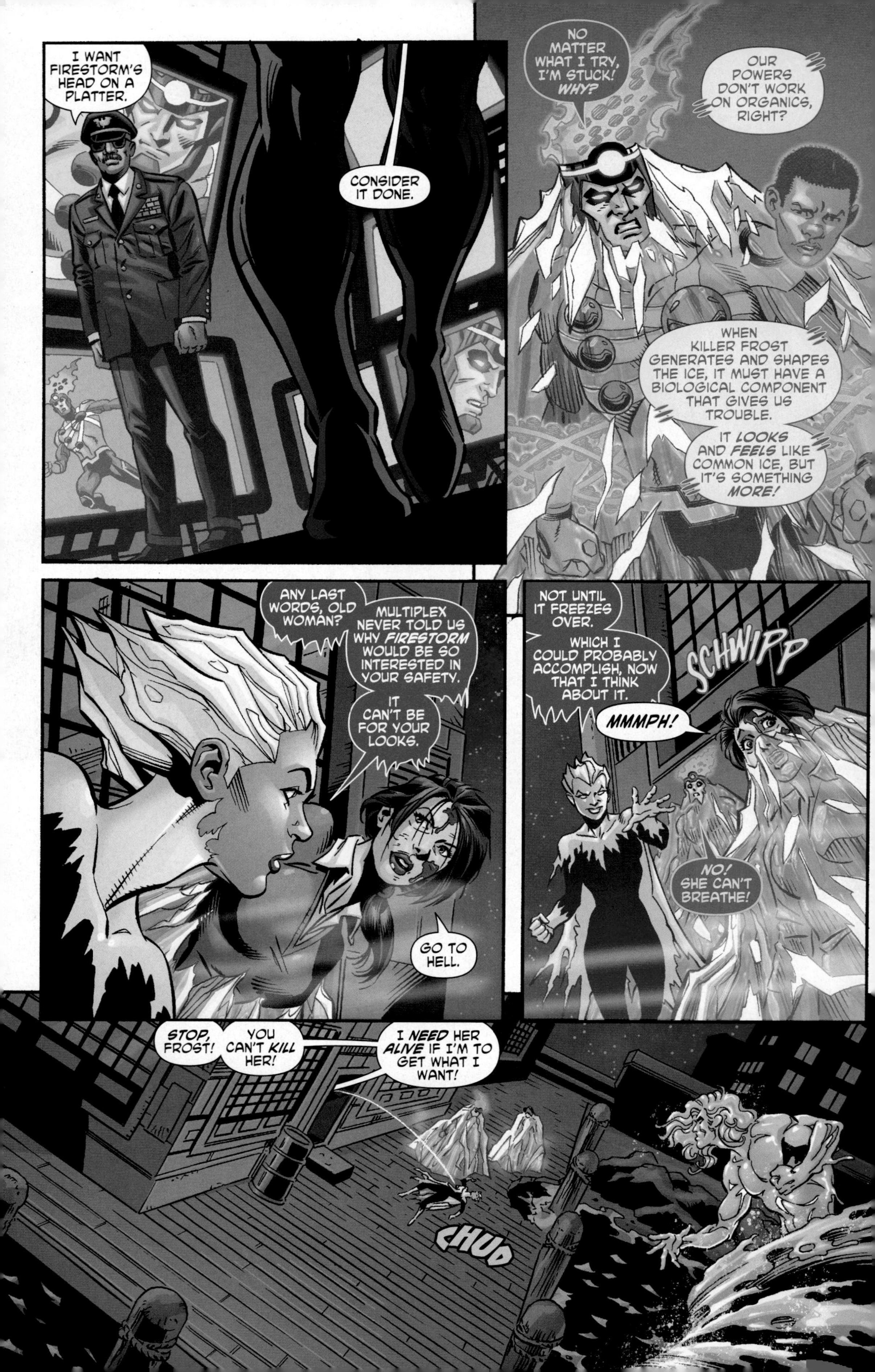
I WANT FIRESTORM'S HEAD ON A PLATTER.
CONSIDER IT DONE.
NO MATTER WHAT I TRY, I'M STUCK! WHY?
OUR POWERS DON'T WORK ON ORGANICS, RIGHT?
WHEN KILLER FROST GENERATES AND SHAPES THE ICE, IT MUST HAVE A BIOLOGICAL COMPONENT THAT GIVES US TROUBLE.
IT LOOKS AND FEELS LIKE COMMON ICE, BUT IT'S SOMETHING MORE!
ANY LAST WORDS, OLD WOMAN?
MULTIPLEX NEVER TOLD US WHY FIRESTORM WOULD BE SO INTERESTED IN YOUR SAFETY.
IT CAN'T BE FOR YOUR LOOKS.
GO TO HELL.
NOT UNTIL IT FREEZES OVER.
WHICH I COULD PROBABLY ACCOMPLISH, NOW THAT I THINK ABOUT IT.
SCHWIPP
MMMPH!
NO! SHE CAN'T BREATHE!
STOP, FROST!
YOU CAN'T KILL HER!
I NEED HER ALIVE IF I'M TO GET WHAT I WANT!
CHUD

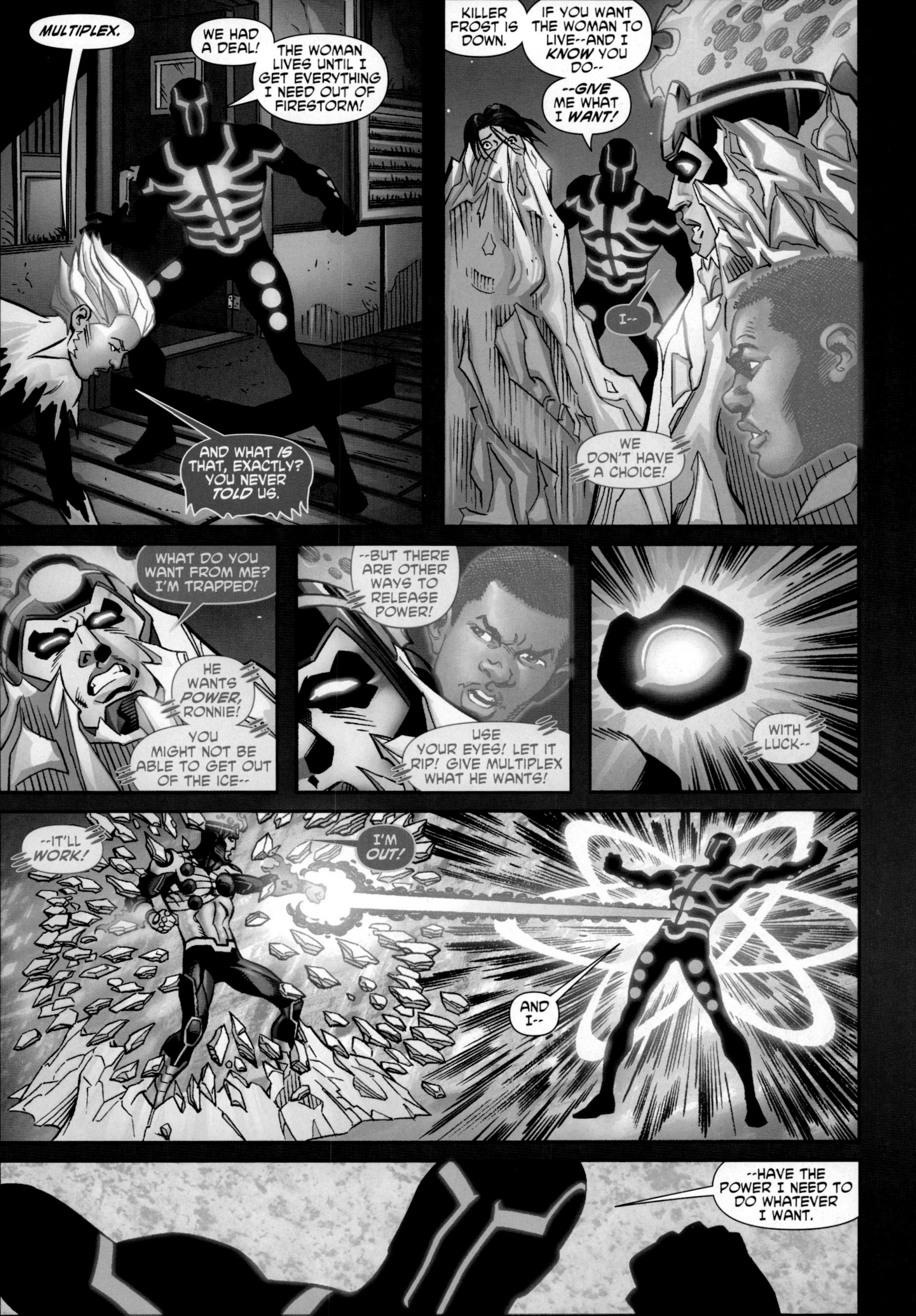
MULTIPLEX.
WE HAD A DEAL!
THE WOMAN LIVES UNTIL I GET EVERYTHING I NEED OUT OF FIRESTORM!
AND WHAT *IS* THAT, EXACTLY? YOU NEVER *TOLD* US.
KILLER FROST IS DOWN.
IF YOU WANT THE WOMAN TO LIVE--AND I *KNOW* YOU DO--
--*GIVE* ME WHAT I *WANT!*
I--
WE DON'T HAVE A CHOICE!
WHAT DO YOU WANT FROM ME? I'M TRAPPED!
HE WANTS *POWER,* RONNIE!
YOU MIGHT NOT BE ABLE TO GET OUT OF THE ICE--
--BUT THERE ARE OTHER WAYS TO RELEASE POWER!
USE YOUR EYES! LET IT RIP! GIVE MULTIPLEX WHAT HE WANTS!
WITH LUCK--
--IT'LL *WORK!*
I'M *OUT!*
AND I--
--HAVE THE POWER I NEED TO DO WHATEVER I WANT.

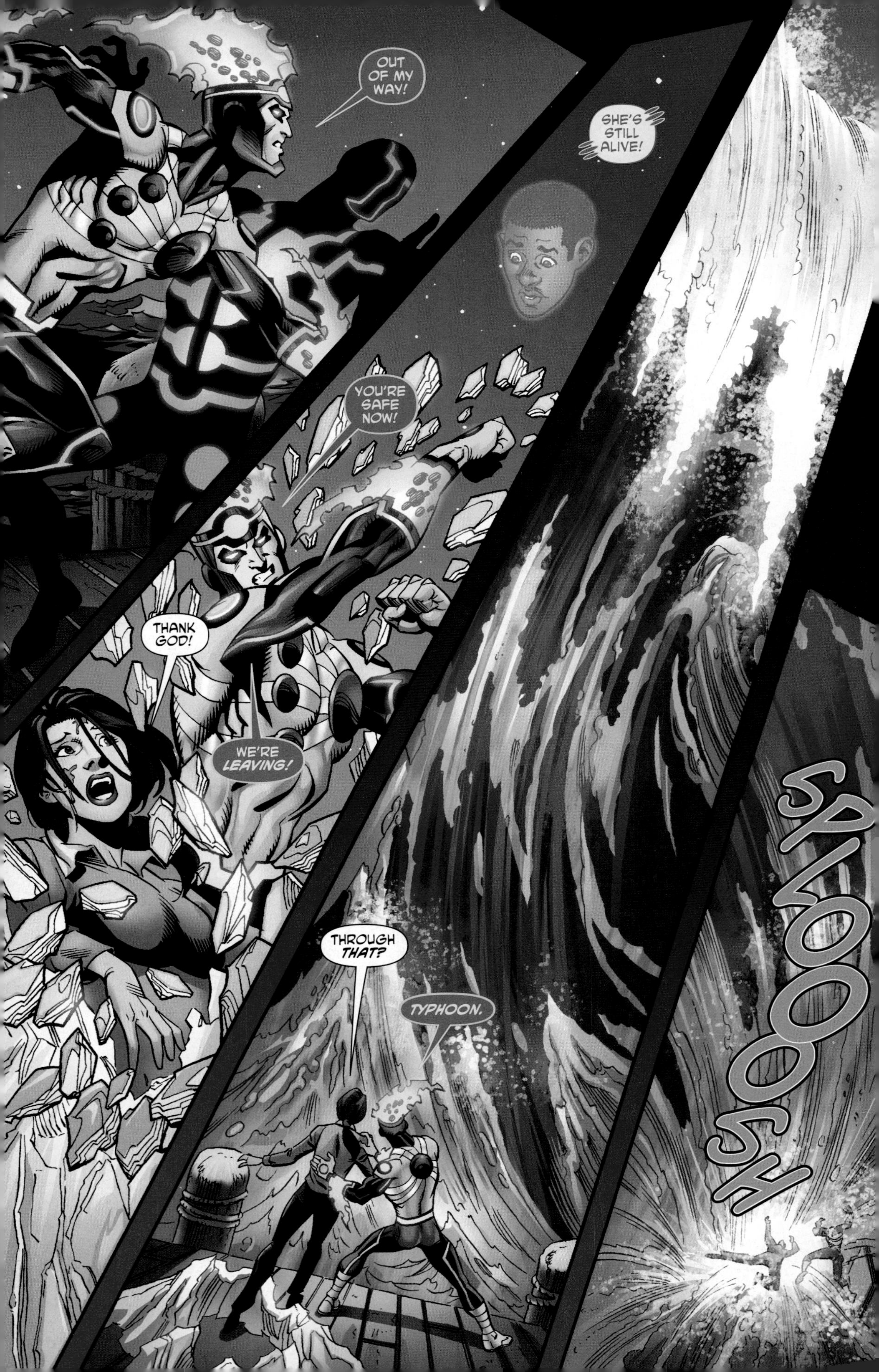
OUT OF MY WAY!
SHE'S STILL ALIVE!
YOU'RE SAFE NOW!
THANK GOD!
WE'RE *LEAVING!*
THROUGH *THAT?*
TYPHOON.
SPLOOOOSH

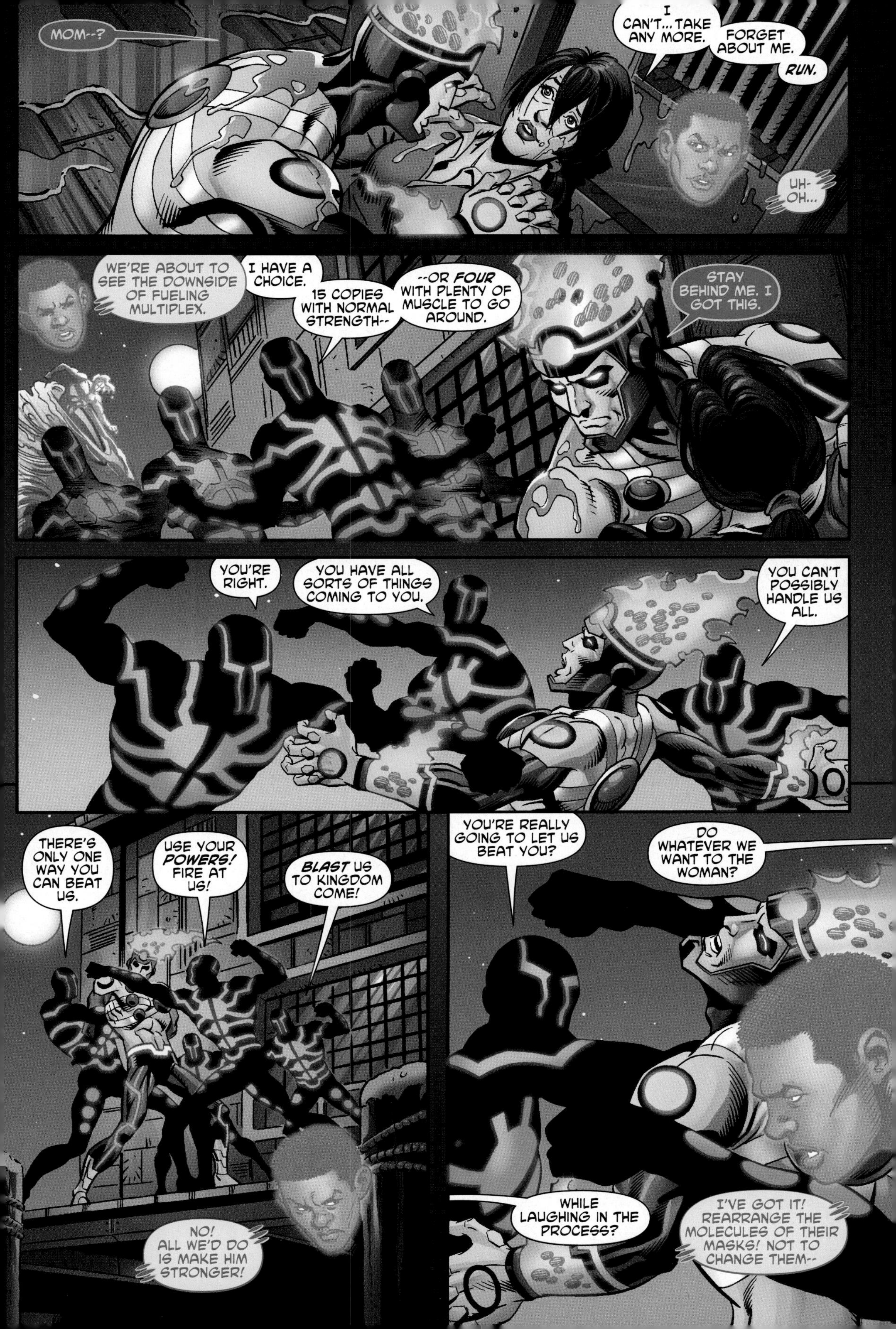

MOM--?
I CAN'T... TAKE ANY MORE.
FORGET ABOUT ME. RUN.
UH-OH...
WE'RE ABOUT TO SEE THE DOWNSIDE OF FUELING MULTIPLEX.
I HAVE A CHOICE.
15 COPIES WITH NORMAL STRENGTH--
--OR FOUR WITH PLENTY OF MUSCLE TO GO AROUND.
STAY BEHIND ME. I GOT THIS.
YOU'RE RIGHT.
YOU HAVE ALL SORTS OF THINGS COMING TO YOU.
YOU CAN'T POSSIBLY HANDLE US ALL.
THERE'S ONLY ONE WAY YOU CAN BEAT US.
USE YOUR POWERS! FIRE AT US!
BLAST US TO KINGDOM COME!
NO! ALL WE'D DO IS MAKE HIM STRONGER!
YOU'RE REALLY GOING TO LET US BEAT YOU?
DO WHATEVER WE WANT TO THE WOMAN?
WHILE LAUGHING IN THE PROCESS?
I'VE GOT IT! REARRANGE THE MOLECULES OF THEIR MASKS! NOT TO CHANGE THEM--

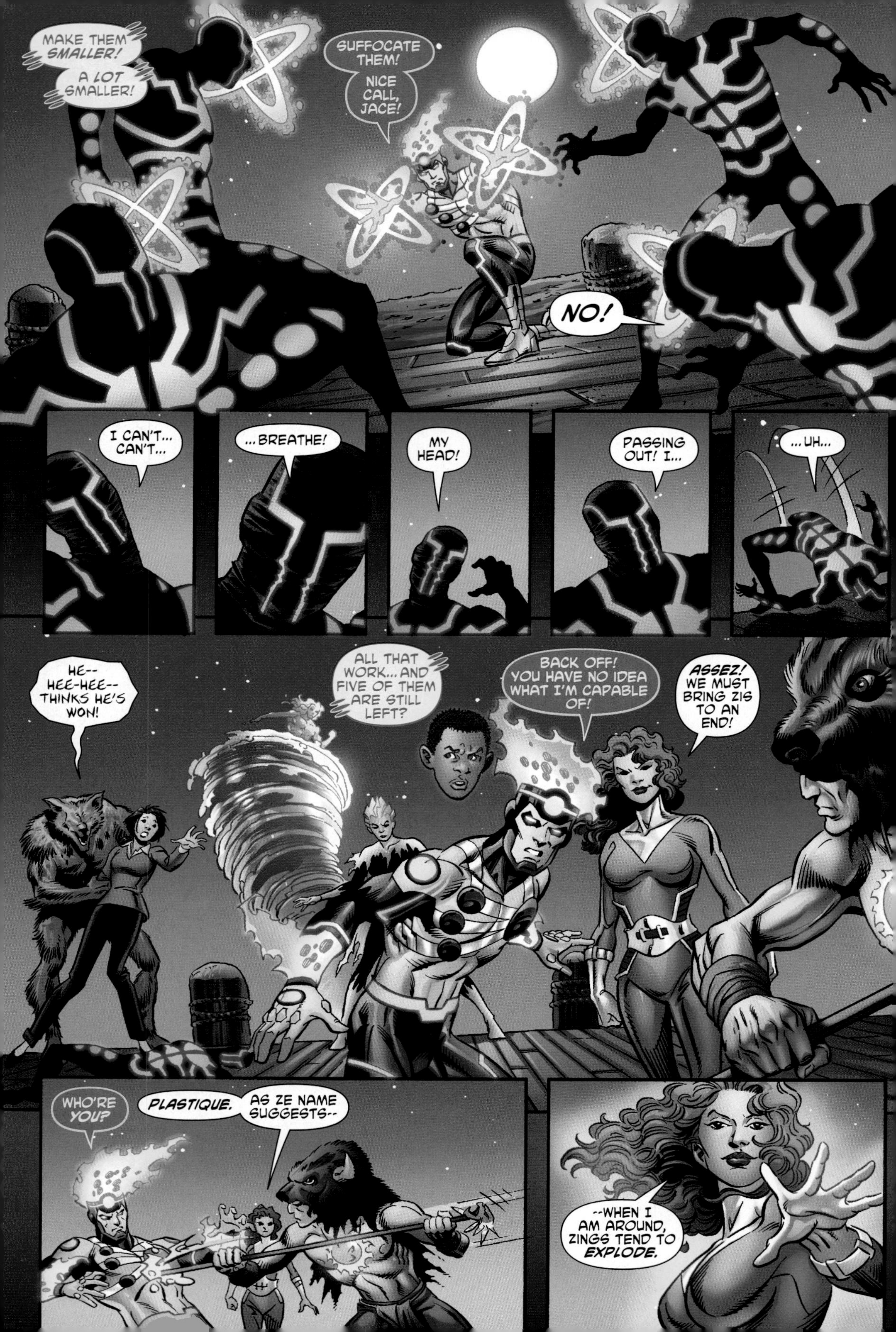
MAKE THEM SMALLER! A LOT SMALLER!
SUFFOCATE THEM! NICE CALL, JACE!
NO!
I CAN'T... CAN'T...
...BREATHE!
MY HEAD!
PASSING OUT! I...
...UH...
HE-- HEE-HEE-- THINKS HE'S WON!
ALL THAT WORK... AND FIVE OF THEM ARE STILL LEFT?
BACK OFF! YOU HAVE NO IDEA WHAT I'M CAPABLE OF!
ASSEZ! WE MUST BRING ZIS TO AN END!
WHO'RE YOU?
PLASTIQUE.
AS ZE NAME SUGGESTS--
--WHEN I AM AROUND, ZINGS TEND TO EXPLODE.

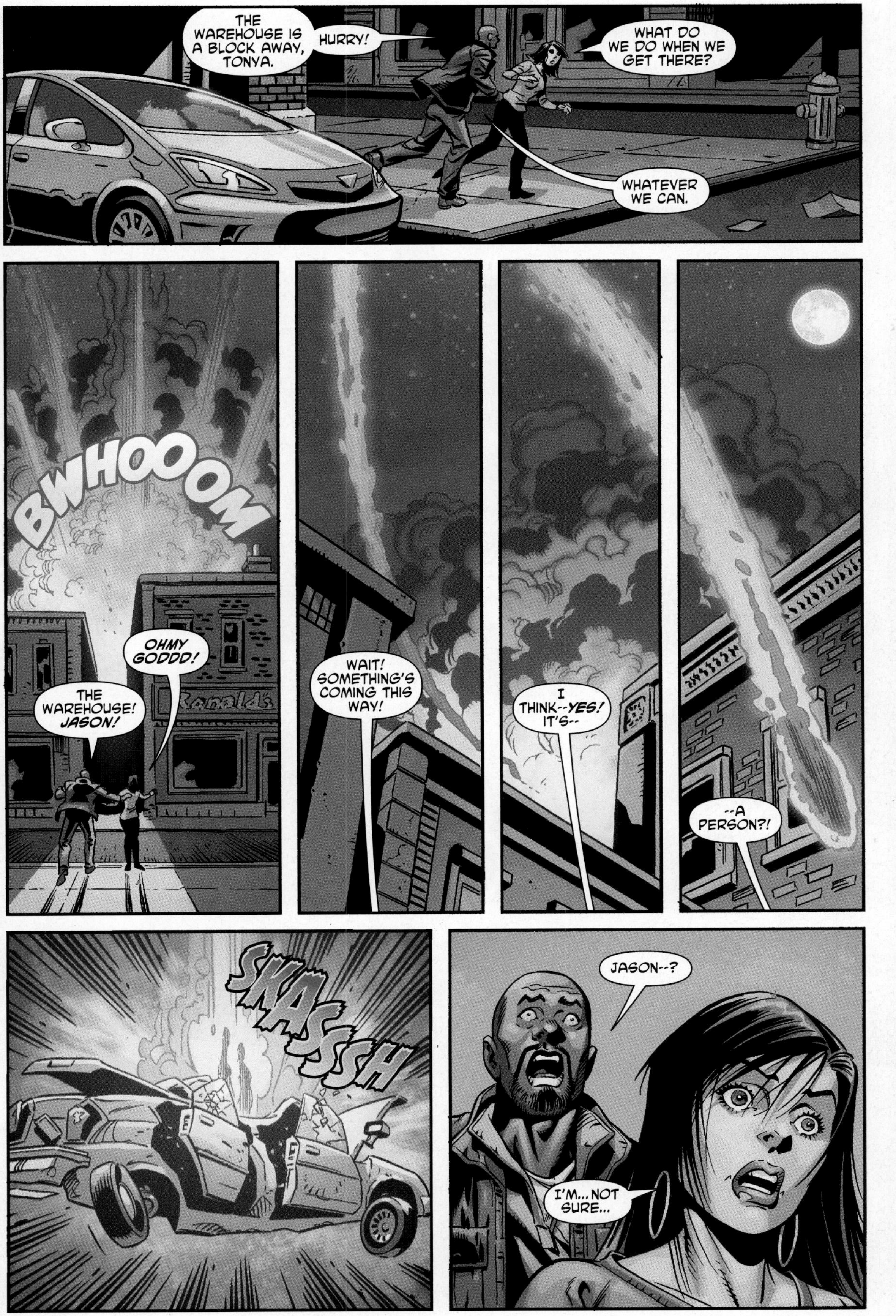
THE WAREHOUSE IS A BLOCK AWAY, TONYA.
HURRY!
WHAT DO WE DO WHEN WE GET THERE?
WHATEVER WE CAN.
BWHOOOM
OHMY GODDD!
THE WAREHOUSE! JASON!
Ronald's
WAIT! SOMETHING'S COMING THIS WAY!
I THINK--YES! IT'S--
--A PERSON?!
SKASSSH
JASON--?
I'M... NOT SURE...

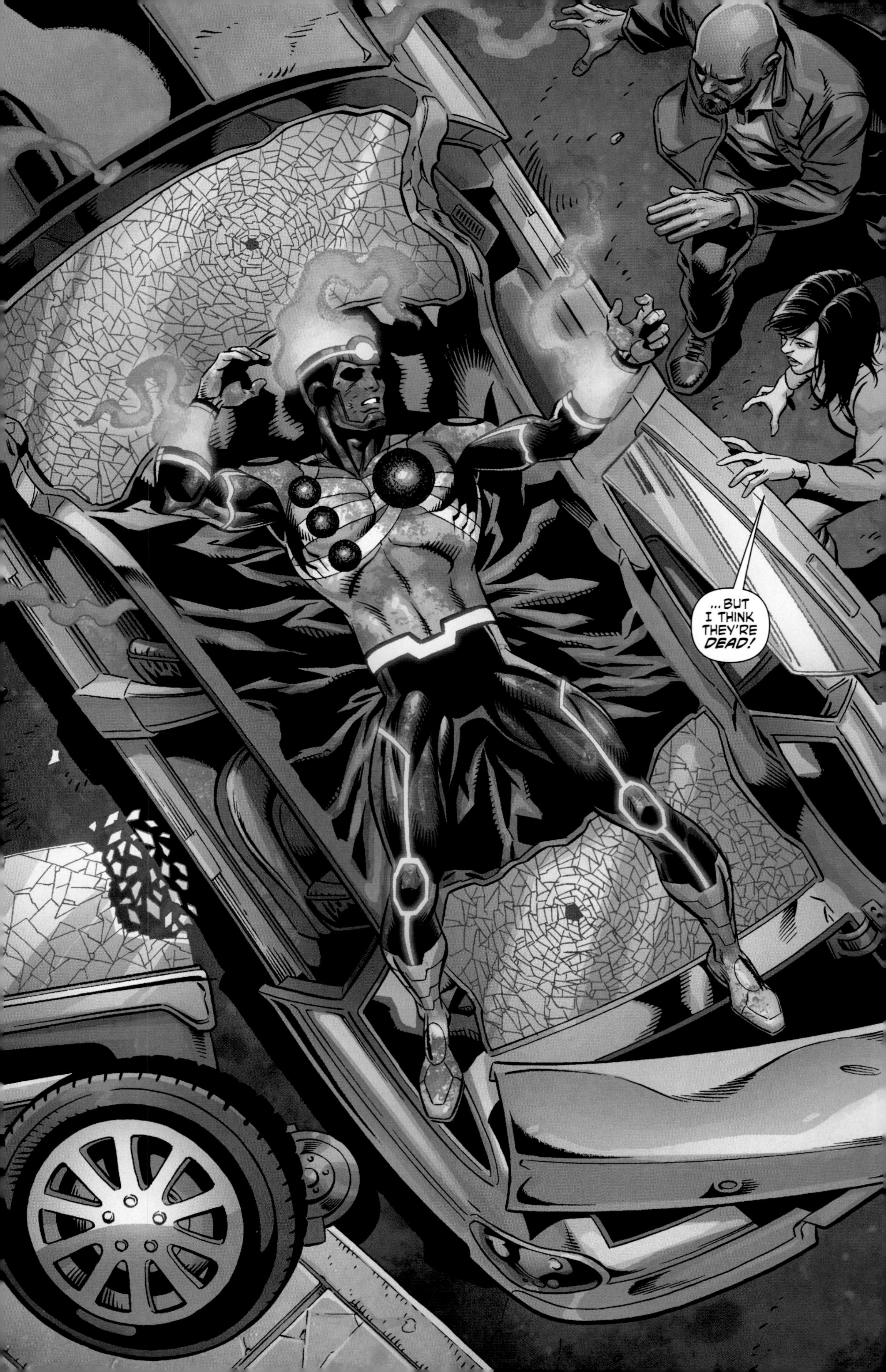
...BUT I THINK THEY'RE *DEAD!*

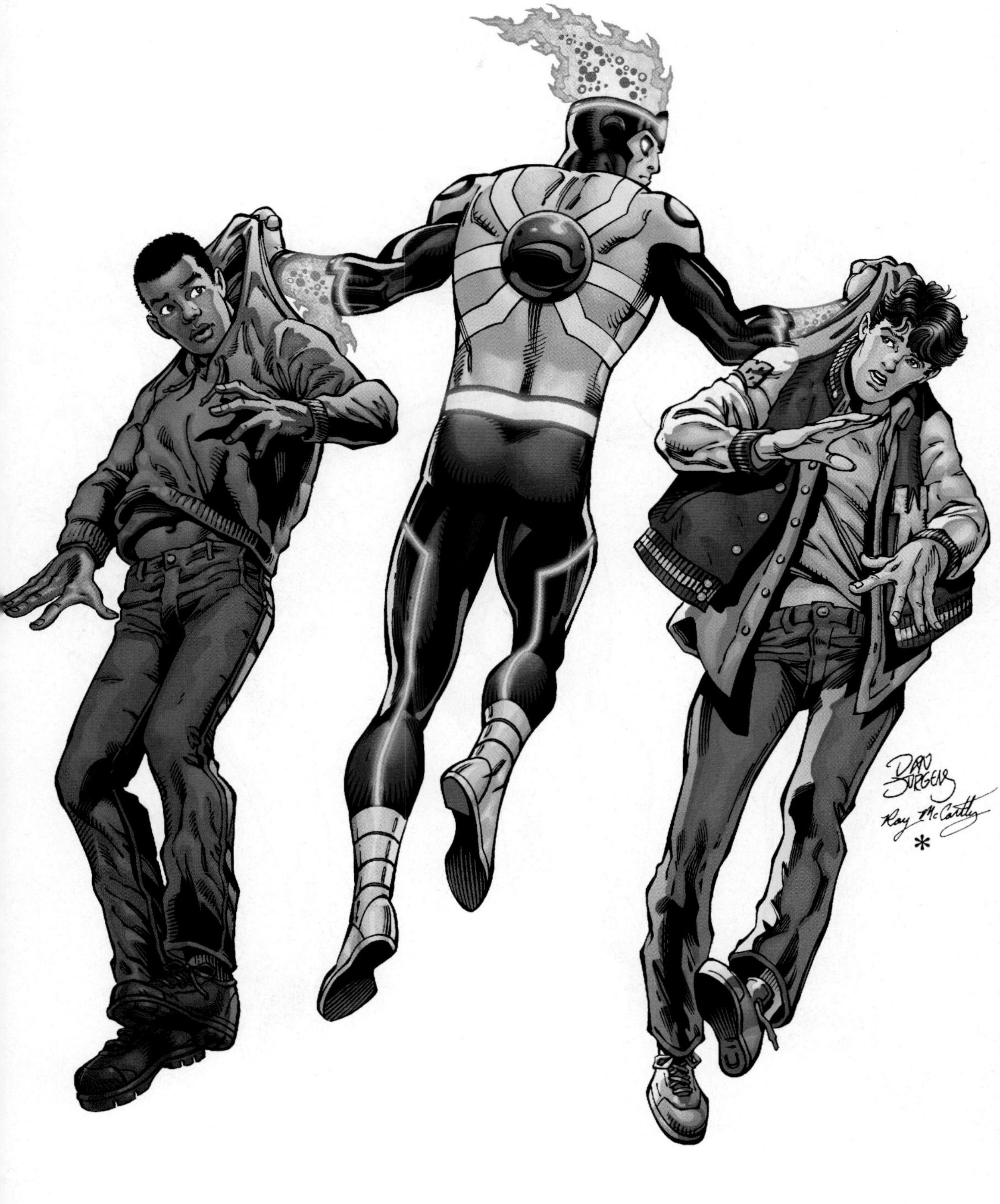
DAN JURGENS
Ray McCarthy

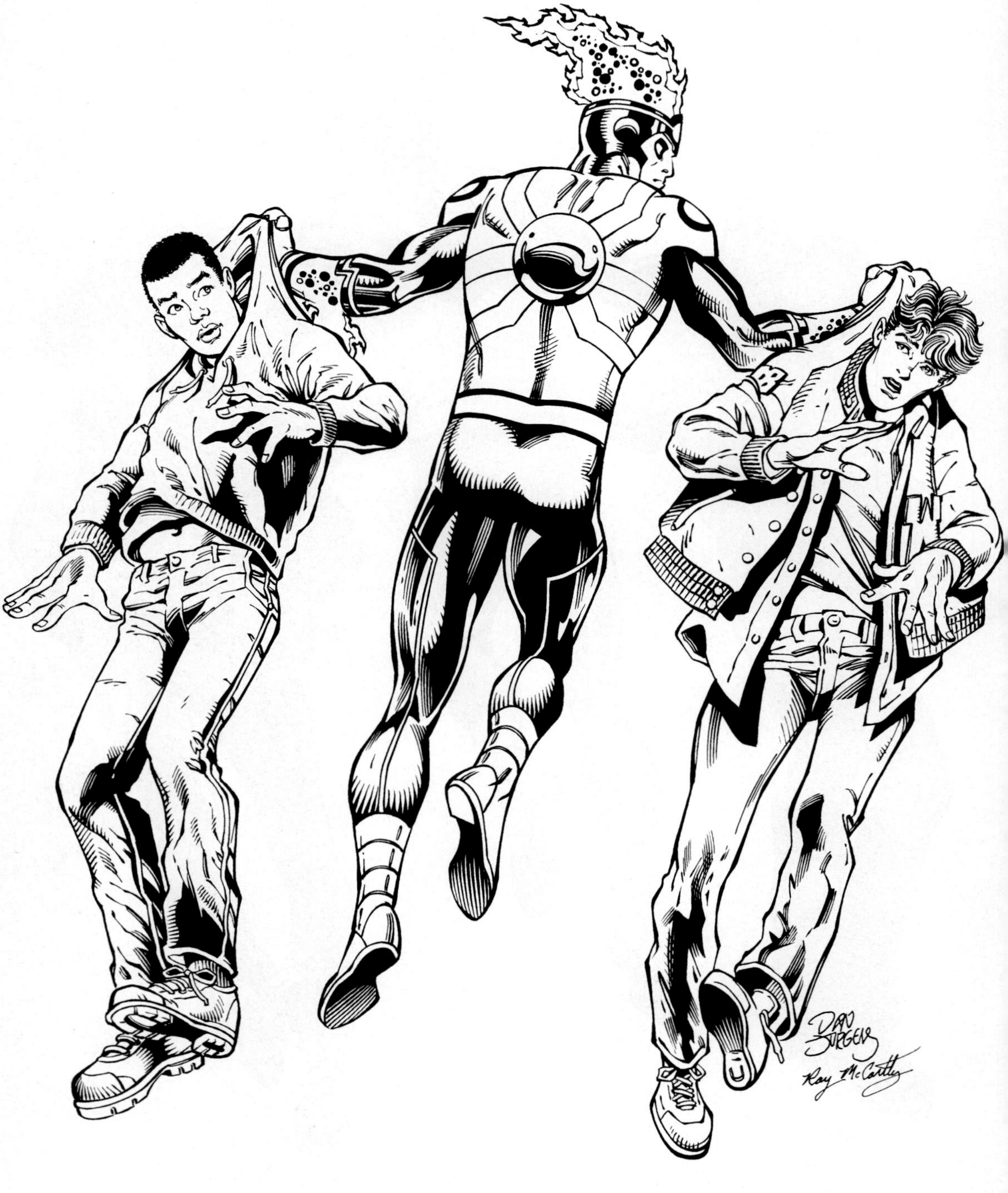
DAN JURGENS
Ray McCarthy

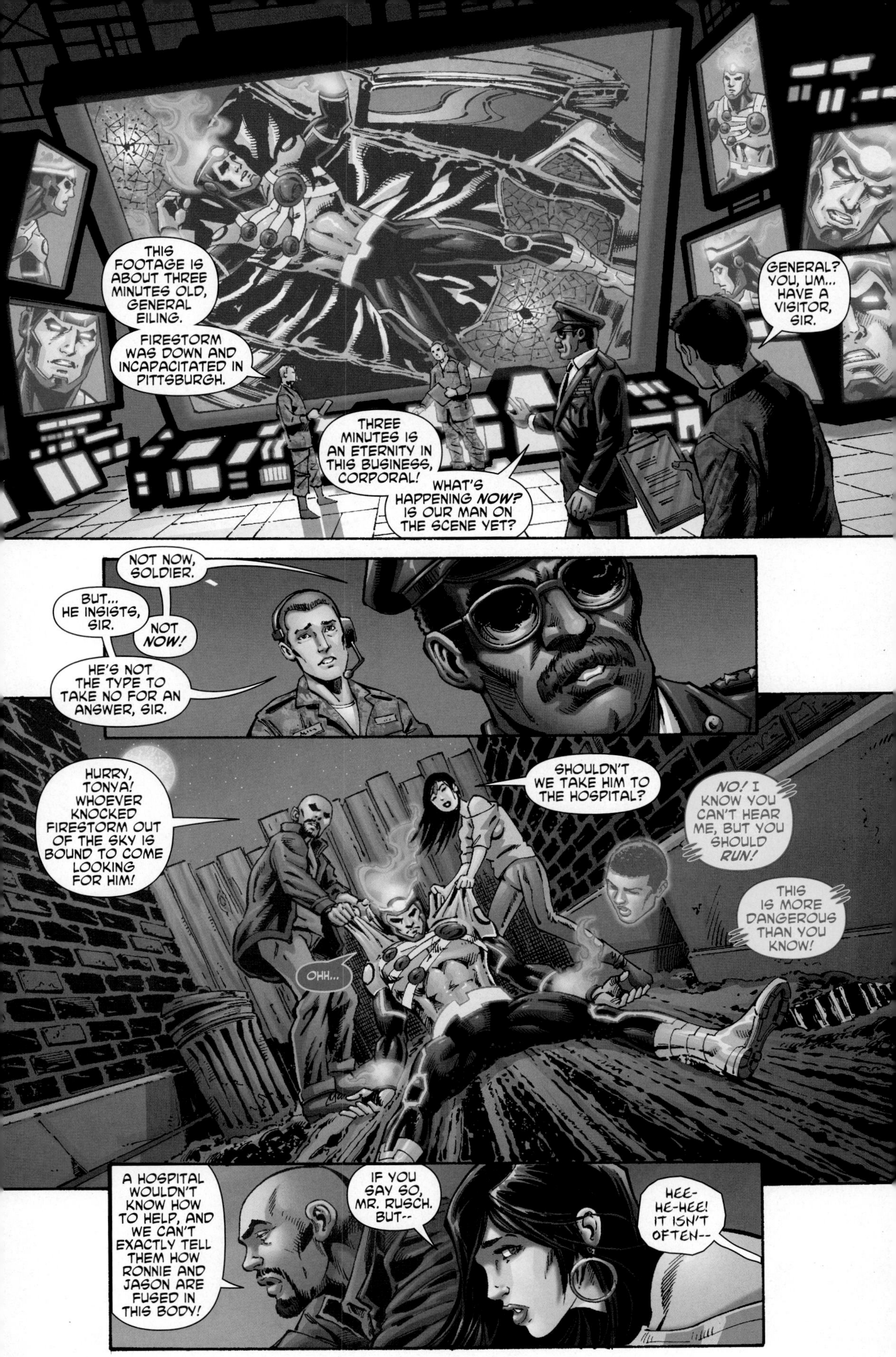
THIS FOOTAGE IS ABOUT THREE MINUTES OLD, GENERAL EILING.
FIRESTORM WAS DOWN AND INCAPACITATED IN PITTSBURGH.
THREE MINUTES IS AN ETERNITY IN THIS BUSINESS, CORPORAL!
WHAT'S HAPPENING NOW? IS OUR MAN ON THE SCENE YET?
GENERAL? YOU, UM... HAVE A VISITOR, SIR.
NOT NOW, SOLDIER.
BUT... HE INSISTS, SIR.
NOT NOW!
HE'S NOT THE TYPE TO TAKE NO FOR AN ANSWER, SIR.
HURRY, TONYA! WHOEVER KNOCKED FIRESTORM OUT OF THE SKY IS BOUND TO COME LOOKING FOR HIM!
SHOULDN'T WE TAKE HIM TO THE HOSPITAL?
NO! I KNOW YOU CAN'T HEAR ME, BUT YOU SHOULD RUN!
THIS IS MORE DANGEROUS THAN YOU KNOW!
OHH...
A HOSPITAL WOULDN'T KNOW HOW TO HELP, AND WE CAN'T EXACTLY TELL THEM HOW RONNIE AND JASON ARE FUSED IN THIS BODY!
IF YOU SAY SO, MR. RUSCH. BUT--
HEE-HE-HEE! IT ISN'T OFTEN--

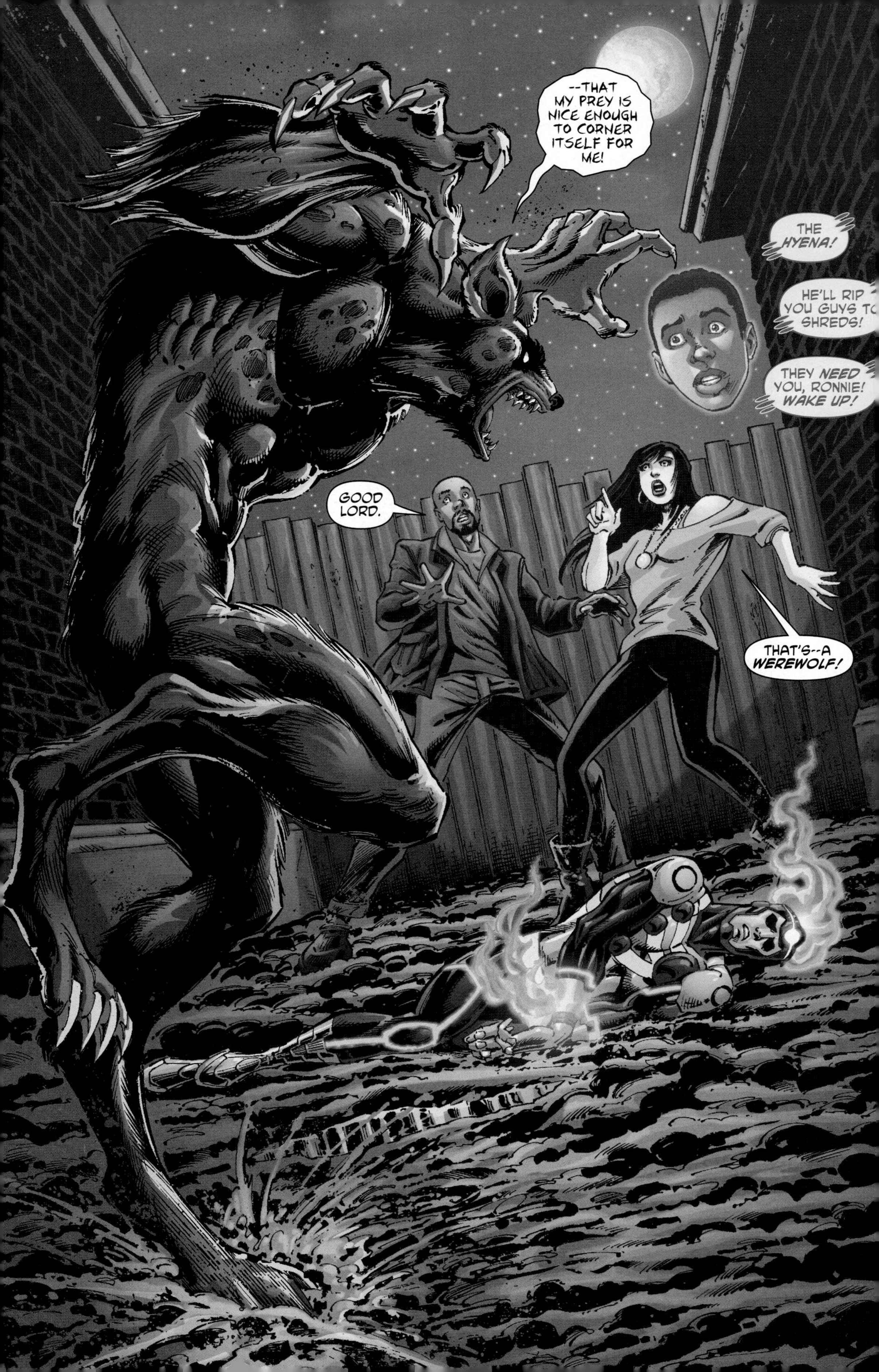
--THAT MY PREY IS NICE ENOUGH TO CORNER ITSELF FOR ME!
THE HYENA!
HE'LL RIP YOU GUYS TO SHREDS!
THEY NEED YOU, RONNIE! WAKE UP!
GOOD LORD.
THAT'S--A WEREWOLF!

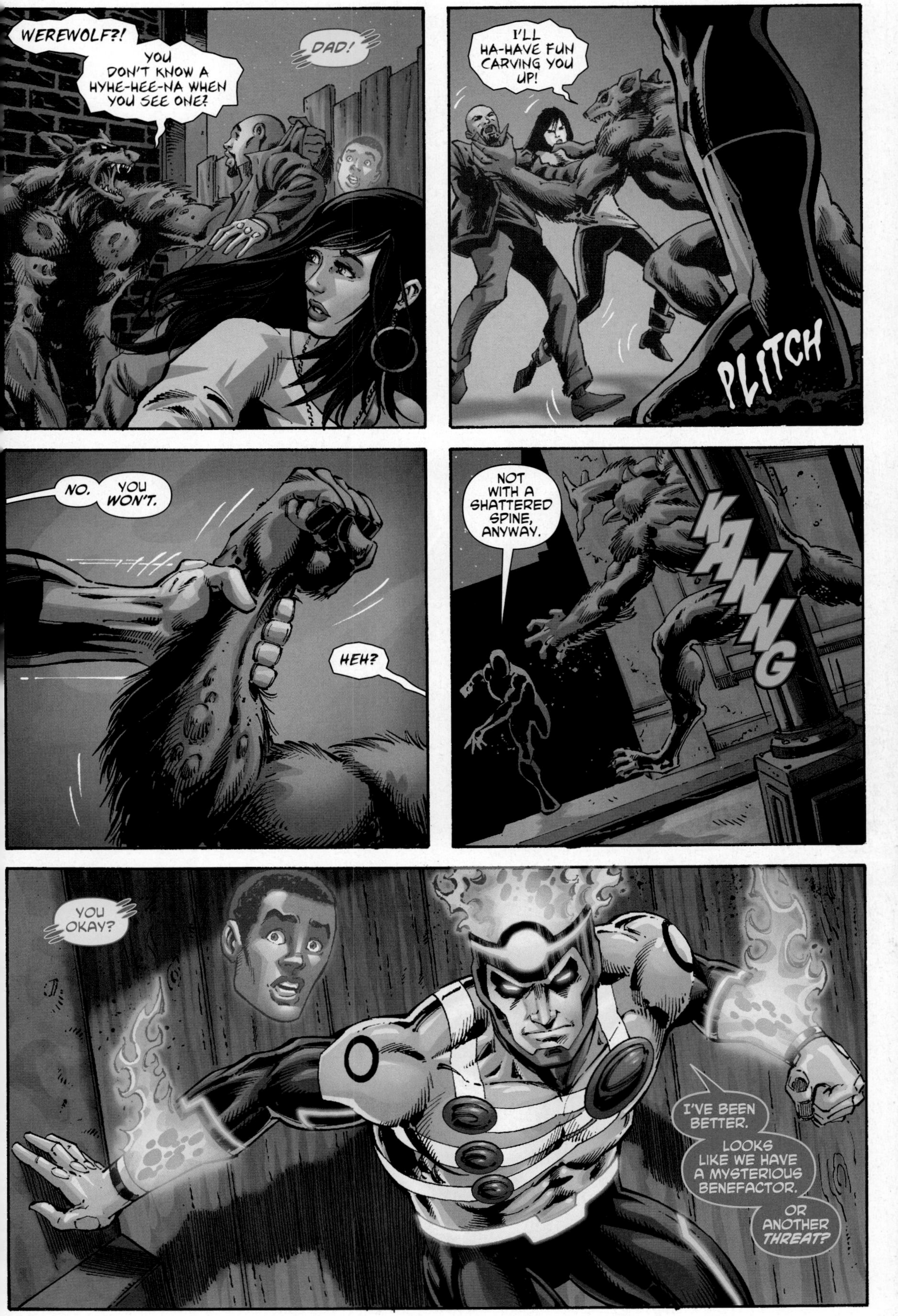
WEREWOLF?!
YOU DON'T KNOW A HYHE-HEE-NA WHEN YOU SEE ONE?
DAD!
I'LL HA-HAVE FUN CARVING YOU UP!
PLITCH
NO.
YOU WON'T.
HEH?
NOT WITH A SHATTERED SPINE, ANYWAY.
KANNG
YOU OKAY?
I'VE BEEN BETTER.
LOOKS LIKE WE HAVE A MYSTERIOUS BENEFACTOR.
OR ANOTHER *THREAT?*

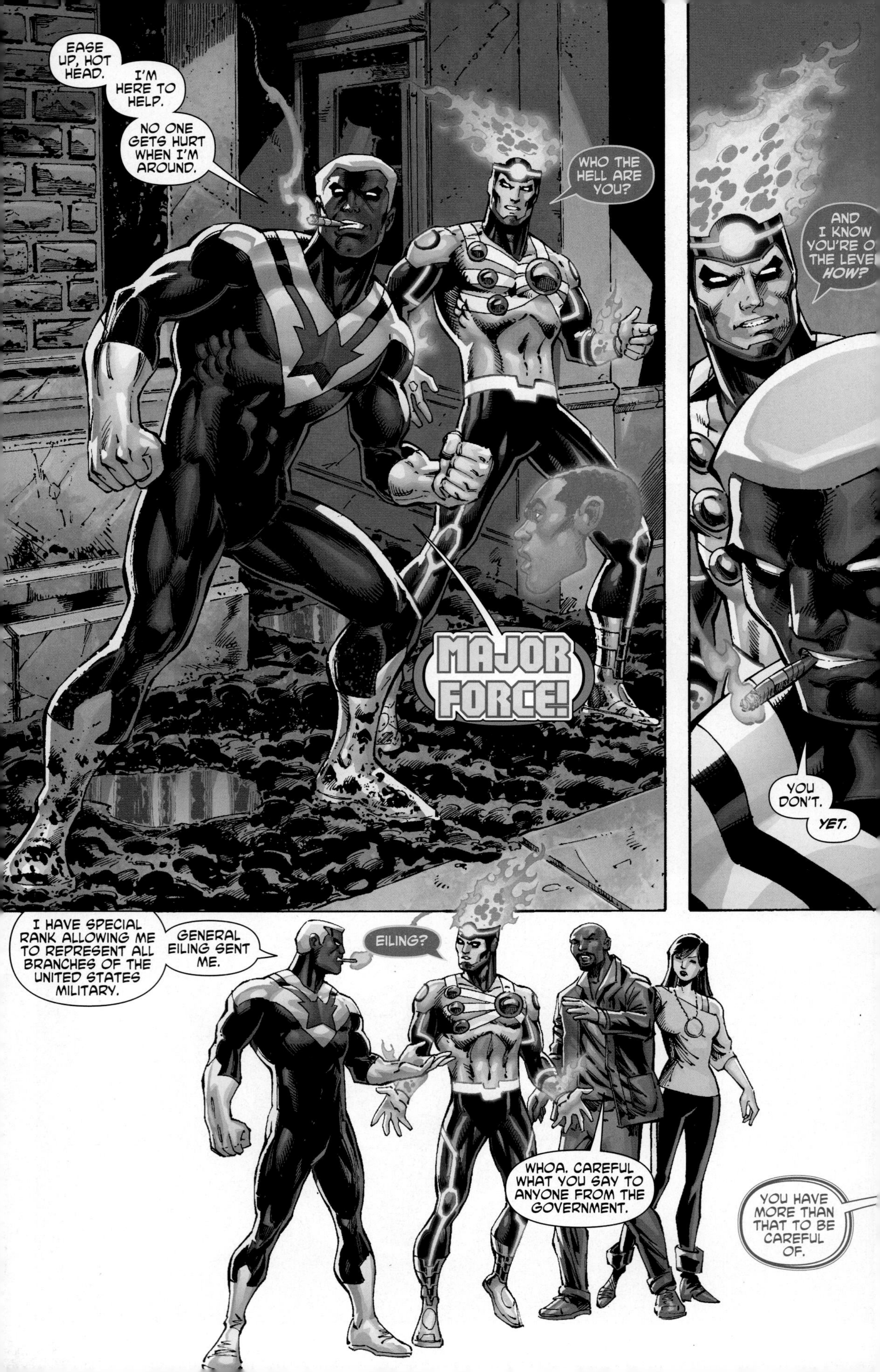
EASE UP, HOT HEAD.
I'M HERE TO HELP.
NO ONE GETS HURT WHEN I'M AROUND.
WHO THE HELL ARE YOU?
MAJOR FORCE!
AND I KNOW YOU'RE O THE LEVE HOW?
YOU DON'T.
YET.
I HAVE SPECIAL RANK ALLOWING ME TO REPRESENT ALL BRANCHES OF THE UNITED STATES MILITARY.
GENERAL EILING SENT ME.
EILING?
WHOA. CAREFUL WHAT YOU SAY TO ANYONE FROM THE GOVERNMENT.
YOU HAVE MORE THAN THAT TO BE CAREFUL OF.

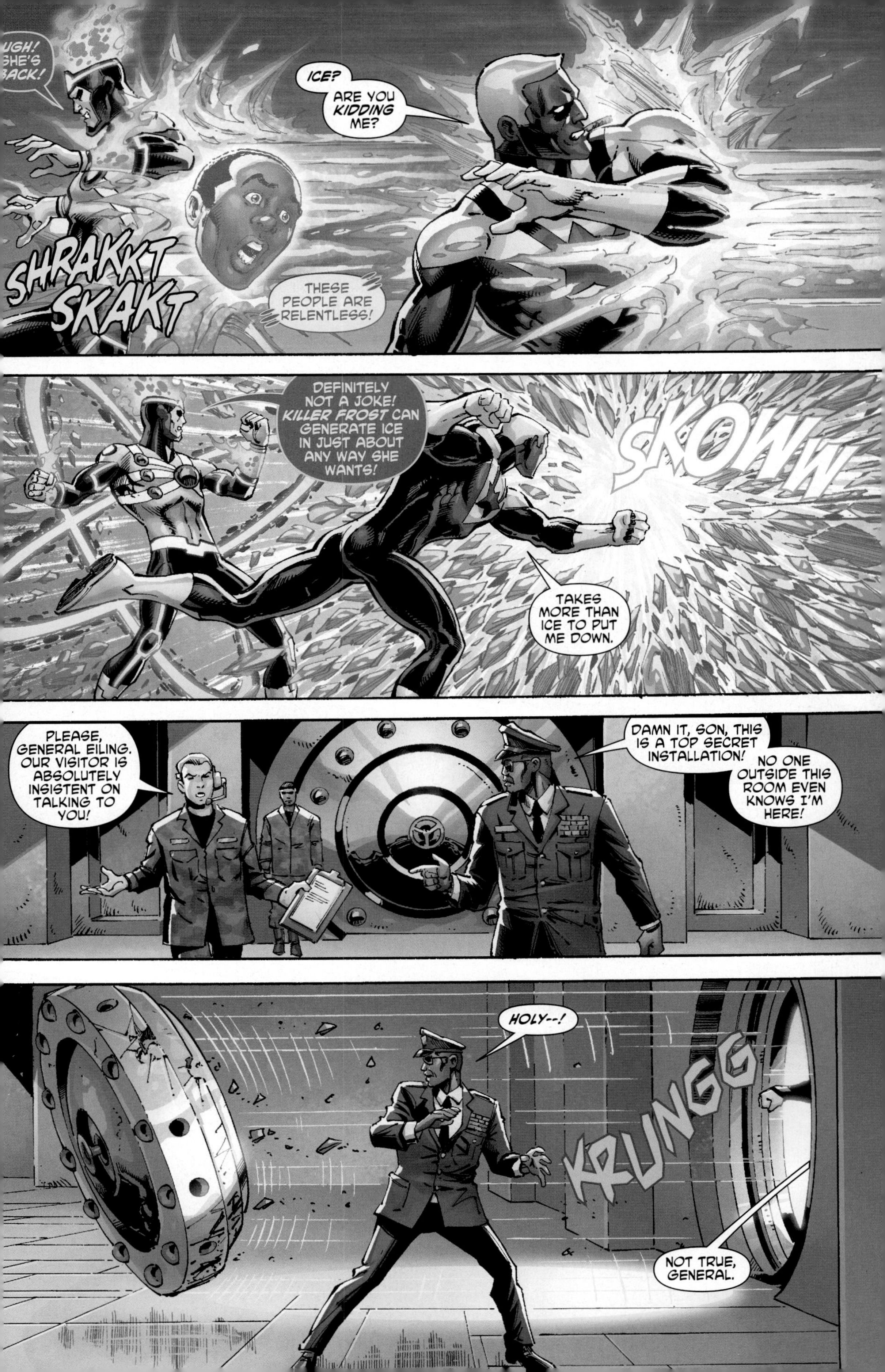
UGH! HE'S BACK!
ICE? ARE YOU KIDDING ME?
SHRAKKT SKAKT
THESE PEOPLE ARE RELENTLESS!
DEFINITELY NOT A JOKE! KILLER FROST CAN GENERATE ICE IN JUST ABOUT ANY WAY SHE WANTS!
SKOWW
TAKES MORE THAN ICE TO PUT ME DOWN.
PLEASE, GENERAL EILING. OUR VISITOR IS ABSOLUTELY INSISTENT ON TALKING TO YOU!
DAMN IT, SON, THIS IS A TOP SECRET INSTALLATION!
NO ONE OUTSIDE THIS ROOM EVEN KNOWS I'M HERE!
HOLY--!
KRUNGG
NOT TRUE, GENERAL.

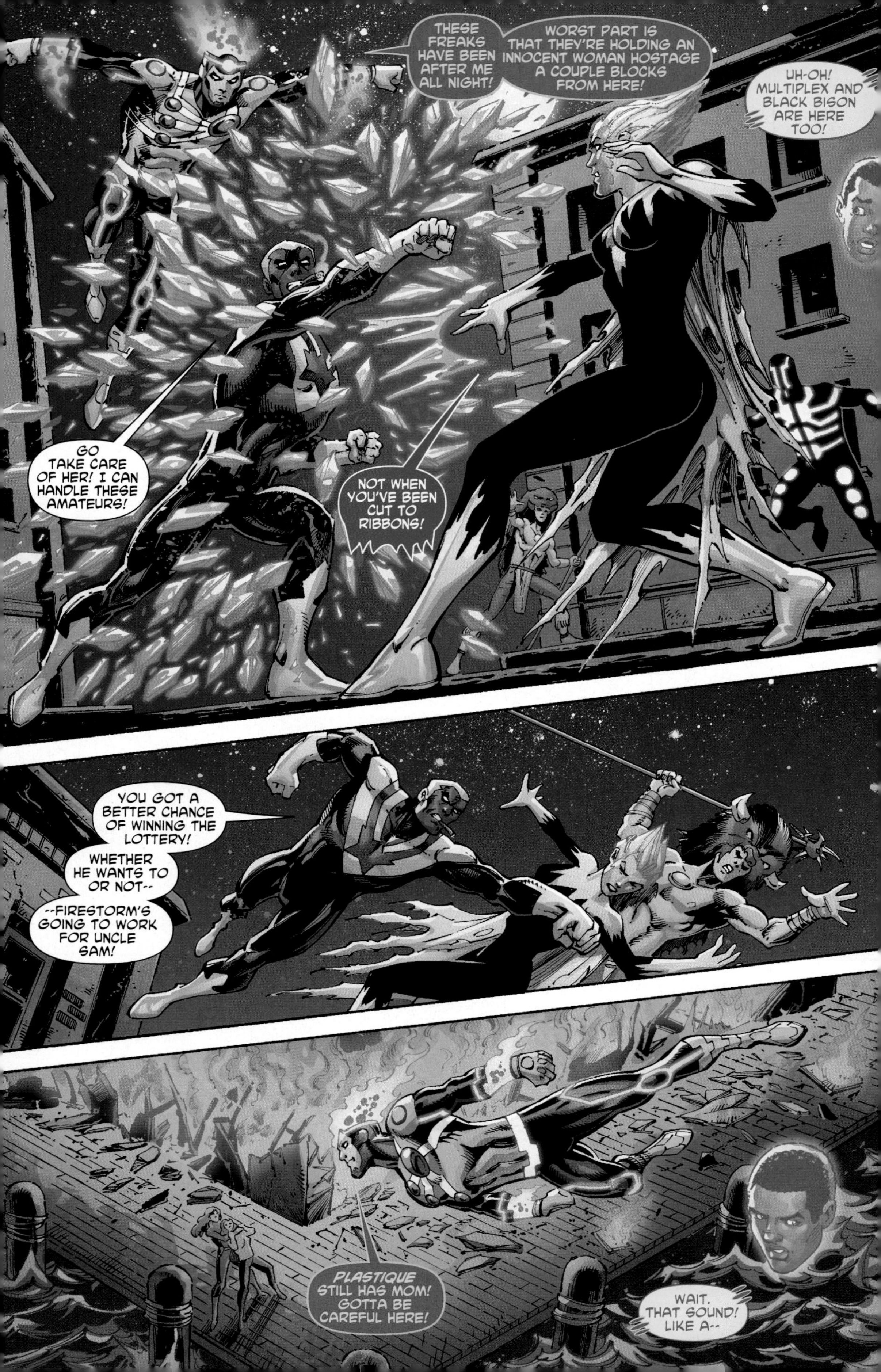
THESE FREAKS HAVE BEEN AFTER ME ALL NIGHT!
WORST PART IS THAT THEY'RE HOLDING AN INNOCENT WOMAN HOSTAGE A COUPLE BLOCKS FROM HERE!
UH-OH! MULTIPLEX AND BLACK BISON ARE HERE TOO!
GO TAKE CARE OF HER! I CAN HANDLE THESE AMATEURS!
NOT WHEN YOU'VE BEEN CUT TO RIBBONS!
YOU GOT A BETTER CHANCE OF WINNING THE LOTTERY!
WHETHER HE WANTS TO OR NOT--
--FIRESTORM'S GOING TO WORK FOR UNCLE SAM!
PLASTIQUE STILL HAS MOM! GOTTA BE CAREFUL HERE!
WAIT. THAT SOUND! LIKE A--

--TIDAL WAVE!

OH.

TOOOSH

THIS IS GETTING OLD.

TYPHOON. MAKES WATER DO WHATEVER HE WANTS!

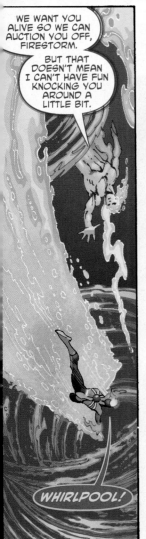

WE WANT YOU ALIVE SO WE CAN AUCTION YOU OFF, FIRESTORM.

BUT THAT DOESN'T MEAN I CAN'T HAVE FUN KNOCKING YOU AROUND A LITTLE BIT.

WHIRLPOOL!

WOULD YOU DO SOMETHING BEFORE WE WIND UP IN ATLANTIS?

AND MEET AQUAMAN? THAT'D BE COOL!

KILLER FROST SEES ME AS SOMETHING OF A LIGHTWEIGHT--

--BECAUSE I WORK BEST IN WATER.

WONDER WHAT SHE'D SAY IF SHE SAW THIS?

WHUD

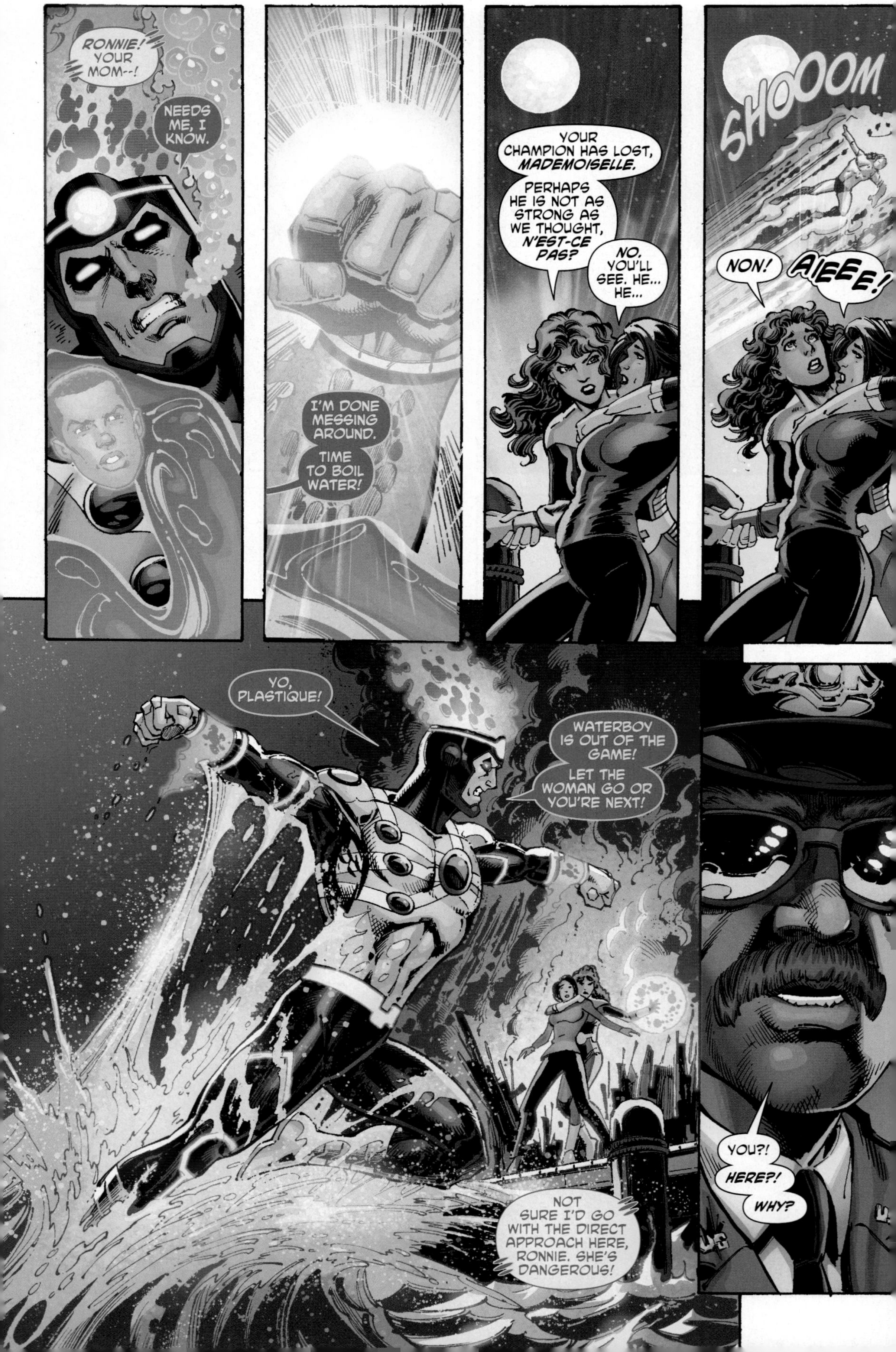
RONNIE! YOUR MOM--!
NEEDS ME, I KNOW.
I'M DONE MESSING AROUND.
TIME TO BOIL WATER!
YOUR CHAMPION HAS LOST, MADEMOISELLE.
PERHAPS HE IS NOT AS STRONG AS WE THOUGHT, N'EST-CE PAS?
NO. YOU'LL SEE. HE... HE...
SHOOOM
NON!
AIEEE!
YO, PLASTIQUE!
WATERBOY IS OUT OF THE GAME!
LET THE WOMAN GO OR YOU'RE NEXT!
NOT SURE I'D GO WITH THE DIRECT APPROACH HERE, RONNIE. SHE'S DANGEROUS!
YOU?!
HERE?!
WHY?

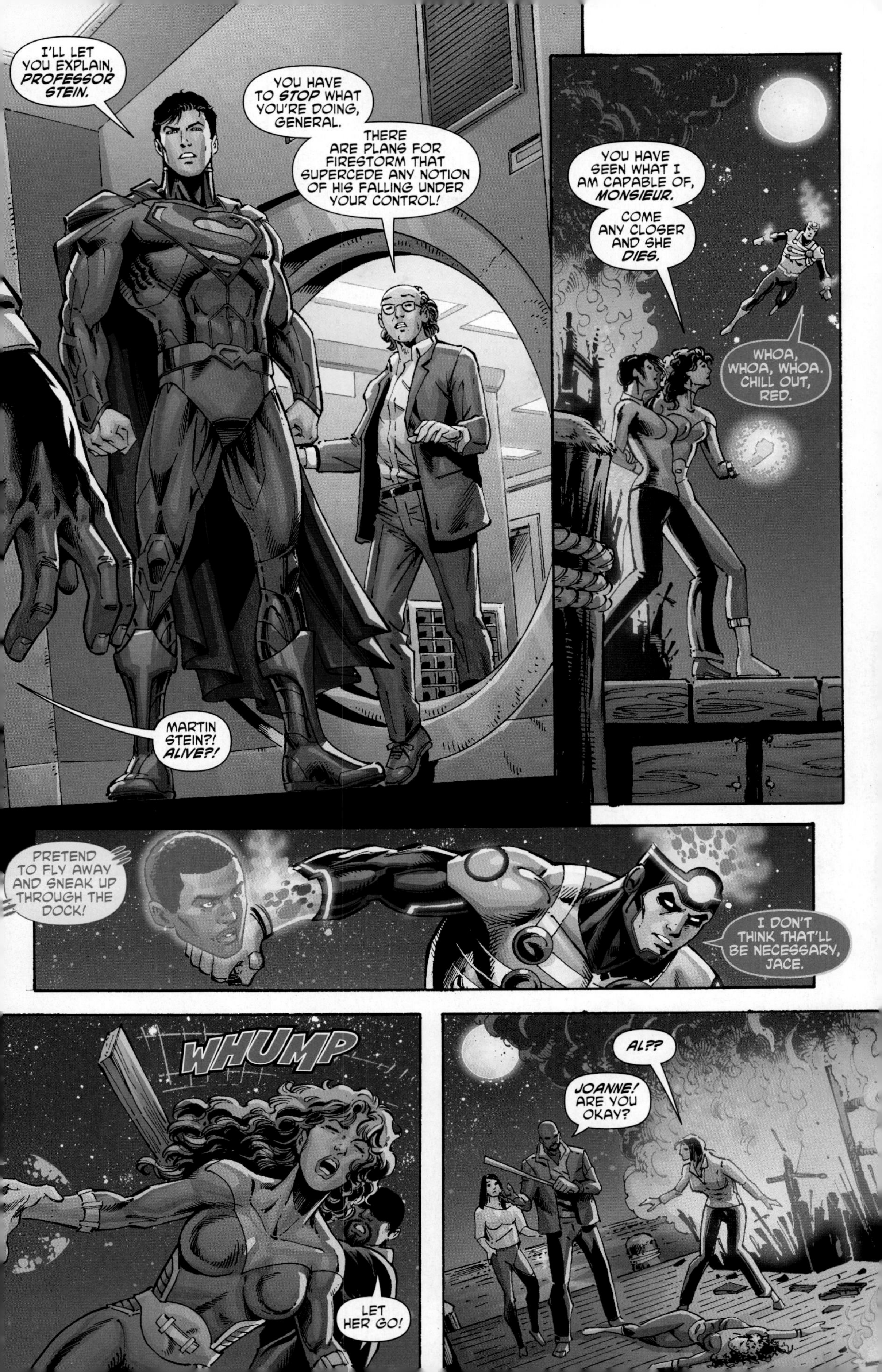
I'LL LET YOU EXPLAIN, PROFESSOR STEIN.
YOU HAVE TO STOP WHAT YOU'RE DOING, GENERAL.
THERE ARE PLANS FOR FIRESTORM THAT SUPERCEDE ANY NOTION OF HIS FALLING UNDER YOUR CONTROL!
MARTIN STEIN?! ALIVE?!
YOU HAVE SEEN WHAT I AM CAPABLE OF, MONSIEUR.
COME ANY CLOSER AND SHE DIES.
WHOA, WHOA, WHOA. CHILL OUT, RED.
PRETEND TO FLY AWAY AND SNEAK UP THROUGH THE DOCK!
I DON'T THINK THAT'LL BE NECESSARY, JACE.
WHUMP
LET HER GO!
AL??
JOANNE! ARE YOU OKAY?

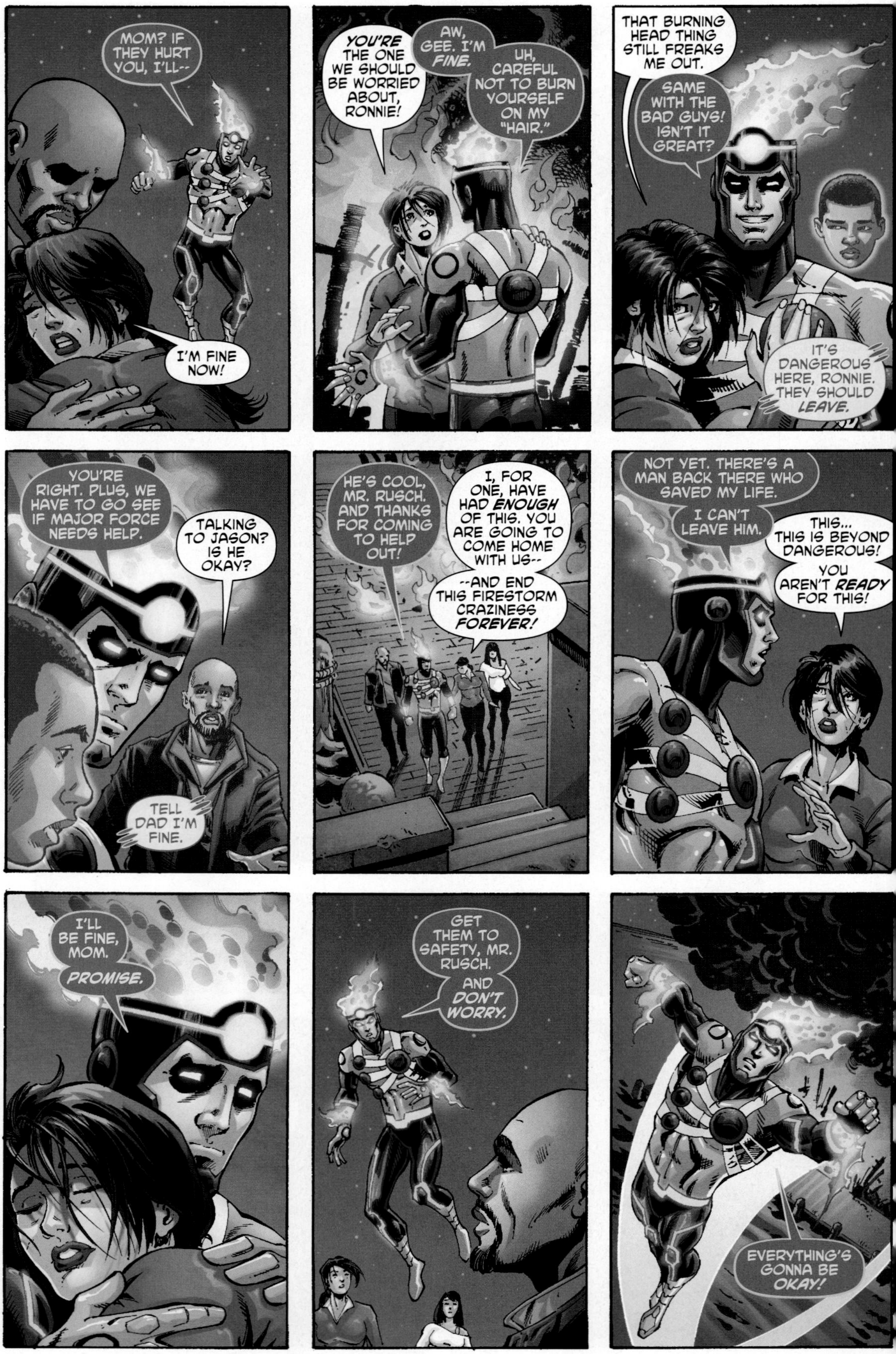
MOM? IF THEY HURT YOU, I'LL--
I'M FINE NOW!
YOU'RE THE ONE WE SHOULD BE WORRIED ABOUT, RONNIE!
AW, GEE. I'M FINE.
UH, CAREFUL NOT TO BURN YOURSELF ON MY "HAIR."
THAT BURNING HEAD THING STILL FREAKS ME OUT.
SAME WITH THE BAD GUYS! ISN'T IT GREAT?
IT'S DANGEROUS HERE, RONNIE. THEY SHOULD LEAVE.
YOU'RE RIGHT. PLUS, WE HAVE TO GO SEE IF MAJOR FORCE NEEDS HELP.
TALKING TO JASON? IS HE OKAY?
TELL DAD I'M FINE.
HE'S COOL, MR. RUSCH. AND THANKS FOR COMING TO HELP OUT!
I, FOR ONE, HAVE HAD ENOUGH OF THIS. YOU ARE GOING TO COME HOME WITH US--
--AND END THIS FIRESTORM CRAZINESS FOREVER!
NOT YET. THERE'S A MAN BACK THERE WHO SAVED MY LIFE.
I CAN'T LEAVE HIM.
THIS... THIS IS BEYOND DANGEROUS!
YOU AREN'T READY FOR THIS!
I'LL BE FINE, MOM.
PROMISE.
GET THEM TO SAFETY, MR. RUSCH.
AND DON'T WORRY.
EVERYTHING'S GONNA BE OKAY!

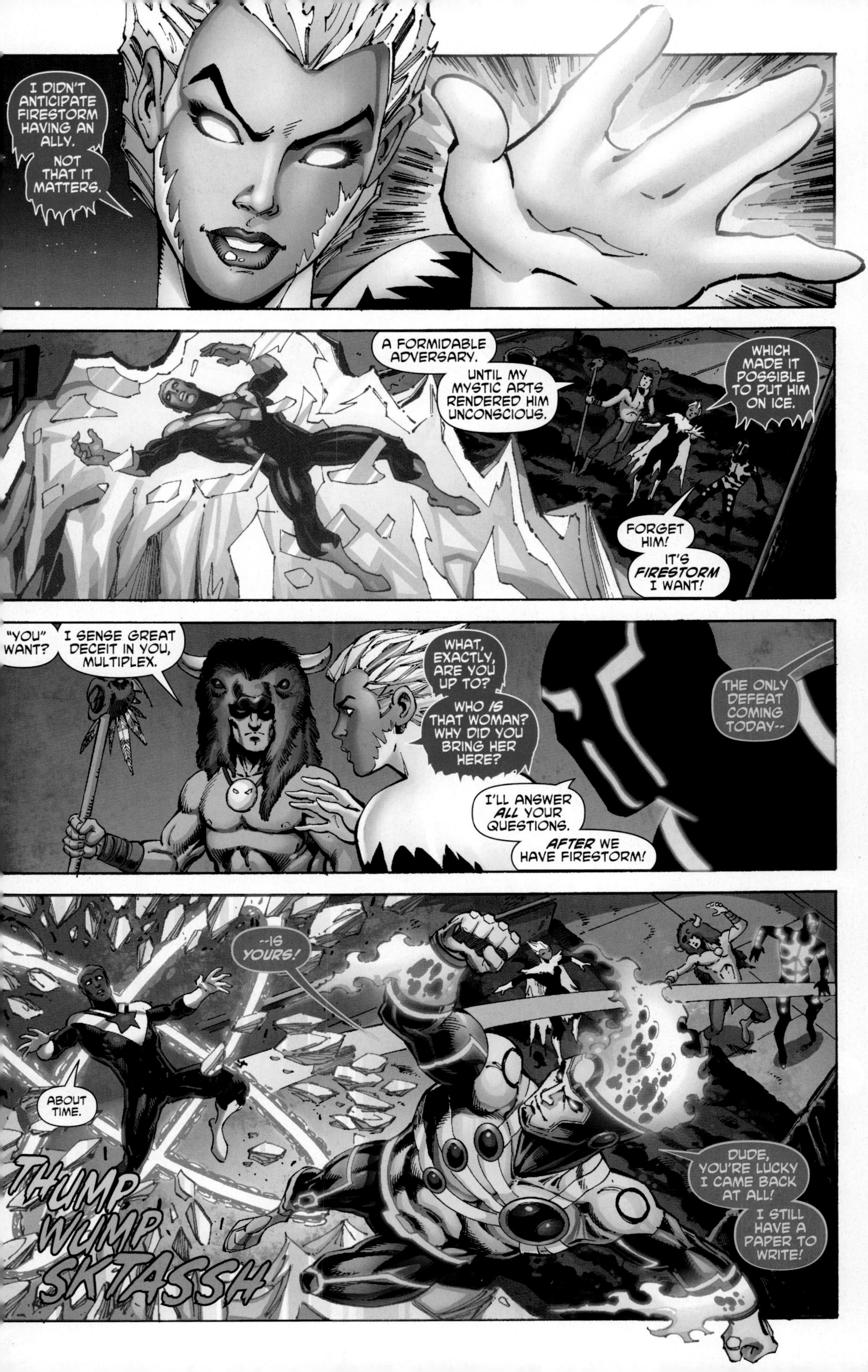
I DIDN'T ANTICIPATE FIRESTORM HAVING AN ALLY.
NOT THAT IT MATTERS.
A FORMIDABLE ADVERSARY.
UNTIL MY MYSTIC ARTS RENDERED HIM UNCONSCIOUS.
WHICH MADE IT POSSIBLE TO PUT HIM ON ICE.
FORGET HIM!
IT'S FIRESTORM I WANT!
"YOU" WANT?
I SENSE GREAT DECEIT IN YOU, MULTIPLEX.
WHAT, EXACTLY, ARE YOU UP TO?
WHO IS THAT WOMAN? WHY DID YOU BRING HER HERE?
I'LL ANSWER ALL YOUR QUESTIONS.
AFTER WE HAVE FIRESTORM!
THE ONLY DEFEAT COMING TODAY--
--IS YOURS!
ABOUT TIME.
THUMP
WUMP
SKTASSH
DUDE, YOU'RE LUCKY I CAME BACK AT ALL!
I STILL HAVE A PAPER TO WRITE!

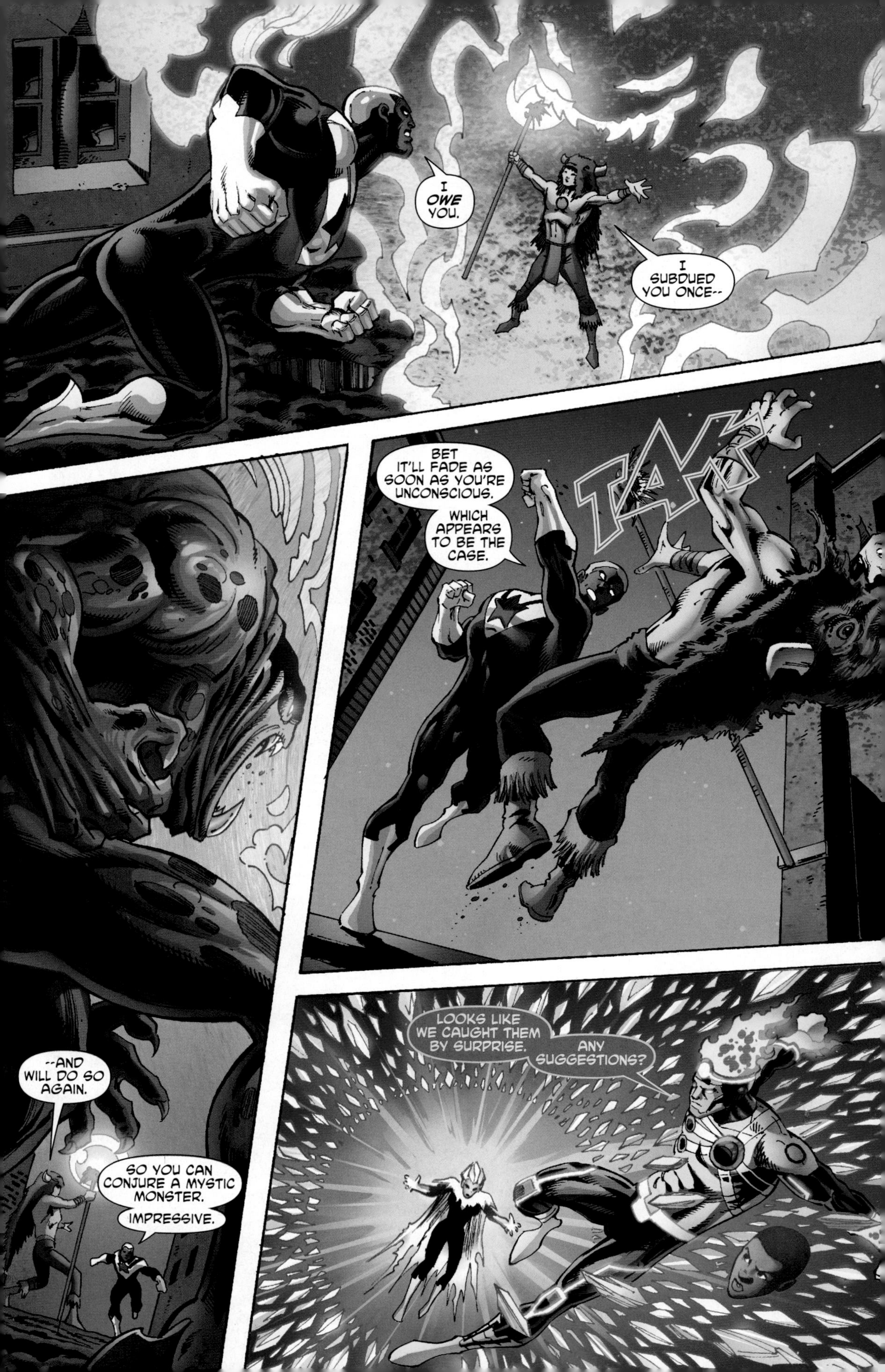
I OWE YOU.
I SUBDUED YOU ONCE--
--AND WILL DO SO AGAIN.
BET IT'LL FADE AS SOON AS YOU'RE UNCONSCIOUS.
WHICH APPEARS TO BE THE CASE.
TAK
SO YOU CAN CONJURE A MYSTIC MONSTER.
IMPRESSIVE.
LOOKS LIKE WE CAUGHT THEM BY SURPRISE.
ANY SUGGESTIONS?

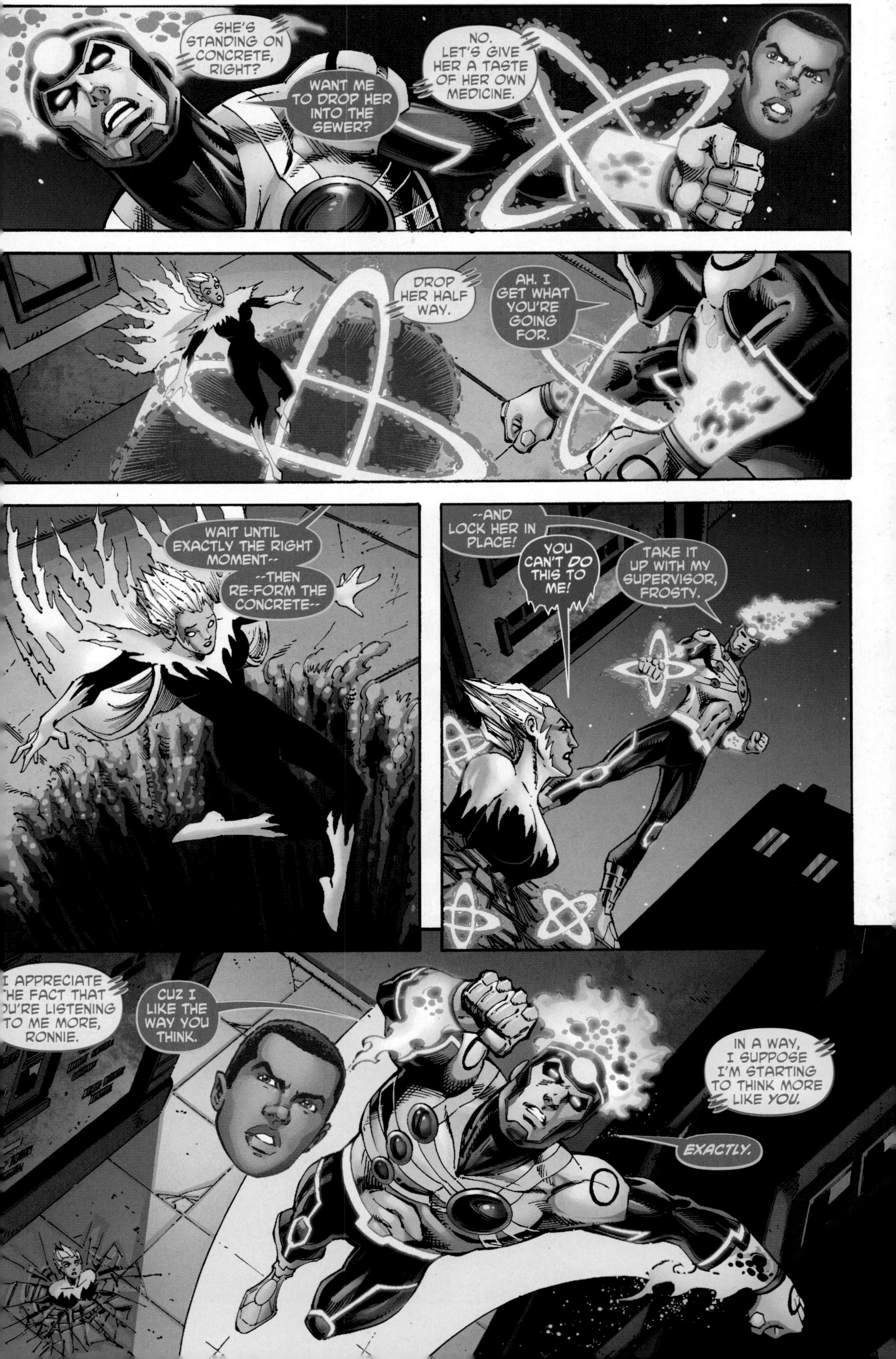
SHE'S STANDING ON CONCRETE, RIGHT?
WANT ME TO DROP HER INTO THE SEWER?
NO. LET'S GIVE HER A TASTE OF HER OWN MEDICINE.
DROP HER HALF WAY.
AH. I GET WHAT YOU'RE GOING FOR.
WAIT UNTIL EXACTLY THE RIGHT MOMENT--
--THEN RE-FORM THE CONCRETE--
--AND LOCK HER IN PLACE!
YOU CAN'T DO THIS TO ME!
TAKE IT UP WITH MY SUPERVISOR, FROSTY.
I APPRECIATE THE FACT THAT YOU'RE LISTENING TO ME MORE, RONNIE.
CUZ I LIKE THE WAY YOU THINK.
IN A WAY, I SUPPOSE I'M STARTING TO THINK MORE LIKE YOU.
EXACTLY.

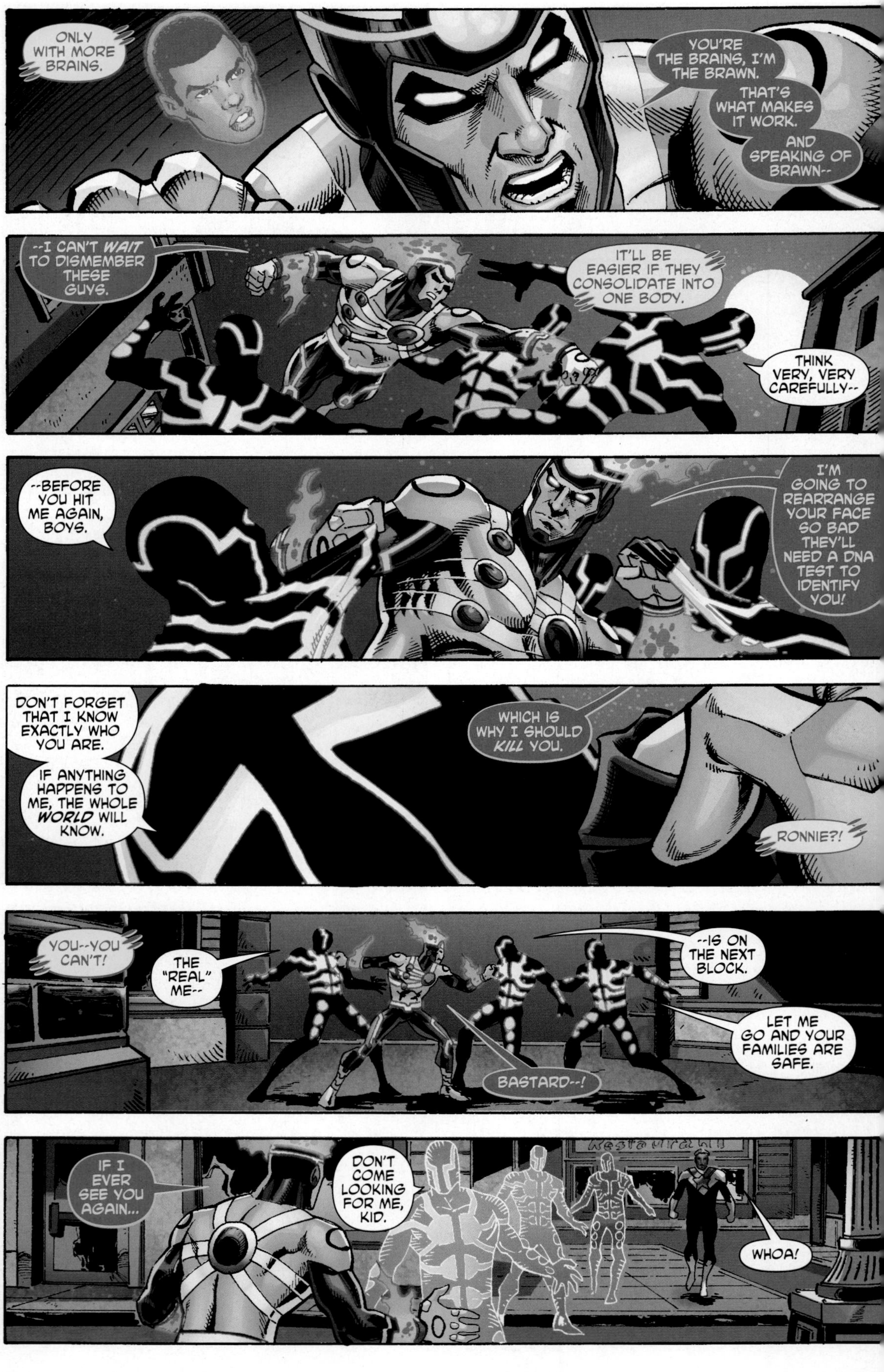
ONLY WITH MORE BRAINS.
YOU'RE THE BRAINS, I'M THE BRAWN.
THAT'S WHAT MAKES IT WORK.
AND SPEAKING OF BRAWN--
--I CAN'T *WAIT* TO DISMEMBER THESE GUYS.
IT'LL BE EASIER IF THEY CONSOLIDATE INTO ONE BODY.
THINK VERY, VERY CAREFULLY--
--BEFORE YOU HIT ME AGAIN, BOYS.
I'M GOING TO REARRANGE YOUR FACE SO BAD THEY'LL NEED A DNA TEST TO IDENTIFY YOU!
DON'T FORGET THAT I KNOW EXACTLY WHO YOU ARE.
IF ANYTHING HAPPENS TO ME, THE WHOLE *WORLD* WILL KNOW.
WHICH IS WHY I SHOULD *KILL* YOU.
RONNIE?!
YOU--YOU CAN'T!
THE "REAL" ME--
--IS ON THE NEXT BLOCK.
LET ME GO AND YOUR FAMILIES ARE SAFE.
BASTARD--!
IF I EVER SEE YOU AGAIN...
DON'T COME LOOKING FOR ME, KID.
WHOA!

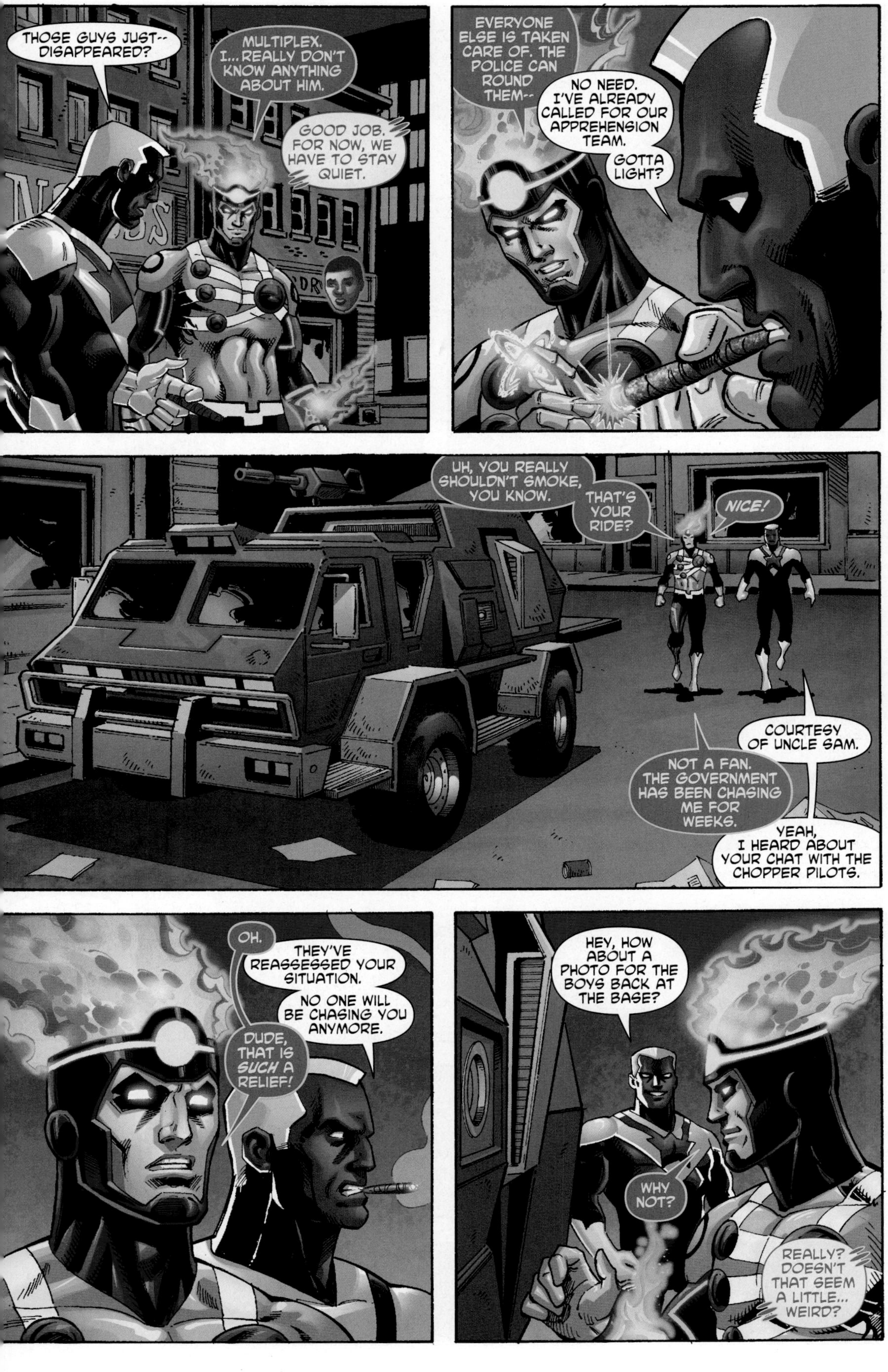

THOSE GUYS JUST--DISAPPEARED?
MULTIPLEX. I... REALLY DON'T KNOW ANYTHING ABOUT HIM.
GOOD JOB. FOR NOW, WE HAVE TO STAY QUIET.
EVERYONE ELSE IS TAKEN CARE OF. THE POLICE CAN ROUND THEM--
NO NEED. I'VE ALREADY CALLED FOR OUR APPREHENSION TEAM.
GOTTA LIGHT?
UH, YOU REALLY SHOULDN'T SMOKE, YOU KNOW.
THAT'S YOUR RIDE?
NICE!
COURTESY OF UNCLE SAM.
NOT A FAN. THE GOVERNMENT HAS BEEN CHASING ME FOR WEEKS.
YEAH, I HEARD ABOUT YOUR CHAT WITH THE CHOPPER PILOTS.
OH.
THEY'VE REASSESSED YOUR SITUATION.
NO ONE WILL BE CHASING YOU ANYMORE.
DUDE, THAT IS *SUCH* A RELIEF!
HEY, HOW ABOUT A PHOTO FOR THE BOYS BACK AT THE BASE?
WHY NOT?
REALLY? DOESN'T THAT SEEM A LITTLE... WEIRD?

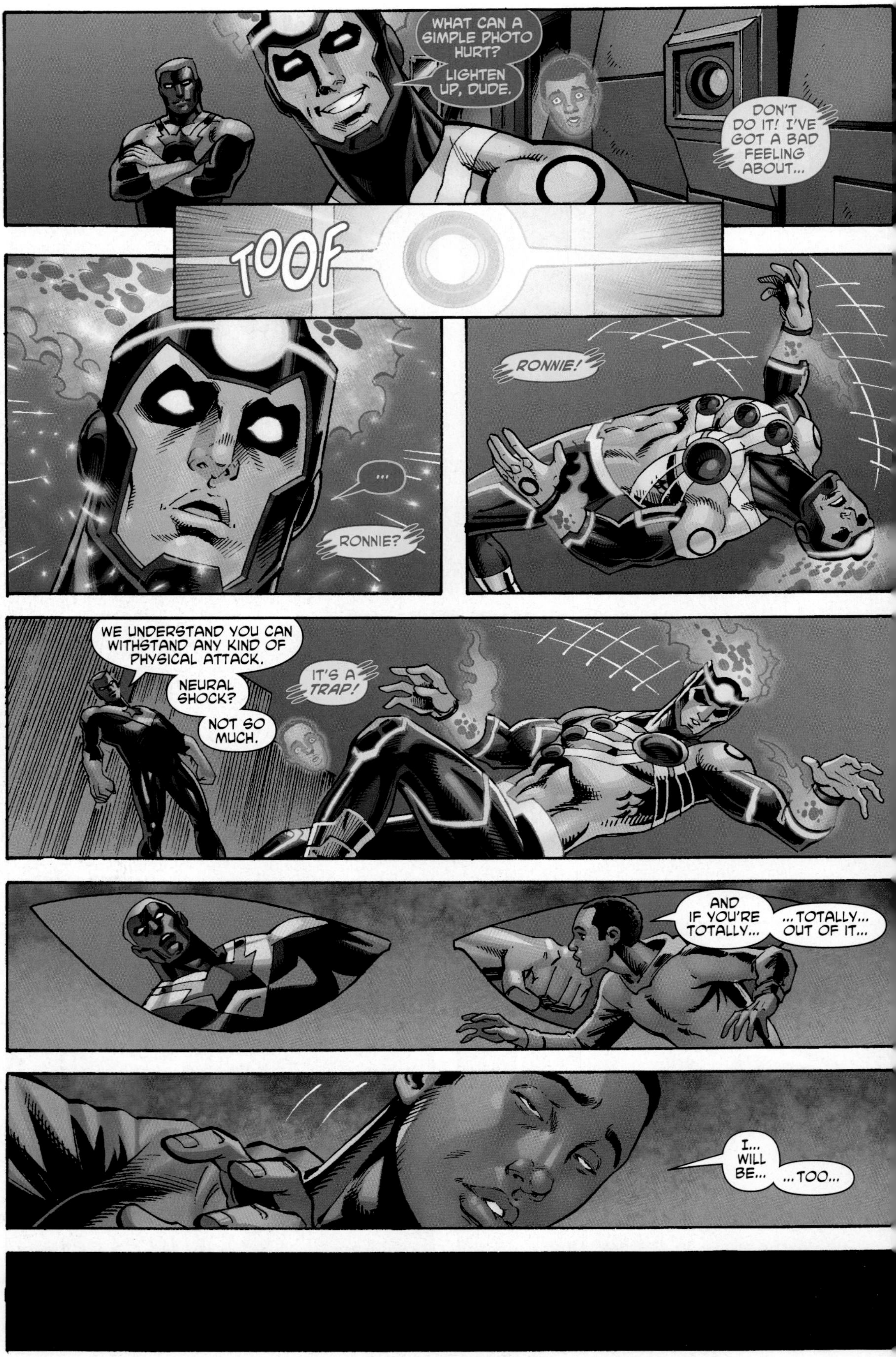
WHAT CAN A SIMPLE PHOTO HURT?
LIGHTEN UP, DUDE.
DON'T DO IT! I'VE GOT A BAD FEELING ABOUT...
TOOF
...
RONNIE?
RONNIE!
WE UNDERSTAND YOU CAN WITHSTAND ANY KIND OF PHYSICAL ATTACK.
NEURAL SHOCK?
NOT SO MUCH.
IT'S A TRAP!
AND IF YOU'RE TOTALLY...
...TOTALLY... OUT OF IT...
I... WILL BE...
...TOO...

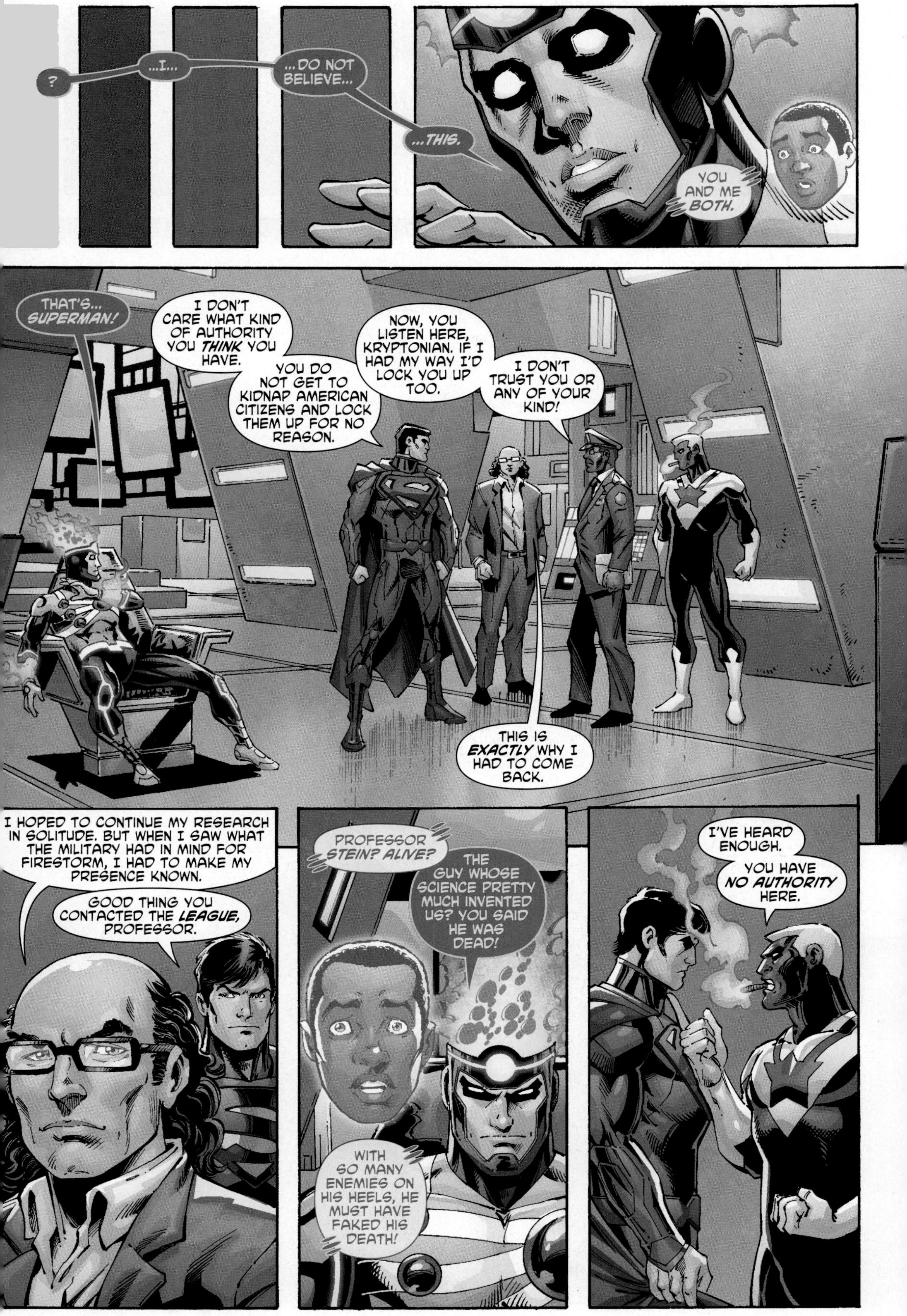
?
...I...
...DO NOT BELIEVE...
...THIS.
YOU AND ME BOTH.
THAT'S... SUPERMAN!
I DON'T CARE WHAT KIND OF AUTHORITY YOU THINK YOU HAVE.
YOU DO NOT GET TO KIDNAP AMERICAN CITIZENS AND LOCK THEM UP FOR NO REASON.
NOW, YOU LISTEN HERE, KRYPTONIAN. IF I HAD MY WAY I'D LOCK YOU UP TOO.
I DON'T TRUST YOU OR ANY OF YOUR KIND!
THIS IS EXACTLY WHY I HAD TO COME BACK.
I HOPED TO CONTINUE MY RESEARCH IN SOLITUDE. BUT WHEN I SAW WHAT THE MILITARY HAD IN MIND FOR FIRESTORM, I HAD TO MAKE MY PRESENCE KNOWN.
GOOD THING YOU CONTACTED THE LEAGUE, PROFESSOR.
PROFESSOR STEIN? ALIVE?
THE GUY WHOSE SCIENCE PRETTY MUCH INVENTED US? YOU SAID HE WAS DEAD!
WITH SO MANY ENEMIES ON HIS HEELS, HE MUST HAVE FAKED HIS DEATH!
I'VE HEARD ENOUGH.
YOU HAVE NO AUTHORITY HERE.

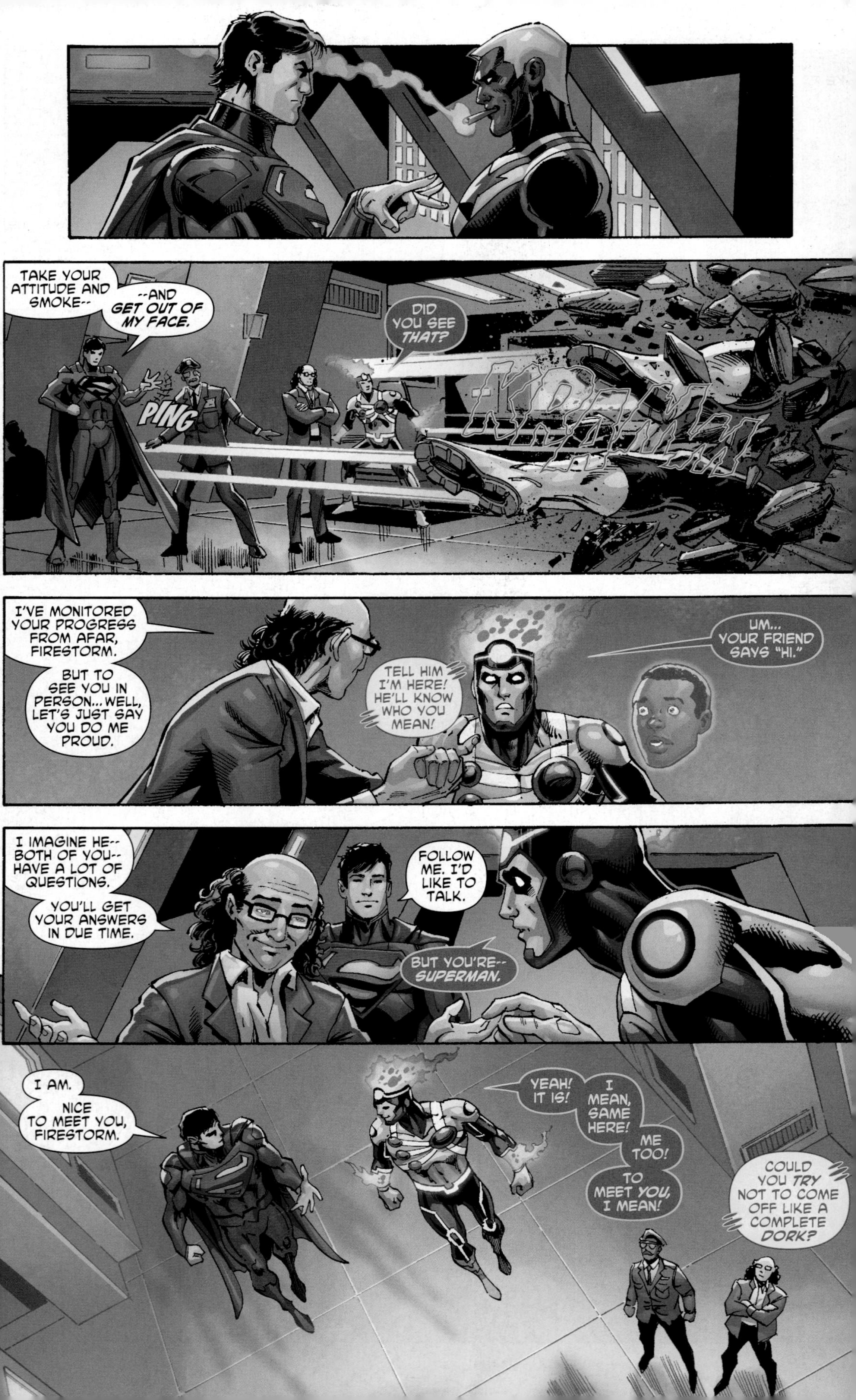

TAKE YOUR ATTITUDE AND SMOKE--
--AND GET OUT OF MY FACE.
PING
DID YOU SEE THAT?
KRAKOOM
I'VE MONITORED YOUR PROGRESS FROM AFAR, FIRESTORM.
BUT TO SEE YOU IN PERSON...WELL, LET'S JUST SAY YOU DO ME PROUD.
TELL HIM I'M HERE! HE'LL KNOW WHO YOU MEAN!
UM... YOUR FRIEND SAYS "HI."
I IMAGINE HE--BOTH OF YOU--HAVE A LOT OF QUESTIONS.
YOU'LL GET YOUR ANSWERS IN DUE TIME.
FOLLOW ME. I'D LIKE TO TALK.
BUT YOU'RE--SUPERMAN.
I AM.
NICE TO MEET YOU, FIRESTORM.
YEAH! IT IS!
I MEAN, SAME HERE!
ME TOO!
TO MEET YOU, I MEAN!
COULD YOU TRY NOT TO COME OFF LIKE A COMPLETE DORK?

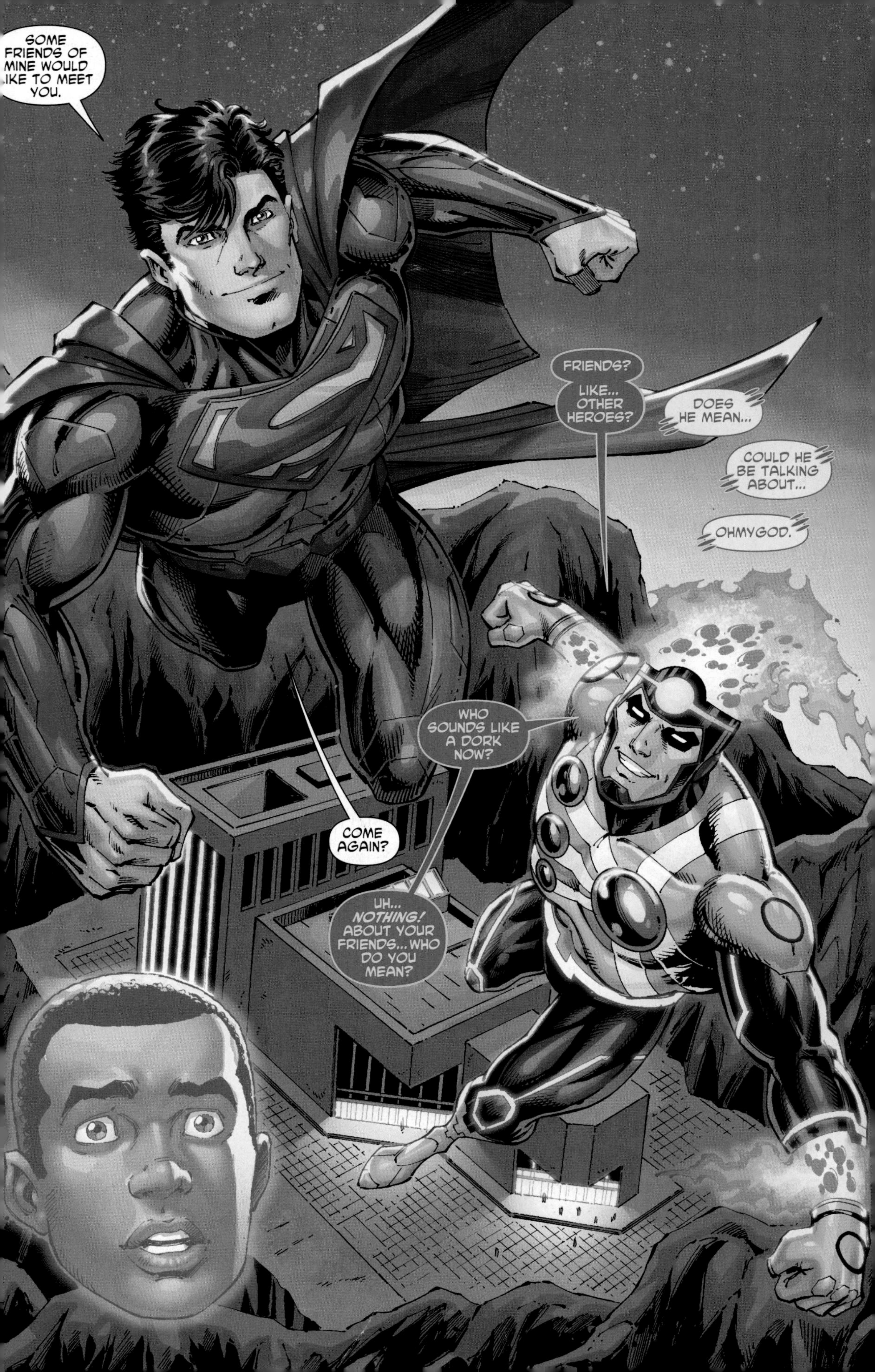
SOME FRIENDS OF MINE WOULD LIKE TO MEET YOU.
FRIENDS?
LIKE... OTHER HEROES?
DOES HE MEAN...
COULD HE BE TALKING ABOUT...
OHMYGOD.
WHO SOUNDS LIKE A DORK NOW?
COME AGAIN?
UH... NOTHING! ABOUT YOUR FRIENDS... WHO DO YOU MEAN?

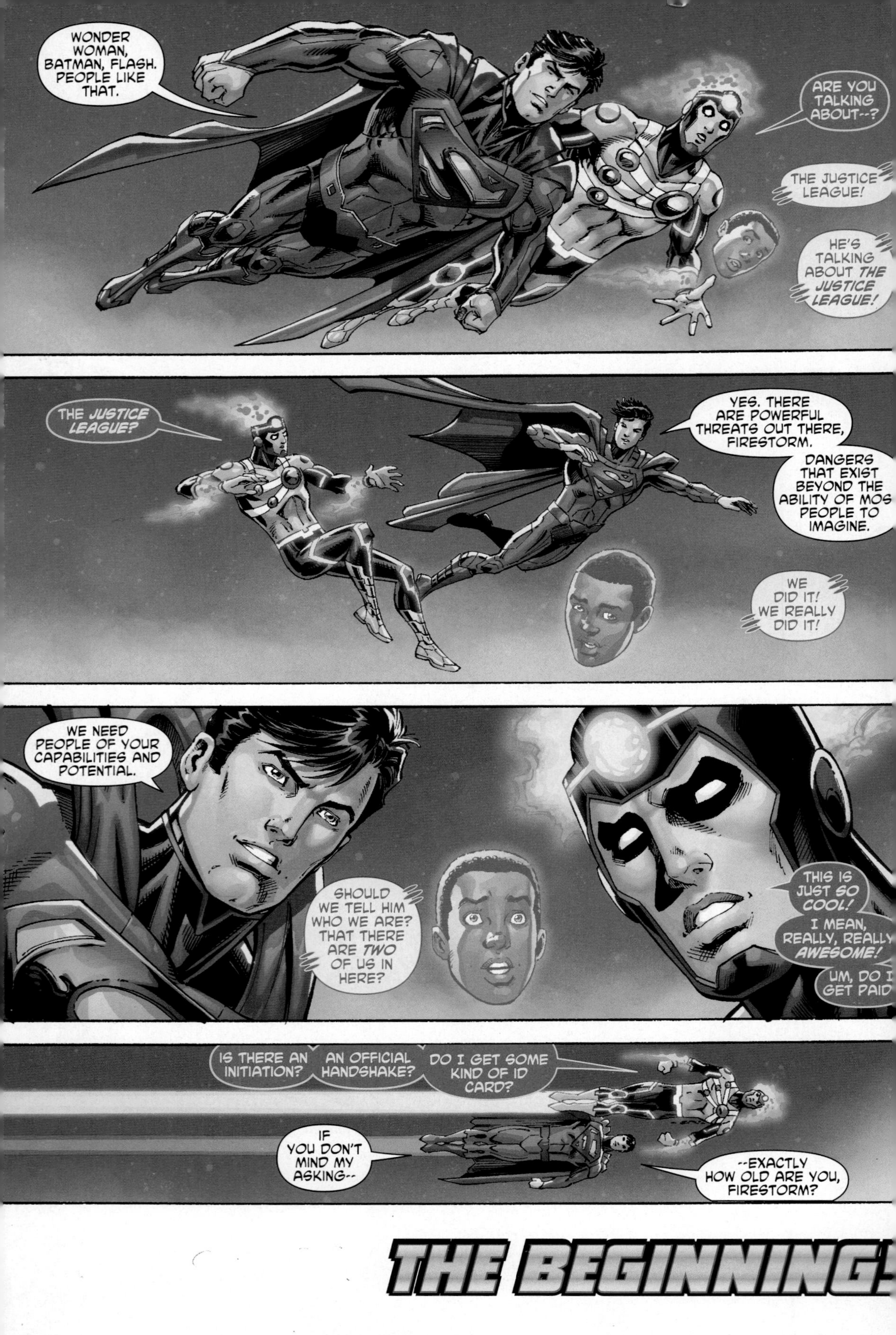
WONDER WOMAN, BATMAN, FLASH. PEOPLE LIKE THAT.
ARE YOU TALKING ABOUT--?
THE JUSTICE LEAGUE!
HE'S TALKING ABOUT *THE JUSTICE LEAGUE!*
THE *JUSTICE LEAGUE?*
YES. THERE ARE POWERFUL THREATS OUT THERE, FIRESTORM.
DANGERS THAT EXIST BEYOND THE ABILITY OF MOS PEOPLE TO IMAGINE.
WE DID IT! WE REALLY DID IT!
WE NEED PEOPLE OF YOUR CAPABILITIES AND POTENTIAL.
SHOULD WE TELL HIM WHO WE ARE? THAT THERE ARE *TWO* OF US IN HERE?
THIS IS JUST *SO COOL!*
I MEAN, REALLY, REALLY *AWESOME!*
UM, DO I GET PAID
IS THERE AN INITIATION?
AN OFFICIAL HANDSHAKE?
DO I GET SOME KIND OF ID CARD?
IF YOU DON'T MIND MY ASKING--
--EXACTLY HOW OLD ARE YOU, FIRESTORM?
THE BEGINNING.